Withdrawal

Withdrawal

Reassessing America's Final Years in Vietnam

GREGORY A. DADDIS

OXFORD
UNIVERSITY PRESS

OXFORD
UNIVERSITY PRESS

Oxford University Press is a department of the University of Oxford. It furthers
the University's objective of excellence in research, scholarship, and education
by publishing worldwide. Oxford is a registered trade mark of Oxford University
Press in the UK and certain other countries.

Published in the United States of America by Oxford University Press
198 Madison Avenue, New York, NY 10016, United States of America.

CIP data is on file at the Library of Congress
ISBN 978–0–19–069108–0

3 5 7 9 8 6 4 2

Printed by Sheridan Books, Inc., United States of America

To
Richard H. Kohn
and
Paul L. Miles

No student could ask for two better
teachers, mentors, and friends

CONTENTS

LIST OF ILLUSTRATIONS

Maps

Figures

PREFACE AND ACKNOWLEDGMENTS

In 2009, while still in the US Army, I had the opportunity—in truth, the privilege—to serve as the command historian for the Multinational Corps, Iraq. As a lieutenant colonel with follow-on orders to teach in the Department of History at West Point, the deployment was a unique opportunity to observe the transition of military control from US to Iraqi forces in a still war-torn country. I studied and read widely to prepare for my assignment. I pored over texts on Iraqi history, read about the British experience in Mesopotamia during the early twentieth century, and worked through the most fashionable books on counter-insurgency. And despite my preparation, I learned more than I ever could have anticipated as I undertook my charge of writing the command's official history. It was all an immensely humbling experience.

The corps commander that year, Lieutenant General Charles Jacoby, proved especially enlightening. A former instructor in West Point's history department himself, Jacoby had a discerning eye, a senior officer who asked penetrating questions in staff meetings that always seemed overburdened by too many slides. (Of course, the US Army fought its long war in Iraq with PowerPoint as one of its major weapon systems.) He also assigned a professional reading list to his principal commanders and staff officers. Throughout the corps headquarters, ensconced within one of Saddam Hussein's former palaces, one could find dog-eared copies of Lawrence Wright's *The Looming Tower* or Stathis Kalyvas's *The Logic of Violence in Civil War*. Only one book on the Vietnam War made the list—Lewis Sorley's *A Better War*.

Sorley's was a congenial narrative for an army coming to grips with its own history in Iraq. Even in 2009, when most officers realized their efforts there would achieve ambiguous results at best, *A Better War* offered a palliative of sorts. Among the many histories on and memoirs of Vietnam, here was the "unexamined" story of a courageous officer who took over a losing conflict, instituted a bold new strategy, and brought the United States to the brink of military victory.

The "tragedy" came from civilian policymakers, a biased media, and antiwar activists who withdrew their support just when their military leaders, and their South Vietnamese allies, needed them most. In this telling, the US Army in Vietnam had fulfilled its wartime obligations. The war had been "won" militarily in Southeast Asia, only to be "lost" politically here at home.

The parallels to Iraq appeared, on its face, unmistakable. Just as General Creighton Abrams had taken over from his misguided predecessor, William C. Westmoreland, so, too, had David Petraeus from George W. Casey Jr. Both Abrams and Petraeus not only breathed new life into a stalled war effort, but also concentrated on the neglected aspects of what mattered most to US military strategy—counterinsurgency. These enlightened warriors, the storyline went, abandoned obsolete conventional tactics, instead directing American combat units to conduct "population-centric security" and "clear-and-hold" operations. The results were near immediate. Abrams, like Petraeus after him, had proved that the right leader with the right strategy could still win wars that seemed hopelessly lost.

But what if those advocating a "better war" in Vietnam, in reality, had manufactured a narrative that misinterpreted the complicated nature of American strategy? What if there existed more continuities than change in how US military leaders approached the complex problems of a political-military conflict? And what if a reevaluation of American strategy found not a war-winning remedy to an internecine struggle over national identity in the modern era, but rather a historical illustration shedding light on the limitations of US power abroad?

In large sense, *Withdrawal* aims to answer these crucial questions. This work, however, is far more than simply a response to the "better war" narrative. As with *Westmoreland's War*, I have aimed to challenge some of the fundamental, and thus more popular, preconceptions held on the American experience in Vietnam. *Withdrawal* then is not just a historiographical riposte. Rather, I hope that a reconsideration of US military strategy in the final years of America's long Southeast Asian war will facilitate a more balanced discussion of a still hotly debated conflict.

Part of such a reexamination might also include asking hard questions about how Americans remember the Vietnam War. Why, for instance, in 2009, when it was clear Iraq would not constitute a traditional military "victory," did many US Army officers want to believe in a particular historical narrative highlighting American accomplishments in Vietnam? A narrative that told of steady commanders who persevered despite lack of support on the home front? Why, in short, has the "better war" storyline remained so compelling?

In the process, it is my sincere hope that a reexamination of the United States' final years in the Vietnam War, still an understudied period in a long and difficult conflict, will offer new perspectives for those looking back to history for wisdom in managing current and future conflicts.

Of course, none of these aspirations would ever have seen the light of day without my benefiting from the assistance of some amazing people. First, my thanks to David McBride, editor extraordinaire at Oxford University Press. This is our third Vietnam outing together and I could not have asked for a more professional, charitable advisor at OUP. Katie Weaver also deserves much credit for shepherding me through the editorial process, as do Patti Brecht and Paul Tompsett for their help in the final production phase.

Having shed my military uniform back in 2015, I still profit from amazing friendships with and mentoring by those still in the West Point history department. A summer 2015 trip to Vietnam with cadets remains one of the highlights of my army career. My thanks still go to Rory McGovern for all his heavy lifting in making the trip such a success. Co-traveler and cherished friend Jen Kiesling continues to challenge my assumptions on a topic I hold dear, though living on the other side of the country doesn't afford me nearly as many cookies as in the past. Other colleagues from the department past and present—Casey Doss, Kevin Farrell, Andy Forney, David Frey, Josiah Grover, John Hall, Tom Moore, Jason Musteen, Cliff Rogers, Danny Sjursen, Chuck Steele, Ty Seidule, and Gail Yoshitani—remain great friends. Very special thanks go to Tom Rider, a longtime companion from my first teaching assignment at West Point, for composing the exceptional maps in this volume.

At Chapman University, I have grown as a scholar and teacher by becoming immersed in a tremendous master's program in war and society. Jennifer Keene had a remarkable vision, planting the seeds for an academic experience that has few rivals in the United States. She is a marvelous collaborator and has become a close friend. So, too, has Alex Bay, who has broadened my understanding of historical myth and memory and helped cultivate my palate to enjoy some fine beer. Additionally, colleagues like Allison DeVries, Patrick and Kelli Fuery, Stacy Laird, Lisa Leitz, Erin Mosely, and Bob Slayton have made our stay on the left coast all the more enjoyable. Perhaps most importantly, the graduate students at Chapman, like the cadets at West Point before them, have motivated me to reconsider the interrelationships between war and strategy and the role society has in both. Finally, my thanks to Chapman's Wilkinson College for granting me scholarly subvention funding to see this work through to its conclusion.

All historians know the value of knowledgeable archivists and library staff and I have benefited from working with more than a few. John Wilson at the LBJ Library helped me find some important documents on pacification and the term "one war." At the Nixon Library, I have been fortunate to work with some amazingly talented folks: Greg Cummings, Pamela Eisenberg, Mike Ellzey, Melissa Heddon, Ida Kelley, Meghan Lee-Parker, Ryan Pettigrew, and Jason Schultz.

Special thanks go to the immensely talented team at Florentine Films—Ken Burns, Lynn Novick, Sarah Botstein, and Geoff Ward—for allowing me to contribute, in a miniscule way, to the very best documentary on the wars in Vietnam.

In helping me navigate through the countless minefields within the Vietnam War historiography, I have incurred quite a bit of debt to some incredibly talented historians. John Carland, Carolyn Eisenberg, and David Elliott were immensely gracious with their time in reading drafts and offering tremendous feedback. Ed Moise went far above and beyond doing the same, saving me from myself in numerous places. Dale Andrade, Pierre Asselin, Andy Birtle, Martin Clemis, Mark Clodfelter, Mai Elliott, Gian Gentile, Kyle Longley, Hang Nguyen, William Rust, Heather Stur, Erik Villard, Jackie Whitt, Andy Wiest, and Marilyn Young have all offered counsel and assistance along the way. Jim Willbanks and Ron Milam are among this list, two veteran-scholars I admire greatly. And so, too, has been my dear friend Bob Brigham. Bob and Monica Church have been like family to me (and to a certain Vassar student) and I cannot thank them enough for everything these past few years.

Of course, my family also helped along this most recent journey through Vietnam. My mom and Robert made trips to Florida a welcome respite from research and writing, while my father's memory still holds sway. Rob Young, more brother than friend, now has to read yet another book on Vietnam. (You're welcome!) The Puryears remain close as ever, as does the entire Chittick clan. Our cats George and Lucky continued on as relentless writing companions, sleeping on documents before sharing treats at lunchtime. My daughter Cameron made sure I balanced work with surfing lessons at the beach and hiking in Yosemite during a busy summer as my version of the Vietnam War neared the finish line. She makes me a proud father every single day. And my wife Susan, indexer supreme (you're also welcome!) who has been on this long journey all the while, has never failed to smile when it was needed most. I am truly elevated by the love around me.

Finally, I want to thank two gentlemen, true gentlemen, who have made such an important impact on my life. For more than a decade now, Dick Kohn has been a constant presence, a sounding board without equal, and an example of grace, intelligence, and warmth. To this day, I continue to ask the most important question he posed to me as my dissertation advisor: "So what?" And for nearly as long, Paul Miles has volunteered more of his time, and shared more of his insights, than I rightly deserve. Paul has read and astutely challenged virtually every word I have written on Vietnam over the years and our near weekly conversations have been, for me, as educational as they have been enjoyable. How so very fortunate I am to have these two amazing people in my life.

LIST OF ABBREVIATIONS USED IN THE TEXT

APC	Accelerated Pacification Campaign
ARVN	Army of the Republic of Vietnam
CIA	Central Intelligence Agency
CINCPAC	Commander in Chief, US Pacific Command
CIP	Counterinsurgency Plan
CJCS	Chairman of the Joint Chiefs of Staff
COMUSMACV	Commander, United States Military Assistance Command, Vietnam
CORDS	Civil Operations and Revolutionary Development Support
COSVN	Central Office of South Vietnam
CTZ	Corps Tactical Zone
DMZ	Demilitarized Zone
DoD	Department of Defense
DRV	Democratic Republic of Vietnam
FLN	Algerian National Liberation Front
FM	Field Manual
FWMAF	Free World Military Assistance Forces
GVN	Government of South Vietnam
HES	Hamlet Evaluation System
JCS	Joint Chiefs of Staff
KIA	Killed in Action
MAAG	Military Assistance Advisory Group
MACV	Military Assistance Command, Vietnam
MAT	Mobile Advisory Team
NCO	Noncommissioned Officer
NLF	National Front for the Liberation of South Vietnam
NSAM	National Security Action Memorandum
NSC	National Security Council

NSSM   National Security Study Memorandum
NVA   North Vietnamese Army; see also PAVN
OCO   Office of Civil Operations
PAAS   Pacification Attitude Analysis System
PAVN   People's Army of Vietnam; see also NVA
PLAF   People's Liberation Armed Forces; see also VC
PRC   People's Republic of China
PRG   Provisional Revolutionary Government of the Republic of
                South Vietnam
PROVN   Program for the Pacification and Long-Term Development
                of South Vietnam
PSDF   People's Self-Defense Force
RD   Revolutionary Development
RF/PF   Regional Forces/Popular Forces
RVN   Republic of Vietnam
RVNAF   Republic of Vietnam Armed Forces
SEATO   Southeast Asia Treaty Organization
VC   Vietnamese Communist, Vietcong; see also NLF
VCI   Vietcong Infrastructure
VVAW   Vietnam Veterans Against the War
USAID   United States Agency for International Development
USIA   United States Information Agency

LIST OF ABBREVIATIONS USED IN THE NOTES

CMH	US Army Center of Military History, Fort McNair, Washington, DC
FRUS	*Foreign Relations of the United States*. Vietnam. US Department of State, Washington, DC
JCSHO	Joint Chiefs of Staff History Office, The Pentagon, Washington, DC
LBJL	Lyndon B. Johnson Presidential Library, Austin, Texas.
MHI	US Army Military History Institute, Carlisle Barracks, Pennsylvania
NARA	National Archives & Records Administration, College Park, Maryland
OSDHO	Office of the Secretary of Defense Historical Office. Washington, DC
RNL	Richard M. Nixon Presidential Library, Yorba Linda, California
TTUVA	The Vietnam Archive, Texas Tech University, Lubbock, Texas
USAAWCL	US Army Aviation Warfighting Center, Aviation Technical Library, Fort Rucker, Alabama
USMA	United States Military Academy, West Point, New York
VNIT	Vietnam Interview Tape Collection, CMH, Fort McNair, Washington, DC
WCWP	William C. Westmoreland Papers
WHPO	White House Photo Office
WPSC	Special Collections, United States Military Academy Library, West Point, New York
WPUSC	William C. Westmoreland Papers, South Caroliniana Library, University of South Carolina, Columbia, South Carolina

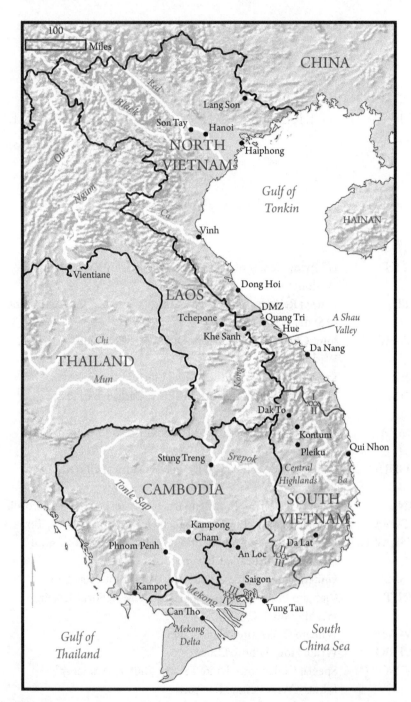

Map 1 Southeast Asia

Introduction

The Limits of Strategy in a Stalemated War

June 6th, 1962. At ten o'clock in the morning, President John F. Kennedy spoke to the graduating class of the United States Military Academy. Kennedy opened by noting the pride he felt in being part of the West Point tradition and, with it, the pride in being a citizen of the United States of America. He then announced his decision, as commander in chief, to remit all confinements and other cadet punishments. Surely, at least a few cadets no longer cared what their president said that morning. Indeed, JFK joked that Superintendent William C. Westmoreland must have been slightly pained to hear this news given that one cadet, who Kennedy predicted would someday head the US Army, had just watched eight months' worth of punishment miraculously expunged from his record.

The president then turned more serious, though certainly no less inspiring. He asked cadets to realize how much America depended on them, how their responsibilities would require a "versatility and an adaptability never before required in either war or in peace." Kennedy also spoke of a new type of war, "new in its intensity, yet ancient in its origin—war by guerrillas, subversives, insurgents, assassins, war by ambush instead of by combat; by infiltration, instead of aggression, seeking victory by eroding and exhausting the enemy instead of engaging him."

Kennedy acknowledged the difficulties ahead, but in 1962 little seemed outside the influence of American power. Moreover, the young president told cadets they had one satisfaction, however difficult future days may be: "When asked by any American what you are doing for your country, no one's answer will be clearer than your own. West Point . . . was built to produce officers committed to the defense of their country, leaders who understand the great stakes which are involved, leaders who can be entrusted with the heavy responsibility which modern weapons and the fight for freedom entail, leaders who can inspire the same sense of obligation to duty which you bring to it."[1]

It would be nine years before another American president spoke to the Corps of Cadets in the spring of their graduating year. Those nine years would see near unimaginable turmoil at home and abroad. A president and his brother would be assassinated, as would the most eloquent and inspirational of civil rights leaders. The war in Vietnam would expose the incapacity of American military leaders to bring about a social revolution aimed at transforming foreign political structures and cultural traditions. Antiwar protests and race riots, raging across the United States, would unmask social divisions at home. It was, to be certain, a tumultuous decade.

Nine long years after Kennedy's commencement address, Richard M. Nixon arrived at West Point to offer his own remarks to a new crop of soon-to-be army lieutenants. Nixon spoke of the long and bitter struggle in Vietnam, and even as US troops were then withdrawing from that war-torn country, he noted how Americans had "stood behind their commitment to the people of South Vietnam in the face of great temptations to turn aside." While the president saw hope for a new era of world peace, none of this, he said, was a cause for euphoria. "The harvest-time of peace is not yet," the president somberly declared.

Nixon told the cadets they could be proud of their country's power and proud of their own uniforms, yet admitted it was no secret that the "discipline, integrity, patriotism, self-sacrifice, which are the very lifeblood of an effective armed force and which the Corps represents, could no longer be taken for granted in the Army in which you would serve. The symptoms of trouble were plain enough," Nixon said, "from drug abuse to insubordination."

Compared to Kennedy's address, Nixon's speech was solemn, even ominous. Clearly, the world had changed over the previous decade. So, too, it seemed how Americans viewed themselves at the most basic of levels. Was it true, as President Nixon suggested, that the United States was still the "keystone of peace"? Could cadets still be proud of their country's power and of their own uniforms? Did the academy's ideals of duty and honor and country still ring true?[2]

Both speeches, each one in a sense bookending the Vietnam conflict, suggested how a decade's worth of war had reshaped presidential narratives on the limits of American power, the role of wartime dissent, and whether the United States still had a unique role to play in global affairs. Nixon's depiction of cadets growing up in "stormy times" seemed a far cry from the soaring rhetoric of Kennedy's Camelot.[3] In fact, by 1975, most Americans agreed with the tempestuous imagery Nixon had employed at West Point only four years earlier. One Catholic journal decried, "There's a lot of blood on American hands," while the Washington Post reported that Vietnam had "left a rancid after-taste," so much so that 72 percent of polled Americans regarded Vietnam as a "dark moment" in United States history.[4] Had visions of American power (and possibilities) abroad changed that much between the two presidencies?

In truth, even before Nixon's resignation from office, Americans already were questioning what the Vietnam experience meant to the nation. Writing in 1970, former National Security Council staffer Chester L. Cooper argued that the "thoughtful American is still groping for reasons, explanations, assurances."[5] The fall of Saigon in April 1975 proved especially shocking. Few could argue that with South Vietnam's collapse, the United States had not suffered an ignominious defeat in Southeast Asia. Still, Americans searched for answers. One senior military officer writing a postmortem on Vietnam hoped to "comprehend what has appeared to be an incomprehensible war." From discrediting military service to undermining Americans' faith in their government, the war had exacted a heavy price on a once proud and self-confident nation.[6]

The postwar challenge, then, became one of crafting a historical narrative that many, if not most, Americans could find palatable. In the process, tough questions needed tackling. If the United States had somehow changed between the Kennedy and Nixon presidencies, what did that mean for US presence abroad? Was the nation in decline? Its foreign policy bankrupt? Perhaps most importantly, was it possible to re-envision the Vietnam War as a noble cause in which the American armed forces had actually won the war, only to have it lost at home by those lacking the will to see a hard-fought conflict through to its rightful conclusion?[7]

Figure 1 STORMY TIMES. President Nixon reviewing West Point cadets at a United States Military Academy parade ceremony, 29 May 1971. (WHPO Master File #6423, RNL)

A Long War's Turning Point

For those seeking answers explaining how the United States lost its first major overseas war, the 1968 Tet offensive increasingly seemed an obvious tipping point. After a year of optimistic reports emanating from the White House and the US military headquarters in Saigon—General William C. Westmoreland described 1967 as a year of "great progress"—surprise enemy attacks ranged across the entirety of South Vietnam in late January and early February.[8] The physical destruction wrought on South Vietnamese society was immense. The psychological trauma to Americans immeasurable. Senior US policymakers expressed "grave doubts" about any further progress being made in the war effort, while correspondents opined that the "scope, the intensity and the tenacious thrust of the Communist attacks clearly caught a supposedly alerted allied command badly off balance." Journalist David Halberstam recalled that for the American public, "the Tet offensive was a rude awakening to the toughness and resilience of the enemy, and a television preview of the long war ahead."[9]

Perhaps unsurprisingly, Americans focused on themselves in the aftermath of Tet, despite the devastation and social upheaval suffered by their South Vietnamese allies. Ambassador Ellsworth Bunker reported in mid-February of the more than 450,000 refugees, the 48,000 homes destroyed, and the civilian deaths numbering in the thousands. Still, Americans turned inward. News editors, quite simply, found a more compelling story to be told in what appeared to be a monumental failure in US leadership. Thus, *The Wall Street Journal* could conclude in late February that the "American people should be getting ready to accept, if they haven't already, the prospect that the whole Vietnam effort may be doomed."[10]

It took only a few short steps to begin searching for someone to shoulder responsibility for such a colossal mistake. Tet demanded a scapegoat. And as *Newsweek* reported, "[T]he figure most conveniently on hand was the commander on the spot, William Childs Westmoreland." If the war was indeed mired in stalemate (or worse), then at least one columnist argued it was time "to send a commander to Vietnam who is capable of plotting a winning strategy or, if there is no such thing, who is capable of telling the President so."[11]

Seeking blame for a miscarried foreign war—a war so different from the one being advertised by senior US officials—cut to deeper questions about America's role in Southeast Asia. No doubt Westmoreland spoke for many military officers when he argued Hanoi had suffered a major military defeat in early 1968. But was Tet truly an American victory? If so, why was the US commanding general in Vietnam reportedly asking for more than 200,000 reinforcements in the offensive's wake? Was the enemy really on the run, thus offering a "great opportunity" for those bold enough to see that victory finally lay within the allies' grasp?[12] Or had the United States been dealt a catastrophic blow? If American military commanders had "gravely underestimated the capacity of the enemy," was it possible the war in Vietnam was now "unwinnable"? Few senior leaders, either in Washington or in Saigon, possessed satisfactory answers to any of these questions dominating the public discourse at home in mid-1968.[13]

The American-centric focus of these inquiries tended to push the Vietnamese, both allies and enemy, into the background. Yet leaders in Hanoi and Saigon equally struggled to find meaning from the battlefields of 1968. Even if the communists had not intended to drive the foreign occupiers out of South Vietnam, their goal of defeating the Americans' "aggressive will" remained difficult to assess.[14] Surely, US newspapers attested to widespread discontent in American cities. But would that popular disaffection translate into policy change? While American generals might complain that "you could have marched on Hanoi and [the media] would have found some way to poor mouth you on it," such griping did not necessarily mean the United States was on the verge of withdrawing from Southeast Asia.[15]

Yet within the first year of Richard M. Nixon's presidency, it became clear to Hanoi, and to the rest of the world, that the United States was, in fact, leaving South Vietnam. If few Americans considered Vietnamese perspectives in the aftermath of Tet, there seemed little doubt of the United States' inability to compel Hanoi into renouncing its aims of independence and national reunification. Slowly came the realization that the long war in Asia might not be won. Tet may have been "the most disastrous defeat North Vietnam suffered in the long war," but inexplicably it didn't seem to matter.[16] The new type of war about which President Kennedy warned seemingly had gotten the best of US soldiers and their civilian masters.

And thus began a decades' long search for answers, a relentless pursuit of the "truth" rivaling Old Thunder Ahab's quest for his white whale. In fact, postwar debates at times rivaled the contentiousness of the war itself. Even core questions remain disputed. Who won? Who should be blamed if the United States did lose? Did defeat in Vietnam mean the United States no longer served as the guarantor of democratic liberalism across the globe?[17]

In the war's aftermath, the paucity of concrete answers seemed only to heighten Americans' angst over what really happened in Vietnam. Thus, some began to seek clarity by asking new questions; in truth, counterfactuals resting more on hope than historical evidence. What if, in the aftermath of Tet, a new American general assumed command in Vietnam and, with a new strategy and determined leadership, had turned around the war effort? Might it be possible that feckless civilian policymakers began to withdraw from a war just as it was being won?

Searching for a "Better War"

Certainly, contemporary media portrayals of General Creighton Abrams endorsed such a proposition. Just two days after President Lyndon B. Johnson designated Abrams as the new commander of American forces in South Vietnam, *The Christian Science Monitor* declared in mid-April 1968 that the United States had regained "strategic momentum on battlefield." Westmoreland's deputy, pictured squinting with a stern look, had not yet officially taken over the war effort, yet miraculously had already turned it around.[18]

Journalists gushed over this "general with a flair." Newspaper readers learned of Abrams's daring exploits as a World War II tank commander in Patton's army, of his "Spartanly simple" approach, and of his penchant for chewing black cigars. (Had not Ulysses S. Grant similarly smoked cigars while saving the Union from disaster?) Abrams was "tough, aggressive, dynamic, spectacular."[19] Even after Tet, reporters took an optimistic tone when describing the new commander of the US Military Assistance Command, Vietnam (MACV). Whereas his West Point classmate Westmoreland looked the part of an aloof, crisp, professional soldier, Abrams impressed with his "candor, humor, self-effacement and common-sense skepticism." Moreover, in the "rumpled and somewhat burly Abrams," correspondents saw the "possibility of a significant change" in military strategy.[20] Thus, scaffolding was already being emplaced for construction of a myth that would endure for decades.

Abrams, in short, would fight a "better war." The story appealed in no small part because of its very simplicity. Despite setbacks in Vietnam and a growing antiwar movement at home, a new general with a better strategy had taken the reins and, through sheer will, had forced the allies back onto the path toward victory.

Abrams's herculean feat mattered because American leaders still depicted the war in Vietnam as a morally righteous crusade. National security advisor Henry Kissinger recalled "the overriding issue was how to keep faith with the tens of millions who, in reliance on American assurances, had tied their destiny to ours."[21] President Nixon argued in September 1969 that the United States could not "accept a settlement that would arbitrarily dictate the political future of South Vietnam and deny to the people of South Vietnam the basic right to determine their own future free from outside interference."[22] For Abrams to lose the war militarily meant a loss of American credibility abroad and, just as importantly, a loss of freedom for young democratic Asians opposing the aggression of global communism.

The "better war" thesis also rested on an overly reductive interpretation of American strategy under Abrams's predecessor. According to the storyline, Westmoreland's failures as a strategist obliged the allies to a wrong-headed approach that produced only a costly stalemate. Concentrating solely on attrition of enemy forces, where body counts served as the gruesome metric of progress, Westmoreland had chosen and pursued a "search-and-destroy" strategy destined to fail. As the Tet offensive's implications became clearer, it seemed obvious the MACV commander had been "strategically outmaneuvered."[23] How else could it be possible the United States was failing to make progress against a Third World nation like North Vietnam? Only a mistaken strategy could explain the "smoldering stalemate" that was Vietnam. Further, Westmoreland apparently had renounced alternative strategies that would have more properly focused the allies on population security.[24] A clear-sighted Abrams, however, waiting patiently in the wings as MACV's deputy, reoriented the entire command soon after taking charge. A change in strategy had broken the stalemate.

For Americans uncomfortable with the idea of a tie, especially on the battlefield, the "better war" narrative proved instantly appealing. With the war costing nearly $2.5 billion a month, and Americans being killed at an approximate rate of 300 per week, Abrams's ascendance to command promised a reinvigorated strategic approach—perhaps even victory.[25] Even if more astute observers realized that the Nixon administration no longer sought a strictly military solution in Vietnam, Abrams could at least win an "honorable peace," of which senior officers had spoken as early as 1967. American commanders might not be able to deliver an unconditional surrender, as had their forebearers in World War II. But they could at least translate the moral commitment to South Vietnam into a tangible outcome that maintained the nation's honor and prestige.[26]

In short, the "better war" premise offered hope at a time when Americans were coming to the uncomfortable realization that the very definition of victory in war might be changing, and not for the better. Critics still maintained the United States was mired in an unwinnable war. The seeming reverses wrought by the Tet offensive—coupled with increasing social and political turmoil at home—shook the confidence of policy elite and general public alike.[27] Yet Abrams and his more enlightened approach to military strategy offered Americans a chance to redeem themselves on the battlefields of South Vietnam. If military victory lay out of reach, the general could nevertheless withdraw from Vietnam in an honorable fashion. The communists would not steal a win in the global contest of good versus evil. The South Vietnamese would remain free. And the Americans could remain proud of fighting for a noble cause.[28]

Hence, the "better war" myth, first constructed by journalists believing they saw a major change with the ascendancy of Creighton Abrams to MACV command, became a functional device for later pundits and policymakers. For instance, the general's reputation rose dramatically after the 2003 US invasion of Iraq. With the war there unraveling as early as 2004, analysts reached back to

Vietnam for "lessons" on defeating a committed insurgency. US Army officers penned articles in professional journals like *Military Review* extolling the virtues of Abrams, while the RAND Corporation issued studies contending the general's "understanding of the war was clearly different from his predecessor's."[29] Consequently, with Iraq on the brink of collapse in 2006, history seemed to be repeating itself. General David Petraeus, just like Abrams, took charge of a losing war at a critical moment and, with a new and enlightened strategy, snatched victory from the jaws of defeat. A "better war" had once more saved the nation from humiliating defeat.[30]

Beyond the Myth

Though the Abrams era has become a convenient historical case study for more present-minded analysts, a reassessment of the Vietnam War's later years presents a far less triumphal narrative. Thus, the purpose of this work is to reevaluate the "better war" thesis and, more broadly, the often overlooked period of the American war in Vietnam between 1968 and 1972. Much of the new scholarship within the United States continues to focus on the inner workings of the Nixon White House (thanks to the release of the president's Oval Office tape recordings) or how the antiwar movement embodied the angst of the post–World War II generation.[31] Additionally, new memoirs have expanded our knowledge of the combat soldiers' experiences, fighting at such battles like "Hamburger Hill," or of the discontent in the ranks that led to the "fragging" of officers and senior enlisted leaders. Yet the relationship between the US military leaders in South Vietnam and the civilian policymakers in Washington, DC, remains an understudied topic.[32]

   Withdrawal, therefore, intends to fill a gap within the existing literature by concentrating on the senior US military command's prosecution of the political-military conflict in Vietnam, in a sense a continuation of *Westmoreland's War*. Far from the conventional-minded officer who cared only for racking up enemy body counts, I have argued previously, Westmoreland "developed a comprehensive military strategy consistent with the president's larger political objectives." In the process, the general "devised an operational plan that accorded well with the complex realities of the Vietnamese revolutionary war."[33]

   In conjunction with the main arguments made in *Westmoreland's War*, this work challenges the long-standing, and overly reductive, proposition that American strategy in Vietnam changed abruptly in mid-1968 from "search and destroy" to "clear and hold."[34] Reassessing the historical record suggests the transition between Westmoreland and Abrams yielded no such categorical breaks. The lure of the "better war" narrative, however, remains strong. Thus, in his recent study of American generalship, journalist Thomas E. Ricks could argue "there were more continuities between Westmoreland and Abrams than not," while still affirming that "Abrams put aside Westmoreland's strategy of attrition." Counterinsurgency advocate John Nagl offered an equally contradictory view. Nagl maintained, "Abrams completely changed the emphasis of MACV strategy," only to state shortly thereafter that the general "was unable to change the strategy of the U.S. Army."[35] It seemed as if contesting the narrative was just too bitter a pill. Myths, of course, have a way of enduring in the popular mindset.

A reassessment contesting these myths is long overdue. At its core, then, *Withdrawal* argues that General Creighton Abrams, and the entire US mission in South Vietnam, were unable to reverse, or even arrest, the downward trends of a complicated Vietnamese war that by 1968 had turned into a political-military stalemate. Despite a new articulation of MACV strategy, Abrams's "one war" approach could not materially alter a war that American political leaders no longer saw as vital to US national security or global dominance. In short, the bloody stalemate in Vietnam persisted during the Abrams years. Moreover, though the war expanded outside of South Vietnam's borders (in part because of this stalemate), the Vietnamese conflict became tangential to larger US national security needs. Surely, Abrams adapted to these changing circumstances. But the slight tactical alterations ultimately mattered little. Once the Nixon White House made the political decision to withdraw from Southeast Asia, MACV's military strategy was unable to change either the course or the outcome of a decades' long Vietnamese civil war.[36]

This work further argues that the "better war" thesis overextends reality. The myth's narrative assumes that military strategy crafted in Saigon could overcome political decisions made in Washington. It could not. Even with over a half-million US troops in Vietnam by 1968, continued fighting there seemed unlikely to attain larger foreign policy objectives.[37] Abrams quite simply could not save a war that at least some US political leaders already had decided was lost—at least in the traditional military sense—or was no longer worth fighting. President Nixon might still believe in the domino theory, but groused that the "real question is whether the Americans give a damn anymore."[38] After years of stalemate, policymakers in Washington had finally grasped that furthering the war in Vietnam was damaging, rather than bolstering, US credibility abroad.

Perhaps most importantly, neither Abrams nor his predecessor Westmoreland could answer underlying questions about Vietnamese national identity in the modern era. In essence, the war had always revolved around this fundamental issue—what did it mean to be Vietnamese in the aftermath of European colonialism? If US military strategy could not transcend policymaking decisions in Washington, it possessed even less influence in the rural countryside and urban cities of South Vietnam where this key question would be settled. The contest over national identity remained central to determining the war's outcome, yet Americans mattered only in that many, if not most, Vietnamese saw outside influence as inimical to their cause. Surely, countless South Vietnamese, especially army officers, viewed US involvement as crucial to sustaining the Saigon regime. Yet by the late 1960s, even under the auspices of a new commander, the American presence appeared as disruptive as it was necessary.

Reassessing the Final Years

If violence remained an integral part of MACV's approach in the years after Tet, other consistencies marked the American experience in Vietnam during the Abrams era. Thus, three themes thread their way through this work. First, political grand strategy fashioned in Washington trumped military strategy conceived and implemented in South Vietnam. Strategy, in truth, unfolds at different levels. US Army doctrine in the late 1960s made clear delineations between "national strategy" and "military strategy." While the former comprised "the long-range plan through which a nation applies its strength toward the attainment of its objective," the latter directed the "development and use of the military means" to "further national strategy through the direct or indirect application of military power."[39]

More recent explorations into the topic have proposed that "grand strategy" supplies the "intellectual architecture that lends structure to foreign policy."[40] Encompassing more than just military matters, grand strategy takes into account all assets of national power and authority—economic, diplomatic, social, and even moral aspects. Thus, as one specialist has observed, " 'Military strategy' and 'grand strategy' are interrelated, but are by no means synonymous."[41]

This argument plays a crucial role when reassessing the United States' final years in Vietnam. While General Abrams held broad authority when crafting military strategy inside South Vietnam, his seemingly unconventional "one war" approach could not transcend political decisions being crafted in the White House. Whether under Lyndon Johnson or Richard Nixon, military strategy remained bounded by parameters set far from the battlefield.

Second, Abrams could not balance a war that was unfolding along numerous (and often competing) lines. Upon taking office, Nixon formulated a wide-ranging grand strategy aimed at achieving multiple goals—reversing the "Americanization" of the war, giving more priority to pacification, destroying enemy sanctuaries, withdrawing US troops from Vietnam, and negotiating a cease-fire and peace treaty with Hanoi and Saigon.[42] Yet even before Nixon's inauguration, Abrams acknowledged the challenge was "to orchestrate our efforts and our resources so that our total goal can be achieved." The general believed that all of his tasks had to be undertaken concurrently. To many critics, Westmoreland had failed, in part, because of his sequential approach aimed at defeating the enemy first before helping pacify and then build a stable South Vietnamese nation.[43]

But Abrams's "one war" approach, while conceptually sensible, proved unrealistic in practice. The MACV commander could never find parity among the opposing imperatives of US troop withdrawals, negotiations with Hanoi, the policy of Vietnamization, and the necessity of fighting an ongoing war.[44] If the purpose of grand strategy was to "achieve equilibrium between means and ends," Nixon had given his military chief in Vietnam an unmanageable task. Even optimists enamored with Abrams conceded that one had to make "hopeful assumptions" when assessing whether or not the general could fulfill the president's wishes.[45]

This crafting of grand strategic objectives outside the capacity of the military command in Vietnam speaks to the final theme in *Withdrawal*. Throughout, this work explores the interrelationships between war and society in both the United States and South Vietnam. If Abrams could not balance the war in Vietnam, at least some of that failure could be attributed to the influence of the American home front. Certainly, much care is needed here, for it is far too easy to blame the antiwar movement or a liberal news media for failures at the grand strategic level. Writing in early 1967, Arthur Schlesinger believed the "proposition that dissent in America is losing the war in Vietnam is, on existing evidence, much less a fact than an alibi."[46] Still, policy decisions and domestic matters held influence over how Abrams (and his South Vietnamese allies) approached the conflict in Southeast Asia.

Nixon and Kissinger, for instance, both lamented the pressures being exerted by an impatient home front. The president, hoping to withdraw from Vietnam while maintaining the nation's honor, complained of "this cancer eating at us at home, eating us abroad." Kissinger equally railed against domestic groups who were pressing the United States to "withdraw unilaterally and dump" South Vietnamese president Nguyen Van Thieu.[47] Even the editor for *The Harford Courant* compared the war in late 1969 to a football game in which the United States was "winning 34-7 in the third quarter just when the game may be called and the other side declared the winner."[48]

This interdependence between military strategy and the home front certainly influenced what the White House and Abrams's headquarters deemed possible as the United States began its slow departure from Vietnam. Less studied, however, has been the role of the South Vietnamese home front on the war's progress and final outcome. In a struggle among the population (and for its support), the South Vietnamese were always more than just passive actors.[49] The political elite in Saigon decided whether or not to accept recommendations emanating from the US Embassy. Local militia and security forces often determined military and political momentum in the countryside. And, of course, the people themselves were the final arbiters in resolving the crucial question of their government's legitimacy. If the United States was winning in the third quarter, it seemed at times they were playing in a completely different stadium from their South Vietnamese allies.

Thus, even for Americans, notions of victory and defeat ultimately depended on local entities. Without question, most US military and civilian leaders in Saigon understood that South Vietnam was "in the midst of a social and political revolution."[50] They worried about sustaining popular will not only at home, but also in the Vietnamese countryside, where war-weary inhabitants might concede to communist demands and revoke their support for the Thieu government. But Americans' grasp of this revolutionary struggle reached only so deep. The complexities of the internal contest over national identity that crossed ethnic, cultural, and social boundaries too often eluded US war managers. Moreover, for officers to consider their own limited influence remained a difficult proposition. As one senior US general recalled, "It was like keeping a gyroscope spinning on this thing. You have to put a little spin on it occasionally if it runs down and wobbles."[51]

Clearly, though, the South Vietnamese proved much more than an inanimate spinning top in need of American energy to keep upright. In this sense, exploring the war's impact on both Vietnamese and American societies helps us reevaluate the successes and limitations of US military strategy during the Abrams era. A more holistic approach contests the popular notion that the United States won the war militarily only to lose it politically. Though Nixon later would complain that "Vietnam was lost on the political front in the United States, not on the battlefield in Southeast Asia," such verdicts tended to diminish the chaotic revolutionary struggle among the Vietnamese.[52] Americans may have pursued an effective and stable Saigon government "like the Holy Grail," but arguing that dissent at home undermined US military accomplishments abroad misses an important point. The intersections between governmental legitimacy and political-military violence in South Vietnam never evolved as neatly as President Nixon might have hoped.[53]

Moreover, if many Americans dissented against US foreign policy in Southeast Asia, the South Vietnamese equally judged their government of South Vietnam (GVN). Far from limp "puppets" represented in enemy propaganda, the South Vietnamese—political leaders, urban elite, and rural farmers alike—made choices that mightily influenced the course of the war. True, local leaders' decisions often "exacerbated the social disorder already generated by the war."[54] But so, too, did the presence of more than half a million foreign soldiers and civilians. And while contemporary Americans generally condemned the "sheer incapacity of the regime we backed," introducing any form of "social revolution," as GVN leaders believed they were doing, was bound to be disruptive. In the process, even a farmer's passive acceptance of communist influence in his village proved to be a choice of great political import.[55]

This larger appreciation for the relationships between war and its affected societies entails reevaluating the evidence (or lack thereof) on which "better war" narratives rest. If Abrams had, in fact, succeeded in refocusing "U.S. military strategy away from search and destroy toward population control," then why did this dramatic shift not lead to substantial increases of support for the Saigon government?[56] Why, in the aftermath of Tet, did a battered National Liberation Front (NLF)—pejoratively dubbed the "Vietcong" or "VC" by the allies— continue to retain political influence in the South Vietnamese countryside? And if Abrams spoke of a "new ball game," why did so much of the rural population see only continued suffering and devastation from a war with seemingly no end in sight?[57]

In the end, a selective use of the historical record, too often ignoring the South Vietnamese voice, has helped craft a misleading story about a new, war-winning strategy in the aftermath of Tet. A more accurate portrayal, however, tells a different tale. No miraculous strategic transformations occurred in mid-1968. American officers did not suddenly gain a newfound appreciation for the war's political facets because of Abrams's rise to command. The Saigon government had not convinced the bulk of the rural population that it alone was the legitimate voice of the more than 17 million people living inside a war-torn country. And no victory had been achieved in South Vietnam, only to have irresolute American politicians, disloyal journalists, and unpatriotic antiwar demonstrators sabotage the nation's last chance to achieve peace with honor in a long, yet noble, war.[58]

War as Politics

Reassessing America's final years in Vietnam requires one final recognition. War is not simply a military endeavor. Political objectives drive the decisions of policymakers, combatants, and even those civilians caught in the path of war.[59] Tet surely demonstrated the incongruity between military operations and political realities in both the United States and Vietnam. But so, too, did post-1968 battles like Hamburger Hill or the allied incursions into Cambodia and Laos. Success on the battlefield rarely translated into political cachet for either Presidents Nixon or Thieu. Nor did these military operations encourage the South Vietnamese people to fully throw their lot behind the Saigon government. Nixon surely intended MACV's military operations to create political opportunities for the allies, such as increased leverage at the negotiating table. Yet the president and his advisors (as well as contemporary military officers) visibly grasped the all too temporary affects that military campaigns had in realizing the war's larger political aims.[60]

Still, Vietnam veterans took aim at their civilian masters after South Vietnam's collapse. They railed against the "fuzzy-headed liberals" and the "great deal of pressure from Washington . . . just to turn tail and run."[61] They blamed political leaders for unnecessary restrictions that undermined military effectiveness. (Wouldn't an unlimited air campaign and a call-up of the reserves, they asked, have altered the course and outcome of the war?) And they impugned policymakers for stabbing them in the back. As one lieutenant general recalled, "We had won the war after the Tet offensive and the mini-Tet, but we weren't permitted to follow it up and actually accomplish the total defeat." Civilian oversight of the military, a constitutional imperative, seemed less important than winning the war at all costs.[62]

Veterans equally denounced the media for cultivating dissent at home, misrepresenting military victories in Vietnam, and pressuring Washington politicians to end the war regardless of the costs to national prestige and influence. One officer protested the "irresponsible journalism" that created a "chaotic image of the US effort in Vietnam."[63] Another believed the communists had used "our freedom of the press to their advantage," while yet another, writing in late 1969, believed the "Cassandras have succeeded in blinding the victorious warrior who cannot see his enemy writhing on the floor in the arena." Not to be outdone, even President Nixon bemoaned how "our worst enemy seems to be the press!"[64]

Of course, blaming political leaders or the media for "losing" the war in Vietnam absolved military leaders of much wrongdoing, especially if under Abrams a new strategy promised victory in Tet's aftermath. While convenient, such claims rested on half-truths at best. Nixon and Kissinger, for example, sought alternative policies not just for winning the war but also for ending it honorably. Allegations of an oppositional media have been generally overblown.[65] Perhaps most importantly, to argue that political defeatism undercut battlefield victories misinterprets a war that always was more political than military in its construct. Such arguments also misconstrue the nature of modern war itself, which is always a political act first and foremost.

In truth, a collective search for blame became part of the long healing process after America's first lost war. The search reached far and wide. If victory was betrayed in Vietnam, a host of villains could be faulted—Congress, which in Nixon's words had "proceeded to snatch defeat from the jaws of victory"; the South Vietnamese government for failing to embrace reforms endorsed by US advisors; peaceniks like Jane Fonda and the misguided journalists who gave them a national voice; even Abrams's predecessor for bungling the war effort and squandering public support.[66]

From within this search for blame arose a reimagining of the Vietnam War. Perhaps the war had been won in Vietnam as Nixon had argued. Perhaps prolonging the conflict had, in fact, demonstrated the nation's credibility by directly confronting communism, thus preventing other dominoes in Southeast Asia from falling.[67] Perhaps Ronald Reagan made sense when he claimed in August 1980 that "it's time we recognized that ours was, in truth, a noble cause." As the Republican presidential nominee declared, "We dishonored the memory of 50,000 young Americans who died in that cause when we give way to feelings of guilt as if we were doing something shameful." Was it possible the United States had won the war in Vietnam?[68]

Such rhetoric found a receptive audience, particularly among military officers. This reframing of the American experience in Vietnam also bolstered claims that a major strategic shift after Tet had wrought significant gains. Though the "American people decided that Vietnam wasn't worth it," tough fighting had produced results. Nixon's decision to expand the war outside of South Vietnam's borders, long an appeal from MACV, had disrupted enemy sanctuaries in Cambodia and Laos and had a marked effect on Hanoi.[69] Even though some argued there "was no intention—no objective—of defeating North Vietnam militarily," Abrams still had led the allies to victory. No doubt many officers agreed with the argument, made in early 1970, that any "acceptance of defeat would be a matter of our own decision and not a necessity."[70]

These assertions, however congenial to veterans who sacrificed so much in hopes of leaving behind a stable and independent South Vietnam, also rest on dubious evidence. Reassessing America's final years in Vietnam presents a more sober account of a struggle that left indelible scars on a number of societies. It may be true, as one British officer remarked in 1967, that the military man "will at times feel that his freedom of action is being unduly restricted by political considerations."[71] But war is a product of politics and military strategy only part of any larger war. Several issues, well outside of MACV's scope, affected American policy toward Vietnam—the political acumen of Hanoi's leaders, the military effectiveness of the North Vietnamese and National Liberation Front armed forces, progress in nation building made by the Saigon government, and the changing global context of the larger Cold War. Quite simply, there were limits to what military force inside South Vietnam could accomplish.[72]

The war surely affected more than just military officers coping with the limits of US strategy. Some Americans saw in the conduct of a losing war the making of a national trauma. Nixon and Kissinger worried extensively about what Vietnam was doing to US credibility abroad. Even before war's end, the president warned that a precipitous withdrawal from Vietnam would "result in a collapse of confidence in American leadership not only in Asia but throughout the world." Faced with the consequences, "inevitable remorse and divisive recrimination would scar our spirit as a people."[73] With the last American troops departed from Southeast Asia, Nixon's words seemed prophetic. One critic lamented the spectacle of defeat in Vietnam, calling it a "highly traumatic experience, since a devaluation of national identity is a loss affecting the very quality of life itself." If maintaining US credibility had replaced a free and independent South Vietnam as the war's ultimate political objective, it appeared the Americans had come up short on both counts.[74]

Contentions of a war won militarily yet lost politically thus fall short of their mark. The inseparable bonds between societies and the war they were fighting came into full view during the conflict's final years. Nowhere was this more evident than in South Vietnam, an unsettled political community that buckled under the combined weight of allied and enemy military action. If armed might could buoy the Saigon government, it could not convince the people that military occupation would lead to their salvation. Nor could minor strategic alterations convert skeptics within the United States to believe their international commitments to the Saigon regime were worth the continuing sacrifice.[75]

More than forty years after the fall of Saigon, it is time for those studying the Vietnam War, especially Americans, to consider an uncomfortable proposition. Only the Vietnamese could resolve the deep political and social differences around which their civil war revolved. Revisionist narratives of a war-winning strategy undone by political imprudence simply don't hold up under closer scrutiny. In the end, the best that American forces were able to achieve, whether under William Westmoreland or Creighton Abrams, was a costly military stalemate. By 1973, the final US troops withdrew from South Vietnam not as victors, but as interlopers in a war that was never theirs to win or lose.

1

Abe's "One War"

Continuity in Change

"Marineland." For years, military operations in the northernmost provinces of South Vietnam fell under the direction of the US Marine Corps. It seemed almost a special preserve, an operational area off limits to intrusive army officers running the war in Saigon. Occasionally, rumors surfaced in the press of marines' dissatisfaction with allied strategy. Some of the Corps' generals, like Lewis Walt, argued that fighting against larger enemy main force units, far away from the population centers, missed the point. Instead, the allies should be concentrating their efforts at the village level. As one reporter described Walt's philosophy, "The main Communist force depends on the support of teachers, nurses, tax collectors and laborers. If these people could be located and won over, Walt argued, the Communists would be hit where it hurts."[1]

But "Marineland," officially known as the I Corps Tactical Zone (CTZ), covered a vast area, roughly 200 miles long and varying in width from 30 to 80 miles. More than 2.5 million inhabitants resided there. More importantly, though, four of the five northern provinces abutted either Laos or the demilitarized zone between North and South Vietnam. By 1967, four North Vietnamese Army (PAVN) regular divisions were pressuring marine positions and outposts guarding the borders against enemy incursions. As much as Walt and his commanders may have wanted to maintain a large presence among the villages, the threat of a full-fledged conventional invasion from the north precluded such aspirations. Still, the marines, believing they had discovered a path toward victory in Vietnam, chafed under the perceived mismanagement of the larger war effort.[2]

The feelings were mutual. General William C. Westmoreland, head of the US Military Assistance Command, Vietnam (MACV), had long been uneasy with the marines' approach in I Corps. As one senior officer recalled, Westmoreland "felt that the Marines needed somebody to guide them. . . . He wasn't getting the response from the Marine outfit that he thought he should in I Corps." With indications of an enemy buildup in late 1967, the MACV commander decided to add a level of oversight in the northern provinces. In essence, Westmoreland was establishing a forward headquarters "to make sure things get under control." Only one army officer possessed the gravitas to handle such a delicate command restructuring—Westmoreland's deputy, Creighton Abrams.[3]

Abrams had been in country since mid-1967 and shared his boss's views, rating the marines' tactical proficiencies below the US Army, the Australian contingent, and the South Korean allies in Vietnam. The former World War II tank commander also agreed on the need to fight the enemy near South Vietnam's borders. As Westmoreland argued in mid-December, the allies "must strike him as soon as he is within reach, and before he can gain a victory or tyrannize the local population."[4] Nor did Abrams deviate from prevalent assumptions on enemy capabilities. Though most of the MACV staff grasped indications of a possible offensive during the upcoming Tet holiday, few believed Hanoi had the capacity to support a countrywide assault across the whole of South Vietnam. Even while ordering tactical adjustments around Saigon, Westmoreland clung to his belief that North Vietnamese forces would attack the marine base and airstrip at Khe Sanh in Quang Tri province. A more far-reaching offensive simply seemed unimaginable at the time.[5]

This concentration of enemy forces along South Vietnam's northern borders held Westmoreland's attention throughout early January. As anxieties rose, the general recommended to President Nguyen Van Thieu that he cancel a planned Tet holiday cease-fire. (Thieu agreed to a shortened 36-hour truce.)[6] The climactic blow against Khe Sanh, however, never came. Instead, with Westmoreland's eyes fixed along the borders in I Corps, the enemy launched their countrywide attack on 30 January 1968. Though not fully caught off guard, the allies clearly had misread the scope of Hanoi's plans. The Tet offensive, though, seemed only to validate Westmoreland's concerns over I Corps. On 3 February, Abrams arrived in Phu Bai and less than a week later formally activated a new headquarters, MACV Forward. Lieutenant General Robert E. Cushman's III Marine Amphibious Force now fell directly under Abrams.[7]

With Westmoreland's deputy "running the I CTZ show," American and South Vietnamese forces hastily recovered from the initial onslaught of the Tet offensive. Hard fighting, though, remained. Khe Sanh came under heavy attack in late January. So, too, did the imperial city of Hue, the liberation of which took nearly three weeks after brutal urban combat.[8] The tense command relationships between MACV headquarters and the marines in I Corps, however, gained attention in US newspapers as the fighting died down in South Vietnam. In early March, *The Washington Post* reported army officers' criticism of marine leaders as "unimaginative." Critics found the marine chain of command "confused" during the recent Tet fighting and "singularly unimpressive." One month later, the *Los Angeles Times* conveyed the "open secret" that Westmoreland's top staff officers were "less than enthusiastic with Marine generals' conduct of the war in the five northernmost provinces." By early April, the MACV commander found it necessary to publicly express his admiration for the Marine Corps leadership.[9]

The command friction between army and marine commanders in early 1968 underscored the complexities of a war now more than two years old for American combat forces. The defense of Khe Sanh surely captured both senior policymakers and the media's attention in the days leading to Tet. Yet a myopic focus on a piece of terrain, with near frantic inquiries over whether Khe Sanh could be held, diverted attention from more fundamental questions. *Should* Khe Sanh be held?[10] More fundamentally, did the war in Vietnam still make sense? Were US foreign policy objectives still being advanced by the hard fighting in Southeast Asia? Was the war truly winnable after more than a year of seeming military stalemate?

This final question proved the most discomfiting in the uneasy days and months after Tet. Fretful Americans wondered, many aloud, if they were seeing the makings of their first lost war. Such a possibility unsettled even the most strident critics. Thus, when Creighton Abrams assumed command of the allied war effort in mid-1968, the transition offered hope that defeat in Vietnam might still be averted. Surely, this gruff, cigar-chomping soldier—who looked so different from the ramrod straight Westmoreland—possessed fresh strategic ideas that would vastly improve the allies' chances for victory. His use of the apparently novel phrase "one war" suggested an innovative approach.[11]

Such optimism, however, rested on false notions. In the end, Abrams's "one war" concept represented more a change in rhetoric than a modification of strategy in practice. As one senior MACV insider rightfully claimed, the "myth of a change in strategy [was] a figment of the media imagination." When pressed, even marines with vast wartime experience at the village level doubted "anyone could really make the case that a great difference existed."[12] Journalists, discerning minor alterations at the tactical level, mistakenly reported a conspicuous change in US military operations under Abrams. Yet in reality, Abrams had simply incorporated a phrase, and with it a strategy, that had long been in place within MACV headquarters. As much as the "one war" approach offered hope to those seeking encouragement in the aftermath of Tet, no new strategy emerged in the dark days of mid-1968.[13] The different looks between William Westmoreland and Creighton Abrams had, in fact, been deceiving.

Making Sense of a Multifaceted War

Not long after the allies brooked the first waves of the Tet offensive, Abrams flew to Washington, DC, to meet with President Johnson and stated, without reservation, that he saw no need for a change in strategy. For nearly two hours on the morning of 26 March, Westmoreland's deputy engaged in a wide-ranging discussion in the White House family dining room with LBJ and Chairman of the Joint Chiefs of Staff (JCS) Earle G. Wheeler. Abrams noted how North Vietnamese infiltrators were replacing losses within the insurgent National Liberation Front (NLF), a sign of manpower difficulties after nearly two months of fighting. Johnson directed Abrams to stress publicly that the South Vietnamese morale was holding, yet worried about the panic caused by Tet. The president then asked, "Is there anything we should be doing that we aren't doing?" "Our basic strategy is sound," replied Wheeler. Abrams concurred. "I don't feel we need to change strategy. We need to be more flexible tactically inside South Vietnam." The following day, Abrams met with the National Security Council and maintained that with currently planned augmentations to US troops already in Vietnam, the "situation can be adequately handled."[14]

Far from a unique episode in the weeks following Tet, Abrams's White House statements accorded with most all senior civilian and military leaders managing the war effort in South Vietnam. Ambassador Ellsworth Bunker recalled the "course we had charted was a correct one." Army Chief of Staff Harold K. Johnson publicly laid out his views on US strategy and the "interdependence of the various levels" of the enemy's forces. To Johnson, the current approach was proceeding in three stages: first, separating the local guerrillas and political apparatus from the enemy main force units; next, wearing down the enemy regional and local forces through smaller-scale operations; and finally, eliminating the political structure of the the NLF inside South Vietnam. The chief of staff was "confident that our concept represents a well-conceived and balanced approach toward freeing the South Vietnamese countryside from domination." Even the commandant of the Marine Corps wrote the president that he "fully support[ed] the concept of operations outlined in General Westmoreland's Campaign Plan for 1968."[15]

Still, Abrams's own role in Tet had exposed him to lingering problems with American military strategy in Vietnam, one that covered the breadth of a geographically diverse country. In 1968, South Vietnam was home to more than 17 million people living in some 250 districts and 44 provinces. The variations among these locales was vast. American soldiers might find themselves fighting in multicanopy forest with dense undergrowth, while their comrades were groping their way through inundated swamps or unfamiliar sugarcane plantations. The land border alone covered more than 1,000 miles and touched neighboring Laos and Cambodia, as well as the demilitarized zone (DMZ) between North and South Vietnam. As one observer put it, each district was "so different in geography, demography, tactical and political situations, and characteristics of the opposing forces and leadership" that there were hundreds of unique campaigns

being fought throughout the battle-scarred country. The "fragmentary information" emanating from these countless wars only undermined attempts to understand larger trends within the overall political-military conflict.[16]

So, too, did disputes over allied strategy that cut to the very core of how well
the war was progressing. Abrams observed firsthand the intraservice strategic
wrangling and shared Westmoreland's disquiet over the leadership in I Corps.
It appears, however, these debates have long been oversimplified. In large sense,
Westmoreland and the marines agreed on more than contemporary reports
would have us believe. Rather than a clash between advocates of attrition warfare and population security, the two services essentially were talking past each
other. Both MACV officers and the marines in I Corps recognized the threat
posed by North Vietnamese Army regulars infiltrating across South Vietnam's
borders. As General Walt acknowledged, "I don't think you can ignore the main
force war."[17] Yet marine leaders also appreciated, as did Westmoreland, the threat
of "a more elusive enemy—the guerilla fighter . . . [who] lives and hides in the
sanctuary of the population." Thus, the commandant of the Marine Corps advocated a "balanced approach" that sought to integrate the main force war with
counterinsurgency and population security operations.[18]

Even those marines—like General Victor H. "Brute" Krulak—who believed
attrition of enemy forces was "peripheral" to the overriding struggle for the population's loyalty, could not ignore the conventional threat posed by PAVN forces
in I Corps. "Search-and-destroy" operations might make unflattering headlines,
but they proved an indispensable element of MACV strategy throughout the
war, even under Abrams.[19] Thus, the innovative combined action program, aiming to merge marine squads with local forces at the village level, never prospered
because the leadership in I Corps simply could not redirect critical resources
away from the main force war. Additionally, more than a few marines found
the grassroots combined action program unrealistic. As one recalled, "The VC
[Vietcong] infrastructure was too deeply entrenched, literally as well as figura-
tively in some places. They had more than 20 years to win hearts and minds
before we blundered onto the scene . . . The cultural gulf was just unbridgeable
out in the countryside."[20]

If American forces had difficulties assessing the depths of the insurgency's
infrastructure, they equally struggled to evaluate the South Vietnamese armed
forces. With Abrams soon to take command of MACV, senior officers continued a long tradition of denigrating their Asian allies. A June 1968 debriefing
report summarized the long-standing defects within the Army of the Republic of
Vietnam (ARVN)—troops fearful of closing with the enemy and uninterested
in the pacification effort; logistical resupply problems with ammunition, food,
and water; and, perhaps most importantly, "spotty" leadership and command
deficiencies "at all levels."[21] Despite the ARVN's generally solid performance

during the Tet offensive, the *Boston Globe* saw "no reason for optimism" of South Vietnam taking over the war in the next few years. Even a general mobilization law, signed on 20 June, that aimed to add more than a quarter of a million men into the armed forces, left senior American war managers uneasy.[22] Abrams surely appreciated the challenges given his work on improving the ARVN while Westmoreland's deputy. Yet any talk of the United States withdrawing from Vietnam rested on dubious assumptions that the South Vietnamese could capably replace the departing Americans. Most US advisors remained skeptical. As one infantry colonel reported that summer, "ARVN battalions still have a long way to go before they can be termed combat ready to go it alone on a sustained basis."[23]

The South Vietnamese Army, of course, was not operating in a vacuum. A war that had long preceded the Americans' entry had left a population reeling from the pressures of constant fighting. Tet seemed only to accentuate the suffering. Nowhere was this more evident than in the imperial city of Hue. Less than 20 percent of the city remained undamaged in the fighting, blasted away by US and ARVN firepower. But the communist presence, and the allied response, brought further depredation to the local population, spawning some 68,000 refugees. Hue citizens were caught between communist death squads, rounding up and killing "reactionaries," and allied bombs, "falling like rain" from the sky. One witness recalled nights of "shouts and screams, exasperation, and flaring gunfire" and an "atmosphere filled with death and panic." The city of Hue was left "screaming and moaning in the throes of death."[24]

Even if American officials and their South Vietnamese allies could declare victory in Tet's aftermath, the destruction wrought on Hue and other cities and towns left a shaky foundation on which to build a stable political community. Here would be Abrams's topmost challenge in the years of American withdrawal—helping build a viable South Vietnamese military institution from a population weary from decades of war. Senior US officers trumpeted the fact that the population had not risen in support of the communists during and after Tet. (A full year before, Westmoreland believed the enemy intended to "discredit and erode GVN political authority at all levels.")[25] Yet the absence of a popular uprising hardly denoted a people willingly throwing their fortunes in with the Saigon regime.

Just prior to Tet, noted journalist David Halberstam traveled to South Vietnam and found cause for concern. "The government of Vietnam is largely meaningless to its citizens." Though surviving the Tet offensive, the GVN labored to regain influence, and thus control, within the countryside. As head of the American civil operations effort, Ambassador Robert Komer reported in May 1968 that the "Tet aftermath resulted in a power vacuum in rural areas; a vacuum the enemy quickly recognized and is attempting to fill."[26] Yet those living in the countryside recognized something as well. As one farmer observed, we "saw that the Government side was weak, and needed to have the Americans support them."[27] If Abrams intended to build a viable military structure atop a sturdy political foundation, he had his work cut out for him.

These lingering problems with the Saigon regime frustrated American military advisors and civilian policymakers alike. Thieu's signing of the general mobilization law in June surely demonstrated the GVN's commitment to the war effort. So, too, did a national plan to arm villagers under the People's Self-Defense Force (PSDF) program. Yet claims of corruption, black market connections, and abuses in land reform programs all hindered building an effective governmental bureaucracy so necessary for the national political struggle. These issues, though, were hardly new.[28]

As early as January 1965, Ambassador Maxwell Taylor had decried the political "turmoil" in Saigon and blamed it on "historical factors growing out of national characteristics and traditions, susceptible to change only over the long run." Two years later, Robert Komer believed the Americans in Vietnam were dealing with "smart crooks, rather than dumb honest men."[29] Even perpetual optimist Ellsworth Bunker, who served as US ambassador to South Vietnam during Abrams's tenure, found Thieu more "used to command as a military man" than an effective politician who could persuade others to join his cause. Bunker consistently urged GVN leaders to remove or discipline corrupt province officials and clean up the police force, all while urging Thieu to set aside his personal rivalry with Vice President Nguyen Cao Ky. The results proved unsatisfying.[30]

In large part, the war itself had created space for crime and corruption to flourish. Urban areas, in particular, seemed to invite social ills that put into question whether Saigon leaders had the proper vision for the nation at large. Moreover, the very presence of Americans appeared to erode traditional social norms, further disrupting the conversation over the future of Vietnamese identity in the modern era. In the process, many local officials blamed their patrons for the GVN's problems. Yet while some Vietnamese believed "corruption and political reforms were simply not high on the American list of priorities," others argued corruption "was necessary for survival in South Viet Nam's war-ravaged economy."[31] For his part, the vice president felt his nation should "win the war first, then make far-reaching social and economic plans." Even some American advisors thought they had contributed to enlarging "the scope for graft and corruption."[32] How military victories on the battlefield would rectify these social problems in the post-Tet era remained to be seen.

So, too, would Abrams's influence on the larger strategic front. For years, American policymakers had assumed Hanoi would eventually break under the weight of US pressure. They had long been disappointed. Despite the increasingly evident setback of the Tet offensive, Le Duan, the Hanoi Politburo's first secretary, remained committed to Vietnamese unification and independence from Western influence. In the months after Tet's opening round, Hanoi sent roughly 85,000 replacements down the Ho Chi Minh Trail. MACV also perceived a decrease in military activity as enemy forces retired to sanctuaries in Cambodia and Laos, all as North Vietnamese diplomats pressed for a halt to the US bombing campaign.[33] Yet while Le Duan altered his tactics in Tet's aftermath, the basic policy objective of toppling the Saigon government had not changed. US soldiers might contend a "more bizarre, eccentric foe than the one in Vietnam is not to be met," but Hanoi's leaders proved far more discerning than most Americans had anticipated.[34]

Thus, Tet exposed for many Americans, not just Creighton Abrams, the complexities of a multifaceted war in Vietnam. Concluding a late February visit to Vietnam, JCS chairman Earle Wheeler could only report that the situation was "still developing and fraught with opportunities as well as dangers." Others offered a more definitive assessment. After his own tour of South Vietnam, respected correspondent Walter Cronkite publicly called for Americans to "negotiate, not as victors, but as an honorable people who lived up to their pledge to defend democracy, and did the best they could."[35] The following month, Undersecretary of the Air Force Townsend Hoopes penned a scathing memorandum titled "The Infeasibility of Military Victory in Vietnam." In a memo for Clark Clifford, who had replaced McNamara as secretary of defense, Hoopes urged a "redefinition of our political objectives" so the United States could achieve "an honorable

Figure 2 A NEW COMMANDER, BUT A NEW STRATEGY? The tough demeanor of General Creighton Abrams elicited hope that he might somehow turn around a stalemated war in mid-1968. (RG737S, MHI)

political settlement." The current policy was succeeding only in destroying South Vietnam and "tearing apart the social and political fabric of our own country."[36]

In the aftermath of Tet, only one thing seemed clear. The continuing war effort left discouraged Americans with more questions than answers. Who was winning? Were the costs worth the returns? Might success not be possible? And, perhaps most hopefully, could a new military commander break the stalemate and guide the allies to victory?

A Commander in Waiting

In late March 1967, the *New York Times*, citing "authoritative sources," reported that Creighton W. Abrams "would be named soon to a key post in Vietnam."[37] The 52-year-old was then serving as the army's vice chief of staff and speculation ran high that he would eventually succeed William Westmoreland, already in his third year heading the US Military Assistance Command, Vietnam (MACV). Since the president had recently laid out plans for an increased effort in nonmilitary pacification programs, reporters inferred that Abrams would be working closely with a "new team of civilian officials" throughout the South Vietnamese countryside. The decision to replace Westmoreland's current deputy, Lieutenant General John A. Heintges, with the full four-star Abrams also held political weight. LBJ could see through his promise to send to Vietnam "additional top-flight military personnel, the best that this country has been able to produce."[38]

In 1967, Abrams certainly epitomized the best the US Army had to offer. Born in Springfield, Massachusetts, the former high school football star graduated from West Point in 1936 alongside his classmate Westmoreland. He commissioned into the cavalry and participated in all of the 4th Armored Division's campaigns during World War II. Returning from Europe, Abrams directed tactics at Fort Knox's armor school, attended the US Army War College, and then went on to Korea as three different corps' chief of staff. As with so many officers, the newly promoted general bounced back and forth in the late 1950s between command and staff assignments before commanding the 3rd Armored Division in October 1960. His mettle was further tested when, in the early 1960s, Abrams twice commanded US Army troops and federalized national guardsmen to deal with racial unrest in the wake of school desegregation in the South. His compassionate yet firm stance impressed the Kennedy administration. Secretary of the Army Cyrus Vance called Abrams "unflappable." Thus, the coveted vice chief of staff position required little second guessing among civilian policymakers and Johnson later held no qualms about posting Abrams to Vietnam as Westmoreland's deputy.[39]

Still, the general's impressive biography—and multiple Distinguished Service Medals and Silver Stars—seemed to matter less than the respect he garnered from across the army. One senior officer described Abrams as having that "rare quality, common sense, the knack of going straight to the heart of a problem, and insisting on a simple and workable solution." If not an intellectual, he was a seasoned combat officer who "could inspire aggressiveness in a begonia."[40] But the presumptive MACV commander also had a temper. As General Bruce Palmer Jr. recalled, "Abrams, a slumbering volcano, would suddenly erupt in an earthy, profane way when necessary to straighten someone out or to spur lagging performance." Staff officers quickly learned to prepare well for their briefings to Abrams or suffer his wrath.[41]

The diversity of Abrams's résumé also alluded to a level of thoughtfulness acquired through years of professional experience. Though gaining his spurs in Patton's Third Army, the general appreciated, as did many of his peers, that the conventional fighting of World War II Europe was not necessarily suited to the complex mosaic of Vietnam. "This was a totally different kind of experience," one division commander illustratively recalled.[42] While historians have tended to criticize Vietnam-era generals for their conventional approach to a multidimensional conflict, evidence suggests senior commanders were much more introspective in managing this new type of war. True, Abrams's past shaped his command style in Vietnam. As one reporter noted, in both Europe and Korea, "Abrams espoused the doctrine that overwhelming firepower saves American lives." Such views did not change in Vietnam. But Abrams—as did his predecessor—consistently worried about the social and political ramifications caused by destructive military operations. The challenge was determining how best to defeat the enemy and save soldiers' lives without ravaging a civilian population already caught in the middle of an ever-escalating civil war.[43]

Abrams received no better introduction to this new environment when Westmoreland assigned him to oversee the training and modernization of the South Vietnamese armed forces (RVNAF). The deputy MACV commander threw himself into a task already worrying many senior US officials. While military officers in Saigon reported on ARVN's operational "tempo" and effectiveness in the growing pacification program, advisors in Washington pondered how to get "more for our money out of ARVN."[44] As General Wheeler wrote later in the year, "Many believe that the ARVN is not carrying its fair share of the combat effort." When Abrams arrived in May 1967, he found a local army dependent on a vast American logistics system and, perhaps ironically, on heavy doses of firepower from the US Army and Air Force. Firepower might save soldiers' lives, but it was also alienating the local population.[45]

With his distinctive energy, Abrams trekked across South Vietnam, questioning, advising, and prodding. The Los Angeles Times reported the general traveled six days out of seven to accomplish the "herculean task of strengthening the Vietnamese army." "He was in the field constantly," MACV Chief of Staff Walter T. Kerwin recalled. "He took it upon himself, I think, more than General Westmoreland told him, to become the sort of godfather of ARVN." Abrams spoke with US advisors and South Vietnamese officers, reviewed ARVN training facilities, and inspected regional and popular forces charged with providing local security to the population. It was a daunting task, yet crucial to larger American goals.[46] As Abrams stressed at a commander's conference, "Our success here is synonymous with the achievements of our programs in assisting the RVNAF take over the defense of their country." Westmoreland concurred, advocating a concept that "puts emphasis on the essential role of the Vietnamese in carrying out a major burden of their war against the Communists." Neither Abrams nor his boss were under any illusions that war would be resolved quickly. But by mid-1967, it seemed Westmoreland had the leadership in place to internally manage MACV's resources, placing Komer in charge of pacification while Abrams attended to the South Vietnamese armed forces.[47]

How best to prioritize the missions assigned to ARVN forces, and the type of support they received, had long concerned senior US officials. Even before Abrams's arrival, MACV staffers wrestled with the decision of which forces should receive the new M-16 semi-automatic rifle, an improvement from the single-shot M-1 carbine. Westmoreland decided priority should go to the Americans. If US troops were focused on combatting enemy main force units while the ARVN and local militia attended to the pacification effort, such an arrangement made sense. Yet as North Vietnamese and insurgent forces became increasingly equipped with the AK-47, arguably the most reliable rifle used by either side during the war, pressures mounted to modernize the ARVN. Thus, in March 1967, the Pentagon earmarked 100,000 M-16s for delivery to South Vietnam, the first shipments arriving at roughly the same time as Abrams. After Tet, Secretary of Defense Clark Clifford pledged even more firepower to Saigon forces, a decision fully supported by the new MACV commander.[48]

In fact, on most strategic matters, Abrams shared the views of Westmoreland. Arguments that he just "languished in the deputy's slot for over a year" simply don't accord with the historical evidence. Without question, as Walter Kerwin recollected, "there was never any deep feeling between the two" generals, "never a warmth between the two of them." Yet claims that Abrams kept his brilliance "under a bushel" until he had a chance to be in charge himself rest on little more than inferences.[49] By all indications, Abrams was loyal, not just to his commander, but to the very mission itself. Even if the new deputy believed "it was really too late to change U.S. strategy," no records have surfaced of any quarrel between the two four-stars over MACV's strategic direction.[50] Moreover, it seems highly doubtful that Abrams would have approached his new assignment in such a selfish manner, hoping for Westmoreland to fail so he could rescue the war effort and wrap himself in glory.

A review of Westmoreland's strategy illustrates the comprehensive approach MACV embarked on not long after the arrival of US combat troops in mid-1965. That autumn, Westmoreland outlined his thoughts on how best to achieve the "ultimate aim" of pacifying the Republic of Vietnam. After halting the enemy's offensive, the allies would destroy insurgent and main force units, pacify high-priority areas, and finally "restore progressively the entire country to the control of the GVN." The tasks to fulfill this strategy were wide-ranging: defending major military bases, purging areas of NLF elements "as a prelude to pacification," and conducting offensive operations against the enemy.[51] In his command guidance for 1967, Westmoreland spoke in similar tones. After acknowledging that "military force alone will not achieve [our] objectives in Vietnam," he noted the importance of "apportioning resources against the *full spectrum* of enemy elements—main forces, local forces, supply system, guerrillas, and the VC infrastructure." Nothing in the historical record suggests Abrams disagreed with any aspect of this strategic approach.[52]

In truth, Westmoreland's use of the phrase "full spectrum" foreshadowed Abrams's penchant for describing the enemy as a "system." Neither officer spoke of supporting an exclusive attritional or counterinsurgency approach. Both types of operations had their place. Thus, the 1968 combined campaign plan, written during Abrams's tenure as MACV deputy, established a long list of basic objectives. Not only would the allies defeat enemy forces in the field, they would also seek to extend Saigon's control throughout the countrywide, deny the enemy rice and other supplies, secure major economic centers, and conduct civic action "to win support of the people to the GVN."[53] In Westmoreland's mind, the South Vietnamese armed forces bore the "primary responsibility for the pacification and security of 'National Priority' areas, or those containing a large majority of the population, food producing regions, and vital" lines of communication. Without question, far too many American officers focused their attention (and firepower) on destroying enemy main force units, thus wreaking havoc on the civilian population.[54] Yet battle remained a centerpiece of US strategy long after Tet had made its impact felt in early to mid-1968.

Thus, Abrams joined a military headquarters at a time when leaders in the US mission already were speaking of the war in holistic terms. At his first council meeting on 1 May 1967, newly arrived Ambassador Ellsworth Bunker expressed his dislike of the term "other war," a phrase then in vogue depicting the nonmilitary pacification effort. "To me this is all one war," Bunker asserted. "Everything we do is an aspect of the total effort to achieve our objectives here."[55] The use of such "one war" language—later appropriated by Abrams—was not intended to prioritize pacification over combat operations, but rather to demonstrate the interlocking dimensions of a complex war. As advisors informed President Johnson that spring, the new ambassador did "not regard pacification as a civil or military problem, but as a civil/military problem. Hence his solution is to have US civilians and military work together." Coordinating his efforts with MACV, Bunker concentrated on pacification planning, increasing the capability to handle refugees, and augmenting the advisory structure to better support the ARVN. "As is so often the case," the ambassador reported in June, "the Government of Vietnam performance remains the crucial factor."[56]

So too, however, was gaining an accurate intelligence picture of the enemy, no easy feat that summer. Westmoreland's staff and the CIA quarreled over accurate assessments, in large part because of a key objective established during the February 1966 Honolulu conference. While the president met with South Vietnamese leaders, Secretaries of Defense Robert McNamara and State Dean Rusk assigned Westmoreland six overriding objectives, the last of those to "attrit, by year's end, VC/NVA forces at a rate as high as their capability to put men in the field." Determining when the allies reached this "crossover point" depended on a careful evaluation of the enemy's "order of battle."[57]

By the summer of 1967, however, CIA analysts were openly contesting MACV's counting system, arguing the military staff was purposefully deciding to exclude local self-defense forces and thus demonstrate progress in the war. To intelligence specialists, Westmoreland should continue tallying self-defense troops, local guerrillas, and political cadre into their overall numbers. The debate reached both the Pentagon and the White House and ultimately led to Westmoreland suing CBS News in 1982 for libel after accusations the general had conspired to falsify order of battle reports.[58]

Far from an intelligence cover-up, the episode highlighted the difficulties of simply defining the enemy.[59] CIA analysts like Sam Adams believed the self-defense militia—roughly 120,000 to 150,000 in strength—should continue to be calculated into the enemy's formal order of battle. MACV disagreed, as did Ambassador Bunker. In August, with Westmoreland in DC, Abrams sent a message to the chairman of the Joint Chiefs questioning the inclusion of the self-defense forces. "These forces contain a sizeable number of women and old people. They operate entirely in their own hamlets. They are rarely armed, have no real discipline, and almost no military capability." Just as importantly, Abrams noted, would be the press reaction if these new figures were incorporated into the enemy order of battle. "The newsmen will immediately seize on the point that the enemy force has increased about 120-130,000."[60] If MACV's deputy underestimated the crucial role played by these irregular forces, he surely understood the increasingly political nature of the war back home. Less than one month later, after much wrangling, the CIA and MACV had squared the circle. A compromise assessed the enemy main and local forces in one category, while separating "guerrillas," "administrative service personnel," and political cadre into others.[61]

The order of battle controversy suggested that doctrinal prescriptions on countering local insurgencies made sense on paper, but often proved far more difficult to implement in the field. Officers confidently affirmed there was "no purely military battlefield in counter-insurgency warfare" and posited that these long campaigns could "only be won by combined civil-military efforts."[62] Doctrine writers valued the importance of support from the local population and emphasized the role of internal defense and development programs. Even Westmoreland's concept of operations followed the counsel of those advocating for a comprehensive approach that linked search-and-destroy missions with "clear-and-hold" operations aimed at securing the population. Yet such operational breadth also inhibited coordination among the allies. How, for example, should MACV confront the enemy's political cadre while also defending against North Vietnamese regiments and securing the rural population from the more provincial threat of the NLF insurgency? Moreover, consigning political cadre into discrete threat categories tended to conceptually divorce them from the main force units to which they were intrinsically linked.[63]

As MACV's deputy commander for more than a year, Abrams surely recognized the dilemmas posed by such a multifaceted threat. He was also, however, heavily influenced by Westmoreland's own approach to this threat. Less than six months after Abrams's arrival, the MACV commander summarized his strategic concept for the Joint Chiefs. He spoke of applying "real pressure on the enemy" and of securing as much rice-producing areas and the population as possible. Westmoreland went on to outline the various task his command had undertaken: "to disrupt communist control over the people, to open roads and waterways, to take the fight to the enemy's main forces, to invade base areas of the enemy in South Vietnam, to block invasion across the DMZ and from his sanctuaries in Laos and Cambodia, and to support the government's revolutionary development program." Westmoreland's strategic concept was nothing if not wide-ranging.[64]

Still, the last objective of supporting revolutionary development efforts became an increasingly vital part of MACV strategy by mid-1967. While civilian and military leaders alike often conflated the term "revolutionary development" with phrases like "pacification" or "civic action," the end-state remained constant—linking South Vietnam's rural population to the Saigon government. Westmoreland, and later Abrams, anticipated that military operations would lead to increased security and thus improve Saigon's credibility in the eyes of the population. The people would then accept the GVN pacification program and, most importantly, the government's "involvement in their own future."[65] Hence, only through a comprehensive approach to the political-military problems inside South Vietnam could the allies break the communists' grip on the local inhabitants and restore democracy to an embattled nation.

Without question, professional officers and soldiers alike became discouraged in their lack of ability to woo the population over to the government side. Many also expressed their frustration in not being able to extend the war into North Vietnam, to their minds the "source" of the southern insurgency. Throughout both Westmoreland and Abrams's tenures at MACV, high-ranking officers railed against the limitations being placed on them by their civilian masters. By 1965, the Joint Chiefs were calling once more on the president to "intensify military pressure" on North Vietnam.[66] Four years later, senior commanders ranted to Abrams that they were "getting tired of the NVA firing at us from across the border." One division commander offered a somewhat bizarre interpretation on the "causative factors" of the southern insurgency. "If you're a hungry Chinaman who has never heard of a vasectomy but who has confronted a burly Russian on the North, then you go South." Clearly, as late as 1969, at least some US officers were still working through the intricacies of international relations.[67]

While military leaders may have falsely assumed Moscow or Beijing was controlling the Hanoi Politburo in its efforts to subvert the free peoples of South Vietnam, they nonetheless remained committed to their views on securing the population. In November 1967, Abrams reported to Westmoreland, then in Washington for consultations, the progress being made in developing an improved "pacification evaluation system" to better manage nonmilitary programs.[68] Yet with the enemy increasingly pressuring Dak To in Kontum province, the MACV deputy felt obliged to focus his attention on the "attrition game" near the Laotian border. Abrams worried the dense terrain might preclude a "decisive engagement should the enemy choose to avoid combat." Deciding not to reinforce the threatened region with more combat troops, Abrams turned to what would become a centerpiece of American post-Tet military strategy—airpower. As the deputy explained, "Attrition can best be accomplished in the area near the border by the use of Arc Light strikes, tac air, and artillery."[69] Security meant safeguarding the population not just from southern insurgents, but from North Vietnamese regulars as well.

Thus, his experiences both before and during the Tet offensive profoundly influenced how Abrams would direct the war after assuming the mantle of MACV leadership in mid-1968. And so, too, did the media's reporting of the war's most dramatic event. Abrams drew hard lessons from the headlines in February and March. Some journalists reported that the allies' pacification program was "dead" and "no part" of South Vietnam was "secure either from terrorist bombs or from organized military operations." In early March, Frank McGee of NBC News questioned President Johnson's "futile policy to destroy Vietnam in an effort to save it."[70] Abrams clearly took note. Despite the media's fawning over the general's selection to command MACV, press relations with the military headquarters worsened over the course of Abrams's tenure. There was no small irony here. The same journalists who would help conceive the "better war" myth increasingly found themselves at odds with the very general they hoped would save the war.[71]

For Abrams, though, the Tet offensive exposed the pitfalls of military commanders sharing their private thoughts with a skeptical public media. As early as August 1967, Westmoreland complained about "the confused or unknowledgeable pundits who serve as sources for each other."[72] Abrams pledged not to make the same mistake. As MACV's commander, he cancelled informal dinners with journalists and, according to Neil Sheehan, "rarely said anything of substance to the newsmen." So hostile had Abrams's headquarters become to reporters by 1970 that even an army broadcaster working for the Armed Forces Network accused the command of "suppressing unfavorable news" from the media. One year later, newsmen were "complaining about being given an official run-around."[73] Abrams's distrust of, if not hostility toward, the media could be tied directly to his experiences as the MACV second-in-command.

Finally, the year-long deputy assignment offered valuable insights into the difficulties of managing a multiprovincial conflict across the more than 66,000 square miles of South Vietnam. Under Westmoreland's command, Abrams realized the war had to be fought and won on multiple levels—within the villages, on the battlefields along South Vietnam's borders, in the air, and, ultimately, at negotiating tables far from Southeast Asia.[74] Just prior to his March 1968 meeting with the president, Abrams wrote to Earle Wheeler, acknowledging "a tough fight ahead against a skillful and determined enemy."[75] He could not have been more correct.

The Strategic Dilemma

Defending South Vietnam's 1,000-mile-long land border had long topped MACV's list of strategic priorities. By the close of 1965, more than 10,000 laborers were working to maintain or extend the Ho Chi Minh Trail, a lifeline of sorts that ran from North Vietnam, through sanctuaries and supply caches in Laos and Cambodia, and finally into the battlefields of South Vietnam. American military commanders pined at the chance for ground troops to conduct cross-border operations and cut the trail. Yet during the Johnson administration, the permissions never came. The president, hoping to limit the ground war and avoid a superpower confrontation with either China or the Soviet Union, repeatedly denied requests from the Joint Chiefs to expand the battlefield outside of South Vietnam. The military brass, for their part, never came to grips with these seemingly imperious political limitations.[76]

As the army's vice chief of staff, Abrams had witnessed firsthand the difficulties formed by what many officers saw as meddlesome civilians narrowing military strategists' options. Indeed, Abrams had urged senior commanders to press MACV to cross into Laos and cut the infiltration routes. Only with US troops sitting astride the Ho Chi Minh Trail could the logistical cords between North Vietnam and the southern insurgency be severed. Westmoreland, however, had already advocated such a proposal and come up empty. As the general diplomatically responded to Abrams, "Such a plan was not in the cards in the foreseeable future because of complex political and other considerations."[77]

Westmoreland, of course, had long operated under political and institutional constraints. His inability to persuade Johnson to expand the war unquestionably influenced the course of the conflict. But to argue the general "gravely damaged the war effort" because of his strategic approach is as misplaced as counterfactuals asserting the war would have been won if only LBJ had permitted offensive operations into Laos or Cambodia.[78] Officers' support for cross-border operations might have rested on solid military logic. As one reasoned, unless you have a plan "that allows you to go after the enemy, then you are just sitting there and that really is just a defensive situation."[79] Yet the president's insistence on limiting the war rested on equally sound political logic. The failure to bridge these two rationalities by mid-1968 helps, in part, to explain the political-military stalemate both sides faced before and in the aftermath of Tet.

Still, two conclusions seemed unassailable after Tet. First, American military operations, by themselves, were insufficient to save South Vietnam from defeat. As Ambassador Bunker recalled, "The impact of the Tet offensive was to make U.S. personnel realize that the problem was probably going to be bigger and more difficult than we had anticipated beforehand, that obviously there was a great deal of damage done throughout the country as a whole."[80] Senior officers also recognized the people had "remained indifferent to the enemy's presence" in the days leading to Tet and in some cases "supported him passively." As a result, in Lieutenant General Fred C. Weyand's estimation, "Allied forces had no information base in the local population." More was needed in gaining the people's allegiance. Even President Thieu's belated decision to create a People's Self-Defense Force (PSDF) alluded to deeper issues with arming the population.[81]

These concerns interlaced with a second conclusion. The people of South Vietnam had rejected Hanoi's call to rise up against the Saigon government. Thus, there appeared little risk of the GVN collapsing in the immediate future. Senior leaders in the US mission believed Hanoi had "made a major miscalculation in expecting uprisings among the people and defections among the Vietnamese forces."[82] In one sense, Tet had afforded the allies breathing room, at least on the battlefields inside South Vietnam. Yet many Americans and ARVN officers took their evaluations one step further, arguing Tet had demonstrated "that

the majority of the Vietnamese were loyal and that the military and paramilitary forces were capable and willing to fight." According to Westmoreland, not
only had the enemy failed to "exert psychological pressure on the RVNAF and
on the people," but also the "populace [had] reacted with 'outrage' at Vietcong
brutality."[83]

Such upbeat assessments, though, masked a larger problem faced by MACV
planners—how to best achieve momentum in a still deadlocked war after Tet.
Hoping to regain the tactical initiative, Westmoreland proposed the allies were
"now in a new ball game" and requested troop reinforcements to support a wide-
ranging counteroffensive in March and April. Not only did MACV intend to
attack enemy base areas inside South Vietnam, but also reinvigorate the pacification program that had taken a beating in February.[84] Westmoreland's request for
reinforcements, however, went public in early March, stirring a debate within the
Johnson administration that the president hardly intended or hoped for. After
an overarching policy review, Secretary of Defense Clark Clifford disagreed
with the MACV commander, seeing only "an open-ended commitment that
seemed to get us deeper and deeper and deeper." Consequently, in the tumultuous weeks after Tet, LBJ decided on a grander strategy of stabilization, even as
Westmoreland was seeking a military victory inside South Vietnam.[85] Far from
unique, these disconnects hinted at larger gaps between presidential policy and
military strategy during the Nixon years.

Perhaps more importantly, the US mission struggled with how to achieve
political momentum from Westmoreland's "aggressive, unremitting" military
operations aimed at applying "pressure on all enemy elements" throughout
South Vietnam. Here, the allies seemed to be making only limited progress. Even
after Tet, according to one ARVN officer, President Thieu "was still working to
consolidate his power. He was struggling to replace Ky's appointees in key positions, especially chief of police, and attempting to gain a majority in the Senate
and House."[86] While LBJ urged Westmoreland after Tet to "reassure the people
here that you have the situation under control," the political intrigue among the
Saigon elite fell far outside his influence. As *TIME Magazine* reported in August,
"Political squabbles, economic pressures and social problems" were all adding to the "government's burden." On top of a massive influx of people moving
into urban areas and Thieu's call for a general mobilization, both forced by the
intensifying war, any hopes for achieving political stability in mid-1968 seemed
improbable as Westmoreland prepared to assume his duties as the army's chief
of staff.[87]

This inability to achieve political headway from battlefield exploits also tor-
mented Hanoi's leaders in Tet's aftermath. For years, Hanoi's First Secretary Le
Duan battled in a "war of words" against political opponents who believed the
Politburo should concentrate on state building within North Vietnam rather

than on the growing rebellion in the south.[88] By late 1967, Le Duan's views gained ascendancy and set the foundation for a Central Committee resolution laying out the Tet holiday objectives. A general offensive aimed at the "total disintegration" of the South Vietnamese "puppet army" and defeat of their American patrons would lead to a general uprising of the southern population, thus crushing the "American will to commit aggression and force the United States to accept defeat in South Vietnam."[89] Ambitious in scale, Le Duan's plans fell short of their purpose. The architect of Tet had achieved neither a decisive military victory nor a political windfall from an offensive that proved immensely costly for both the NLF and, to a lesser extent, the North Vietnamese Army.[90]

While Tet exposed Le Duan to criticism from rivals opposed to his unyielding pursuit of a knockout battlefield blow, the offensive also drove the first secretary to reluctantly accept negotiations as a primary strategic objective. In the process, each side adopted a "fighting while talking" strategy that seemed only to lengthen an already protracted conflict.[91] The prospect for negotiations, however, held long-term implications not just for Hanoi, but also for Creighton Abrams and the entire American enterprise in Vietnam. The possibility of a negotiated settlement, too tantalizing for US policymakers to ignore after years of costly stalemate, would leave MACV little chance of achieving victory in the traditional military sense. There would be no battlefield triumphs leading to the enemy's surrender, a point made increasingly visible with the first US troop withdrawals in July 1969.

Yet Le Duan's unenthusiastic move toward the negotiating table held crucial implications for the North Vietnamese as well. As one party document accurately predicted, "Victory will come to us, not suddenly, but in a complicated and tortuous way."[92]

Abe's War

Creighton Abrams ascended to the US Military Assistance Command's top post in Vietnam at a time of great political uncertainty at home. Tet had shaken the American public's faith in its government; in March, the president announced he would not run for re-election, and that spring, assassins' bullets struck down Martin Luther King Jr. and Robert F. Kennedy. King's death proved especially traumatic, as both the civil rights and the antiwar movements lost one of their most inspiring voices. Reporters covering Abrams's elevation to command thus seemed eager to expose a bright spot in an otherwise dismal political landscape. The "odds-on choice to succeed Westmoreland," Abrams "had a reputation for aggressive and unorthodox command." President Johnson described him as "the man most competent to assume this very heavy responsibility." When reports

surfaced in mid-May that the North Vietnamese were prepared to begin prelimi-
nary negotiations in Paris, a wave of anticipation swept the country. With a new
commander, might the deadlocked war finally be nearing its conclusion?[93]

The command change certainly offered hope. As *The Christian Science Monitor*
declared that spring, Westmoreland's departure "will open the way further to new
approaches to strategic problems of the conflict."[94] Such hopes were bolstered by
Abrams's seemingly fresh depiction of the war. Having adopted Bunker's "one
war" vocabulary, the new MACV commander appeared to be re-conceptualizing
the entire conflict. He spoke to soldiers, diplomats, and journalists alike about
attacking the enemy's "system" and viewing the war as a multidimensional affair.
Parroting Bunker, Abrams reported in October that the enemy understood "that
this is just one, repeat one, war. He knows there's no such thing as a war of big
battalions, a war of pacification, or a war of territorial security. Friendly forces
have got to recognize and understand the one war concept and carry the battle
to the enemy, simultaneously, in all the areas of conflict."[95]

In this sense, Abrams had learned well from his former boss. Westmoreland
had never been able to command the strategic narrative—to persuade the media
to think of the war in terms other than "attrition," "search-and-destroy," and
"body counts." While his campaign plans proved far more comprehensive than
such phrases suggested, Westmoreland had failed to articulate the complexities

Figure 3 TOURING THE FRONT. Abrams visiting an American firebase and soldiers
from the US 25th Infantry Division. (RG737S, MHI)

of a war that seemed so nebulous to the American public. Abrams's employment of the "one war" phrase offered just enough clarity to inspire hope that a strategic change was in the offing.[96]

So, too, did talk that Westmoreland's appointment as the US Army chief of staff offered proof he had become a "political liability" to the president and was being "kicked upstairs." The *Los Angeles Times* noted that while the MACV commander had been one of the president's key political assets, Tet had "somewhat diminished Westmoreland's luster."[97] Still, senior administration officials rallied to the general's defense—McNamara judged the speculation and criticism "quite undeserved"—but the reporting only furthered expectations that Abrams would overhaul US strategy in Vietnam once in command. For his part, Abrams refused to be drawn into the debate. While reporters conjectured and military analysts called "talk of dropping search-and-destroy operations in favor of clear-and-hold . . . just a lot of bull," the general offered up little. Queried about a potential change in strategy, Abrams would only say, "I look for more fighting."[98]

Indeed, more fighting would not be hard to find in the years ahead. Asked during a late March press conference if the United States was any closer to peace, the president replied, "I cannot answer that question."[99] One week later, Johnson announced he would not pursue re-election. Thus, Abrams's elevation to command must be placed in this larger context. If, for instance, Ho Chi Minh announced in mid-1968 his decision to step down as president of the DRV, replaced his top general, capped the number of North Vietnamese troops inside South Vietnam, and sued for negotiations, Americans likely would have thought they had won the war. The script, however, had been flipped. Abrams was assuming the reins of MACV at the very moment the war in Vietnam appeared stalemated—if not irretrievably lost. Hence, journalists expectantly reported on the "military experts, and many civilian officials, urging a variety of drastic revisions of war policy." Insiders, however, regarded such talk as "exaggerated."[100]

After Abrams officially assumed command on 3 July 1968, he published a series of memoranda outlining his operational guidance. The messages would prove the insiders right. The new MACV commander issued no formal order dictating a major strategic change. In truth, his guidance spoke in familiar terms. Westmoreland's final advice to the command recommended improving the local militia forces, supporting pacification by "all elements" of the government, "of which the RVNAF is a major part," and maintaining "the offensive spirit."[101] Abrams followed suit and, in truth, proved far more aggressive than his predecessor. In late July, he related his intent to "accommodate the enemy in seeking battle and in fact to anticipate him wherever possible." He exhorted his troops to do more than just repulse the enemy. "We must defeat his forces, then pursue them and destroy them." Abrams looked to incorporate local regional and popular forces by "becoming heavily engaged in aggressive patrolling and night ambushes." In August, he continued "emphasizing offensive operations" and the following month requested all subordinate commanders to expand their "spoiling and pre-emptive operations" against enemy main forces units and the NLF infrastructure. Abrams was hardly shying away from a fight.[102]

Yet Tet had also altered the operating environment. Officers reported difficulties in finding an enemy that had slipped back into Cambodia or broken down into smaller units to avoid contact with US forces. Abrams may have wanted to "pile on" the enemy, but the enemy refused to cooperate.[103] Moreover, units struggled with how best to rank the multiple tasks of the "one war" concept, the major aspects of which included pacification, elimination of the enemy's political infrastructure, expanding and improving the South Vietnamese armed forces, and, not the least, combat operations. "Each," Abrams directed, "is to receive the highest priority." Yet if all these tasks required equal emphasis, how was a company or battalion commander to avoid dispersion of effort? Abrams never said. To him, the enemy's setbacks after Tet presented an opportunity of which bold military commanders must take advantage.[104]

In reality, Abrams's command guidance proved mostly tactical in nature. According to pacification chief Robert Komer, the new head of MACV "said he didn't intend to make any [strategic] changes unless he saw that some were necessary." Many officers agreed, seeing Washington-based calls for a "clear-and-hold" strategy as "naïve in face of the local realities." Besides, Abrams's "one war" idea was scarcely new. Even before the change of command at MACV, journalists discerned tactical modifications being made in Tet's wake. Moreover, by July, it appeared the enemy was avoiding contact to conserve their resources and manpower. A major shift in strategy, at least from senior officers' perspectives, did not seem all that warranted.[105]

And yet any thoughts inside MACV headquarters, if there were any, of crafting an alternate strategy were ultimately abandoned due to political decisions made in Washington. For the time being, cross-border operations remained off limits—Abrams asked in August to pursue enemy units into Cambodia—as did requests to call on the strategic reserve and bolster US troop strength in Vietnam. In fact, Secretary of Defense Clark Clifford instructed MACV's new commander to reduce American casualties to help subdue domestic criticism of the war.[106]

Even disagreements over the defense of Saigon in the spring and summer of 1968 did not equate to a change in military strategy. A centerpiece of the "better war" myth, that Abrams changed tactics "within fifteen minutes" of taking command, rests on a false reading of historical events in the chaotic months after Tet. True, the new MACV chief abandoned the Khe Sanh position in early July and countermanded Westmoreland's directives concerning the fighting in Saigon. Since early June, the Pentagon had been relaying the "considerable concern here in Washington at the destruction being wrought in the course of searching out and eliminating infiltrating enemy units in the urban Saigon."[107] Harassing fire against the South Vietnamese capital was taking its toll, while heavy attacks in May—dubbed "mini-Tet"—left a civilian population increasingly demoralized. Westmoreland had already issued orders to Fred Weyand, then commanding the Saigon defense forces, directing him to storm the outskirts of the city and clean up the enemy threat. Within an hour of taking command, Abrams countermanded the order, fearing the risk of civilian casualties outweighed the likely benefits of costly urban street-fighting. Nonetheless, the defense of Saigon rated as one of the general's top priorities that summer. As Abrams railed to one senior officer, "I want you to clean up the Goddamn hot spots in the city, and I want you to stop the Goddamn infiltration."[108]

Better war proponents erroneously point to this dispute over how best to defend the capital city as proof of a newly conceived strategy. Weyand, however, never spoke of a change of strategy in either his official debriefing report or in speeches after returning home in late 1968. At best, the general only conceded that a "strategy of all-round pressure" changed "only in emphasis from time to time."[109] MACV Chief of Staff Walter Kerwin equally recalled that when "Abe took over, there was no lifting the light, no shade or pulling down the shutter or anything like, well, now, he's gone, now we're going to change things. Nothing like that at all." Even the presumptive MACV commander reported to the Joint Chiefs back in March that he felt "compelled to avoid any implication of 'great change,' 'new strategy.'"[110]

Abrams's actions matched his words. The new MACV chief made no mid-year change to the 1968 allied campaign plan, nor did he request any major reallocation of resources or seek to alter the command structure between the RVNAF and American headquarters. As had his predecessor, Abrams sought to link military operations to expanding government control over the population. Underscoring the assumptions underlying the "one war" approach, a contemporary report maintained that "destroying, dispersing, or pushing back the enemy main force units" would ensure "gains in the control war became possible."[111]

Abrams, though, never formalized any new concept of operations in writing. Instead, he sent monthly directives to his commanders, pressing them to maintain and expand the momentum of pacification, increase security for the South Vietnamese population, and relentlessly attack the enemy. Yet critics alleged this final military task remained at the heart of US strategy, to ill effect. As one correspondent believed, demoralization among troops actually increased under Abrams because he "kept pushing American soldiers into the bunker-complex killing grounds the NVA prepared."[112]

It is important to note, however, that so much of the war's major contours had already been dictated before Abrams's arrival. The broader mission of maintaining an independent, noncommunist South Vietnam required a host of supporting efforts—defending Saigon and the nation's borders, promoting pacification, training the ARVN and local militia forces, uprooting the NLF political infrastructure, and defeating enemy main forces units in battle. None of these requirements changed after Tet. MACV officers understood this point. One of the commander's aides recalled that by "the time Abrams arrived on the scene, there were few options left for changing the character of the war."[113] Another officer stated bluntly in mid-July 1968 that the basic strategic approach outlined under Westmoreland would continue. "At this point there is very little that we can do with what we have that would drastically change policies." The officer admitted there would be minor alterations—"whenever a new general takes over there have got to be changes"—but differing command styles and personalities were hardly enough to fundamentally alter the foundations on which the American war in Vietnam had been built.[114]

While Abrams proved flexible in reacting to an ever-shifting political-military landscape, he could not avoid a simple truth. His opponent, Le Duan, remained committed that summer to a decisive military offensive that might undermine the American presence in South Vietnam and discredit Thieu's "puppet" regime. The impacts of the early May "mini-Tet" were still being felt after the MACV change of command. Then, in August, another enemy offensive, the third of the year, swept across South Vietnam. Abrams intended for "spoiling operations" to disrupt Hanoi's plans for further attacks, yet journalists reported heavy fighting in three of the country's four military regions.[115] As rockets and mortar fire fell on the capital city, one Saigon businessman could only say, with an air of resignation, "We are sitting on the fire." Though Abrams spoke of increasing attention to the pacification effort, he acceded that the enemy's ability to continue his attacks "causes the allocation of an inordinate amount of combat assets to the defense" of the command.[116]

It was not in Abrams's nature, however, to sit passively on the defensive. Thus, throughout the summer of 1968, Americans aggressively patrolled the South Vietnamese countryside, seeking to provide a shield behind which the GVN could regain its political footing after Tet. As the allies contended with some 1,500 enemy ground assaults in 1968, Abrams intended to fix the enemy's "major forces as far away as possible from our vital areas, and defeat him decisively." Rather than recoil from Hanoi's renewed attacks, Abrams pushed his troops to strike the enemy a "crushing blow." By now routine, communist forces refused to cooperate with MACV planning. Lieutenant General Julian Ewell recalled how Americans "would flog through the jungle and the enemy would just part before you like water before a ship's bow."[117] Already in this first summer of his command, Abrams was finding it difficult to shape the conflict according to his "one war" designs.

The general, nonetheless, pressed forward with plans enacted by Westmoreland to recuperate allied losses from Tet. Project Recovery, initiated back in February, aimed to offset the psychological and physical damages wrought during the offensive. But progress came slowly, if at all. A late October report on rural Vietnam found the NLF still holding the psychological advantage in the countryside, and though American units might "prowl around to thwart main force gatherings," they rarely seemed "to influence the local balance of power."[118] Moreover, Le Duan's vow to keep military pressure on the allies meant Abrams had to reply in kind. The general's midsummer forecast proved telling. Abrams reported to the Joint Chiefs his plan for the marines in I Corps to "find, fix, and destroy enemy forces in the area." In III Corps, the 9th Infantry Division would mount "brigade sized operations in the eastern Plain of Reeds," while in the southernmost tactical zone, the allies would "continue to focus on destruction of VC forces and interdiction of enemy [communication] liaison routes."[119]

All through the summer, Abrams preached a gospel of aggressive action. He congratulated his commanders for their "spirit of the offensive," while Ambassador Bunker reported on the effectiveness of allied interdiction and spoiling attacks. In the process, the weekly average of battalion "days of operation" nearly doubled over the course of 1968.[120] The ARVN chief of staff took notice. In a closed-door meeting with a colleague late in the year, he shared a message from Abrams "ordering any U.S. officer commanding a company or higher to explain why he lost contact with the enemy after a short engagement." One MACV officer even intimated that Abrams would resign from command "if they cut back on friendly actions like [in] Korea." If journalists covering the transition at MACV headquarters glimpsed any changes in US military strategy, clearly they did not include a reduction in fighting.[121]

Nor did Abrams abandon "search-and-destroy" operations. Reporters inaccurately boasted that the new MACV commander had "abandoned the tactics of his predecessor," opting instead for a "more flexible, diversified approach that employs smaller roving units." Yet in August, 3,000 soldiers from the 101st Airborne Division and the ARVN 1st Infantry Division swept into the A Shau Valley for a major assault on enemy base camps near the Laotian border.[122] (A similar excursion in May 1969 would lead to public outcry over casualties incurred at Hamburger Hill.) Though Abrams spoke of the need to "go beyond smashing up the enemy's main-force units," he still advocated "pile on" operations to crush his foe. Likewise, subordinate commanders continued using "kill ratios" of enemy to friendly casualties to track their progress. Thus, major combat operations remained an integral part of US strategy even if the language had changed. As one infantryman recalled, "American units were still sent on Search-and-Destroy Missions, though that term might not be officially used since, like Free-Fire Zones, it had bad connotations."[123]

Distasteful undertones aside, Abrams had long advocated for increased fire-power against the enemy. Just before taking command, he expressed concern over "recent messages from Washington . . . urging economy and curtailment in the application of US military power in one form or another." At an early July MACV staff meeting, the general deemed the "payoff" was "getting a hold of this fellow and killing as many of them as you can." By March 1969, Abrams was call-ing for a "resumption of air and naval gunfire" against North Vietnam and a full-blown assault against the Laos sanctuaries.[124] Abrams certainly intended to limit collateral damage and the risk to civilian lives. In October 1968, for instance, MACV placed restrictions on the controversial harassment and interdiction (H&I) fire program in which artillery units shot rounds, mostly at night, against likely, yet unobserved, targets. Still, critics derided the reliance on heavy arma-ments. Lieutenant General A. S. Collins Jr. condemned the army for carrying "the use of firepower to the extreme," finding it "wasteful, inefficient, and lacking the stamp of the true professional."[125]

While officers like Collins remained unimpressed with MACV's profligate use of firepower, Abrams pressed for an increasing role played by tanks and heavy bombers. Under the command of Colonel George S. Patton, son of the famed World War II general, the 11th Armored Cavalry Regiment took on a dizzying array of missions—route and bridge security, armed reconnaissance, mounted ambushes, pacification, and area security. Patton himself was a fan of the "pile on" technique and the regiment's operational reports spoke often of applying "heavy pressure" on the enemy.[126] Gordon Livingston, however, found the unit's performance judged by only one metric: the body count. A West Point graduate and army physician, Livingston gained notoriety for handing out a satirical prayer at a regimental function that asked God to "Help us bring death and destruction wherever we go, for we do it in thy name and therefore it is meet and just." Immediately relieved of his duties, the doctor returned home, penning a letter to *The Saturday Review* in which he quoted Patton as stating, "The present ratio of 90 percent killing to 10 percent pacification is just about right."[127]

Abrams, in attendance when Livingston handed out his "Blackhorse Prayer," no doubt questioned Patton's math—and the good doctor's character. Yet the "one war" approach relied on keeping the enemy off balance militarily so pacifi-cation and ARVN training could progress. To accomplish this, Abrams turned more and more to airpower. Staff officers called the massive B-52 strategic bombers MACV's "reserve" force, and their commander used them with little restraint. In 1968, B-52 sorties rose from 800 to 1,800 per month. According to one account, by "March 1969 the total level of bombardment had reached 130,000 tons a month—nearly two Hiroshimas a week in South Vietnam and Laos."[128] Abrams responded to any talk of bombing halts with the threat of increased enemy capabilities and US casualties. The B-52s were effective not only in disrupting NVA infiltration routes, he argued, but also in breaking enemy sieges of allied firebases and defending Special Forces camps. "Hell, Abe uses them for almost anything—he goes for B-52s," quipped a fellow general officer.[129]

Still, Le Duan's commitment to a decisive battlefield victory in 1968 required a military response, especially in terms of protecting political centers like Saigon. Thus, MACV directed subordinate commanders to expand their "spoiling and preemptive operations . . . to include an intensive drive against the VC infrastructure and political apparatus aimed at eliminating it just as rapidly as possible."[130] Here was the core of the "one war" approach—to simultaneously attack the military and political components of the enemy's strategy, while preparing for the eventual withdrawal of US troops from South Vietnam. Although Abrams correctly believed his tactical operations were "punishing the enemy," he still worried Hanoi would steal a "political victory" despite his lack of success on the battlefield. Moreover, time seemed an increasingly limited commodity. Already in July, Ambassador Bunker was expressing his concern about "negotiating from a position of weakness" given that diplomatic meetings in Paris had begun.[131]

Bunker's apprehensions, while shared by his military counterpart, resulted in no major changes to US military strategy during Abrams's first year in command. Comparing the 1968 and 1969 combined campaign plans reveals few substantial differences. The new plan restated the previous year's mission to "defeat the VC/NVA forces and to assist the GVN to extend control throughout the Republic of Vietnam." Supporting tasks remained consistent as well. Thus, both campaign plans spoke of conducting "sustained, coordinated and combined offensive operations" and of maintaining "security of areas in which pacification has been conducted."[132]

Without question, Abrams emphasized pacification and improving ARVN forces as equal parts of his "one war" approach. The new campaign plan also sought, for the first time, to eliminate the "separation of responsibilities" between allied forces. "To prepare for the time when it must assume the entire responsibility," the plan stated, "the RVNAF must participate fully within its capabilities in all types of operations necessary to accomplish the mission." Altering the operational emphasis, however, hardly constituted a revolutionary change in strategy on which journalists hopefully reported in the months leading to Abrams's rise to MACV command.[133]

In truth, Westmoreland had bequeathed to Abrams a war that proved stubbornly resistant to American influence. A third enemy offensive in August once more uprooted South Vietnamese society, suggesting the Tet offensive was not a singular event at the beginning of 1968 but a year-long escalation of violence. Still, senior military leaders remained confident. As General Wheeler reported to the president in October, "Abrams' assessment is highly favorable. If we haven't won the war militarily we are well on the way to it."[134] But despite the public and professional optimism inspired by the MACV change of command, the killing continued. In December, US deaths in Vietnam topped 30,000. (American newspapers remained typically silent on Vietnamese casualties.) The incessant fighting and rising death toll seemed only to inspire more serious questions about the war itself. Was it possible the war was a "lost cause"? Was victory "impractical"?[135]

The slow strategic evolution leading to a "one war" approach proved insufficient in helping senior war managers answer such questions.[136] Nor could Abrams convince the incoming president of the United States that military victory lay within reach. The war's course would change greatly in the aftermath of the 1968 Tet offensive. But those changes would emanate not from the MACV headquarters, but rather from a White House now under the leadership of Richard M. Nixon.

2

Vietnamization

Policy of Withdrawal or Strategy for "Victory"?

The relationship between Creighton Abrams and the White House got off to a rocky start as the general took charge of the US Military Assistance, Command (MACV). In June 1968, Clark Clifford, who had replaced Robert S. McNamara as secretary of defense after Tet, asked the chairman of the Joint Chiefs for ways in which the military command might reduce civilian casualties. (The president worried over negative press on what appeared to be MACV's undue use of force in populated areas.) General Earle Wheeler forwarded the request to Abrams, who lashed out in what Clifford later called a "rambling, emotional, and angry reply." The general ranted against the US Embassy for sending military-related reports to Washington without MACV's concurrence and appeared to scold civilian policymakers for naively relying on "raw data."[1] According to one source, Abrams's boldness "sent Clifford into orbit." The defense secretary shot back to Wheeler, informing the chairman of his "uneasiness" with the MACV commander, who immediately apologized for his undiplomatic language. As Clifford recalled, "This storm blew over" and by mid-July the secretary was reporting to President Johnson that he was "most favorably impressed with General Abrams."[2]

The storm, however, proved to be just a precursory tempest that would rage throughout much of Nixon's time in office. Even Clifford, kind in his memoirs to Abrams, protested the "garbage" coming from MACV on expanding the war into Cambodia. "They keep sending accounts of new offensives and other crap none of which are accurate or mean anything." Abrams, for his part, complained to fellow senior officers that "Washington has been very stubborn about getting on board with all of this that's going on. . . . And, in my viewpoint, this can *no longer* be tolerated."[3]

Thus, while White House officials admired the general's record and his fighting spirit, important figures privately held deep reservations over Abrams's capacity to carry out the new administration's policies. Already in the fall of

1969, reports surfaced of "disagreements about the pace and size of [US] withdrawals" from South Vietnam. In September, Abrams had to publicly squash rumors he was resigning because he was "dissatisfied with the administration's handling of the war."[4]

By early 1972, the civil-military relationship had become toxic. Richard Nixon's White House chief of staff, H. R. Haldeman, noted in April that the president was planning to "bypass Abrams" on important military matters and that Nixon "did not have confidence in Abrams," even if he had been a "great commander" in World War II.[5] As a strategist, the MACV commander appeared to be falling short of civilian policymakers' expectations.

Abrams, though, had been in a difficult spot. The secretive nature of both Nixon and his national security advisor, Henry Kissinger, meant that few individuals could be fully trusted to coordinate military strategy with larger foreign policy objectives. Moreover, the continuing war in Vietnam seemed to be placing national policy and military strategy at odds with each other.

While interwoven, these two crucial aspects of war require different intellectual inputs. Policy, in large sense, delineates the purpose of war. It also, however, establishes the parameters for the use of a nation's instruments of power and for how that nation establishes its long-term interests. Strategy, in contrast, is a mechanism to achieve policymakers' objectives.[6] While grand strategy aims to link all national resources—military, political, economic, diplomatic—into one cohesive whole, military strategy more often focuses on what Vietnam-era doctrine writers deemed the "art and science of using the armed forces of a nation" to secure larger policy objectives. While both policy and strategy require a collaborative intellectual effort, modern strategy, according to Colin Gray, "ultimately derives its power from the realm of politics."[7] The war in Vietnam proved no exception.

If policy can be seen as a definition of some future state of peace, while strategy is an articulation of how to get there, the ambiguity between the two in Vietnam contributed to the deteriorating relationship between MACV and the Nixon White House. Consider Abrams's forecast at the beginning of January 1969. The general spoke of operations intended to interdict enemy supply routes, search out enemy forces, and clear contested provinces of insurgent influence, and to work with South Vietnamese Army (ARVN) units in hopes of accelerating the pacification program. The near-term results appeared to support continuing an offensive strategy. As Abrams noted less than two months earlier, "We have the enemy in real trouble. Through unrelenting effort and at a substantial cost, we have gained initiative, put the enemy under pressure and off balance, forced him to move and uncovered him." The general urged the Joint Chiefs of

Staff: "We should grant him no respite or surcease that allows him to overcome his difficulties."[8]

This emphasis on a hard-hitting military strategy, however, soon came at odds with a national policy that deemed the war in Vietnam no longer worth the human and material sacrifices required to wage it. By mid-1968, more and more Americans questioned whether the deaths of young men and women in a limited, overseas conflict for little practical gain made sense. Thus, even before taking office, Nixon told US Embassy officials the South Vietnamese "should understand that American public opinion was in a highly critical condition."[9] Antiwar sentiment at home, however, did not directly lead to the circumscription of US military force in Southeast Asia. As important, the president-elect hoped to redefine American Cold War foreign policy, plans for which South Vietnam played only a relatively small part. In the process of Nixon implementing these designs, Abrams's strategy proved increasingly incapable of delivering what policymakers asked of the general.[10]

When the new president thus first spoke of his intention to begin withdrawing American forces from Vietnam, he bestowed on MACV a mission well outside its capacity to accomplish. Abrams did his best to ensure his strategy advanced larger policy, but the schisms were hard to overcome. For instance, the MACV chief reported in June 1969—no doubt disappointing those hoping for less violent methods to countering the southern insurgency—that he would "continue to minimize casualties through exploitation of superior firepower and mobility."[11] Clearly, an approach that exploited firepower valued American lives at the cost of Vietnamese civilians and the larger pacification effort. Such inconsistencies would deepen as Abrams wrestled with the competing demands of fighting a war while simultaneously withdrawing from it.

Yet the plan to de-Americanize the war, soon dubbed "Vietnamization" by the Nixon administration, had long roots. Even before the creation of a military assistance command in 1962, US advisors looked to a day when they could extricate themselves from Vietnam. By 1967, Westmoreland spoke, presciently, of trends where "conceivably in two years or less the Vietnamese can shoulder a larger share of the war and thereby permit the U.S. to begin phasing down the level of its commitment."[12] Within this process, however, controversy arose over a central question during Abrams's tenure at MACV. Was Vietnamization, as policy, an admission that the American war in Vietnam would likely end in a "barely concealed surrender"? Or was it well-crafted strategy to achieve a newly defined conception of victory in the post–World War II era?[13]

Figure 4 THE TRIALS OF VIETNAMIZATION. Abrams on an inspection tour of the South Vietnamese Air Force. Doubts of the RVNAF's capabilities would endure throughout Abrams's tenure. (RG737S, MHI)

A "Secret" Plan to Win the War

In late October 1968, with the presidential election less than one week away, Abrams met with Lyndon Johnson and top advisors in the White House to discuss a potential halt to the US bombing of North Vietnam. The wide-ranging discussion demonstrated clearly the linkages between policy and strategy. Could it be possible Hanoi was ready for a "tactical shift from the battlefield to the conference table"? Did Abrams feel the president could order a bombing halt without increasing the risk to Saigon or causing further causalities? "Yes, Sir, we can," replied the general. What was the relationship like between Thieu and Ky? How would the US elections affect Hanoi's stance on possible negotiations?[14]

The meeting, instrumental in Johnson's final decision to end the bombing campaign, illustrated how the relations between tactical, strategic, and political issues were not so neatly hierarchical as some political science theorists might expect. In fact, within a room including the secretaries of state and defense, the CIA director, and the chairman of the Joint Chiefs of Staff, Abrams's advice proved most influential. As President Johnson told the general, "I am going to put more weight on your judgment than anybody else."[15]

This civil-military interchange, so necessary for effective strategy, would disintegrate over the course of Nixon's time in office. The often uneasy dialogue between MACV commander and Johnson's successor—when it occurred at all—demonstrated that policy and strategy were increasingly in tension with each other as the US withdrawal from Vietnam began to take hold.

Abrams's October White House meeting suggested problems lay ahead. Discussions with LBJ contradicted advice the general had given to national security advisor Walt Rostow just one week earlier. In a back-channel message exchange, Rostow asked the MACV commander for his thoughts on bombing North Vietnam. Perhaps unsurprisingly, Abrams fully supported the air campaign. Portions of the general's remarks made their way to Chicago, where the Democratic Party was then deciding its policy platform for the upcoming election. A minority plank proposal—backed by Senators Eugene McCarthy and Edward Kennedy—called for a pledge to stop the bombing of North Vietnam.[16] Enter Abrams. The day before MACV's chief met with the president, the Democratic Party's platform chairman introduced the general's "testimony" into the political debate. According to the *Boston Globe*, Abrams apparently warned that "a bombing halt would be an unacceptable risk for U.S. troops." "I cannot agree to place our troops at the risk which that enemy capability would then possess." Party delegates then summarily voted down the peace plank.[17]

Abrams's "testimony" illustrated the ways in which the war was becoming increasingly politicized. As negotiations with Hanoi inched forward, the US delegation in Paris kept the MACV commander apprised of its work. Negotiators hoped that a bombing halt would induce Hanoi into substantial talks that included both the Saigon government and the National Liberation Front. Abrams assented, as long as he retained authority to counter violations of the demilitarized zone and could maintain pressure on the enemy inside South Vietnam. Such nuances, though, never made it to print. Instead, reporters quoted US officers in Vietnam as unanimously praising the Democratic Party's refusal to endorse a bombing halt. "You won't find anyone here who wants to halt the bombing," one officer said.[18]

Lyndon Johnson thought differently. Hoping to tempt Hanoi into serious negotiations, the president announced a total bombing halt on 31 October. Moreover, demonstrating progress toward peace might offer a boost to Vice President Hubert Humphrey, then trailing Nixon in the polls. That day, Johnson ordered Abrams to "use his manpower and resources in a maximum effort" to "keep the enemy on the run."[19] The MACV commander, however, would have his work cut out for him. Rather than discontinuing their infiltration of troops into South Vietnam and agreeing to formal representation of Thieu's government at the negotiating table, Hanoi viewed the bombing halt as a political victory. The embattled American president seemed desperate to end the stalemated war. A Politburo declaration on 2 November trumpeted Johnson's unilateral action as "a great victory for the Vietnamese people in both parts of the country." A "shocked and angry" Saigon political leadership agreed it was a victory, but only for the northerners.[20]

In fact, presidential candidate Nixon had been working behind the scenes to curry favor with government of South Vietnam (GVN) leaders in hopes of subverting Johnson's plans. In a now infamous episode of political subterfuge— some considered it treasonous—the Republican nominee, working through an intermediary, communicated to President Thieu that he would best be served with hardliner Nixon in the White House come January. If the GVN balked at the unfolding peace process, Saigon could rest assured that a Republican administration would stand firm against the communist enemy.[21] Meanwhile, Nixon benefited from critics who derided Johnson for playing politics, calling for a bombing halt only to help vault Humphrey into the Oval Office. Aware of Nixon's political maneuvering, LBJ ultimately decided to keep the matter quiet. "It's despicable," the president stormed, "and it if were made public I think it would rock the nation." On 2 November, the same day Hanoi's Politburo declared the bombing halt a "great victory," South Vietnamese president Nguyen Van Thieu announced he would boycott any peace negotiations. The American election was just three days away.[22]

With no "October Surprise" to upend Nixon's campaign, the Republican nominee slipped into the White House by less than a 1 percent margin in the popular vote over rival Hubert Humphrey. (Independent George Wallace earned more than 13 percent that year.) The president-elect surely benefited by remaining vague on the topic of Vietnam. Back in March, Nixon had pledged that "new leadership will end the war and end the peace." Throughout the campaign, he pivoted between a hawkish stance, criticizing Johnson for not pursuing the war more aggressively, and a more dovish position, advocating a negotiated settlement. Since he would not be inheriting "errors of the past," Nixon could install an "administration that can make a fresh beginning free from the legacy of those errors." Moreover, the candidate had promised that he would "bring an honorable end to the war in Vietnam."[23]

Discerning observers no doubt questioned whether Nixon truly had a "secret plan" to win the war, yet one truth seemed increasingly evident as the 1968 election campaign wore on. Any notion of winning seemed to have increasingly little in common with traditional definitions of wartime victory. Many Americans, including some military officers, certainly aspired to a total victory in the style of 1945—subjugation of North Vietnam—but that never came close to becoming US government policy. Rather, for Kennedy, Johnson, and Nixon, "victory" meant sustaining an anticommunist government in South Vietnam. No American president was willing to pay the cost in money and blood of actually conquering North Vietnam. This was not, on its face, an abandonment of victory as a goal. Rather, American forces would create the conditions that would allow the South Vietnamese to achieve victory after the US withdrawal.[24]

Nixon, for his part, no doubt saw himself caught in a trap set by his predecessor, though surely less moral than strategic and political. The new president had inherited, in Kissinger's words, a "cauldron" from Johnson, a disastrous policy that left few, if any, opportunities for true military victory.[25] As one Nixon aide recollected, "LBJ only had to think about negotiations for Vietnam. We had to think of what could be done to restore peace in three countries, and we had less troops, less diplomatic clout than LBJ had, and he failed." Certainly, more than negotiations weighed on Johnson's mind. The war in Vietnam proved never so simple. Yet Nixon and Kissinger knew they had been dealt a weak hand, one that would require skill—and perhaps a little bit of cunning—to leave the negotiating table with their nation's credibility intact.[26]

Though the new president recalled in his memoirs that a lasting peace in Southeast Asia rested on the opposing goals of ending the war quickly and not abandoning South Vietnam to the communists, he nonetheless made no mention of the ongoing war in his inaugural address. (As a portent of things to come, 10,000 protestors staged a "counter-inaugural" in Washington, DC, the day before.)[27] Nixon focused his remarks on mastering the moment so as to "make the world safe for mankind." Yet the United States, though "rich in goods," found itself "ragged in spirit." The president thus called on the country to unite and, as a forecast of his foreign policy, for Americans to consider how their nation had suffered "from inflated rhetoric that promises more than it can deliver."[28]

Still, delivering some semblance of victory in Vietnam, though absent from Nixon's address, ranked foremost among the new administration's foreign policy objectives. By retaining all of the war's key managers—Abrams, Bunker, pacification chief William Colby, Army Chief of Staff Westmoreland—the new president signaled a policy of continuity with his predecessor. But he also expressed his willingness to engage in a form of brinksmanship with North Vietnam and its patrons, to include signaling the possible use of nuclear weapons.[29] As vice president, Nixon believed Dwight D. Eisenhower's threat to breach the nuclear threshold helped end the Korean War. A similar tactic of coercive diplomacy might produce the same result in Vietnam. If Nixon could convince Hanoi he was "unpredictable and capable of the bloodiest brutality," then perhaps the communists would more readily enter into negotiations for fear of the consequences in continuing their war effort.[30]

Much care, however, needs to be taken when considering this "madman theory" that supposedly underpinned Nixon's foreign policy approach. Without question, the new president shared with advisors plans of threatening his enemies with "excessive force" to break the stalemate in Vietnam. And Nixon most certainly distrusted potential political adversaries at home, even obsessively so, throughout his presidency. Nevertheless, claims that the "madman theory" lay "at the core of Nixon's notions" quite simply are not supported by historical evidence.[31] Yes, the president considered how coercive diplomacy might advance his larger foreign policy goals. Yes, he lashed out when frustrated and he bullied friends and foes alike—too often, he saw himself surrounded by enemies. But Nixon also carefully considered his options, both military and diplomatic, when it came to Vietnam. Deliberations with his chief consultant, Kissinger, were more often than not contemplative and attentive to the complexities and political realities of the Southeast Asian conflict and the larger Cold War.[32]

Take, for example, the Duck Hook episode. In February and March 1969, the White House instructed the Joint Chiefs of Staff (JCS) to develop plans for increased military operations against North Vietnam, to include the mining of Haiphong harbor and an expanded bombing campaign against Hanoi. With peace negotiations stalled, national security advisor Henry Kissinger pushed "for some escalation, enough to get us a reasonable bargain for a settlement within six months."[33] Nixon concurred. Over the summer, the national security staff, in conjunction with the JCS, drafted a study under the code-name Duck Hook. The planned four-day attack against North Vietnam would involve a massive expansion of violence, to include the possible use of tactical nuclear weapons. In July, Nixon sent a personal letter to Ho Chi Minh seeking a "just peace," but threatening "measures of great consequence and force" if the North Vietnamese leader rebuffed the American entreaty. The president set 1 November, the anniversary of LBJ's bombing halt, as Hanoi's deadline to break the diplomatic impasse.[34]

Hoping the Soviet Union would apply pressure on Hanoi, Nixon leaked word of his planned escalation to the press, while Kissinger shared the Duck Hook scheme with Russian ambassador Anatoly Dobrynin. Yet not all presidential advisors shared Kissinger's faith in a "go-for-broke" strategy.[35] The Joint Chiefs worried about losing credibility if their civilian leaders did not follow through with such intimidating talk. The new Secretary of Defense, Melvin Laird, thought such a massive escalation would ignite antiwar dissent at home. Moreover, the National Security Council (NSC) study group (and, ultimately, Kissinger) expressed concerns that Duck Hook might not achieve quick, decisive results as initially hoped. With Hanoi refusing to bend under Nixon's threats, the president reluctantly abandoned the contingency plan and turned toward the more long-term designs of Vietnamization.[36]

Far from establishing the president as an irrational actor, the "madman" dialogue and Duck Hook planning demonstrated Nixon's belief that military power could still be useful, even necessary, to his larger policy goals. The war itself might no longer be worthwhile, but the use of force certainly so. Throughout the new administration's first months in the White House, the president's advisors remained convinced that Hanoi would only negotiate if pressured militarily. Kissinger believed the enemy "could only be brought to compromise by being confronted by insuperable obstacles on the ground."[37] Further, the national security advisor refused to accept "that a little fourth-rate power like North Vietnam does not have a breaking point." Nixon agreed, arguing the United States had to demonstrate further resistance by Hanoi would be "costly and unrewarding." Both men believed diplomatic leverage in Paris rested on military progress inside South Vietnam.[38]

Such assumptions on the linkages between the battlefield and the negotiating table offer clues into why military action remained so important to Nixon. Even if destroying North Vietnam's military power no longer seemed plausible, Nixon (and Abrams) could still rely on military means in seeking a tolerable negotiated settlement. As one embassy official put it, "There isn't much point in just standing still and letting the other side grab the initiative while you wait for peace. That's when your losses go up."[39] Moreover, the image of a forceful, determined Cold Warrior rested on strength and the courage to use that strength—the president and his national security advisor both feared looking weak in the international arena. Thus, strong military action could help Nixon refute suspicions of irresolute American power overseas.[40]

Additionally, the South Vietnamese still considered battle an indispensable facet of allied strategy. As principal authors of the 1969 combined campaign plan, the RVNAF leadership followed earlier precepts on defeating enemy forces and extending governmental control. While criticized during the Westmoreland years for blindly pursuing a "crossover point" on the battlefield, under Abrams the allies continued to seek combat and "inflict more losses on the enemy than he can replace." Thus, the allies' 1969 campaign plan spoke of sustained offensive operations, of detecting and destroying enemy incursions into South Vietnam, and of protecting cities from enemy attack. South Vietnamese and American forces would work side-by-side to accomplish these goals.[41] True, pacification remained a centerpiece of allied strategy, but some US officers felt "winning the hearts and minds of the people" went only so far. As Lieutenant General Julian J. Ewell recalled, "It's a nice concept, but in fighting the Viet Cong and NVA, if you didn't break their military machine you might as well forget winning the hearts and minds of the people."[42]

Ewell, in fact, spent most of his efforts as the 9th Infantry Division commander trying to break the enemy's military apparatus. Based in the southern tactical zone's Mekong Delta, the 9th Infantry commenced Operation Speedy Express in late 1968 to take full advantage of the dry season. With indications already in the air of US troop withdrawals, Ewell aimed to clean out as much of northern Delta as possible before redeployments began. Ground patrols and helicopter gunships roamed across the southern provinces.[43] But word of the 9th Infantry's heavy-handedness made some US advisors question whether Ewell's approach was alienating the local population. One critic believed the division followed a "shoot first, ask questions later policy," thus earning Ewell the nickname "Butcher of the Mekong Delta." The aggressive commander, however, retorted that he had two rules. "One is that you would try to get a very close meshing of pacification . . . and military operations. The other rule is the military operations would be given first priority in every case."[44]

Body counts for Speedy Express validated Ewell's claims. Final statistics tallied nearly 11,000 enemy dead at a cost of 267 "friendly KIA." Yet the division reported only 748 weapons captured, prompting suspicious journalists to inquire about the enormous gap between body and weapons counts. Officers explained that Vietcong were often shot "before they could get to their weapons" or that many guerrillas were "not equipped with individual weapons." *Newsweek* in 1972 later countered that "the first explanation is highly implausible and the second is patently false."[45] It seemed increasingly plausible that civilian noncombatants made up no small percentage of the 9th Division's casualty figures. The unit's chief of staff, Ira A. Hunt Jr., dismissively recalled that in "the populated Delta area, where it was often extremely difficult to differentiate friend from foe, there was always an opportunity for collateral damage." MACV, trying to clarify policy, directed that enemy dead would be "determined from actual body count of males of fighting age and others, male and female, known to have carried arms." Abrams, however, sent a slightly different message when he promoted Ewell to command II Field Force, noting that the 9th Division's performance "has been magnificent."[46]

On the opposite end of South Vietnam, in the northern provinces of I Corps, the MACV commander similarly demanded offensive action. In late January 1969, Abrams launched a regimental-sized attack into the A Shau Valley. Dewey Canyon, a "search and clear operation," aimed at cutting enemy supply routes between the Laotian border and the contested valley while also intercepting two NVA regiments that allied intelligence believed were operating in the area. Multiple battalion-size heliborne assaults opened the offensive, followed by a "simultaneous attack of three battalions."[47] In March, as the 56-day operation was nearing its conclusion, Abrams reported the allies had "uncovered some of the most significant caches of the war." MACV further touted the "high totals for both enemy KIA and enemy/friendly kill ratio." The apparent success whetted Abrams's appetite and in February he cabled the Joint Chiefs, requesting to move into Cambodia. The new administration, though, was not quite ready to expand the conflict so publicly after Nixon had campaigned on a pledge to end the war.[48]

Besides, Abrams had his hands full. Hanoi launched yet another countywide offensive on 22–23 February, the day Nixon embarked on his first official trip to Europe as president. Allied intelligence picked up wind of the attack, yet the enemy still fired rockets and mortar rounds into Saigon and seventy other South Vietnamese cities. One MACV officer mockingly called "it more of a fizzle than an offensive," yet 1,140 American soldiers lost their lives in the next three weeks of fighting.[49] Kissinger later questioned the decision to call off Duck Hook, but Nixon would not let Hanoi's offensive go unanswered. While Abrams proposed resuming the bombing of North Vietnam, the president decided to send American B-52s elsewhere—against the enemy's sanctuaries inside Cambodia. If presidential candidate Nixon had indeed devised a secret plan to win the war in Vietnam, few at the time contemplated the likelihood of widening the war into Cambodia and Laos to achieve such a victory.[50]

A Contentious Strategic Review

The ongoing battles, stretching across the expanse of South Vietnam, indicated to Nixon's national security advisor that the Southeast Asian fighting was doing little to further US foreign policy objectives. Henry Kissinger thus sought to turn his office into a power base from which to end the Vietnam War and re-conceptualize America's role with the larger world. In the process, the NSC would surpass the US Embassy in South Vietnam, the State Department, and even the Joint Chiefs of Staff in manipulating presidential wartime decision-making for the next four years.[51] Kissinger's desire to be *the* indispensable advisor to Nixon fueled the NSC's ascent. His remarks to a security council planning group proved telling. "If there is to be a negotiated settlement, if the war is to end," Kissinger declared, "I am convinced that I have to do it. I must take the president along with me." If the Harvard faculty alumnus sought an end to the war in Vietnam, institutional power within the Nixon White House would be a necessary step in achieving such a crucial strategic outcome.[52]

Kissinger had positioned himself well for the NSC appointment, even if his earlier support of Nixon's rival, Governor Nelson Rockefeller, seemed to disqualify him from any position in the new administration. In 1966, he consulted with the State Department after a second trip to Vietnam, reporting on the lack of progress in the pacification program and the "backbiting" among the GVN leadership. A January 1969 article in *Foreign Affairs* further cast doubt on any resolution other than a negotiated settlement. Ending the war "honorably," however, was "essential for the peace of the world."[53]

Here, Kissinger's views on the changing international environment induced the realpolitik proponent to champion a cease-fire in Vietnam that would facilitate new relationships with the United States' global rivals. With the world becoming increasingly multipolar thanks, in part, to the emergence of China and the Soviet Union as international powers, American statesmen could ill afford to direct their energies and resources to a stalemated conflict in Southeast Asia. In short, supporting South Vietnam had become, at best, a peripheral strategic concern for the United States.[54]

Kissinger also appealed to Nixon because of his background as a national security scholar. A US Army counter-intelligence analyst in World War II, the German-born émigré gained notoriety with his 1957 publication *Nuclear Weapons and Foreign Policy*. Kissinger warned against the dangers of living in the nuclear era and of the challenges of bringing American power into balance with national interests. "It is the task of strategic doctrine," he wrote, "to translate power into policy."[55] Kissinger was not alone in calling on Washington to develop a strategy for conflicts falling below the nuclear threshold. Political scientists like Robert Osgood and defense intellectuals like General James Gavin equally counseled policymakers on the need to approach "limited wars" holistically, "combining military power with diplomacy and with the economic and psychological instruments of power within a coherent national strategy that is capable of supporting the United States' political objectives abroad." Little had changed since the mid-1950s. More than a decade later, Kissinger would contend with these same issues as Nixon attempted to extricate the nation from an ongoing "limited" war in Vietnam.[56]

It did not take long, however, for the new administration to widen the war into neighboring Cambodia. Aggrieved after Hanoi launched its February 1969 Tet attacks—Nixon saw the "savage offensive" as a "deliberate test designed to take measure of me and my administration at the outset"—the president retaliated. With the backing of Kissinger and Abrams, Nixon ordered a secret bombing of Prince Norodom Sihanouk's Cambodia to begin in mid-March. The operation, code-named Menu, lasted over a year and set the stage for a full-scale allied incursion in 1970.[57] The bombing campaign also aimed to fulfill several ambitions. Not only did Abrams and the Joint Chiefs hope to eliminate the North Vietnamese Central Headquarters for South Vietnam (COSVN), but Nixon also sought to demonstrate a willingness to break free of constraints that held back his predecessor. To avoid "domestic uproar" and avoid putting Sihanouk "in a perilous political position," the president kept the air campaign hush-hush. (How to conceal the bombing from Cambodians experiencing the onslaught of American airpower, Nixon never said.) In large sense then, Operation Menu became Nixon and Kissinger's first foray into coercive diplomacy.[58]

The bombing campaign unfolded not long after Kissinger's staff had undertaken a comprehensive review of the war in Vietnam. Even before the inauguration, a Vietnam Special Studies Group began compiling data on a host of strategic issues relating to the war—population control and territorial security in the South Vietnamese countryside, the meaning of "political development" in the context of rural Vietnam, and the capabilities of the GVN's armed forces. Experts from the RAND Corporation—among them, Daniel Ellsberg, who would leak *The Pentagon Papers* in 1971—developed a series of penetrating questions that Kissinger distributed to MACV, the US Embassy in South Vietnam, the CIA, and key State Department officials after Nixon's inaugural ceremony.[59] How much influence did Moscow and Beijing have over Hanoi? What were North Vietnamese capabilities for launching a large-scale offensive? To what extent could South Vietnamese forces handle the enemy threat with or without US combat support? How adequate was American information concerning the political atmosphere in Saigon? Kissinger's team left few stones unturned in seeking information, and thus policy options, for the new president. As the *New York Times* observed, the "Nixon administration will have no shortage of advice . . . on a possible shift in Vietnam strategy."[60]

The *Times* report certainly hit the mark. Nixon's formal dissemination of the "Situation in Vietnam" questionnaire, National Security Study Memorandum 1 (NSSM 1), elicited sharp disagreements from responding agencies. Optimistic feedback from MACV and the embassy contradicted more sobering assessments from the CIA and State Department. (Abrams's command omitted or downplayed critical appraisals from subordinates in its final report.)[61] The enemy order of battle controversy, pitting MACV staffers against the CIA since mid-1967, resurfaced, as did disagreements over the quality of the South Vietnamese armed forces. Abrams complained in November 1969 that he still could not "make any sense out of what we carry as [enemy] strength." Still, the general believed Hanoi would submit if faced with a strong riposte to their military interdiction campaign and progress in ARVN training and the allies' pacification programs. Kissinger seemed less certain. As he told Nixon that May, "In Saigon the tendency is to fight the war to victory. It has to be kept in mind, but you and I know it won't happen—it's impossible." Still, the national security advisor conceded, "Even Gen. Abrams agreed."[62]

If the NSSM 1 process illustrated that the American mission in Vietnam, as a whole, remained uncertain about the war's progress and eventual outcome, it equally advanced few strategic alternatives. Kissinger certainly laid out policy choices on political and territorial accommodations with Hanoi and how they might be influenced by accompanying factors such as an improved RVNAF. Yet alternatives for a truly new military strategy seemed bleak. Kissinger laid out only two basic possibilities— "to continue pressures on Hanoi through the current strategy, threats of escalation, or actual escalation; or to reduce the U.S. presence in South Vietnam, which, by making U.S. presence more sustainable, could be another form of pressure." While Abrams pushed for retaliation against

Hanoi's February offensive—"it would give a clear signal of our resolve"—the extensive policy review offered few, if any, real options in terms of reimagining the allies' military strategy.[63]

Perhaps more fundamentally, the sweeping interagency evaluation left unanswered larger questions on how the United States would achieve peace with honor as it disengaged from South Vietnam or, for that matter, how the Nixon administration would even define an honorable settlement. As Kissinger noted, "We could not simply walk away from an enterprise involving two administrations, five allied countries, and thirty-one thousand dead as if we were switching a television channel."[64] But how to achieve an "honorable" peace agreement when it was the performance of the South Vietnamese government and armed forces that increasingly mattered most? This crucial question, one centered on redefining the term "winning," would bedevil the US mission in Vietnam for the next four years.[65]

Claims, however, that altering the definition of victory meant achieving nothing but a "decent interval" before South Vietnam survived or collapsed on its own seem slightly overblown. As the Nixon administration entered into serious negotiations with Hanoi, the president desired more than just a convenient off-ramp from the war. Throughout, Nixon spoke of upholding "other nations' confidence in our reliability" and warned against a precipitate withdrawal that would "inevitably allow the Communists to repeat the massacres which followed their takeover in the North."[66]

Without question, the stalemated war ultimately forced US policymakers' hands. Even before entering Nixon's White House, Kissinger urged a "reasonable time for political consolidation" that would allow the South Vietnamese "an opportunity to work out their own destiny in their own way." And as he confronted Hanoi's tough negotiators in Paris, the national security advisor slowly came to confront the limits of American influence over North Vietnam. It seems neither the president nor Kissinger willingly embraced a "decent interval" solution as a way to militarily disengage the United States from Southeast Asia. Yet as they met head-on the enduring political problems undermining the Saigon regime, both men increasingly accepted that an interlude, decent or otherwise, might be the only achievable outcome of a negotiated settlement between Hanoi and Washington, DC.[67]

Nixon certainly found himself pressured by a growing antiwar movement that no longer saw *any* honor in the Vietnam War and thus pushed for its rapid conclusion. Kissinger, too, was "well aware of the popular pressures for a prompt settlement of the war and consequent time limitations placed upon the Administration in carrying out its strategy." While the majority of Americans, silent or not, continued to believe global communism should be contained as a matter of policy, opponents of the war questioned how Vietnam was advancing such goals. Was it possible, as journalist Frances FitzGerald proposed, that the "American government did not want to face the consequences of peace"?[68]

Even military officers, historically an apolitical fraternity within the United States, increasingly expressed their private "bitterness and frustration" at not being "permitted" to win the war. Almost certainly, many, if not most, professional soldiers still sought honor in the only active conflict of the Cold War since Korea. A losing war could still bestow on the most cynical of officer accolades and tribute useful for promotion and a personal sense of valor. Yet on the eve of Nixon's inauguration, journalists already were hearing, some for the first time, "majors and lieutenant colonels speaking of the war's absurdity."[69]

These cracks within the military establishment seemingly raised questions over the president's policy aims even before Kissinger's strategic review neared completion. If the war was indeed absurd, how could the nation achieve an honorable peace and maintain its credibility with allies abroad? At this point in a long, stalemated war, what did credibility even mean anymore? Aides worried that a unilateral withdrawal from Vietnam would be interpreted as betraying an ally, while Kissinger insisted the "principles of America's honor and America's responsibility were not empty phrases."[70] The choice, however, between precipitate retreat and continuing stalemate left the administration with few attractive options. By persevering in a protracted, costly war where traditional military victory no longer seemed possible, the administration ran the risk of sacrificing American (and South Vietnamese) lives only for vague platitudes like "prestige" and "credibility." As one observer asked, how could such a course not be viewed as "a sort of slow-motion defeat"?[71]

Arguments to prolong the war, of course, retained a practical edge. Staying true to the South Vietnamese cause avoided political backlash. As Kissinger figured, "If we were to pull out of Vietnam, there would be disaster, politically, for us here, at home." But influential voices in Washington, DC, already were casting doubt on Nixon's plan to achieve peace with honor. Though benefiting from post-election goodwill thanks to his campaign promises, the new president faced a growing chorus of policy elite willing to challenge him publicly. In March, Senator J. William Fulbright challenged the administration to produce a "new and different policy in Vietnam," protesting what he called "an old broken record."[72] Two months later, Averell Harriman, the former chief American negotiator in Paris, appealed for a "reduction in the violence leading to a ceasefire." Recently departed Defense Secretary Clark Clifford followed suit in June, asserting Nixon's present policy resulted only "in a continuation of the high level of U.S. casualties without any negotiations in Paris." By July, Senator George McGovern was calling for a thirty-day cease-fire.[73]

Without question, Nixon saw the legislative branch as a special danger looming in the wings. As an institution most responsive to public opinion, the

House of Representatives could transmit pressure from its constituencies to the White House. Thus, antiwar activism at the congressional district level could prove especially threatening. Few administration advisors understood this better than the new secretary of defense, Melvin R. Laird. Reporting to Nixon on the "vocal opposition to the war" in September, Laird argued the "actual and potential antipathy for the war is, in my judgment, significant and increasing." Thus, the defense secretary petitioned for "a positive and understandable program, even if its dimensions are not fully defined and are subject to change, which will appeal to the U.S. people."[74] In Laird's mind, only one program fit that bill—Vietnamization.

"De-Americanizing" the War in Vietnam

A "midwest Machiavelli." So *The Milwaukee Journal* described Melvin Laird in early 1966. A politician marked by "subtlety and cunning," the Wisconsin congressman took over the Department of Defense at a time when influence over foreign policy resided increasingly within the national security staff. Laird, however, proved Kissinger's equal, at least from a bureaucratic infighting standpoint. He also possessed a keen sense of public opinion and understood the social and economic imperatives of ending the war in Vietnam.[75] While Kissinger's aides complained that Laird favored "domestic tranquility" over "the survival of South Vietnam," the new defense secretary "knew that time was running out for us because the public wasn't going to support the war any longer." American credibility must surely be upheld as the United States withdrew from Vietnam, but the Nixon administration had to tangibly demonstrate its commitment to ending the war lest it squander any chances of a second term.[76]

Thus, when Laird made his first official visit to South Vietnam in March 1969, he went straight to Abrams's headquarters with a clear agenda—"our withdrawal program and when we're going to start." For five days the secretary of defense met with senior US officials and President Nguyen Van Thieu, toured the corps tactical zones, and received a host of briefings. His message remained consistent throughout. The US effort had to make real effort toward "our overall objective, which is the self-determination of South Vietnam." Yet in the near future the command also would have to "reduce the United States contribution, not only in the form of men, but in casualties and matériel and in dollars."[77] Upon returning home, reporters claimed Laird had run into a "buzz saw of opposition" from both MACV and the South Vietnamese government. While overstated—Abrams certainly abhored firm withdraw timetables but respected the secretary's stance—clearly the process of disengagement was going to expose deep anxieties about what the Americans were leaving behind.[78]

Laird's report to the president opened with a connotation purely of victory far below what most military officers likely had envisioned when President Johnson sent ground troops to Vietnam in 1965. "A satisfactory conclusion," the secretary emphasized, "means to most Americans the eventual disengagement of American men in combat." Thus, to sustain domestic support, MACV had "to find the means by which the burden of combat must promptly, and methodically, be shifted to the South Vietnamese." While Laird highlighted reports of "steady progress" in allied military efforts, the basic problem remained "that of achieving permanent South Vietnamese control over the country. . . . This would be a difficult task under peaceful conditions. It is herculean while hostilities continue at the present level." Laird's conclusions were unambiguous. "To enhance the vital interests of our country . . . plans should be drawn for the redeployment of 50-70 thousand U.S. troops from South Vietnam this year." A "substantial replacement" of American with ARVN forces should follow in subsequent years.[79]

Senior military officers contested such views, both privately and publicly. Even before Laird's visit, newspapers reported that Abrams opposed "a reduction in American forces until he [was] certain such a move would not jeopardize the war effort." While the MACV commander believed a cutback in American strength an "inevitable eventuality," the *New York Times* conveyed military officers' opposition to any withdrawal before July.[80] Chairman of the Joint Chiefs of Staff Earle Wheeler went further. After Laird's departure, the general recommended Abrams be authorized to "operate offensively" in the southern demilitarized zone and be "tasked for plans to attack and destroy . . . critical enemy base areas" in both Laos and Cambodia. The political-minded defense secretary no doubt grimaced at what sounded like a broken record from his most senior of uniformed advisors.[81]

The president, however, could not dispute Laird's logic and in late March authorized plans to "de-Americanize" the war. So "to put the emphasis on the right issues," the secretary of defense recommended the phrase "Vietnamization," a label that stuck. Yet a broad definition of the term put into question whether this was presidential policy or military strategy.[82] Vietnamization not only included the extension of governmental presence and control across the South Vietnamese countryside, but also the improvement of military capabilities so Vietnamese forces could "deal with the enemy they face." As one administration official testified, "These two things, together, mean a lessening need for a U.S. role and are thus what enable us to bring about a reduction of our forces without endangering the existence of this program." Thieu and Abrams might object to such a program, but they both would prove to hold little influence over Nixon's decision-making on the US withdrawal.[83]

Nixon, for his part, was still hoping to achieve a similar goal as Kennedy and Johnson before him: enable the anticommunist government in Saigon to regain full control of South Vietnam. But he and his spokesmen tried to make that goal look as modest as possible. Still, senior officials like Ellsworth Bunker attempted to place American efforts in a satisfying light. "When we talk about winning the war," the ambassador noted during Laird's Vietnam trip, "we mean it in the sense of an acceptable political settlement which gives the Vietnamese people the opportunity to choose freely their own government."[84]

There certainly were Americans who would have liked to see a total victory in the style of World War II, a complete subjugation of North Vietnam. But what really disturbed them, and disturbed South Vietnamese officials and officers, was a sense that the moderation of official rhetoric marked a weakness of will, that the Nixon administration was not going to do what was necessary to achieve even its limited conception of victory. They feared that Nixon was putting the war on a path that might end in the worst possible way: with complete communist victory.[85]

One ARVN general, doubting the Americans could achieve such a settlement as outlined by Bunker, believed Vietnamization was "a way for the United States to pull out with a nebulous plan and uncertain support." A US veteran likened the plan to "running the Vietnam War movie backwards, except we would leave an American clone army in our wake." A negotiated political settlement, in short, appeared unsatisfying compared to the unconditional surrender Americans had won over their enemies in World War II. No surprise, then, that as 1969 wore on, American officers were still saying the prospects for defeating the enemy in South Vietnam had "improved strikingly in the past year."[86]

In an address to the nation on 14 May 1969, though, Nixon ruled out a purely military solution for the war in Vietnam. Pledging not to abandon South Vietnam, the president defined his essential objective as the "opportunity for the South Vietnamese people to determine their own political future without outside interference." Nixon insisted there should be no rigid formula for peace, quietly leaving open the possibility of escalation to achieve his aims. He thus asked Americans for their patience. "A war that has raged for many years will require detailed negotiations and cannot be settled by a single stroke." The United States would not even object to reunification, as long as that decision reflected the free choice of all Vietnamese. Nixon concluded with a proposal to withdraw all non-South Vietnamese forces from South Vietnam and to create an international body to supervise a cease-fire leading to peace negotiations. As the *Los Angeles Times* reported, the president's speech blended toughness with a conciliatory tone.[87]

The process of Vietnamization, however, comprised only one stake of a multipillar plan to end the decades' long conflict—at least from the American perspective. Even before the election, Nixon had outlined what he would later call a "five-point strategy . . . to end the war and win the peace." Inside South Vietnam, Vietnamization and pacification would support each other. A maturing ARVN and Saigon government would allow not only a US withdrawal, but also serve as an incentive for the local population to back the GVN. Globally, the administration intended to isolate North Vietnam from its Soviet and Chinese benefactors. While Nixon saw "rapprochement with China and détente with the Soviet Union [as] ends in themselves," he also "considered them possible means to hasten the end of the war." Peace negotiations comprised the fourth leg of the president's strategy. Finally, a "new key element" of the American approach entailed "the complete withdrawal of all American combat troops from Vietnam." And though the United States was ending its involvement in the war, Nixon pledged to uphold his nation's commitments to South Vietnam.[88]

Nixon realized that his grand designs rested on keeping US casualties in Vietnam low. Yet MACV still considered battle a necessity. Throughout the spring of 1969, Abrams sent several missives to the Joint Chiefs warning against "adoption of a purely defensive posture." Moreover, the MACV commander felt aggrieved for not being consulted on the process of Vietnamization. In March, Abrams sent General Wheeler a stinging message objecting to any decrease in allied operations. "From here, we see nothing in the current military situation in SVN that warrants our making a unilateral reduction in combat power at this time."[89] The following month, he told a reporter that "when we have maintained the initiative . . . our kill ratio is spectacular." No surprise then that in April, B-52s dropped some 2,000 tons of bombs on Tay Ninh province alone. Abrams certainly intended to give "maximum support and effort" to the pacification and ARVN modernization programs, but his strategic outlook envisioned hurting the enemy as badly as possible.[90]

The enemy, of course, had to keep pace with Nixon's changes as well and realized the dilemma Abrams faced in balancing so many competing demands. Just because the Americans "had been forced to passively deescalate," did not mean they no longer posed a threat to the National Liberation Front (NLF) or North Vietnamese Army (PAVN) forces operating inside South Vietnam. Thus, Hanoi intended to place pressure on Saigon's "puppet army" while recuperating from the 1968 Tet offensive. In the process, Politburo leaders posed the same question, as did many officers in MACV. Winning control of the population and occupying land required the Americans and South Vietnamese to resume the offensive. Yet the imperative to reduce US casualties placed pressure on Abrams to take a more defensive stance. "Since their offensives and counter offensives had been defeated, how could a defensive strategy help the U.S. attain its aggressive goals?"[91]

Though American troop levels in Vietnam peaked in April 1969, Abrams's answer was to maintain the battlefield initiative. As one MACV briefing officer recounted, the guidelines for allied military strategy were "aggressive pre-emptive operations by attacking the enemy in his base camps and dislodging his logistical system." American advisors continued to evaluate ARVN units based on "kill ratios," while Abrams reiterated advice to maintain his command's combat potential as the Nixon administration considered withdrawal proposals.[92] Thus, to keep "maximum pressure" on the enemy, the allies once more entered the A Shau Valley. As more than 2,000 US and ARVN soldiers descended on the enemy stronghold near the Laotian border, MACV planners hoped this latest strike would uncover communist base camps and force their soldiers to battle. They were not to be disappointed.[93]

American commanders had long operated under the assumption that to protect the South Vietnamese population, they had to construct a shield behind which pacification and other development programs could grow. Thus, to ignore the enemy's use of A Shau Valley invited trouble. A string of allied firebases and special forces camps dotted the valley, but the presence of at least nine enemy infantry regiments within I Corps in the spring of 1969 demanded a military response. Most importantly, US commanders saw the need to protect the imperial city of Hue, in eastern Thua Thien province, from an assault similar to that endured during the 1968 Tet offensive.[94] As American forces moved deeper into the valley, they set their sights on two enemy battalions occupying the major terrain feature of Dong Ap Bia. Plotted as Hill 937 on American maps, the mountain "dominated the local area in the west central A Shau" with the enemy there "preventing friendly forces from gaining control of an infiltration route into South Vietnam from Laos." As one veteran of Operation Apache Snow recalled, Dong Ap Bia "was a perfect defensive position."[95]

Beginning on 10 May, US tactical air and artillery fires pounded the battle area. Far from backing off, however, the enemy reinforced their positions nightly from Laos. Days of hard fighting followed for soldiers of the US 101st Airborne Division and 1st ARVN Regiment. As casualties mounted on both sides, Major General Melvin Zais, the 101st commander, pushed hard toward Hill 937. Frank Boccia, a young lieutenant in the assault, recalled the fighting on 14 May. "The spitting barks of the M16s became one voice; the hammering of the M60s merged into a sheet of sound, a smothering curtain of noise. It seemed as if one cold *walk* across the sound, as if it had, in fact, crystallized the very air into something ponderous." Still, the allies pressed forward. By the 18th, US infantrymen finally had closed in on the southern base of Ap Bia mountain. The final assault would unleash some of the heaviest fighting of the war—and some of the most vocal political criticism as well.[96]

After days of continuous artillery fire and air support, the worn-down troopers from the 101st began their assault up Hill 937. The weeks of fighting through heavy jungle undergrowth already had taken their toll. A coordinated assault against Ap Bia on 18 May followed probing attacks that had alerted the NVA to the Americans' intentions. Now, battalion commanders urged their tired men forward into the face of a well-planned enemy bunker system. The defenders repulsed assault after assault, as US troop leaders pressed their men on. One battalion commander, Lieutenant Colonel Weldon Honeycutt, shouted over the radio to a subordinate officer, "Damn it, get those men moving! You are being paid to fight this war, not discuss it." Zais, not willing to let go of his prey despite the rising casualties among his ranks, committed fresh battalions into the battle. Still, the enemy would not relent.[97]

Hearing of the fighting in progress, Associated Press correspondent Jay Sharbutt made his way into the A Shau Valley. What he found shocked both him and the Americans back home who read his reporting. One soldier railed against Honeycutt: "That damn Blackjack won't stop unless he kills every damn one of us." Another dazed trooper expressed disbelief at the tactics being used by his officers. "All of us are wondering why they just can't pull back and B-52 that

Figure 5 "A PERFECT DEFENSIVE POSITION." The aftermath of fighting on Dong Ap Bia, what Americans soldiers would call, in macabre fashion, "Hamburger Hill." (RG489S, Box 4, Zais Collection, MHI)

hill." In macabre fashion, "that hill" had been renamed by shaken men who saw themselves as meat being chewed up in a steel grinder. On 20 May, the allies assaulted "Hamburger Hill" once more, nearing a charred summit that looked like the worst of any World War I battlefield. They swept over the war-torn hill the next day. Lieutenant Colonel Honeycutt believed his troops had performed "heroically" as the enemy finally retreated back into Laos.[98] Yet as news of the battle emerged, critics were far less acclamatory of the military leadership's performance.

Condemnations were not long in coming after the fighting on Hamburger Hill. MACV's officers, however, closed ranks, arguing that offensive tactics ultimately saved lives, despite the fact that some 70 US soldiers were killed and another 372 wounded during Operation Apache Snow. An enemy body count of 630 dead did little to assuage observers who saw the battle as a repetition of past mistakes.[99] But MACV stood firm in its defense. As Abrams boomed during a staff meeting later in the year, the South Vietnamese simply couldn't handle NVA divisions "with administration and police! I mean, I don't care *what* kind of a damn genius you are, you can't get out here and give them tickets or arrest them or what the hell ever you do with police. I mean, these are just mean bastards with a lot of firepower and a lot of strength." In truth, then, the battle at Dong Ap Bia demonstrated the difficulties of balancing the idea of US withdrawal from South Vietnam with the military requirements of keeping the enemy away from the country's population centers.[100]

These contradictions, though, mattered little as a political firestorm swept across Washington, DC, in the aftermath of Hamburger Hill. Edward M. Kennedy led the charge. The Massachusetts senator denounced the casualties as "senseless and irresponsible," fulminating that "American boys are too valuable to be sacrificed for a false sense of military pride." Zais defended himself: "I don't know how many wars we have to go through to convince people that bombing alone can never do the trick." But the damage was done.[101] Kennedy received scores of letters from disgruntled soldiers asking his support to "extricate ourselves from this mess." As a foreshadowing of greater unrest to come within the army's ranks, an underground newspaper placed a $10,000 reward offer to assassinate any officer ordering similar assaults to Ap Bia. Others saw in Hamburger Hill a microcosm of the larger war. How, they asked, were the fighting, and the seemingly incessant casualties, furthering the president's aims in Vietnam?[102]

Such questions offered few easy answers. Reports of progress on the South Vietnamese armed forces appeared uneven at best. Worse, President Thieu continued to struggle in building a broad-based foundation for a stable, noncommunist government capable of contesting the NLF. Americans harshly blamed the Saigon leadership. Pundits accused Thieu of not integrating opposition groups into his government, even while these elements proved unwilling to cooperate with Saigon. Moreover, US analysts assailed a political system "based on personal ties and loyalties rather than on differentiation in programs and objectives."[103] Even South Vietnamese castigated the GVN for failing to cultivate consensus among the population. As one central Vietnamese political leader noted in 1969, Thieu's regime presented the image of a centralized government, filled with power, yet in reality was "cowardly, incapable, confused, and closed." No wonder American advisors worried over the GVN's capacity to face political competition with US backing to diminish in the not too distant future.[104]

The Thieu government, however, faced a host of issues in mid-1969 as it called for a "constructive solution" to the ongoing conflict. Perhaps most urgent, the South Vietnamese economy appeared progressively incapable of sustaining a society long at war. Mobilization increases not only upended social structures, while decreasing available workforce manpower, but also added further burdens to an already weakened economy. In July, Kissinger' staff quoted a "wide variety of sources indicating that the problems of inflation, budget deficit, mismanagement and other economic woes have sharply increased in intensity over the last few months." Such problems were already "beginning to sap some of the Government's vitality in attempting to build a competitive position against Communists in a future post-war environment."[105] On the ground, the more than 1.3 million refugees only exacerbated the GVN's woes. One American correspondent found it "staggering" that refugee care was comparatively a low priority when "pitted against continuing military operations, intensified peace negotiations, and political skirmishing in Saigon." If Creighton Abrams found it difficult to balance a multidimensional war, so, too, did Nguyen Van Thieu.[106]

The president's worries only deepened given the problems associated with land reform. Long an issue in Vietnam, land ownership had ties to French colonialism, with tenant farmers suffering under high rents and corrupt landlords. After the French-Indochina War ended in 1954, South Vietnamese president Ngo Dinh Diem, hoping to redistribute fertile acreage to farmers, issued decrees that limited an owner's holdings to 100 hectares. Improvements to farmers' lives, however, came slowly, if at all. Additionally, the NLF land allocation program possessed a mass appeal the GVN could not match. According to one study of Long An province, "Under Party practice land redistribution was essentially a local matter, decided by local people at the village level . . . By contrast, the government land redistribution was carried out by cadres of the central government, on the basis of an inflexible law which made no provision for the differing needs of each locality."[107]

Many of these localities, dependent on peasant farmers for harvesting rice, saw land cultivation drop precipitously as the war forced workers to flee toward the relatively safer confines of urban areas. Reform efforts buckled as "liberated areas" often had more land than people to farm it. Thus, as early as 1965, South Vietnam had found it necessary to import rice. By 1969, the GVN, under pressure from American advisors, took action. Thieu froze occupancy rents and in June backed a Land-to-Tiller bill that aimed to increase land ownership throughout the country. Still, these major reform policies, set for implementation in early 1970, worried many officials inside the US mission. As Abrams reported before the Land-to-Tiller legislation went into effect, the "land reform program has tremendous political and economic potential, but is, as yet, essentially unrealized."[108]

Similar anxieties tarnished the Saigon government's political reform efforts. Here, Americans found no shortage of troubles over which to rebuke their wartime allies. Reports emanated from Saigon, almost weekly, on Thieu's inability to build political coalitions, his failure to create a sense of national community, or his refusal to find some common ground with communist sympathizers living inside South Vietnam. Critics condemned the president and his coterie for lording over an "ill-defined" governmental structure, but Thieu had little personal incentive to preside over any policy that might lead to his own removal from power. In the process, a disappointed Ambassador Bunker watched helplessly as a September cabinet re-shuffling, expected to "forge a more united front that could compete with the Communists," in fact, narrowed the government to "military men, obscure technocrats and former associates of the late President Ngo Dinh Diem."[109]

Thieu, and by extension his American backers, faced further political challenges with the creation of the Provisional Revolutionary Government (PRG) of the Republic of South Vietnam in early June 1969. This parallel "government" took direct aim at Nixon's Vietnamization plans. If the US withdrawal depended on building a stable, credible GVN, the additional political competition came at an inauspicious time. As one National Liberation Front official recalled, the Thieu "administration's efforts to portray the Saigon regime as an autonomous, legitimate government would now be answered by another Southern government fighting hard in every international forum to establish its own claim to legitimacy." Less than a week after the PRG's creation, the Soviet Union officially recognized the new revolutionary government.[110]

While unsettling to be sure, developments on the diplomatic front mattered far less to the US military command than the political struggle across South Vietnam's rural areas. MACV strategy ultimately depended on a political solution at the grassroots level. Yet there seemed little to celebrate in the rural countryside. Officers begrudgingly compared the sincerity of the "idealistic as hell" NLF cadre to the GVN and found the Saigon government wanting. Moreover, as one observer wrote in *Foreign Affairs*, Vietnamization made "no provision for a political accommodation between the communist and non-communist forces in South Vietnam. It therefore leaves the central issue of the Vietnam struggle unresolved."[111] Coupled with continuing security challenges, the political factionalism forced the Saigon regime to increase its military presence throughout the contested provinces. Yet this "militarization of the population" came at a price. Augmenting the republic's armed forces only stripped more young men from their homes and the workforce. Worse, the government's main instrument of power illustrated the tolls a long war already had taken on a battered South Vietnamese society.[112]

A Disparaged Army

The Army of the Republic of Vietnam had long suffered in the eyes of most Americans. As Creighton Abrams fumed in February 1968, "For too long the cynics, the self appointed tacticians and strategists among our civilians, the ignorant and the press have been writing the fitness reports of the Vietnamese armed forces."[113] In truth, to most US advisors, even after years of working in tandem with their allies, the ARVN remained an opaque military organization. After the 1968 Tet offensive, both Abrams and Ambassador Bunker spoke approvingly of progress being made in the ARVN's ranks, while subordinate officers reported on the crippling ineffectiveness of the Vietnamese army's leadership. Many Americans wondered aloud if Thieu's military could compensate for the planned US withdrawals. Most had little idea. Efficiency reports on Vietnamization were so inconsistent, some inherently so, that by September 1969, Henry Kissinger could only convey to the president that while MACV could "measure progress in numbers of men and equipment, we have great difficulty assessing motivation, aggressiveness, leadership skills."[114]

The rapid expansion of the RVNAF between 1967 and 1970—a 60 percent increase—only furthered assessment problems. US officers continued to use body counts as a metric for evaluating ARVN performance, but such gruesome appraisals only told part of the story. Abrams therefore remained careful not to oversell South Vietnamese military improvements. The withdrawal of US forces, however, depended on the ARVN assuming more of the combat burden. Yet the MACV commander introduced no new mechanisms to promote reform within his ally's armed forces.[115] Worse, civilian advisors working in the pacification program shared with Kissinger their concerns over "the low level of competence of the U.S. personnel detailed to train" the local and provincial militia. It seemed no surprise then that in late June 1969, the national security advisor sent the president a pessimistic note on the ARVN's readiness to oppose more than the internal Vietcong threat. "I do not believe," Nixon's aide warned, "the Vietnamese armed forces will be able to achieve the necessary combat effectiveness within the timeframe visualized under the Vietnamization game plan."[116]

Regional and Popular Forces, akin to local militia, comprised roughly 48 percent of the RVNAF in early 1969. Spread across the breadth of South Vietnam, the status of the RF/PFs—"Ruff Puffs" in American jargon—demonstrated the complexities of assessing Vietnamization. MACV's strategy had long been built on clearing contested areas with conventional forces, leaving the mission of holding and controlling the newly liberated space to territorial units. The former task, however, had always remained easier than the latter. American field advisors too often reported on insurgent forces resuming their activities as soon as US or South Vietnamese army units moved out of the operational area.[117] Others worried that the need to "nurse the territorials along" would undermine mobility and an "offensive spirit" among the ARVN's ranks. RF units were generally more familiar with the local enemy and terrain, but as one US Army colonel observed, "Many of their daylight operations result in unproductive 'walks in the sun' and their night operations are frequently executed merely to satisfy quotas imposed by higher headquarters."[118]

Such problems raised a fundamental question for senior American officials. If the ARVN was successfully trained to repel a possible North Vietnamese invasion yet the RF/PF remained incapable of providing adequate local security, were the goals of Vietnamization truly being met? Critics protested the "insular self-cohesion" of an army seemingly out of step with the general population, while analysts pointed to increased casualty rates as indicators that "the combat load of the ARVN is increasing."[119] Kissinger, though, worried about throwing too much weight on the South Vietnamese armed forces for fear it "might well start a fatal unraveling of RVNAF effectiveness and morale." Nixon agreed but responded that the US "military should quit trying to build ARVN in their own image." Any evaluation of Vietnamization thus had to balance long-held preconceptions on the military effectiveness of the South Vietnamese with the demands of a diminishing US presence.[120]

Moreover, Abrams decided not to alter any of the key command relationships between wartime allies. Westmoreland had recognized from the beginning of his tenure at MACV that the Americans could only consult and advise, not direct. Thus, the US military command did not assume control over the South Vietnamese joint general staff. Critics condemned such faulty command relationships, but as one officer noted, "It must be recognized that the US does not dictate strategy in Vietnam. The Republic of Vietnam has a functioning government headed now by proud military leaders who have positive nationalistic feelings."[121] This advisory role rankled many Americans who believed their taking over the war would produce better results, but Abrams made no change given the end state toward which he was proceeding. Even though officers grumbled that combined operations between allied forces were no "more than superficial," MACV's commander retained a parallel rather than integrated command structure. The Americans' position would thus remain as consultant on the process of Vietnamization for the war's final years.[122]

If the advisory role illustrated the limits of American power, US officers tended to view the local army as *the* impediment to progress. Commanders scoffed at the ARVN's "lack of aggressive leadership at all levels," its failure "to carry the fight to the enemy," and their leaders' canny ability to stay in command despite poor performance. Rising desertion rates among ARVN soldiers only furthered advisor worries. Abrams rightfully spoke of the "cultural chasm" between allies, as evidenced by the Americans' use of terms like "dink" and "slope" to describe their Vietnamese compatriots. Even if a "great many who use it don't use it intentionally to offend," the general opined, "there's no question but what it does."[123] Thus, after the Nixon White House published its formal national security memorandum "Vietnamizing the War" in April 1969, the secretary of defense surfaced a number of "unknowns" on the quality of South Vietnam's armed forces. "With such unknowns, we must recognize the possibility that even with additional training, improved equipment, and increased combat support, the RVNAF will not be able soon to stand along against the current North Vietnamese and Viet Cong force levels."[124]

Laird's candid appraisal left little doubt of the difficulties ahead. Yet the evaluation also suggested inequalities inherent in how those within the US command defined the fundamental term "allies." In the eyes of many American soldiers, the South Vietnamese acted more like dim understudies than true partners. One battalion commander recalled that his troopers hated the ARVN soldiers who "were 'search and avoid' experts or thieves or lazy bastards." Another officer found his subordinates derisively calling local militia forces "the second team," while a lieutenant admitted that over the radio the South Vietnamese army "were usually just 'the fucking ARVNs.'"[125] Abrams continued to stress combined operations as a way to build the RVNAF into a "militarily mature" organization, but results varied by corps tactical zone. One postwar questionnaire found that nearly a third of surveyed US officers rated their South Vietnamese as "inadequate." If Vietnamization was to succeed, Thieu's armed forces would have to become more than just an "obstruction" to US military efforts.[126]

Reports in the American press, however, did not help matters. Irate officers shared with journalists their frustrations over an army that "only seems to fight," and in late 1969, *Newsweek* ran a representative story under the byline "Baby-Sitting with ARVN." The open criticism forced Abrams to brainstorm with the Joint Chiefs on "more effective ways to publicize the progress and achievements of the RVNAF."[127] Of course, the GVN reaction to such harsh depictions was predictable. As Vice President Ky seethed after the war, "The American advisory program was a lamentable disaster that contributed largely to the eventual debacle in Vietnam. It was worse: it was a gigantic con trick foisted on American popular opinion." If Ky's assessment seemed harsh, it nonetheless hit on an important, and accurate, point. In the process of a long war, Americans both at home and in Saigon had turned the South Vietnamese armed forces into a convenient scapegoat as they argued about the prospects of successful Vietnamization.[128]

A Policy of Withdrawal

The fate of the South Vietnamese government, its armed forces, and its people became intertwined with global events as the Nixon administration gained its footing in mid-1969. Without question, the civil war inside Vietnam had always ebbed and flowed within the larger currents of the Cold War. Yet Nixon's reconceptualization of US grand strategy clearly drove many, if not most, of the decisions leading to Vietnamization. In short, a changing global context was forcing the new White House occupants to reexamine what a "meaningful victory" in Vietnam meant. As Kissinger recalled, a sense of national unease was born from the realization "that we were becoming like other nations in the need to recognize that our power, while vast, had limits." Thus, in an effort to "shape a global equilibrium," Nixon's foreign policy team necessarily weighed the ongoing, even rising, costs of prolonging the war in Vietnam against the expected benefits from a global perspective. Vietnamization might calm US and world opinion, allowing for a long-term American presence in Southeast Asia. But the war might also derail Nixon's designs for a reimagined relationship with the major communist powers China and the Soviet Union.[129]

As part of his decision-making, the president had to weigh treaty commitments with Southeast Asia Treaty Organization (SEATO) nations. While Abrams told the Joint Chiefs in July that he saw no need for a revolutionary change in military strategy, Nixon certainly thought otherwise at the grand strategic level. Disengagement from Vietnam, if accomplished with US credibility intact, would grant more flexibility in American foreign policy. The administration thus needed to balance interests with commitments and Nixon firmly believed the former shaped the latter. Naturally, talk of withdrawal from Southeast Asia caused concern among America's allies, especially those in Europe. If the United States withdrew precipitously from SEATO because of unbearable domestic pressure, might it be possible similar forces would drive an American decoupling from NATO? Nixon, however, seemed less interested in pursuing a neo-isolationist policy than redirecting the nation's interests toward forming new relationships with the major communist powers.[130]

This process suggested the president envisioned Vietnamization as a policy of withdrawal rather than a strategy for victory in South Vietnam. The distinction matters. Nixon's policy aimed at restructuring Cold War relationships, of which extraction from Vietnam was a crucial component. The goal of strategy fell to Abrams—to disengage from a war without causing a collapse to either the South Vietnamese nation or American prestige. Pundits might condemn Vietnamization as doing nothing more than changing "the color of the bodies," but Abrams's task was to make the war, as best as possible, "useable" by the new administration.[131] To do this required, in the general's words, the Americans to depart "in an orderly way, in a way that makes sense, and a way that doesn't let the Vietnamese down—doesn't collapse the whole system." Whether the philosophy guiding Vietnamization, in truth, rested on underlying imbalances between policy ends and strategic means remained to be seen in mid-1969.[132]

Nixon, however, set Vietnamization in motion during an 8 June meeting with Thieu on Midway Island. The two presidents agreed on the "principle of self-determination," which meant the South Vietnamese people would "be able to choose without interference or terror." Talk of a negotiated settlement, though, belied a sense of solidarity the Midway meeting intended to portray. Even before the six-hour summit, US sources reported that Saigon political leaders had "long been hypersensitive in their concern for American constancy and what they think of as the US willingness to stay the course." Thieu, in short, was "genuinely afraid of being sold out."[133] News of the Provisional Revolutionary Government's establishment the same week as Midway did little to alleviate GVN fears. Yet the South Vietnamese president had few options but to give Nixon his consent. As Ambassador Bui Diem recalled, if Thieu "was not happy about the move toward Vietnamization, he had by that point accepted the inevitable."[134]

The Americans' intentions became patently clear when Nixon announced at Midway the first pullout of 25,000 US troops to be completed by the end of August. Linking the cutback directly to Vietnamization, journalists reported that "the equivalent of a combat division could leave Vietnam because of progress in the training and equipping of South Vietnam's army."[135] Behind the scenes, though, the Joint Chiefs implored Secretary Laird to go slow on subsequent rounds of troop withdrawals because neither "the assessment of the military situation nor the [ARVN's] capabilities" justified a sizable redeployment. It would not be the first time public narratives on Vietnamization's progress diverged from more private assessments among senior military commanders.[136]

The first phase of the US withdrawal, however, illustrated not only the politicized nature of Vietnamization but also the quickly fraying bonds in civil-military relations. In Midway's aftermath, commentators at once denounced the "token withdrawals" while knocking the loss of military pressure Abrams could exert on the enemy. Long-time newspaper columnist Joseph Alsop likened

Nixon's policy to "the Russian woman who threw the wolves a child from time to time to keep the wolf-pack from catching up with her troika."[137] Simultaneously, senior military officers reproached civilian officials for not understanding the war. During an October visit to Vietnam, Joint Chiefs Chairman Earle Wheeler groused to the MACV staff over "the attitude of a considerable segment of the Congress who are always shooting off their mouths about things they know nothing about." Six months later, Alsop publicly warned the president he would be "asking for trouble by refusing to heed Gen. Abrams" and his call for a pause to further troop withdrawals. If the process of Vietnamization included a good deal of policy, it also came with a heavy dose of politics.[138]

One month after the Midway summit, the president put a finer edge on his foreign policy objectives by issuing what would become known as the Nixon Doctrine. Flying to Guam after the splashdown of Apollo XI, the commander in chief held a press conference on 26 July laying out his vision for the US role in Asia after the war in Vietnam. The United States would continue to play a significant part, yet Nixon intended to avoid the "kind of policy that will make countries in Asia so dependent upon us that we are dragged into conflicts such as the one that we have in Vietnam."[139] In large sense, the president was calling for a course that would have been viewed as heretical a decade earlier. His "doctrine" suggested there were, in fact, limits to American power. As one army colonel later described the policy, the United States would "assist our allies in shoulder-ing their responsibilities [but] with less direct involvement abroad."[140]

If Nixon anticipated his remarks would signal less of a withdrawal from Asia than a search for local self-sufficiency, the political message it sent to Thieu's regime and the people of South Vietnam rang clear. There was no turning back from the initial steps taken under Vietnamization. The Americans were leaving. Yet long-standing problems remained, consigning Abrams's command with the colossal task of transferring the war fully over to the Vietnamese, a war in which the Americans themselves had achieved only limited success. Thus, perhaps for the first time, US military officers were being confronted with a hard truth. They might be departing South Vietnam without having achieved victory in any tradi-tional sense of the word.[141]

Such a possibility grew that summer as Abrams received a formal change to the MACV mission statement. Against the Joint Chiefs wishes—the senior brass still craved cross-border operations into the DMZ and North Vietnam—the secretary of defense sent Abrams new marching orders to take effect in mid-August. Rather than seeking an outright defeat of the enemy, the US military command would provide "maximum assistance" in developing South Vietnam's armed forces while continuing to support pacification and security missions.[142] Military operations would now be "designed to accelerate improvement in the RVNAF and to continue to provide security for US forces." Laird also directed

Abrams to reduce the infiltration of men and materiel into South Vietnam. In the end, success depended on defeating enemy efforts "intended to deny self-determination to the RVN people."[143]

The policy of Vietnamization thus outlined for Creighton Abrams a difficult strategic road ahead. The general held little influence over the president's decision-making process leading to the US drawdown. Nor had his command devised a new strategy to leave behind a South Vietnam capable of sustaining itself without the benefits (and trappings) of overt American assistance. Ultimately, the general had been assigned the job of getting the United States out of a stalemated conflict regardless of whether his soldiers were winning or losing. If Vietnam would produce no "glorious victories," a major question thus confronted Abrams and his command.[144] Was it possible that a war-torn South Vietnam could at least be "pacified" before the Americans finally departed?

3

Pacification without Peace

The Travails of Nation Building

Even in defeat, the French cast a long shadow over American involvement in Southeast Asia. Not only had the French-Indochina War, ending in 1954, left behind a collapsing French empire and a divided Vietnam, but a host of European veterans who had bequeathed to their US inheritors a number of treatises on "modern warfare."[1] No French star shone brighter among this group than the young Saint-Cyr graduate and army lieutenant colonel David Galula. Five years before the 1968 Tet offensive, Galula had penned a detailed memoir of his experiences in North Africa titled *Pacification in Algeria*. Fresh off the heels from their ignominious defeat in Indochina, many French officers had deployed to a rebelling Algeria with hopes of forestalling the loss of yet another colony, all the more important as many in France considered the African territory a fully integrated part of the metropole. Those hopes would be wildly disappointed.

Though Galula had missed service in Vietnam, he volunteered for duty in North Africa and for two years commanded a company in Greater Kabylia, east of Algiers. By his own account, he was tremendously successful. At least on the surface. *Pacification in Algeria* portrayed its author as a methodical counterinsurgent who not only struggled, successfully, to control the rebelling population but also actively won over their support. Perhaps most useful for his American readers, Galula concluded with a list of "essential 'laws' of counterinsurgency warfare," suggesting that in "all probability" they would have global application. The first law declared that the "objective is the population," while other principles spoke of the need to organize popular support and for the counterinsurgent to "concentrate his efforts area by area." As Galula concluded, "I set out to prove a theory of counterinsurgency warfare, and I am satisfied that it worked in my small area."[2]

Yet discerning readers might have questioned the French officer's self-assured claims. Even as he outlined a meticulous process for the prospective counterinsurgent, Galula not once defined the crucial term "pacification." Other question arose. Why did Galula's short-term district gains not translate into sustainable progress at the strategic level? How reliable were the local officials who the French recruited to their cause? Did military presence in a village truly mean the population there fell under governmental control? And what to make of other officers' testimonies that proved far less heartening? Take, for instance, the reflections of Lieutenant Jean-Jacques Servan-Schreiber who reported that "without the population's active cooperation, the problem faced by the forces of order was insoluble."[3]

Such gloomy commentary could be dismissed by Americans who deployed to Vietnam with not only a confidence bordering on hubris but also a handy guide that Galula himself had published in 1964. *Counterinsurgency Warfare: Theory and Practice* outlined in precise detail a "step-by-step procedure" to defeat an insurgent threat and win over the local population. As in his earlier work on Algeria, though, Galula never defined, or in this case even mentioned, the word "pacification." Americans might applaud the Frenchman's pedagogical approach in his exposition on counterinsurgency, but a crucial element in the tutorial seemed to be missing. If Galula defined ultimate success as building (or rebuilding) a "political machine from the population upward," what was entailed in pacifying the people so those mechanisms could be constructed? Surely, such a process included more than just destruction or expulsion of the insurgent threat.[4]

This vague definition of pacification would dog allied nation-building efforts throughout America's final years in Vietnam. Military officers and civilian policymakers alike continued to use terms, many legacies from Westmoreland's tenure, interchangeably—pacification, nation building, civic action, and revolutionary development to name but a few. Nearly all considered nation building a sequential process. Even "one war" advocates like Creighton Abrams tended to agree. As an early 1968 MACV pacification pamphlet advised, "Without initial military security operations to establish the essential secure environment, the civil aspects of pacification cannot progress." The root word of pacification might be peace, but the US military command's strategy, even under Abrams, was hardly pacific. Security remained at the core of Abe's "one war" approach.[5]

Thus, despite "better war" claims that the new MACV commander approached the political-military problem in South Vietnam with a more restrained, even enlightened, outlook, the process of "pacifying" a war-torn country remained as violent as ever. As Abrams told the president at a National Security Council (NSC) meeting in September 1969, "Where we are in South Vietnam is due to the application of raw power. That is why the enemy is where he is, why pacification has moved. . . . When you turn off the power, you have got an entirely new ball game."[6]

The Chimera of Nation Building

The ball game of leaving behind a stable, noncommunist South Vietnam actually had changed little since the early days of American intervention. Even with

Vietnamization the stated American policy, nation building remained a component of both US Army doctrine and MACV strategy. The September 1968 version of the army's principal field manual, *FM 100-5*, concluded that land forces
would "play a predominant part in the U.S. military effort to encourage and assist
indigenous armed forces in their nation-building role."[7] A spate of topical articles
appeared in the army's professional journal, *Military Review*, during the following years. Officers argued they could "help build a nation's economic and social
resources until adequate civilian capabilities are developed." Others saw nation
building as "one of our major strategies in halting the spread of communism,"
while still others spoke of using the US Army to establish training programs
aimed at increasing agricultural output in "emerging nations."[8]

Of course, the Nixon Doctrine sought to limit direct military assistance, hoping instead to foster a sense of self-sufficiency that would preclude future interventions into Southeast Asia. Contradictions, however, threatened to undermine
the president's larger aims in Vietnam. Because of congressional pressure to
reduce the federal deficit, economic aid to South Vietnam dropped by more
than $100 million between 1968 and 1973. Yet, somewhat paradoxically given
the larger objectives entailed in nation building, military aid increased over
the same time span from $1.2 billion to more than $3.3 billion.[9] Critics levied
charges that the president's Vietnamization program "was in effect creating a
social upheaval and exposing more Vietnamese to those very dangers [Nixon]
claimed to be saving them from." But, as with army doctrine, the "do-it-yourself"
security doctrine rested on a sequential approach to nation building that had
long been part of the American approach in Southeast Asia.[10]

For well over a decade, senior US officials subscribed to a concept calling for the
modernization of emerging states as a way to contest rising communist sentiment in
the Third World. With colonialism's demise in the aftermath of World War II, global
instability seemed likely to threaten US interests abroad, only made worse by the
supposed backwardness of "traditional" societies. Advocates of this new "modernization theory" thus saw nation building as a tool to catalyze "stagnant" social orders
and, with the appropriate doses of foreign aid and American advice, place them on
a path toward becoming progressive, democratic societies.[11] The United States,
unsurprisingly, served as the universal model. Consequently, many American officers in Indochina could easily portray themselves as modernizers "providing every
Vietnamese with the means for improving his standard of living in an effort to help
the country resist guerrilla attacks by North Vietnam Communists."[12]

While most modernizers agreed on a traditional society's evolutionary end-
point, they often differed over the best path toward American-inspired enlight-
enment. In short, should foreign aid focus at the national or grassroots level?
Even while many early US advisors saw themselves as exporting New Deal-era
reforms to Southeast Asia, they still disagreed with one another over where

to focus their efforts and resources. Moreover, nearly all Americans came into conflict with South Vietnamese leaders who held their own ideas on nation building.[13]

Such discord should not have been surprising. Early US advisors working on "civic action" programs—a catchall phrase linking together military forces and local inhabitants to improve the civilian community—proved especially intrusive from the South Vietnamese perspective. One US report listed the "essentials" of a viable civic action plan. Americans would provide the means for the South Vietnamese Army (ARVN) to "earn the friendship of the people," to "make the village a dynamic, willing part of free Vietnam," to "establish a permanent government structure," and to "help the people help themselves." No wonder Saigon leaders balked at US nation-building plans. American advocates of modernization theory aimed at no less than a complete restructuring of South Vietnamese society, too often with little input from those most affected by any social revolution, whether homegrown or externally imposed.[14]

Moreover, the American theory of development rested on a set of assumptions that looked exceedingly optimistic when viewed through the lens of South Vietnamese politics. Early modernization proponents, like Walt Rostow, author of *The Stages of Economic Growth: A Non-Communist Manifesto*, presumed the United States could steer "politically inert" populations in "constructive rather than destructive directions." Despite evidence to the contrary, many modernizers also continued to accept that foreign aid and assistance would guarantee local economic growth.[15] Perhaps most importantly from a military viewpoint, such notions matched the belief that "various types of economic and social programs can prevent the loss of popular support for established institutions, or win popular support away from the insurgency." Thus, US Army officers could maintain that the ARVN was capable of assisting any program "designed to win the people over to more active support of the fight against the Communists within the country."[16]

But did modernization theory and its attendant programs truly equate to nation building? As Richard Nixon entered office, the US mission in Vietnam had yet to fully parse out the differences between a popular will to continue the war and a true sense of nationalism to inspire the majority of South Vietnam's population. In truth, US and ARVN forces were still preoccupied with providing security to the people so those in the countryside could become more involved in government-sponsored social and economic programs. In this sense, so little had changed from the early years of American involvement. Efforts to simply gain control of the population were still surpassing efforts to inspire nationalistic feelings among the people. Without question, the inklings of South Vietnamese nationalism were present by the late 1960s. Yet American observers, in particular, questioned whether a combination of national pride, loyalty to the government, and plain endurance would be enough for South Vietnam to survive on its own.[17]

Such reservations hinted at an important truth of the Vietnam War. Building state structures—the organizational bureaucracy of the state, its economy, its security forces—was not the same as nation building. Americans certainly were quick to spotlight the failures of the government of South Vietnam (GVN). Critics in 1969 and 1970 questioned whether the GVN even deserved the name "government" at all and faulted Saigon leaders for not developing a "meaningful political structure in the villages."[18] One US Army officer, writing in June 1970, even took a swipe at modernization theorists in casting blame for an enfeebled political culture inside South Vietnam. "While the Communists worked to capture men's minds," the major argued, "the West was preoccupied with economic and military aid—with outer needs. The West attempted to redesign the structure of society while ignoring the functional bases underlying the structure."[19]

By mid-1969, however, the Americans in Vietnam were still searching for these functional bases from which to help build a lasting political community in South Vietnam. Even at this relatively late stage of the war, when US troops already had been designated to redeploy home, the search continued for a sturdy, local sociopolitical foundation. The population's lack of reverence for the government and its armed forces certainly undermined this ground-level aspect of nation building. Yet the war itself complicated these endeavors. According to one US advisor, the war had become "a way of life" for far too many Vietnamese, especially for those soldiers who struggled to grasp GVN leaders' political vision of the future.[20] The government's narrow social bases of support did little to arouse patronage from a population unconvinced their hopes and dreams would best be served by President Thieu's regime. American officers working among the rural villages thus found "the vast majority of the people . . . quite capable of supporting whichever side seemed to be winning the political-military struggle."[21]

This seemingly fickle attitude toward a struggle that would define their futures illustrated how millions of South Vietnamese never quite embraced the GVN's vision of a postwar world. In fact, there were many competing visions of what an ideal southern political community should entail, conceptions that far exceeded the government's ability to instill security and stability. The withdrawal of US troops suggested that any transition to peace would require essential decisions on the GVN's future relationship with communist sympathizers living in the south. The same held true for the host of religious sects, noncommunist political opposition groups, and even the armed forces. Here lay yet another fundamental challenge of the conflict. To be successful, the allied pacification program depended on the government to articulate to its people a postwar vision that encouraged their willing participation. That essential task had not yet happened by 1969. Nixon thus inherited not only a stalemated war but also an ongoing political struggle for the very future of South Vietnam.[22]

Without question, American officers in MACV headquarters had difficulty understanding the nuances of this competition over postwar visions. They surely conceived of pacification as a program involving the insurgency's defeat and the building of a viable political community. Yet too often Americans continued to view rural farmers as impassive pawns rather than active agents in the larger struggle. Additionally, official documents tended to offer sweeping generalizations rather than practical steps toward political reconciliation. Take, for instance, the Combined Strategic Objectives Plan published in the summer of 1970. The document listed several GVN aims that likely mattered little to villagers who, like Le Ly Hayslip, "not only had to contend with keeping government officials happy, but also had to pacify the local Viet Cong." Thus, vague strategic objectives like developing and preserving democracy or reforming society to achieve improved social justice tended to sound hollow for those caught in the crossfire between government forces and the National Liberation Front (NLF).[23]

If neither the people nor the government nor US officials fully grasped the end state of these wartime political reform efforts, senior Americans in Vietnam still clung to the belief they could confer on the South Vietnamese a nation-state capable of effective (and anticommunist) governance. The absence of a secure political structure, even at this late stage in the war, did not yet mean failure. Though modernization theory, so in vogue during the early 1960s, may have been tested and found wanting, hope remained that with the correct doses of organization and leadership, the GVN would harness the political potential of the rural countryside and create a durable nation. But a fundamental question remained as the war persisted. On a deeper level, was pacification the same thing as nation building or simply a step in a much more complicated process?[24]

A Long History of Pacification

As a means to helping build a stable, noncommunist South Vietnam nation, pacification had a long history within the American military command. As early as mid-1961, for example, the US mission had assisted in publishing a field command directive titled "Concepts of Pacification Operations." Such facts contest one of the key arguments in the "better war" thesis—that only after Abrams took command did the American military machine properly focus on pacification.[25] In truth, military officers serving in Vietnam had long considered the political aspects of the conflict, even as they too often took a heavy-handed approach to fighting a war among the South Vietnamese population. While US ground troops were first deploying to Southeast Asia, rural pacification planners worked on melding security operations with civic action and economic activities, reeducating defectors from the NLF, and training local militia forces to hold areas cleared of insurgent influence.[26]

Such an emphasis evolved from nearly a decade of advisory work in the aftermath of Vietnam's 1954 partition. True, American officers worried at length over the external threat from Ho Chi Minh's Democratic Republic of Vietnam. But they also understood that defeating the internal insurgency, even if resourced and directed from outside, required a strategy "to win the active and willing support of the people and to deprive the guerrilla of that support."[27] Thus, US advisors sought ways to coordinate military efforts with government agencies and to resolve the "paucity of talent in the civil service for duty in the provinces." They envisioned local Civil Guard units as becoming "an integral part of the community" and winning "the confidence of the people by providing public security." Even West Point cadets enrolled in counterinsurgency courses read articles proclaiming that "The Peasant is the Key to Vietnam."[28]

Far from starry-eyed social engineers, American officers were well aware of the challenges they faced. In helping prepare a basic counterinsurgency plan for Vietnam, published in early 1961, military leaders pointed to the Saigon government and the ARVN as the main obstacles to, and potential for, success. Not only was the GVN dealing with political discontent "rising among the peasantry," but its armed forces were also "committed to pacification missions" that forced them into "static guard and security roles."[29] (Abrams would echo these concerns about the need for ARVN leaders to be more offensive-minded.) The counterinsurgency plan circulated the following year mirrored the 1961 plan in its emphasis on shoring up local political structures. Thus, even as early US advisors tended to focus on military operations, they still aimed to improve the selection and training of village officials, the living standards of the rural population, and the overall effectiveness of South Vietnamese governmental structures.[30]

These trends continued after William C. Westmoreland took charge of the MACV in mid-1964. That spring, MACV, in coordination with the American embassy and the military junta under General Nguyen Khanh, instituted a pacification program dubbed "Hop Tac." Meaning "cooperation" in Vietnamese, Hop Tac aimed to pacify the strategically important provinces around Saigon. Following a clear-and-hold approach, the plan espoused a sequential method of neutralizing NLF forces, securing the population and critical resources, and then developing the newly controlled area so as to raise living standards.[31] As with other pacification endeavors, Hop Tac ran into problems. Local militia forces struggled to gain a footing against the insurgents. American officials worried that the "military manpower necessary to provide security as well as to clear areas in the initial phases of pacification operations was [being] diverted to replace battle losses inflicted by the stepped up pace of Viet Cong military action." And, just as troubling, Westmoreland feared that his ARVN counterparts were hardly giving Hop Tac their full attention.[32]

Despite these difficulties, the pacification effort remained a central component of the US mission's strategic planning. After years of bureaucratic wrangling, involving disputes over whether pacification would be a civilian- or military-run operation, MACV took control as the "single manager" of what one senior official called "the heart of the matter."[33] In early May 1967, President Johnson signed a national security action memorandum establishing the Office of Civil Operations and Revolutionary Development Support (CORDS). As a result, Westmoreland assumed control of all pacification-related programs. The president assigned Robert Komer, a veteran NSC staffer, to head the new organization, an interagency clearing house that established a "single chain of command for civil operations and RD support from Saigon to district level." With ambassadorial rank, Komer reported directly to Westmoreland.[34]

This massive organizational restructuring took place just as Abrams had arrived in South Vietnam to assume duties as the MACV deputy. Amid reports that the "shift of pacification to the military reflects security woes in [the] countryside," the general had a front row seat as the implementation of CORDS unfolded. Not only was MACV planning to integrate revolutionary development support "at all levels," but the headquarters also aimed to coordinate South Vietnamese military efforts with the larger pacification program.[35] As the 1968 combined campaign plan, published not long after Abrams's arrival, stated, "The pacification campaign to provide sustained territorial security in the countryside and concurrently to introduce political, economic and social reforms which will establish conditions favorable for further growth and stability, is just as important as anti-aggression operation." If the allies believed military operations, "while clearly essential to pacification," were "by themselves inadequate," they faced a major challenge in coordinating such a diverse range of activities.[36]

In fact, the very definition of pacification alluded to the difficulties MACV faced, under both Westmoreland and Abrams, in synchronizing its efforts across the expanse of South Vietnam. The headquarters defined this key term as "the military, political, economic, and social process of establishing or re-establishing local government responsive to and involving the participation of the people." In his official report on the war, Westmoreland called pacification a "very difficult process" that aimed to "reassert lawful governmental control by removing the enemy's underground apparatus." No doubt the military component ranked high in the struggle over population control. But the nonmilitary aspects of pacification raised serious questions over how much social and economic impact allied soldiers and marines truly had when implementing such a multifaceted program.[37]

Any failures were not for a lack of trying. Far from focusing solely on military operations against their enemies, American commanders followed MACV's guidance of supporting, as best they could, the pacification effort. Mobile Advisory Teams (MATs) worked with Regional and Popular Forces (RF/PF) to improve their "administrative and logistic support procedures." Intelligence analysts targeted the insurgency's political infrastructure. While Westmoreland envisioned the RVNAF as having "the primary responsibility of participating in and supporting pacification," he nonetheless charged American units with military tasks that possessed distinctly nonmilitary aims. As one official report noted, the "opening and securing of roads, railroads and waterways must be done as a matter of priority to facilitate movement of people and commodities, thus strengthening the economy, reducing inflation and enhancing the security of the countryside."[38]

Even major combat units became intricately involved with pacification efforts. Take, for instance, the 1st Cavalry Division, which won fame during the late 1965 battle in the Ia Drang Valley. Nearly a year before CORDS took shape, the division had launched Operation James Bond in early July 1966, the unit's planners clearly enamored with Sean Connery's most recent performance in *Thunderball*. While some troopers launched raids against suspected insurgents, others engaged in civic action activities "to show the Vietnamese people that the government of Vietnam, the US military forces, and the district officials were interested in their overall welfare as well as their security." Hamlet chiefs concurrently distributed food to local farmers while emphasizing "the interest that the South Vietnamese government had in their welfare." A second James Bond operation, begun at the end of July, included counterintelligence raids, medical team assistance, and the dissemination of agricultural pamphlets and toys. The division even helped organize a local Boy Scout troop. If such efforts seem quaint in retrospect, they at least illustrate the willingness of some commanders to incorporate pacification into their larger operational concepts.[39]

Such experimentation, however, too often foundered as CORDS began implementing its pacification programs across South Vietnam. On one level, MACV faced a tremendous civil-military coordination problem. Prosecuting the "other war" required unified direction of near countless projects. CORDS chief Robert Komer oversaw efforts to buttress Vietnam's economy, train revolutionary development cadre, restore law and order, and care for war refugees. US advisors strove to incorporate ARVN battalions into local security missions, while at the same time facilitating village and hamlet elections, strengthening police units, and helping to build an industrial base.[40] All the while, a war raged on at full force. Thus, MACV officers complained of the "long lead time necessary to allow coordination on the province and district levels before US forces

are permitted operational access to an area." The lag times, one report stated dis-
approvingly, were "often of great advantage to the enemy."[41]

On another level, simply fighting the enemy worked at cross purposes with
the pacification program. Destruction wrought by constant battle ruptured social
structures and undermined stability in South Vietnam's countryside. Marine
propaganda illustrated the bind in which military operations placed rural villagers. Dropping leaflets on rural areas, the marines threatened to destroy homes
that harbored NLF insurgents. As one small flyer read, "If you allow the V.C. to
hide in your hamlet, you can expect destruction from the air from mortars and
artillery. Do not let your hamlet be destroyed. Point out the V.C. who bring
death and destruction to your home."[42] Such threats surely wore down the resiliency of a population long at war and certainly put into question whether the
GVN truly had the people in its best interests. While violence remained at the
heart of US strategy under Abrams—the allies needed to weaken the enemy so
Vietnamization and US withdrawals could proceed—the constant fear of death
pervaded a political community still uncertain of its future identity.[43]

In the process, American soldiers often had a difficult time reconciling their
roles as armed social engineers in a combat zone. Few could even tell who they
were supposed to be supporting. As veteran correspondent Ward Just put it, the
"American Army ended up fighting the entire country, because it was impossible to tell who was on the right side and who was on the other side."[44] A common refrain among GIs thus denounced the untrustworthy South Vietnamese
population. "We learned to trust no one, not even children," recalled one US
advisor. Another soldier, writing home in mid-1969, called the people "treacher-
ous," smiling during the day, "but at night the dirty little rats are VC." Even advisors assigned to CORDS spoke contemptuously of their allies. One lieutenant
colonel reported on his evaluation trip to Kien Hoa province in March 1970,
complaining of a US advisor who called his Vietnamese driver "shithead" and
another who habitually spoke to his counterpart thusly: "Goddammit, why the
fuck can't you do something right once in a while?"[45]

Such attitudes clearly worked against the overriding mission of pacification—
to convince the majority of South Vietnamese to throw their lot behind the
Saigon government. Some officers might laud "high-impact, short-term projects" that got "to the heart of the problem and the needs of the people," but
such optimistic calculations seemed overstated when compared to Vietnamese
appraisals that American soldiers "did not seek to create favorable relations with
the common" people.[46] Officers unmistakably worried about the psychological aspects of military operations, especially those among the hamlets and villages. Yet the indifference to, if not scorn of, the local population surely undercut
MACV pacification programs and the larger nation-building mission. As one
soldier recalled, "I began to hate them, because I couldn't stand the idea that we

were coming into these people's lives and totally disrupting them. You began to sense that these people wouldn't give a shit if we were there or the Viet Cong were there or anybody else."[47]

Ultimately, this inability of Americans, whether in the field or in Saigon, to help foster a sense of political community began to cast doubt on MACV's strategy. Robert M. Montague Jr., a highly respected officer working on pacification, noted the challenges he and his peers faced in guiding the efforts of so many different, if not competing, agencies. "Given the particularly nasty situation in South Vietnam," the lieutenant colonel noted in an Army War College student essay, "with its deep-rooted contradictions, a very well organized and powerful enemy, and a weariness brought on by two decades of conflict, one can imagine the difficulty found in developing a rational strategy favored by all factions."[48]

Yet American strategy prior to Tet, contentious as it may have been, was based on not just MACV's command guidance but also accepted doctrinal theories and

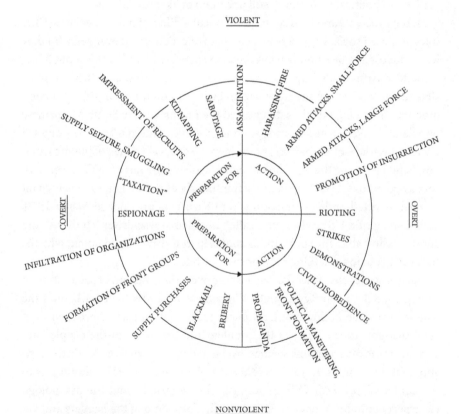

Figure 6 "No *Single* VC Operational Threat." A late 1968 village defense study demonstrated the multiple threats to the allied pacification effort. (RG472, Box 3, CORDS Historical Working Group Files, NARA)

academic writing concerning the prospects of modernization and nation building. Army doctrine advised that pacification and nation-building efforts were best left to local entities, supported by US agencies assigned to reinforce them. American military power would serve as the buffer between the enemy and those allies restoring government presence in their country. Scholars concurrently wrote of the need to see any rebellion as a "system" and to appreciate the "triple disloca-tion" of social, economic, and political upheaval that undeveloped countries were experiencing "in telescoped time."[49] Those officers bridging the gap between doctrine and scholarly writing counseled that "destruction of the revolutionary organization must be followed by construction of a counter-revolutionary substi-tute." In this sense, American military strategy before Tet rested on a fairly broad consensus among professional officers and academics alike.[50]

Though some of the assumptions on which modernization theory rested had fallen out of favor inside the Nixon White House—senior policymakers saw far too many gaps between abstract concepts and the reality in Vietnam— David Galula's ideas on pacification did not suffer from equivalent criticism. At least early on. Though counterinsurgency slowly declined in importance as the Abrams years wore on, pacification remained a crucial element of US military strategy despite limited evidence that strong bonds were being built between Saigon and the country's rural communities.[51] With enough resources and American oversight, US advisors hoped a South Vietnamese nation could still be built. Galula's methodical approach of gaining security for, then control over, and finally support from the population remained valid to a broad constituency. And the population still held the key. As one marine colonel noted, "To win this war, you've got to get the people behind their government."[52]

A Renewed Emphasis

The US military command's long history with pacification left an indelible mark on Abrams and his key subordinates as they took over the war effort after the 1968 Tet offensive. Obstacles surely endured. A dearth of effective leadership at provincial and district levels continued to frustrate CORDS officials, as did the chasm between GVN bureaucrats and the rural population. One American advi-sor in the Mekong Delta believed "the people in this district don't give a damn for the Saigon government because that government never does anything for them. The Viet Cong thrive off of Saigon fuck-ups."[53] Despite these impediments, senior leaders saw glimmers of hope within the ashes of a fragmented pacifica-tion campaign. Not long after Abrams assumed command, Secretary of Defense Clark Clifford discerned "an obvious shift in the emphasis on and importance of the pacification program." As Clifford saw it, this shift resulted "from the reaction of all to the change in the enemy tactics and the enemy's attempts to bring down the government of Vietnam by his attacks upon the cities."[54]

Few others' faith in South Vietnam becoming a viable nation after Tet matched that of Robert Komer. Even after President Johnson's decision to limit additional US manpower being sent to Vietnam, the head of CORDS remained as optimistic as ever on pacification. The brash Komer, however, did not enjoy a close relationship with the new MACV commander. Far from it. The CORDS chief found Abrams less "imaginative militarily" than his predecessor, while the general expressed an almost immediate dissatisfaction with Komer's autonomy inside the US command.[55] Critics charged the ambassador "was trying to run his own war." The MACV chief of staff, for instance, believed the outspoken pacification advocate was "volatile"—Komer undoubtedly earned his nickname the "Blowtorch"—and "often had difficulty separating good ideas from bad ones."[56]

Moreover, Komer's enthusiasm, combined with his brazen assertiveness, worried Abrams that CORDS was overselling its product. In fact, according to one aide, the MACV commander "blamed Komer for much of the surprise of Tet" because of the ambassador's overly optimistic reporting to the press. Even after the 1968 offensive, the CORDS chief reported pacification was "definitely on a recovery curve" and "generally back on track and moving again."[57] Yet the program faced a host of weighty problems—regaining territorial security, relocating refugees, reviving the rural economy, and enhancing the image of the GVN in the countryside. All these efforts were basically a continuation of earlier pacification planning, but Komer's inclinations to exaggerate progress tended to undermine his own policies. Volney Warner, working with the CORDS program, wrote to Komer in July 1968 and frankly stated the ambassador had a credibility problem. Interrogators in Washington, the lieutenant colonel said, "honestly believe that you juggled and continue to jiggle statistics to present a pretty picture of success."[58]

Abrams no doubt agreed with Warner's candid remarks. As the relationship between the CORDS chief and MACV commander soured during the summer months, Komer began seeking an out from Vietnam. With the president soon departing office, and the Defense Department seemingly having little interest in pacification, a disheartened Komer sent entreaties to Johnson's advisors asking for help in finding a new assignment. The lobbying paid off. On 28 October, LBJ appointed his longtime supporter as the US ambassador to Turkey. Komer's departure from Vietnam came with not a small hint of irony. Pacification's biggest proponent for more than two years could not maintain his position within a military command that was trying to place increasing emphasis on the very programs Komer had helped to install.[59]

Correspondents were quick to pick up on the differences between the abrasive CORDS ambassador and his successor, William E. Colby. They highlighted his "muted style" that contrasted "sharply with that of the ebullient Robert Komer." The Princeton-educated Colby had served in the OSS during World War II, joining the CIA after the Korean War's outbreak before landing the chief of station post in Saigon. The new "soft-spoken" pacification chief had also gained valuable experience in Washington as the head of the CIA's Far Eastern Division before serving as Komer's deputy. As with Abrams, reporters hoped the personnel change hinted at a new direction, if not greater progress, in allied strategy. Though pacification had "long been a sneer word" according to one observer, Colby's assignment as head of CORDS meant the program was taking a "more realistic turn."[60] Old habits, though, marked correspondents' reporting. A little more than a year after Komer's departure, the *New York Times*, while admitting the "long-term success of the pacification program may be in doubt," still reported that revolutionary development was "making marked progress in some of its aspects."[61]

Moreover, such hopeful reporting obscured the fact that little had changed between the two CORDS ambassadors. While the 1969 pacification plan concentrated on the village rather than hamlet level, it still emphasized three long-standing "mutually supporting principles: self-defense, self-government, and self-help."[62] The language used and overarching objectives also remained exceptionally similar. MACV spoke in terms of securing and controlling the population, establishing local government, eliminating the NLF infrastructure, and increasing the People's Self-Defense Force. Quantitative metrics persisted as well. The command would "rally" 25,000 defectors, increase rice production from 5 million to 6 million tons, and resettle at least 300,000 refugees. As in earlier campaign plans, the 1969 version stated that the allied pacification and development program was "designed to expand the GVN controlled population by the aggressive deployment of territorial security forces." Pacification would thus retain its violent edge.[63]

In these ways, Colby's vision of pacification hardly differed from that of Komer's. The basis for the 1969 campaign returned to similar themes of the past—upgrading territorial security, stepping up attacks on the NLF political infrastructure, developing strong local government, and expanding self-defense. None of these were new objectives. Nor did Colby's pacification plan relate any differently to allied military strategy from years past. Friendly forces were still charged with keeping the North Vietnamese Army (NVA) off balance and away from populated areas so pacification programs could proceed.[64] The GVN's Pacification and Development Plan for 1969 thus offered few new ideas while outlining ambitious aims. "We must build democracy," the plan declared, "reform society, and end the war." To confront the political struggle, the government thus sought to "instill in the people a sense of responsibility for their community for it is the people themselves who must actively combat the Communists." Even this objective had long been a goal of allied strategy.[65]

Of course, the aftermath of the Tet offensive offered an opportunity to concentrate on pacification given the degradation of NLF main force units in 1968, perhaps the allies' greatest achievement that went underreported that summer. Yet the insurgency was far from defeated, prompting Abrams to emphasize that security was "vital to pacification" and the "first objective" of the 1969 Pacification and Development Plan.[66] But despite suffering a defeat during Tet, the NLF infrastructure, according to one political scientist, was "still the most extensive and effective political network in the country." Abrams and Colby thus both realized that a period of recovery, reestablishing security throughout rural areas, would have to precede the more ambitious aims of nation building. As one US advisor noted, "There is no point in building schoolhouses if there are no teachers and if the buildings are in an area where the city-minded teachers are afraid to enter."[67]

Such observations pointed to familiar contradictions long intrinsic within the allied pacification program. CIA operatives, continuing to recruit spies inside the National Liberation Front, worked at cross purposes with MACV officers trying to destroy the same organization. American negotiators worried that any failures in pacification would weaken their position in Paris. But, perhaps most importantly, military operations persisted in such ferocity as to tear apart the very social bonds the Saigon government was hoping to create. American officials were keenly aware of the problem. A national intelligence estimate highlighted the "increased hostility toward the government and the ARVN for failing to provide protection against the Viet Cong, for looting, and for widespread destruction from air strikes and artillery. And the US is also blamed for destruction of urban areas."[68] Yet combat operations, like the 9th Infantry Division's Speedy Express, endured, racking up high body counts while ostensibly, though not actually, facilitating pacification of the countryside. As one farmer responded when asked about the allies' civic action efforts, "How can I remember anything good about the Americans when they do so much bad?"[69]

Abrams certainly did his best to promote the expansion and improvement of the revolutionary development cadre, to put a Vietnamese face on pacification in the hamlets and villages. But, as in so many other areas, long-standing problems persisted. As MACV placed increasing emphasis on the RD cadre, so, too, did the insurgency, targeting the local militia for intimidation, kidnapping, and assassination. The NLF equally spent considerable effort trying to plant agents into the Regional and Popular Forces. All the while, wary villagers watched on the sidelines as best they could, knowing they risked death if openly cooperating with the GVN.[70] Able administrators thus became special targets for coercion and terrorist activity. The killing of a pro-government village official sent a strong message to others, perhaps even more powerful than the allies' indiscriminate use of artillery or airpower. In the process, a vicious cycle took hold as the NLF responded to Abrams and Colby's growing attention on pacification. "As the hamlet ratings began to improve and climb upward," one US advisor recalled, "the level of assassinations would also go up and force the short-lived improvements back down."[71]

Hoping to spark momentum in the program that might be more lasting, the Saigon government, with MACV's input, initiated an Accelerated Pacification Campaign (APC) in November 1968. Though Colby reported it was "the first integrated civil-military program to move into the country," the APC actually borrowed heavily from Project Takeoff, a similar "crash program," initiated back in 1967, "to show better results in pacification." Both plans, ushered in by Komer, were envisioned as a "short-term surge effort" to upgrade village security throughout the country and reinvigorate the pacification program.[72] The APC's objectives proved especially hopeful—to upgrade, by 31 January 1969, at least 1,000 contested hamlets to "relatively secure ratings"; to neutralize at least 3,000 VCI cadre each month during the three-month campaign; to induce at least 5,000 defectors to rally to the government's side; to arm at least 200,000 "self-defenders"; and to "conduct an information campaign to demonstrate to the people and the enemy that GVN has seized the initiative and is moving rapidly toward the end of the war."[73]

In large sense, the new Accelerated Pacification Campaign revealed the enduring hold of quantitative metrics to demonstrate progress in a war largely without front lines. Political inducement to show forward momentum had long been part of the reporting process in Vietnam and the APC was no different. Abrams conceded that "pressures to achieve accelerated campaign goals could introduce a favorable bias into some district advisor ratings," even with "strong command emphasis . . . to remain objective."[74] Yet despite the "softness" of pacification statistics, MACV continued to rely on them. As part of the APC, units reported on the numbers of cordon and search missions they ran, of insurgent KIAs, and of the civic action projects they initiated. According to one evaluation system, the population living in secure areas rose by 1.7 million people during the last quarter of 1968. But such a "fast-and-thin" approach to pacification, and its quantitative assessment mechanisms, had long bred suspicion among more perceptive commentators. Even before Project Takeoff, one investigation had noted that "Villages, often haphazardly, have been labeled as enemy or pro-government when in reality they are neither or both."[75]

The US military command's emphasis on territorial security, however measured, was intended to complement the GVN's efforts at controlling and ultimately winning support of the people. Abrams thus hoped that a successful accelerated pacification program would establish a foundation on which the

Saigon leadership could promote its social and economic plans, none more important than the land reform plans enacted by President Nguyen Van Thieu in March 1970. The Land-to-the-Tiller bill sought to give landless peasants a stake in their country's future by improving their own. One South Vietnamese official called Thieu's land reform a true "rural social revolution" for it built "an ownership society almost overnight."[76] Without question, the NLF had long used the land problem as a valuable propaganda tool to disparage the Saigon government. But the Land-to-the-Tiller legislation, attacking landlordism and awarding five free acres to all farming families, made only modest gains. According to one ARVN general, many poor farmers "praised the new law" but others still "complained about corruption and red tape." Perhaps most importantly, Thieu's overdue efforts did little to sway the population's loyalties away from the NLF and toward the Saigon government.[77]

Criticism suggesting that the GVN discounted pacification efforts thus seems to unfairly condemn governmental leadership for ignoring a crucial component of allied strategy. Though Americans derided the Saigon elite for being out of touch with the rural population, Thieu, in fact, acknowledged the importance of gaining the people's allegiance. Abrams, Bunker, and even Nixon all agreed that the South Vietnamese president was "working along generally similar lines" as the US mission. While Thieu took heat for temporarily abolishing village elections in the aftermath of the 1968 Tet offensive, he still authorized manpower increases to the National Police and to the Regional and Popular Forces.[78] Such acts suggested a growing appreciation of the villagers' struggle and its relation to the overall war's outcome. Equally important, as Nixon recalled, "Thieu recognized that while protecting the rural population was critical in the short term, it would not be enough in the long term." As a consequence, the GVN leader had to focus on more than just consolidating his own power and therefore "took steps to give [the people] a stake in the war."[79]

But how best to provide for more personal freedoms, and thus tie the masses to their government, while simultaneously fighting off a concerted political-military challenge from the communists? Here, Thieu, similar to his many predecessors, faced an immense administrative challenge. Building bonds between the people and the GVN required better political leadership at the provincial and district levels. Though MACV manuals claimed, rather simplistically, that successful pacification was "essentially a problem of counter-organization," producing effective local leaders required more than just finding managerial talent. The war, however, became a convenient pretext for the GVN to install army generals in key leadership posts throughout the country. The ascent of this new political class received few applauses. Civilian politicians complained about "the clannishness and insensitivity of their military competitors," while ordinary people grumbled that the generals were "more interested in self-enrichment than in fighting the war."[80]

This competition over political power at the provincial and district levels pointed to yet another question concerning pacification. How did the allies know they were making any progress? The Hamlet Evaluation System (HES) worksheet served as the basic evaluation tool for many US advisors. Hamlet inspectors filled in a matrix of eighteen separate indicators falling under two categories of security and development. Americans, few with Vietnamese language skills, completed forms assessing a village's political infrastructure, medical services, education, and public works to name but a few. Introduced in 1967, early HES data, according to one pacification expert, "was incomplete, inaccurate, and inconsistent since the system was in a formative state and subject to varying interpretation." Fine-tuned over the years, the evaluation system still had its doubters as the accelerated pacification campaign took shape. Statistics, quite simply, could not accurately measure intangibles like political loyalty or popular will.[81]

CORDS officials, however, did their best to compute the figures, even creating a Pacification Data Bank that incorporated information from several reporting and evaluation systems. Analysts thus pored over reports from the HES, the Territorial Forces Evaluation System, the People's Self-Defense Force System, and many others. If commanders struggled to gauge their operational effectiveness, it was not for a lack of trying on the part of the system analysts.[82]

Yet contradictory reports continued to plague evaluation efforts. Even Bill Colby, highlighting the success of the accelerated pacification campaign, hedged in his appraisals. "Nobody claims that the 1,000 hamlets upgraded are secure forever," the ambassador conceded. But if the APC was a "once-over-lightly," as Lieutenant Colonel Montague called it, then how did the allies know when a more lasting pacification would take hold? Moreover, a late February enemy offensive in 1969 left roughly 4,500 civilians killed and 6,800 homes destroyed in its wake. American newspapers might boast that the Vietcong were "now fish in a hostile sea," but the additional 27,500 South Vietnamese refugees suggested that the foundational blocks of nation building were as fragile as ever.[83]

One year later, discouraging reports cast further doubt on the pacification campaign's long-term success. The NLF infrastructure, "far more important than the fighting guerrillas," had been "largely untouched" in certain key provinces. Even as late as the spring of 1970, the VCI remained a fairly opaque organization. "Picking them off is like shooting a moving target while blindfolded," quipped one report. This intelligence aspect of pacification illustrated the depths to which the National Liberation Front had entrenched itself into southern society. Since the insurgency had metastasized within South Vietnam during the early and mid-1960s, if not sooner, the post-Tet era pacification advocates found it nearly impossible to surgically separate the NLF from its host body politic.[84]

Despite MACV's renewed emphasis on pacification under Abrams, the population seemed no closer to the Saigon government. Senior US officials complained, as they had for over a decade, about "the apparent indifference of the people" and how they "don't care who wins." It appears likely, though, that these Americans too often conflated political ambivalence with simple war weariness. Regardless, US soldiers and officers alike became increasingly frustrated as they considered themselves fighting and dying for a "politically inert" population that cared little if the GVN prevailed.[85] While such judgments unfairly belittled the hardships of a people who had been at war long before the Americans arrived, disappointments in the pacification campaign surely facilitated a turn toward what soldiers thought they could at least partially achieve—security through destruction of the enemy. As one US Army officer wrote in early 1970, "It seems clear that we can no longer afford to withhold our regular combat forces from participating in the decisive conflict over control of the population."[86]

Security versus Control

Despite Creighton Abrams's "one war" rhetoric of simultaneously attacking all elements of the enemy "system," MACV officers still followed established theories advocating a sequential approach to pacification. Securing an area, they believed, would lead to population control and ultimately the people's support. A 1970 NSC study group concurred, arguing that public "support tends to follow rather than lead control." Yet long after Tet, Americans were still struggling with securing contested areas so they could "control" the population.[87]

Moreover, senior officials continued to debate the very meaning of the word. Kissinger's Vietnam Study Group defined control as "the ability of either the GVN or the Viet Cong to have unimpeded day and night access to the rural population." Yet another report saw it as the "level of combined political and military strength within the population that when possessed by one side excludes effective strength by the other side." The 1969 Combined Campaign Plan, for its part, explained control through its related tasks—to secure political, economic, and population centers; to clear and secure areas undergoing pacification; to identify and eliminate the VCI; to develop self-defense forces; and to conduct civic action. Clearly, "control" required more than just mere presence in a contested area.[88]

Yet presence, permanent or otherwise, depended on security and in this realm pacification under Abrams remained a violent affair. In no small way, the MACV commander's guidance empowered soldiers to take an aggressive stance against the enemy. Abrams believed that success in "bashing the VC down" would allow the government to "raise its head up." His instructions to subordinates left little room for restraint. "Reponses are to be so prompt and decisive and the punishment of the enemy so severe," Abrams exhorted, "that he will realize that any time he assaults a hamlet, village, resettlement project, or other community, or an RF/PF element he will receive a massive response from friendly forces."[89]

Such an approach, however, came with a high cost. One analyst of the NLF revolutionary movement found that "'pacification' was more due to bombing and shelling that drove much of the rural population into safer areas . . . than improved GVN performance." In fact, a closer examination of MACV's accelerated pacification campaign finds little talk of "revolutionary development," instead placing emphasis on the establishment of governmental presence in the countryside.[90] Without question, the US mission understood the importance of "keeping civilian casualties and damage to property down" as it opened new areas to the GVN. But Abrams and his key staff concluded that security, and thus control, depended mostly on levels of force. And yet, at least by MACV's own definition, security alone could not be a substitute for true pacification. No wonder then that journalist Michael Herr called pacification just "another word for war."[91]

These details matter because the "better war" thesis presumes, incorrectly, that Abrams somehow approached counterinsurgency and pacification in a more progressive and less violent way than his predecessor. In truth, MACV's pursuit of security as the first step toward pacifying the country meant violence remained a centerpiece of US strategy. As one American advisor recalled, "I knew no pacification program would ever work unless security became a reality in the outlying hamlets and villages."[92] Abrams thus continued to report on enemy killed in action and used body counts as a key metric, among many others, to show the allies were making progress. Military operations, according to one senior officer, were the Americans' "best contribution to pacification" and necessary to "lessen the security threat." In the process, CORDS officials like John Paul Vann criticized the command's excessive use of firepower as damaging to the government's political aims.[93]

Nowhere did this violence more support Vann's claims than at the village level. While MACV never condoned the murder, rape, or torture of civilians as a matter of deliberate policy, the war in Vietnam had long taken a devastating toll on the population. Young American soldiers unable to tell friend from foe too often lumped all Vietnamese together as "gooks." As one veteran put it, "You can't tell who's the enemy. You got to shoot kids, you got to shoot women."[94] This racialization of the population proved especially frightening for Vietnamese women, "the lowest people on the planet" according to one sympathetic GI. Sexual violence, while perhaps not widespread, came to be seen as unexceptional by indifferent soldiers. One remembered there "were a few rapes" but nothing "out of the ordinary." Though senior officers might dismiss their soldiers' sexual assaults as the result of ordinary, young fighting men being "faced with opportunities and temptations," such violent behavior had long-term consequences when unit commanders spoke of "sanitizing" stubborn villages that supported the Vietcong.[95]

Violence toward the civilian population thus became all too common even as Abrams sought to limit the damage. Supposed advances in pacification, however, tended to overshadow the people's suffering. The Hamlet Evaluation System, revised in early 1970 to gain "increased accuracy" in reporting, showed a notable rise in rural security. By December 1971, MACV was counting 98 percent of South Vietnamese hamlets as "relatively secure."[96] Yet enduring doubts plagued the system. How, for example, could quantitative metrics accurately assess "control" in a hamlet or village? The revised HES, seeking objectivity, perhaps went too far. "Instead of asking how effective the local self-defense forces are in a local area, the new questionnaire asks the adviser to report, within fixed numerical ranges, how many operations the defense forces mounted, how many contacts they had, and so forth." Of course, numbers could be misleading. Upon conclusion of the accelerated pacification campaign, Ambassador Colby embarked on a widely reported trip through a former NLF-controlled area. Though reporters "waxed enthusiastic about an unescorted tour," a senior MACV officer admitted later that "armed teams and helicopters" had preceded and followed Colby "just out of sight."[97]

Abrams certainly realized the limitations of mathematical modeling and followed through on earlier attempts to gauge popular opinion in the struggle for "hearts and minds." The Pacification Attitude Analysis System (PAAS), its first results reported in October 1969, hoped to "provide a capability for determining trends in rural Vietnamese attitudes" on everything from GVN development programs to the impact of ARVN military operations. Trained Vietnamese interviewers asked if villagers "felt more secure as the year passed," if they saw security as a "joint people-government undertaking," and if they were aware of national programs like land reform.[98] While the PAAS suffered from limitations inherent in the semi-structured interviews and the relatively small sample sizes, some trends did emerge. Systems analyst Thomas C. Thayer found that roughly "75 percent of the respondents expressed a desire for peace or security as their first aspiration," while few (11-13 percent) "thought fighting harder against the communists was the main problem." By 1972, nearly a quarter of respondents still felt that security ranked as the "most severe rural problem."[99]

Both Abrams and Colby, though, were doing their level best to confront the security problem, even at the cost of being charged with overseeing a MACV-sponsored "assassination program." The Phung Hoang or Phoenix program, initiated and expanded under Westmoreland, sought to cripple the NLF's political infrastructure (VCI) by targeting the insurgency's leadership. In its objectives, Phoenix became an integral part of pacification. "The defeat of the VC infrastructure," MACV reported, "is essential to preclude re-establishment of an operational or support base to which the VC can return." Dismantling the VCI would allow "the Vietnamese people to carry on their way of life and thereby [make] them more resistant to VC pressure."[100] While ostensibly an intelligence operation—Abrams noted that attacking the VCI "involved detailed intelligence work"—Phoenix proved one of the more violent of allied programs related to pacification. As Abrams remarked, "It's a ruthless business, similar to elimination of the Nazi infrastructure during World War II. In order for it to be successful, each individual VC has to be physically removed from the area."[101]

Such a high bar for success, though, meant that nearly anyone could be named a Vietcong agent and thus targeted for elimination. Colby might argue that identifying VCI members was the "main effort" of Phoenix, but those involved in the program, according to one senior MACV officer, "got into the body count syndrome."[102] If the CORDS chief saw Phung Hoang as "more akin to police work than normal military operations," it nonetheless left a swath of destruction in its wake. Between 1968 and 1972, more than 80,000 NLF cadre were "neutralized," of those over 20,000 killed. (Nearly two-thirds of the total had been captured.) And yet a disappointed Colby could only report in mid-1969 that such seemingly impressive statistics "represented only one and one-half percent of the total VCI strength each month."[103]

CORDS also attempted to coordinate Phoenix with the Chieu Hoi ("Open Arms") program, an effort commenced back in 1963 to "induce Viet Cong followers to return to the government's side and rejoin the open society of Vietnam." Senior US officials hoped this carrot-and-stick approach might weaken the National Liberation Front and create an opening for the GVN. And, in fact, the NLF viewed the Chieu Hoi program as a considerable threat. By 1972, more than 200,000 former Vietcong had rallied to the South Vietnamese government.[104] Yet Americans found their allies none too keen on fully supporting a program that brought untrustworthy defectors into the fold. As one US advisor wrote, "Government military and political authorities had little use for ralliers, whom they regarded with suspicion and contempt." A communist returnee might be a "priceless source of information," but also a risk simply not worth pursuing. In such instances, "neutralization" seemed the more prudent course than reintegration.[105]

If claims Phoenix was a "bloody-handed assassination program" proved overstated, the campaign to defeat the insurgent infrastructure still left a noticeable chill among the population. Faulty intelligence resulted in false arrests and, once detained, suspects lost nearly all their legal rights. Corrupt officials used the cover of Phoenix to rid themselves of political rivals, while others, hoping to curry favor with Saigon, focused their counterinsurgency efforts on producing a high number of NLF captives to demonstrate progress in their province or district.[106] Perhaps most importantly, Phoenix never resulted in the capture of high-level cadre—though it did force them to move to safer areas—nor did the government ably fill in the political holes created by the program's successes. In the end, while the campaign disrupted the VCI, it also tended to further the social destabilization already causing anxieties at the village level.[107]

So, too, did operations conducted by more conventional US Army units. Here, Abrams pressed his division commanders to become further involved with pacification. Hoping to better coordinate the CORDS effort with military planning, the general directed his subordinates to embrace the "one war" approach at the tactical level. Divisions like the 25th Infantry, stationed in Hau Nghia province, were already following Abrams's intent. As early as 1966, the "Tropic Lightning" division's leaders spoke of extending government control, focusing on local security, and contributing to the revolutionary development program.[108] By 1967, the 25th was undertaking combined operations with local Popular Forces even as it participated in large-scale operations like Junction City to defeat the NLF main force threat in War Zone "C." Operation Toan Thang III, commenced in February 1969, continued these trends. The division coordinated with district officials, struck at the NLF infrastructure, and worked closely with both the 25th ARVN Division and the National Police. Here was Abrams's "one war" vision in practice.[109]

Other units followed the 25th Infantry's lead. In December 1969, the 101st Airborne Division initiated Operation Randolph Glen, "a departure from the more conventional approach to the role of US forces in Vietnam." Cooperating with the 1st ARVN Division, the "Screaming Eagles" directed their efforts toward two main objectives: maintaining a "shield of security for protection of the people" in Thua Thien province and providing "maximum support for the pacification and development goals established by the Government of Vietnam."[110] That same year, soldiers in the 173rd Airborne Brigade followed a similar tack during Operation Washington Green. Operating in Binh Dinh province, the airborne troopers focused nearly all their efforts on pacification. As MACV acknowledged, the "absence of major main force enemy elements in the brigade AO [area of operations] made this commitment possible." Thus, the brigade employed a "saturation concept for area security," complete with "intensive patrolling and ambushing."[111]

The results of these operations, however, were mixed at best, placing into question whether pacification and Vietnamization could proceed simultaneously. Randolph Glen suggested pacification-related missions "necessitated close and continuous coordination and cooperation with ARVN and civilian and paramilitary agencies," a tall order given the competitive political nature of South Vietnam. And though the 173rd Airborne Brigade's commander believed the enemy was "steadily losing ground" thanks to Washington Green, such optimistic reporting proved overly ambitious as the unit began its redeployment home. Territorial forces proved inadequate to backfill the declining US presence, while the level of security, and thus control, seemed all too dependent on aggressive military action that reduced soldiers' emphasis on true pacification work.[112]

Just as important, the increasing role played by the ARVN meant a necessary decline in American influence. Though the "one war" approach envisioned an integrated allied effort, officers still saw deficiencies in the "sequential manner of attacking one critical phase or threat at a time." If both pacification and Vietnamization relied on a secure environment in which to flourish, then it made sense to defeat the enemy's military threat. Yet the combined campaign plans continued to place the primary responsibility for pacification on the ARVN's shoulders. In large sense, the South Vietnamese armed forces were being pulled in two opposite directions. Abrams surely expected to reduce the presence of the "counterproductive 'ugly Americans' who can do great harm," but his senior officers still found an ARVN leadership incapable of assuming the full burden of a complex war.[113] One lieutenant general reported that he was impressed with few ARVN commanders who "seldom get out to see what's going on." While the individual South Vietnamese soldier had demonstrated his courage, he still served in a system that promoted far too many incompetent leaders. As the general lamented, "He deserves better leadership."[114]

Yet it seems hard to argue against the idea that South Vietnamese forces, despite all their flaws, indeed were best suited for pacification, always a process of negotiation between the host government, its army, and the people. Realizing the "population had to be provided with more than temporary security," MACV had always intended the ARVN to work closely with local territorial forces. But with US forces withdrawing, Abrams and his staff grappled with whether the South Vietnamese army should focus on pacification or improving its ability to react to the more conventional NVA threat.[115] Numbers offer a glimpse into what the allied command decided. In the first half of 1969, ARVN infantry battalions spent, on average, 47 percent of their time on combat missions, 21 percent on security missions, and 24 percent on pacification. (They also spent a small number of days in training, reserve, or rehabilitation.) All the while, Regional and Popular Forces "were employed to perform a multitude of different tasks" that became "truly burdensome," according to one ARVN officer, and "demanded too much of the RF and PF." No surprise then that Kissinger's staff recommended in July for a "wholesale reorganization of all the Vietnamese security forces."[116]

The US mission, however, remained in an advisory role and could hardly dictate such comprehensive reform without President Thieu's active support. Moreover, a shakeup of the GVN defense structure, this late in the war, hardly accounted for the dilemma faced by every field commander—"how to destroy the enemy without causing casualties or damage to the civilian population." Abrams, instead, concentrated on training and education programs for both the ARVN and RF/PF to better grapple with this predicament. Commanders in I Corps, following guidance to better merge allied efforts, also introduced the Combined Unit Pacification Program that paired US infantry platoons with the Popular Forces.[117] The results, though, left much to be desired. Casualty rates among the local militia units soared. A furious Abrams seethed in November 1969 that PF platoons were "coming out of those goddamn training centers, and they couldn't fight their way out of a paper *sack*!" Worse, a high-level US delegation to Vietnam two months later concluded pacification momentum might be "faltering" and "though dislocated, the enemy's infrastructure remained intact."[118]

Such assessments illustrated the immense challenges Abrams and other senior officials faced during the Vietnamization era. Partly a military confrontation, pacification proved a political test as well. And in this arena, the ARVN was ill-equipped. Critics might judge South Vietnam's army a "paper tiger," but its underpaid, uneducated, and poorly indoctrinated soldiers had "little concept of nation" and thus even less sense of why they were fighting. An American-sponsored "Motivation Indoctrination Program," dating back to 1965, had made little progress by the time Abrams assumed command.[119] Thus, even while reports suggested that the ARVN had become "more competent and more aggressive," the army still suffered from a lack of political education that might have committed its soldiers ideologically to the Saigon government. This political void came at a high price. As one South Vietnamese enlisted man recalled, "Most soldiers that I knew understood little about why we were fighting."[120]

It seems plausible then to suggest that the government of South Vietnam never fully succeeded in controlling either the physical or political landscapes on which the pacification war was fought. In a contest to "dominate the land," the allies were coming up short. Not that senior US officials could fully support or dispute such a claim. More than a year after Abrams's ascension to MACV command, words like "control" remained uncertain terms. In reality, no hard lines existed between enemy-controlled or GVN-liberated areas. Instead, both insurgent and government forces intermeshed in hundreds of villages and hamlets across South Vietnam, fighting pockets of resistance on a daily basis. In the process, the political side of "pacification" remained as turbulent as the military effort violent.[121]

Figure 7 A DIFFICULT ALLIANCE IN NATION BUILDING. President Nixon shaking hands with Nguyen Van Thieu at the Midway Island Naval Terminal as Henry Kissinger and other officials stand in the background, 8 June 1969. (WHPO Master File #1284, RNL)

The Continuity of Political Instability

In sum, MACV under Creighton Abrams introduced no new initiatives for the pacification program, even as US headquarters expended considerable effort helping to build a viable South Vietnamese political community. The 1970 Pacification and Development Plan, for instance, outlined only one change. Rather than allied units supporting pacification, the new plan called for their active participation. Yet the campaign plan's major goals remained consistent—territorial security, protection of the people against terrorism, greater national unity, improving local administration, and prosperity for all. MACV staffers trumpeted the fact that the Vietnamese were directly involved in the planning, but one could hardly tell from the outcome.[122]

Thus, little had materially changed from Westmoreland's days. A review of the Pacification and Development Plans from 1969 to 1971 surely reveals a US military command appreciating the necessity of building a strong political society to compete with, and eventually outperform, the NLF. Yet MACV remained focused on the security aspect of pacification throughout the final years of withdrawal. Though Abrams spoke in "one war" terms, he retained Westmoreland's sequential approach to counterinsurgency and pacification—security first, followed by population control, and then sociopolitical development. Two years after Tet, CORDS was still allocating 80 percent of its resources to security programs. Even Colby later admitted that while the 1970 pacification plan "offered more of a chance to integrate" government programs into MACV's strategy, that goal "could only be met if there were continued improvements in the security situation *and* if there was also progress in the political and economic aspects" of the war.[123]

The allies, however, never attained such a lofty goal. The combined campaign plans, and guidance emanating from Abrams's headquarters, certainly spoke of efforts leading to a political end-state and units in the field did accomplish a number of nonmilitary tasks at the tactical level. But Abrams, much like his predecessor, could never resolve the security problem. Thus, estimates in the Nixon White House always seemed much less optimistic when compared to what was being reported by the NSC staff to Lyndon Johnson. Abrams and his commanders may have wanted to do more on the political front, but they simply could not surmount the hurdle of a lack of security in the countryside—even after winning a military "victory" during the 1968 Tet offensive.[124]

In part, the main obstacle remained Saigon's inability to harness the energies of a civil society that was actively engaged in the cultural discussion and production of what it meant to be South Vietnamese. The population's response to the government had always been the key assessment of wartime progress. This reality had not changed in the period of American withdrawal, nor had the insurgency's ability to maintain its access to the population. "While [the enemy] cannot seize and hold a location for any period of time," one US advisor wrote in mid-1970, "he does maintain his presence through these tactics."[125] Thus, the seemingly permanent existence of a shadow government contesting the GVN's political authority left most claims of pacification's success in doubt. How could the allies gain sustainable momentum in the political struggle when, according to an American officer in the Mekong Delta, "Saigon doesn't mean shit out here"?[126]

These frustrated Americans, however much they labored to couple the people to their government, simply could not fathom the ebb and flow of the undercurrent political war. Despite years of service in Vietnam, MACV officers were still only touching the surface when it came to pacification. Nearly all senior US officials, for instance, missed how the social revolution itself was changing after 1968. Without question, the allied pacification campaign damaged the NLF infrastructure, as "liberated areas shrank" and the insurgency's ability to tax and recruit declined. But the slow development of a rural middle class also affected interest in the revolutionary struggle, as did the wane of landlordism in the countryside. In short, the war itself was causing such vast social changes that neither the Americans nor the revolutionaries themselves could fully understand them or channel them to their needs.[127]

Thus, while pacification made inroads—"1969 was the worst year we faced" admitted one communist official—the revolution's woes were due only in part to allied operations. Perhaps more importantly, MACV was unaware how and why these changes indeed were occurring. Intelligence analysts continued to believe the Front held influence only because of coercion and terrorism. But the war's social impact left a population, in many instances, focusing mostly on its own familial and individual needs.[128]

The overwhelming dislocation caused by the war consequently undermined not only the very foundations of the revolution but Abrams's "one war" approach as well. CORDS evaluators doubted whether effective pacification programs could be instituted in provinces with one-fifth of their population living as "uprooted refugees." By mid-1970, Colby estimated that "something between three and four million people have been in refugee status in this country some-time in the past three years."[129] That same summer, another observer offered a sobering picture of victims displaced from the ancestral homes. "The people fled insecurity more than war. Not knowing what would happen from day to day was worse for these people living in the midst of a battlefield. Insecurity meant they were pressed by both the government and the communists."[130]

The emphasis Abrams placed on pacification simply could not overcome these wartime political realities. HES figures might denote 8.2 million people "made secure" between 1967 and 1972, but statistics based on questionable data hardly accounted for the plight suffered by the bulk of South Vietnamese society. Relocating a rural farmer into an area deemed "secure" by the GVN likely did not create any affinity for the Saigon government. In fact, among the villages in which the pacification campaign unfolded, the population fared no better during the withdrawal era than in years past. The revolution may have lost some support among the people, especially in 1969, but that support never shifted to the gov-ernment of South Vietnam. Rather than political unity, pacification only begot socioeconomic dislocation.[131]

Ultimately, the Saigon government proved unable to formulate a national consciousness that could inspire a people living in a politically fragmented soci-ety. As much as MACV wanted, defense and security forces could not indeed "provide a focal point for active commitment of the people to the Government of Vietnam."[132] This inability to gain a political constituency, more than any other factor, destined the allied pacification campaign to failure. While the com-munists surely had a popular cause reinforced by an effective political-military organization, as Duong Van Mai Elliott suggests, the revolution maintained its countrywide influence thanks to GVN deficiencies as well. "We were losing because of ourselves," Elliott recalled, "because we had been unable to come up with a system, an ideology, and a leadership that could tap the same qualities in the people, inspire them, and pull them together in the same direction to win the struggle." In the end, MACV's focus on security could not inspire allegiance to a questionable local government.[133]

A protracted conflict therefore left most South Vietnamese people worried more about mere survival than political loyalties. The psychological costs of daily suffering through war were likely beyond the comprehension of most Americans. The emotional toll was staggering and nothing Abrams or his command did in reviving the pacification program could undo this trauma. American soldiers might see the paradoxes of a land "so lovely and yet so full of death and destruction," but it seems unlikely they fully appreciated the true essence of the village war.[134] Mass death, social dislocation, collapsing family structures. These, ultimately, were the hallmarks of MACV's violent pacification campaign. Creighton Abrams surely aspired to a time when the war would lead to a better state of tranquility for the South Vietnamese people. Yet disillusioned and alienated individuals, like poet Thuy Yen, just as surely questioned how "the dead corpses would fertilize for peace." In the process, the soil of South Vietnam had become soaked with blood to the point of saturation.[135]

4

Balancing a War

The Coordination of Force and Diplomacy

While the ongoing war ravaged the Vietnamese countryside and its people, it likewise tormented Richard Nixon and his chief national security advisor, Henry Kissinger. As South Vietnam continued to face an existential threat, both from within and without, the Nixon White House confronted a changing global environment that appeared equally menacing. True, the shifting geopolitical environment might not jeopardize the United States' basic survival. But Kissinger, in particular, saw a world in which American authority was becoming less prominent thanks to an international diffusion of power in the post–World War II era. The war in Vietnam seemed only to aggravate these unwelcome trends.[1]

Both Nixon and Kissinger worried incessantly that Vietnam was undermining the United States' position across the world and at home as well. As Kissinger told the president in 1971, "The manner in which we end the war, or at least our participation, is crucial both for America's global position and for the fabric of our society." One year later, Nixon spoke in similar terms. After years of backing South Vietnam, if a "Soviet-supported opponent" defeated a US partner, "this could have considerable effect on our allies and on the United States. Our ability to conduct a credible foreign policy could be imperiled." Again and again as the 1970s unfolded, senior White House officials touted words like "credibility" and "prestige" in arguing that *how* the American war in Vietnam ended mattered just as much as *when* it ended.[2]

While maintaining national prestige remained a core issue during the US military withdrawal from Southeast Asia, geopolitical realities determined that the Vietnamese war was rapidly losing value for senior American policymakers. A quick and honorable end to US participation, even if not an outright military victory, would allow the president to free himself from a war no longer advancing a re-envisioned grand strategy. For Nixon, the outcome in Vietnam mostly carried weight because it "may well determine what happens to peace and freedom in all of Asia."[3] A credible United States could not tolerate an Asian expansion of communism. But perhaps more importantly, with Sino-Soviet relations deteriorating in 1969, unburdening the United States from Vietnam offered the prospect of greater flexibility in foreign policy and a chance to reconsider US relations with Beijing and Moscow. Thus, Nixon's consistent theme of permitting the "Vietnamese to choose freely their future course" made most sense when placed in a global context.[4]

In truth, from a realist perspective, South Vietnam no longer mattered to Nixon and Kissinger's long-term global designs. The relative importance of the embattled Southeast Asian country to America's well-being had diminished greatly since the early 1960s. So, too, had the appeal of politically heated anti-communist rhetoric. Looking to "de-ideologize" US foreign policy, the president aspired to break from "an abstract crusade" against a vague Red menace and instead interact with communist nations on an individual basis. To do this successfully, however, required extricating the United States from Vietnam with the nation's honor and credibility intact.[5] But, as the *New York Times* observed in March 1969, to avoid a precipitous withdrawal, Nixon was forced to negotiate on three fronts—with the enemy in Paris and on the battlefield, with his allies in Saigon, and, finally, with American public opinion. If the president hoped to succeed in stabilizing a new, multipolar world order, he would have to accomplish a delicate balancing act when it came to abandoning the war in Vietnam.[6]

Nixon's global aims impacted not only the pace and manner in which the United States withdrew from Southeast Asia but also, as importantly, the relationship between the White House and MACV headquarters. The president's concept of negotiations on three fronts meant Creighton Abrams's primary concern, military strategy inside South Vietnam, was only part of a much larger whole that often worked against the general's best laid plans. Abrams might aspire to a truly pacified South Vietnam, one capable of building state institutions in a secure environment that would lead to a strong nation capable of defending its borders and defeating the insurgency. Nixon and Kissinger, however, were willing to settle for much less. As long as they maintained US credibility during the withdrawal phase, senior policymakers could accept a policy that aimed at political equilibrium between the two Vietnams rather than outright military victory.[7]

But in the process, the president's balancing act left Abrams in a difficult spot. It seemed doubtful the war ultimately would end on the basis of equilibrium. Without either Hanoi or Saigon abandoning its main political objectives, the war would go on, each side fighting to tip the balance in its favor. This reality would incite tensions between Nixon's inner circle and MACV headquarters. While the White House viewed Vietnamization and GVN control over the population as sufficient to expedite the American departure from Vietnam, Abrams still clutched onto notions that winning the war might still be possible.

Nixon's decision to expand the war in 1970 no doubt fed the general's hopes. But even a military incursion into Cambodia only seemed to complicate the White House's search for equilibrium at the grand strategic level. The offensive set off a shock wave of protest in the United States, further broke down Cambodia's frontier with Vietnam, and complicated the United States' budding relationship with China. Kissinger may have wished to withdraw from Vietnam "as a matter of policy and not as a collapse," but the adverse relationships among diplomacy, military strategy, and politics at home (and in Saigon) tended to counter such aspirations.[8]

All told, decisions made within the Nixon White House made balancing the war inside South Vietnam a near impossible task for MACV's commander. Abrams's military strategy simply could not balance the competing demands of defeating a resolute enemy on the battlefield while negotiating with Hanoi and withdrawing American units from Indochina. All the while, US commanders and advisors had to focus on the process of Vietnamization, a task seemingly at odds with diplomatic aims in Paris. As one RAND analyst noted, "Negotiations and Vietnamization cannot be pursued simultaneously, with equal chances of success."[9]

These tensions between grand and military strategies ultimately helped to undermine a functioning civil-military relationship so necessary to accomplish the White House's goal of departing Vietnam as a matter of policy. Senior military officers argued that substantial US withdrawals could not be made "without considerable risk." How, they asked, could the Americans support pacification and development, Vietnamization, and provide security to the population, all while they were preparing to leave?[10] Kissinger, for his part, worried about the loss of leverage at the negotiating table since there was not "enough of a prospect of progress in Vietnam to persuade Hanoi to make real progress in Paris." In consequence, military strategy and national policy seemed more and more out of alignment for nearly every American involved in the withdrawal from Southeast Asia. If Abrams was hoping to fight a "better war" in 1969 and 1970, he and the troops he commanded would soon find themselves sorely disappointed.[11]

The Risk of Negotiating

In November 1970, US Army rangers and special forces launched a helicopter raid on Son Tay prison, a compound twenty miles north of Hanoi. That summer, defense intelligence analysts confirmed the presence of some fifty to sixty American prisoners of war (POWs) and, not long after, the Joint Chiefs of Staff recommended a rescue operation. The president, seeing political value in bringing home captured American servicemen, approved the plan. Yet three days before the operation was set to commence, intelligence sources sent a distressing report—Son Tay appeared to be empty. Relying more on faith than recent information, the raid went forward anyway. The intelligence analysts proved correct. A meticulous search of the prison cellblocks found no Americans, all of whom had been relocated back in July.[12]

The failed Son Tay raid implied that POWs, in part because of their service and sacrifice, could be useful political tools in seeking to maintain the nation's honor in Vietnam. Defense Secretary Melvin Laird, for instance, suggested the president "consider the need to define more precisely the relationship between the prisoner issue and US troop withdrawals." Kissinger agreed. South Vietnam's release of sick and wounded North Vietnamese POWs, and their "openness to international inspection," might stir international pressure for Hanoi to reply in kind and be used as a leverage point during negotiations.[13]

Championing the release of American prisoners of war, however, could also display Nixon's humanity as commander in chief. By the late 1960s, several family-led grassroots organizations arose, gaining a national voice over the issue of POWs and soldiers missing in action (MIA). One group in particular, the National League of Families of American Prisoners and Missing in Southeast Asia, led a campaign to make POW release a top priority of the Nixon administration. Ever sensitive to potential political advantages, the president embraced the cause. Who would be willing to contest Nixon's Vietnam policy if the White House was pressing for the liberation of prisoners of war prior to an agreement on other matters like a cease-fire or the withdrawal of US forces? In a war with few, if any heroes, POWs might conveniently fill that role and afford the president breathing room by challenging the antiwar movement's demands for a rapid, unconditional retreat.[14]

This politicization of American prisoners hinted at Nixon's deeper convictions on the war. Vietnam was more a political, and less a military, problem. The use of armed force still mattered of course, but extricating the United States from a long-stalemated conflict required political acumen. In this sense, the POW issue proved both an opportunity and a danger. On the stump, Nixon could win favor by claiming "the early release of seriously sick and wounded prisoners" was "not a political or military issue, but a matter of basic humanity."[15] POWs, quite simply, could mollify public opinion. But the very public concern over prisoners also brought political risks. In April 1971, Nixon confided to Kissinger that "the POW stuff" was "our Achilles heel. If those POW wives start running around, coming onto this general election, and veterans, you're in real—we are in troubles like you wouldn't. . . ."[16]

The prospect of prisoners' wives and families coordinating their efforts with the flourishing veterans' antiwar movement highlighted the fact that negotiating an end to the war was as much a domestic problem as it was a foreign policy one. National honor became interlaced with the fate of American POWs, any dissent at all deemed unpatriotic. Thus, prideful war supporters could vehemently label Jane Fonda a perfidious dissident—or worse, a criminal—for visiting North Vietnam and speaking out against the war. Yet more than 300 antiwar activists had made a similar trek before Fonda did in the summer of 1972. (Of course, images of "Hanoi Jane" sitting atop an anti-aircraft gun seemed to set her apart.) Nor did critics acknowledge that by the time of the actor's visit, fewer than 35,000 US troops were still in South Vietnam, most of them serving in non-combat roles. Little that Fonda did had a direct impact on POWs, Hanoi having officially ended the torture of prisoners back in 1969.[17]

Perhaps most importantly, Fonda spoke in terms that more and more Americans saw as indisputable. (Only after the conflict ended, when the "better war" narrative took increasing hold, did she become the exemplar of wartime treachery and disloyalty.) In July 1972, for example, the actor pleaded with Americans to "understand that the people of Vietnam are peasants. They live with the land—the land is part of their lives, as it has been for thousands of years. Every time you drop a bomb on the heads of these peasants it becomes clearer to them who the enemy is." To antiwar activists listening to Fonda, and her husband Tom Hayden, such arguments made imminent sense. End the war. Bring home American prisoners. Stop the suffering of the rural Vietnamese and let them live in peace. Few of these activists saw any reason to continue fighting when a negotiated settlement could achieve all these aims.[18]

In fact, senior White House officials had been thinking along parallel lines. In the summer of 1969, Alexander M. Haig Jr., military assistant to the national security advisor, offered Kissinger his thoughts on strategy for Vietnam. "Ultimately we must accept a coalition government," the soon-to-be promoted brigadier general wrote, "or something that is tantamount to a coalition government if the other side is to agree to a negotiated settlement and the fighting is to be brought to an end." In one sense, the POW issue later provided political cover for not only the US withdrawal but also a policy "accurately reflecting the different tendencies now existing in Viet-Nam." As long as the president brought American prisoners home, he could still negotiate an honorable end to a frustratingly stalemated war.[19]

The problem, though, remained one of sequencing. Nixon wanted the return of POWs to precede any talk of peace. North Vietnamese diplomats thought otherwise. Le Duc Tho told the *New York Times* in July 1971 that the release of prisoners could be "rapidly settled" once Nixon agreed to set a final date for total American withdrawal. Nixon knew he had little leverage. "They're not going to do a damn thing on prisoners," he told Kissinger. "You know why? They know they've got us by the balls."[20]

In this way, military operations still mattered as a way to support negotiations. Even if battlefield progress might not lead to outright military victory, they could offer a sense that the United States was terminating the war on its own accord. Such were hardly novel views. In the immediate aftermath of Tet, Secretary of State Dean Rusk argued, "We will not get a solution in Paris until we prove they can't win in the South." Even American POWs agreed. Former prisoner and US Air Force Colonel Robinson Risner recalled that the communists only "respected strength. They respected a person who was unyielding, who upheld those things that he believed in, who did not yield, who did not weaken, who did not compromise." Yet long before Risner's homecoming in February 1973, the president saw little choice but to compromise and negotiate an end to the war.[21]

Nixon was not alone in his begrudging acceptance of a negotiated settlement. 1969 had not been a good year for the Vietnamese communists. Abrams's focus on placing maximum pressure on the enemy after the 1968 Tet offensive was taking its toll, as were anti-infiltration operations along South Vietnam's borders, forcing the Hanoi Politburo to readjust its strategy while consolidating its losses.[22] In the summer of 1969, the North Vietnamese army "launched a wave of political training" while avoiding costly large-scale offensives. American analysts viewed these "economy-of-force" tactics as proof of a military corner being turned, the chairman of the Joint Chiefs crowing at an early October meeting in Saigon that the enemy was "in deep trouble and knows it."[23]

Hanoi Politburo General Secretary Le Duan may not have been quite so pessimistic; still, he clearly understood the search for a decisive military victory and general uprising in South Vietnam had come up far short of expectations. Party resolutions in 1969 thus cautioned that "under no circumstances should we risk our entire force in one attack," instead conducting operations "intended to compel the enemy . . . to accept serious negotiations with us, to withdraw troops, to recognize the Front, and to accept a coalition government."[24] Like Nixon, Le Duan continued to see value in military operations. Targeted main force and insurgent attacks would cause American troops and Saigon's "puppet army" "increasing difficulties in all fields, and prevent them from carrying out their 'clear and hold' strategy and their plan of de-escalating step by step and prolonging the war in order to secure a strong position." Concurrently, however, Hanoi would concentrate on the diplomatic front, thus embracing a "talk and fight" strategy aimed at negotiating a favorable end to the war.[25]

In sum, Tet and its aftermath had forced Le Duan to reluctantly accede the importance, if not necessity, of negotiations in Hanoi's overall grand strategy. If Nixon arrived at similar conclusions, he was equally wary of the political pitfalls. To discuss, for example, any issues with the newly established Provisional Revolutionary Government (PRG) ran the risk of recognizing a viable alternative to the Saigon regime. Kissinger worried that if revolutionary forces gained and held territory, the PRG could fashion itself as a "major instrument in the political process." De facto recognition of the National Liberation Front and the PRG would make it all the more difficult to contest a coalition government in South Vietnam. Thus, even if Abrams could not achieve a military victory with the forces under his command, he might at least give American diplomats a better position from which to negotiate.[26]

Such was the hope when Kissinger initiated secret negotiations with North Vietnamese envoys in Paris on 4 August 1969. From the start, the national security advisor faced a tricky balancing act. Antiwar activists at home pressed for a rapid conclusion to the war, yet prolonged negotiations, which Kissinger believed inevitable, might allow time for the Saigon regime to solidify its political base and for the South Vietnamese Army (ARVN) to mature. The Americans also hoped to confine talks to "military matters," yet Nixon and Kissinger knew full well that political issues mattered most to Hanoi. Finally, the White House hoped to place diplomatic pressure on Moscow, which had recently surpassed Beijing as Hanoi's main source of economic and military supplies. Kissinger believed the Soviet Union could do more in forcing North Vietnam to accept US demands such as a mutual withdrawal of troops from the south. The national security advisor, though, had little practical experience in negotiating for such high-level stakes.[27]

The death of Ho Chi Minh in September 1969 only muddied the waters for American negotiators. Kissinger thought Ho's death would "deal a blow to North Vietnamese morale" and perhaps result in a power struggle within the Politburo.[28] He was wrong on both counts. Le Duan quickly enshrined the popular revolutionary leader, linking his death with the ongoing fight for independence. At the funeral service, the first secretary read Ho's last testament, "Our People's Struggle," which called for new sacrifices and continuing resolve to achieve "total victory." The people's efforts would be worth the costs. "The American aggressors defeated, we will build a country ten times more beautiful."[29]

Insiders also knew that Ho's death would result in no major power struggle in Hanoi. According to one North Vietnamese colonel, Le Duan "had already long asserted his dominance over the Politburo."[30] Far from comprising a monolithic governing body, party leaders certainly argued over the best way forward during the difficult year of 1969. CIA analysts rightly judged that "there has been considerable debate in Hanoi over a correct strategic line and its proper tactical implementation." Yet Le Duan had already solidified his position among the party elite and he ultimately would decide, in the CIA's estimation, "whether Hanoi should adopt an 'offensive strategy' looking once again for dramatic military results, or adopt a more flexible combination of political and military tactics."[31]

That decision came soon enough given the temporary setbacks of late 1968 and 1969. Negotiations might be just as risky for Le Duan as for Nixon, but the

Figure 8 A MULTIFACETED GRAND STRATEGY. Aboard Air Force One, President
Nixon confers with Ambassador Ellsworth Bunker, General Creighton Abrams, Assistant
Secretary of State for East Asian and Pacific Affairs Marshall Green, and Henry Kissinger,
30 July 1969. (WHPO Master File #1630, RNL)

general secretary realized, even before Ho Chi Minh's death, that a decisive general offensive-general uprising strategy would have to wait as long as the balance
of forces remained in the allies' favor. The American president's rapprochement
with China would further complicate Le Duan's calculations. Hanoi's Politburo
chief had long understood that any people's revolution "must use both political
and military forces to secure victory."[32] Yet recent battlefield setbacks, along with
the threat of a successful Vietnamization policy leaving behind a more stable
South Vietnam, meant the general secretary had to redouble Hanoi's efforts in
the international arena while maintaining a strong negotiating position in Paris.
Richard Nixon surely appreciated the delicate nature of Le Duan's political-
military balancing act.[33]

The Price of Withdrawing

With the military scale inside South Vietnam weighted against Hanoi for the
moment, Politburo members had good reason to argue for patience. Battlefield
losses aside, it became increasingly clear as 1969 wore on that domestic discord
in the United States was forcing Nixon's hand, a point not lost on Le Duc Tho.

The North Vietnamese negotiator, in Kissinger's words, understood that the US "strategy was to make the war bearable for the American people while simultaneously strengthening the Saigon forces so that they could stand on their own." But as Le Duc Tho perceptively asked, how could the South Vietnamese prevail on their own if, after years of fighting alongside their American allies, they had barely achieved a costly stalemate?[34] Both Abrams and Kissinger knew such arguments made sense, but political pressures at home left little chance for an open-ended commitment. As the national security advisor recommended to Nixon that spring, "We must convince the American public that we are eager to settle the war, and Hanoi that we are not so anxious that it can afford to outwait us."[35]

Hoping to offset "the pace of public opinion" against South Vietnamese gains and Hanoi's intransigence, Nixon ordered a second round of American troop withdrawals in September. Another 35,000 GIs would be coming home by year's end. Abrams, consistently dour in his assessment of the enemy situation, highlighted the dangers posed by the "estimated 234,500 troops posing a direct, military threat to South Vietnam." Worse, the MACV commander believed the enemy had a "capability in-country and adjacent to South Vietnam which he has not fully used recently."[36] To the secretary of defense, however, Abrams would have to accept the risks inherent in troop cuts. As Laird later told the media, "We had to go ahead with withdrawal regardless of what North Vietnam did in response, because we did not have domestic support." Kissinger, for his part, doubted whether the White House could disentangle "the insoluble dilemmas of fighting both North Vietnam's army and domestic critics."[37]

If the US drawdown linked to Vietnamization worried the national security advisor, the troop cuts alarmed Creighton Abrams. In one sense, a myopic view of South Vietnam and its place in the global Cold War led to the MACV commander's anxieties. Yet demands on the ground seemed only to be increasing. A November 1969 assessment proved telling. Abrams believed the NVA could initiate "a major offensive on relatively short notice" (though he could not sustain such an attack for long) and reported an increase of thirty-three enemy combat battalions inside South Vietnam since January. Because the enemy likely would rely on "small unit attacks designated to inflict maximum allied casualties," the threat to pacification security forces remained high. Thus, even if pacification was making "slow but steady" progress, Abrams saw potential hazards in Hanoi's "effort to undermine the confidence of the people in the ability of the GVN to protect them." Moreover, the strength, size, and effectiveness of the South Vietnamese army remained a "matter of continuing concern." "From the foregoing analysis," Abrams concluded, "the situation is such that it would not, repeat not, be militarily sound to recommend further U.S. troop redeployments at this time."[38]

The competing demands of US withdrawal—the enemy threat, the status of negotiations, the success of pacification, the progress of Vietnamization—equally pulled American units in multiple directions throughout much of 1969. The 101st Airborne Division, for example, spent a busy twelve months between the summers of 1969 and 1970 juggling manifold tasks. The "Screaming Eagles" not only fought a stubborn enemy in the A Shau Valley, but also worked with neighboring ARVN and US marine units, as well as local Regional and Popular Forces, to advance the pacification effort. The division supported "health, cultural and social programs" in I Corps while bringing "every aspect of airmobility" against the enemy. Young troopers patrolled South Vietnam's borders "to stop enemy movement from Laos and North Vietnam" and slogged through "the lowland rice-producing areas of Phu Tu District." There seemed little the 101st had not covered in prosecuting the allies' combined campaign plan for that year.[39]

These multiple concurrent operations, however, suggested much more work needed to be done before US troops could safely redeploy home. Abrams, thinking in terms of purely military logic, genuinely disagreed with the rapid pace of troop withdrawals. He had long viewed battlefield success as the best help to negotiations. But now it appeared to many senior officers that Laird was "obsessed with getting out of Vietnam for political reasons as soon as possible."[40] Though MACV's mission had not changed, Abrams watched helplessly as his resources diminished with every soldier who redeployed home. Indeed, to the general, the unilateral US withdrawal was working against the crucial goal of improving South Vietnam's armed forces. At least some journalists shared Abrams's concerns. *TIME Magazine*'s Saigon bureau chief, reporting in early 1970, noted, "It is far too early in the game to tell whether, when we yank out some of the props, the South Vietnamese structure will be able to stand on its own."[41]

While surely they saw themselves as more than "props," uniformed leaders gradually, if still only privately, began to wrestle with an uncomfortable proposition. What would it mean if their generation was the first to lose an overseas war? Peace with honor might be a convenient political turn-of-phrase for President Nixon, but it meant something viscerally personal for professional military officers, many of whom had won their spurs in the Second World War. Simply negotiating "victory" implied they had come up short in defeating their enemy on the battlefield. What if the negotiations civilian policymakers forced on them came too soon, leaving behind a South Vietnam incapable of sustaining itself in a time of only nominal peace? How, in this scenario, could honor truly be achieved?

Importantly, Abrams and other military officers found support from Nixon's senior-most advisors. Ambassador Ellsworth Bunker warned that if the US withdrawal outpaced progress in Vietnamization, it could destroy Vietnamese leaders' "self confidence and all that we have built up here step by painful step." National Security Council aide Alexander Haig equally expressed concern that the RVNAF needed time to gel before the president approved more American troop reductions.[42]

No advisor, however, advocated a harder line than Henry Kissinger himself. Citing potential loss of leverage at the negotiating table, Kissinger consistently warned against unilateral de-escalation. In March 1969, he advised Nixon against troop reductions. "Our military effort leaves a great deal to be desired, but it remains one of our few bargaining weapons." Later that summer, the national security advisor worried about approaching a point "where we may be forced to choose between Vietnamization and political negotiations."[43] Other communications with the president spoke of "the presence of our troops in South Vietnam" as "our main asset" and of unilateral withdrawals weakening the US position in Paris. Even newspapers got wind of the counsel from "Kissinger the Hawk." As Jack Anderson of *The Washington Post* reported in late 1969, "If the anti-war movement can be soft-pedaled and the American public will be patient, in Kissinger's opinion, the United States can force the Communists to negotiate."[44]

Patience, however, was running out. In truth, the arguments promoted by Kissinger and Abrams in 1969 and early 1970 rested on a weak political foundation both at home and abroad. Manipulating opinion at home proved just as difficult as developing a potent South Vietnamese army. Moreover, from a grand strategy standpoint, Vietnam seemed only to be keeping the president from concentrating on his larger Cold War designs. Thus, on 14 February 1970, Secretary of Defense Laird declared: "the withdrawal of American troops from Vietnam would continue despite the stalemate in the Paris negotiations and the persistence of a substantial enemy threat on the battlefield." The previous day, the *New York Times* revealed a "suggestion" from a US Army staff agency in Vietnam that units stop emphasizing "hard combat news" and replace it with "reports of the progress of our efforts in the fields of Vietnamization, pacification, and civil action." It seemed as if Abrams's deepest fears of a rapid departure from Vietnam, regardless of potential defeat, were coming to fruition.[45]

This increasingly public civil-military quarrel over troop withdrawals hinted at what would become a major pillar in the "better war" narrative—officers blaming Washington for their strategic misfortunes. With Abrams more and more at odds with the president, journalists picked up on the discord. Worse, they took sides with the general. Thus, veteran correspondent Joseph Alsop argued in early 1970 that "Nixon will be asking for trouble by refusing to heed" Abrams's call for a "pullout pause." At least three major newspapers ran Alsop's column pitting general against commander in chief. Nixon, not one to take criticism lightly, especially from a uniformed officer in the field, held his tongue, but the episode did little to alleviate an already fraying relationship between the White House and MACV headquarters in Saigon.[46]

The president, of course, knew the political risks of withdrawing troops against the advice of his top general in Vietnam. He also grasped, though, his diminishing ability to maintain public support for a war clearly ending. While Abrams fretted over his own capacity to "assure the security of the Vietnamese people" and effectively participate in allied pacification plans, Nixon declared he would not be cowed by antiwar activists seeking to make government policy "in the streets."[47] In the meantime, his caustic vice president, Spiro Agnew, lashed out against peaceniks who had "a masochistic compulsion to destroy their country's strengths." Kissinger, for his part, later savaged the "unpacifiable doves . . . quickening demands in the media and the Congress for unilateral concessions in the negotiations." According to the national security advisor, public protestors espoused one common theme: "The obstacle to peace was not Hanoi but their own government's inadequate dedication to peace."[48]

That autumn, antiwar demonstrations reached a new level despite Nixon's decision to withdraw additional troops from Vietnam. On 15 October 1969, a nationwide Moratorium to End the War in Vietnam unleashed a torrent of protests and demonstrations across the country. Senator George McGovern delivered three major speeches in Washington, Boston, and Bangor, Maine, that day, calling Vietnam "our worst hour."[49] Tens of thousands of protestors gathered in New York City, Philadelphia, and Los Angeles, while some 100,000 assembled in Boston Common to listen to music and speeches. Audience members at the matinee showing of the Broadway hit *Fiddler on the Roof* joined the cast in marching to a rally. Although White House Chief of Staff H. R. Haldeman noted the news media "were obsessed with the whole thing," the Moratorium clearly stuck a chord with many Americans. As *TIME* quoted Eleanor Bockman, "a middle-aged Atlanta housewife: 'I think people are thoroughly tired of the war.'" Brandeis University professor John P. Roche agreed. "The moratorium was a legitimate symbol of the war-weariness of the American people."[50]

Nixon, however, refused to believe vocal protestors spoke for the bulk of patriotic Americans. Purposefully scheduling a major address between the October Moratorium and a second mass demonstration later the next month, the president spoke to the nation on the evening of 3 November. Making his case for winning "America's peace," Nixon argued that "precipitate withdrawal from Vietnam would be a disaster not only for South Vietnam but for the United States and for the cause of peace"; the president blamed Hanoi for refusing "to even consider our proposals." The withdrawal of American forces would be made "from strength and not from weakness," he said. Nixon then asked for support from "the great silent majority of my fellow Americans," contending that "the more divided we are at home, the less likely the enemy is to negotiate at

Paris." A self-satisfied Nixon recalled the speech as "the most effective of my presidency." Journalist Jonathan Schell, however, quipped just one month after the address a different estimation. "Never before in our democracy has silence had such a high reputation."[51]

While Nixon's "silent majority" speech garnered relatively positive reviews, it nonetheless failed to stem the momentum building for another moratorium against the war. Between 13 and 15 November, demonstrators once more took to the streets in major cities, including, by some estimates, roughly 500,000 protestors in Washington, DC. Flooding the nation's capital, they filed down Pennsylvania Avenue in a "March of Death" under a banner "Silent Majority for Peace." The crowds heard Coretta Scott King and Senator McGovern speak, listened to the cast of *Hair* sing selections from the Broadway musical, and chanted along as Peter, Paul, and Mary led a rendition of John Lennon's "All we are saying is give peace a chance."[52]

But the moratorium protests also engendered a backlash of sorts from those increasingly at odds with the "demo" culture and the anti-American sentiments held by some protestors. On the Penn State campus, for example, the unversity's Young Americans for Freedom criticized the peace movement, instead supporting one college dean who ardently defended US military intervention in Vietnam: "Our withdrawal now without a peace settlement would set the stage for North Vietnam to overrun South Vietnam and could lead to another horrendous bloodletting. It would also encourage other aggressive nations to overpower their weaker neighbors." Elsewhere, a loose coalition of Nixon supporters rallied to the president's side under the slogan "the home team." And, demonstrating the fissures expanding in American society over a hotly debated war, Merle Haggard's pro-war song "Okie from Muskogee" shot to number one on the charts the same week as the second moratorium. As the country musician crooned, "We don't burn our draft cards down on Main Street / We like livin' right, and bein' free."[53]

Draft cards, however, would soon become a thing of the past as Nixon moved toward an all-volunteer armed forces. Conscription, quite simply, had become a political burden. Earlier in 1969, the president appointed a commission to review the Selective Service System and worked with Congress to terminate most student deferments and adopt a lottery draft system based on the birth dates of men reaching eighteen the coming year. Nixon argued that the lottery's random selection would "end the agony of suspense over the draft," though it seems doubtful many young men with a low draft number prized their draw.[54] On 1 December 1969, Selective Service officials randomly selected a sequence of birthdays for those being drafted in 1970. The system would serve as a bridge to conscription's end in 1973. While critics argued that an all-volunteer force would become either an "elite corps of killers, dangerously isolated" from society or an army "staffed predominantly by the poor and the black," Nixon, with congressional support, had taken a bold step in easing antiwar sentiment at home.[55]

The president took yet another hopeful stride toward ending the war with his political standing intact by announcing a new round of troop withdrawals on 15 December. Fifty thousand more Americans would be coming home from Vietnam over the next four months. In Saigon, however, senior officials in MACV headquarters watched with dismay at the unrelenting pressures imposed by the antiwar movement. Staff officers believed Hanoi was "attempting to fan the flames of what he's read as a growing U.S. impatience and discouragement with the war," while Abrams railed against critics who focused more on "the *cosmetics* of the thing . . . than what's *accomplished*—in a great many ways."[56] To some in MACV, the "get-out-of-Vietnam-at-any-cost" philosophy was, in fact, damaging the war effort. "While it could not be stated unequivocally that the anti-war movement in the US was responsible for the reluctance of the NVN to negotiate," the command history noted, "there was ample evidence that the disproportionate attention gained by the vocal minority gave great comfort and certainly lent propaganda support to the enemy."[57]

Despite all the calculations in squaring the loss of public support at home with military requirements inside South Vietnam, the balance sheet remained ill-defined as 1969 drew to a close. According to veteran correspondent Peter Arnett, Saigon had made "major territorial gains" during the year but only because "relentless use of firepower and the vigorous deployment of American troops" made this possible. Reports indicated two North Vietnamese regiments now operating in the south's Mekong Delta, a first in the war. Worse, observers saw "no sense of national unity" in South Vietnam, where "political maneuvering" remained "standard procedure."[58] On 15 December, the president addressed the nation to report, regretfully, "that there has been no progress whatever on the negotiating front." While the MACV commander and his staff lamented the costs of withdrawing more US troops from Vietnam, few could perceive any real benefits. A frustrated Abrams, though conceding the South Vietnamese people were tired, roared that they had to do more: "The truth of the matter is, if they're going to *really* come out on top of this, *goddamn it*, they've still got to *sacrifice*, and *they've got to sacrifice a lot!*"[59]

Abrams need not have worried. Richard Nixon was about to ask the South Vietnamese people, and the neighboring Cambodians as well, to sacrifice quite a lot more in the coming year.

Incursion

Cambodia had long played a complicated role in the larger Indochinese conflict. Since at least the 1954 partition of Vietnam, Khmer Prince Norodom Sihanouk had maintained an uneasy neutrality in an increasingly violent Cold

War Southeast Asia. Nonalignment proved a difficult proposition for any political leader neighboring the two Vietnams. By the early 1960s, fighting grew more and more intense along Cambodia's eastern border, as communist forces took control of frontier territories and established bases from which to attack South Vietnam.[60] By the time of Nixon's inauguration, Sihanouk had his hands full preserving his nation's dominion and territorial integrity while simultaneously avoiding formal commitments with either Hanoi or Saigon. All the while, rice exports dropped precipitously as the prince confronted growing opposition to his domestic and foreign policies. Hanoi took advantage of the Khmer turmoil, in MACV's estimate, developing "large enclaves, permanently garrisoned and over which Cambodia has limited or no sovereignty. In these areas Cambodia is experiencing a de facto occupation of her country."[61]

Sihanouk's limited control over his nation's borders troubled American officers who viewed the Cambodian frontier as an exposed flank from which North Vietnamese forces could assail South Vietnam. Well before Abrams's tenure, both the Joint Chiefs and MACV had been advocating for cross-border operations to destroy communist sanctuaries and to cut the logistical lifeline of the Ho Chi Minh Trail. The chorus changed little after Tet. In early November 1968, Abrams thought it "criminal to let these enemy outfits park over here, fatten up, reindoctrinate, get their supplies, and so on."[62] Another high-ranking MACV officer concurred, maintaining that "the enemy's long-standing violation of the neutral territory of Cambodia and Laos justified like action by the US." So constant was the refrain that Secretary of Defense Laird expressed his displeasure during a February 1970 visit to Saigon that the military command had not developed any new approaches to the seemingly sluggish Vietnamization program. To military officers, taking the war beyond South Vietnam's borders appeared the remedy for all their problems.[63]

Nixon and Kissinger, of course, early on realized the advantages Cambodian sanctuaries provided to Hanoi's forces. Operation Menu, the secret bombing of Cambodia that had begun in March 1969, served not only as retaliatory action against North Vietnamese aggression but also a furtive display of the new administration's strength and determination. As long as the aerial campaign remained clandestine, Sihanouk could retain his nominal impartiality while Nixon safely (albeit deceitfully) expanded the war. The consequences of the bombing, however, were not long in coming.[64] Though Kissinger foresaw the possibility of domestic critics decrying the war's enlargement or the start of an "escalatory cycle" with Hanoi, he failed to consider the second-order effects of attacking the NVA's sanctuaries. Only in 1972 did the national security advisor privately admit the Menu operation "led to the collapse of Cambodia because it pushed the North Vietnamese deeper into Cambodia"—a point Kissinger later denied in his memoirs, arguing instead that NVA forces moved back into North

Vietnam. How the Khmer people might deal with the costs of thousands of acres of rubber plantations being defoliated and destroyed by US planes remained an unexamined inquiry.[65]

The social implications of what the bombing meant to Cambodians, in fact, mattered little to military officers more concerned with dismantling the Ho Chi Minh Trail running just outside of South Vietnam's borders. At the White House, Alexander Haig minimized "favorable statistics on the internal security situation in South Vietnam . . . even if they were accurate." To Kissinger's military aide, the "chief threat to Saigon came not from within South Vietnam but from enemy sanctuaries in Cambodia. It was from Cambodia that NVA and Viet Cong operations had always been planned, manned, supplied, and managed."[66] MACV's commanding general tended to agree. As Abrams spoke of attacking the enemy "system," he kept a wary eye on the North Vietnamese supply network running through Cambodia and Laos. Intelligence analysts tabulated the number of NVA troops "being put into the pipeline," observing a "sharp upturn" during the early months of 1969. Less than a year later, Abrams saw evidence "pointing toward a major offensive effort early in 1970."[67]

This "sharp increase" in the enemy's logistical activities suggested that US bombing efforts had not quite lived up to what airpower advocates had been promising since early 1965 with the commencement of Operation Rolling Thunder. That vicious aerial campaign, averaging more than 500 tons of bombs dropped daily on North Vietnam, had neither brought Hanoi to terms nor helped to strengthen the Saigon government. In fact, the bombing may have benefited Le Duan, allowing the Politburo leader to obtain greater material support and resupplies from China and the Soviet Union.[68] Perhaps as important, though, infiltration rates along the Ho Chi Minh Trail actually increased despite the horrific attacks endured by the North Vietnamese porters and construction workers who maintained the shelled road network. The Joint Chiefs estimated that infiltration rose "substantially" near the end of 1969. Just over two years later, a frustrated Kissinger told the president that the bombing campaign was "one of the worst disgraces, that here the great U.S. Air Force can't keep a road from being built." South Vietnam's western flank seemed as vulnerable as ever.[69]

Still, the inability to sever the Ho Chi Minh Trail proved only one of several reasons that Nixon finally decided to move against Cambodia. The president and his senior staff understood the potential of a political backlash at home if he expanded the war and, in Haldeman's words, that there would be a "monumental squawk on the Hill."[70] But by nearly all accounts Cambodia had become an "untenable situation," requiring a "bold move." Kissinger believed a strike would "induce uncertainty and worry in the enemy," while Abrams thought the time ripe since there had been a "public exposure of VC/NVA presence in Cambodia."[71] Moreover, according to one source, the general insisted to Nixon "that if he were to assure the safety of his men and still meet the 12-month withdrawal schedule he required permission to liquidate the enemy sanctuaries in Cambodia."[72]

Sensing an opening for the military's long coveted approval to take the strategic offensive, Abrams hammered home his points in mid-March. The enemy had made "no positive reciprocal response . . . to allied initiatives to de-escalate the conflict." The main bases of supplies for forces inside South Vietnam remained in the north and in Cambodia. Potential hazards endured with four NVA infantry regiments operating in the Central Highlands and ARVN units, focusing on pacification, being "largely untested" in combating the conventional threat. MACV's commander also linked Cambodia to the key allied effort in 1970. "The destruction of enemy supplies before they can be brought to bear against friendly forces in SVN," Abrams argued, "is one of the pre-requisites for maintaining the pace of Vietnamization." Though Kissinger's own staff objected to the type of "deep penetrations" senior military officers were recommending, Nixon felt compelled to act in a forceful manner.[73]

Political events inside Cambodia only bolstered Abrams's claims. Suffering from a volatile political climate and a tanking economy, Prince Sihanouk, en route from Moscow to Beijing in hopes of pressuring Hanoi against further intrusions, watched helplessly from afar as a military coup overthrew his government on 18 March 1970.[74] Former general and current Prime Minister Lon Nol assumed control, promising to oust the communist occupation forces while maintaining his country's neutrality in the Vietnamese war. Though Nixon later argued the "coup came as a complete surprise," Hanoi diplomats in Paris leveled charges the United States was fomenting insurrection. Less than a week after the overthrow, North Vietnam withdrew its envoys from Phnom Penh.[75]

It did not take long for Nixon to use the coup for his own purposes, believing the anticommunist Lon Nol would be more accepting of a US offensive than his predecessor. Abrams responded to a late-March "urgent requirement from higher authority" for his plan to attack the Cambodian sanctuaries with a positive assessment: such an assault was "the military move to make at this time . . . both in terms of the security of our own forces and for the advancement of the Vietnamization program." At least some observers agreed. Max Lerner of the *Los Angeles Times* imagined "the loss of the sanctuaries could mean a radical transformation of the war."[76]

The president used similar arguments in trying to build support for a full-scale Cambodian invasion. Despite protests from Secretary of State William Rogers, who believed an expanded ground campaign would "cost great United States casualties with little gain," Nixon decided to "go for broke." As he later reasoned, "North Vietnam was threatening to convert all of eastern Cambodia into one huge base area, with convenient supply lines and favorable geography,

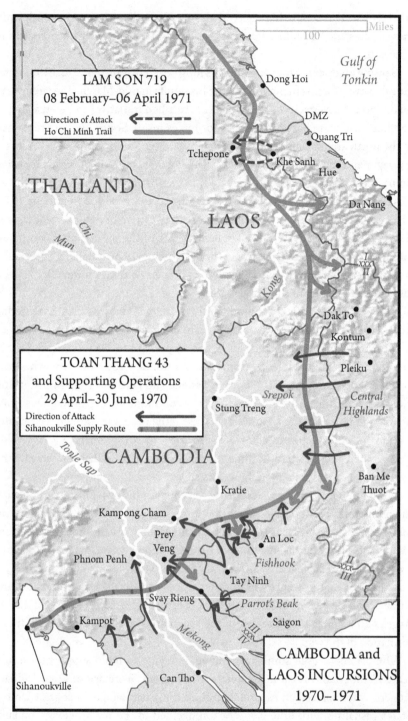

Map 2 Incursions

that would enable its forces to strike both Phnom Penh and South Vietnam at will. This would have been a disaster."[77] MACV intelligence estimates of the enemy's stockpiles in Cambodia only reinforced Nixon's decision. So, too, did Nguyen Van Thieu's enthusiasm on hearing the news of a potential offensive. "If Cambodia and South Vietnam and its allies cooperate along the border," the GVN president stated, "then I believe the Communists would find it impossible to stay."[78]

In truth, far from acting like a "madman," Nixon, in a calculated manner, surmised that increased military pressure could wrench political concessions from Hanoi. Political calculations always had been at the center of the president's wartime leadership. The incursion into Cambodia proved no different. Indeed, artfully formulated, Nixon's decision to attack NVA sanctuaries could be blamed on Hanoi. When one White House staffer questioned whether the offensive actually violated the Nixon Doctrine, Kissinger snapped, "We wrote the goddamn doctrine. We can change it." Besides, the national security advisor argued, "The basic substance of all this is that we have to be tough."[79]

But simultaneously negotiating while fighting complicated the White House's aim of communicating both American strength and compassion to the rest of the world. Military operations might still be necessary to force Hanoi leaders to the negotiating table and keep them there, yet they hardly were sufficient alone for ending the war on favorable terms to the United States. As one South Vietnamese general recalled, "A few sporadic escalations of too short duration served simply as a means of intimidation to stimulate continuation of the peace talks."[80]

This ARVN critique correctly hinted at several issues with the Cambodian incursion even before military planning got underway. Defense Secretary Laird sought limited American participation, believing now was the time to test Vietnamization. Nixon countered, arguing that only with US forces working alongside the ARVN could the enemy's sanctuaries be cleared. Yet Abrams's staff excluded their South Vietnamese counterparts from the initial planning—citing operational security—and, worse, "had absolutely no idea of the manner in which the NVA had established their storage areas."[81] Additionally, the president intended to blunt domestic criticism by limiting the duration and geographical depth of the allied assault. The mission might be simple—"Kill all the dink-bastards you can!" recollected one boorish American officer—but the operational details already were testing the capacity of Abrams's staff to compose a workable plan confirming the progress being made in Vietnamization.[82]

While Kissinger hoped a successful operation would "probably have a highly favorable effect on RVNAF morale and confidence," the president sought a similar aim on the American home front. Returning from a 19 April Hawaii trip to welcome home the Apollo 13 astronauts, Nixon announced the pullout

Figure 9 EXPANDING THE WAR TO SHORTEN IT. President Nixon delivering a televised address from the Oval Office to the nation while pointing to a map of Cambodia, 30 April 1970. (WHPO Master File #3447, RNL)

of another 150,000 American troops to be completed by the following year. A force of 284,000 would remain come May 1971. As the president recalled, the pronouncement was intended "to drop a bombshell on the gathering spring storm of antiwar protest."[83] Abrams predictably warned against further troop reductions, worried about keeping Vietnamization on track given the worsening situation inside Cambodia. The president, however, insisted the war was under control and the "risk for peace" justified the new withdrawals. As the *New York Times* reported, "Militarily speaking, it was not a particularly good time to be talking about removing more American troops from Vietnam. But politically, the President had little choice."[84]

The bombshell to the antiwar movement, though, came not from Nixon's withdrawal announcement but from a speech less than two weeks later revealing that US troops were now fighting inside Cambodia. The broadcast shook the nation. Inspired by watching his favorite movie *Patton*, Nixon spoke on 30 April of the ground operations in Cambodia he had authorized only four days earlier. The reasons were clear. "These Communist occupied territories contain major base camps, training sites, logistics facilities, weapons and ammunition factories, airstrips, and prisoner-of-war compounds." The president saw only one option—"to go to the heart of the trouble." Yet the offensive was "not an invasion of Cambodia." Rather, the allies would depart once the enemy had been driven out of his sanctuaries and his military supplies there destroyed.[85]

Then, speaking to the critics whom the administration predicted would denounce the president's actions as soon as the speech concluded, Nixon declared the offensive was "not for the purpose of expanding the war into Cambodia but for the purpose of ending the war in Vietnam and winning the just peace we all desire." Inaction would destroy US credibility. "If, when the chips are down, the world's most powerful nation . . . acts like a pitiful, helpless giant, the forces of totalitarianism and anarchy will threaten free nations and free institutions throughout the world."[86]

With a "minimum of publicity," more than 5,000 South Vietnamese and 10,000 American troops, ushered in by waves of B-52 bombers, crossed into Cambodia beginning on 29 April. The allied plan envisioned two near simultaneous assaults. A main attack into the "Fishhook" salient comprised elements from five US and ARVN infantry divisions, two cavalry regiments, and an airborne brigade, all of which would conduct a coordinated pincer movement to entrap the 7th PAVN division, capture supply caches, and, if possible, find and destroy the revolutionary party's southern headquarters (COSVN). To the south, three ARVN task forces would assault the "Parrot's Beak," a second salient extending between South Vietnam's Hau Nghia and Kien Tuong provinces. Forward momentum would rely heavily on allied artillery, helicopter gunships, and tactical air support. As directed by Nixon, no US forces would advance farther than thirty kilometers into Cambodia. The Americans also needed to return to South Vietnam by 30 June.[87]

Early assessments of the Cambodian incursion—codenamed Operation Toan Thang 43 (Total Victory 43) by the ARVN—proved ambiguous at best. North Vietnamese troops avoided contact when they could, and though dodging a major engagement, still suffered more than 11,000 casualties. From Saigon, a visiting Alexander Haig reported to Kissinger that the allies had captured over 11 million rounds of ammunition, more than 6 million pounds of rice, and 24,000 pounds of medical supplies. Compared to earlier MACV operations in 1967 such as Cedar Falls and Junction City, the operation already appeared wildly successful.[88]

Yet undercurrents of doubt were quickly rising to the surface. By mid-May, a perplexed Abrams admitted to his staff that he doubted the statistics flaunting so much progress. Instead, it felt as if the command was "talking about a basketful of fog." The hunt for COSVN had come up empty. Knowing of the Americans' 30 June deadline, the communists took cover, limiting their response to harassment and tactical retreats. Worse, one US general worried about what was fast becoming a "delicate problem" in the offensive's first two weeks. The 25th Infantry Division's assistant commander was turning away Cambodians asking

for assistance, realizing that when his soldiers withdrew, "there will be very serious reprisals against the local Cambodian officials if the VC/NVA think there
has been the slightest cooperation with the Americans."[89]

Nor did a new round of US airstrikes against North Vietnam gain much
advantage. The president ordered the bombing of supply depots just north of the
demilitarized zone for the first four days of May to coincide with the Cambodian
incursion. These "protective reaction strikes," the first major aerial assault since
the November 1968 bombing halt, targeted not only Hanoi's air defenses but its
logistical system as well. Hanoi appeared unmoved. While intelligence analysts
assumed the strikes were successful, they could only estimate the damage done,
ranging widely between 10,000 and 50,000 tons of supplies. On 5 May, an emotional Nixon took a solitary early-morning stroll to the Lincoln Memorial, oddly
mingling with student protestors and defending his decision that led to MACV
hitting the enemy with the "hardest blow possible."[90]

The Cambodian blow, however, seemed less and less substantial by month's
end. In Saigon, General Haig warned Abrams's staff of providing the president
with "faulty or lagging information." A clearly frustrated officer retorted, "We
have two of your messages. One of them says 'go get 'em' and the other one says
'hurry up and get out.'" To his boss, Haig related the military situation was "not
bright." Relaying the political conditions in Cambodia to the president, Kissinger
described them as "grave but not altogether hopeless." If Nixon had intended to
shore up South Vietnam's western flank, a month of military operations clearly
had only achieved so much. Moreover, a Gallup poll in May found that nearly
60 percent of surveyed Americans disapproved of the Cambodian operation.[91]

Summoned back to the United States, Abrams gave his commander in chief
a personal assessment in San Clemente, California, on 31 May. The general
believed that the ARVN performed extremely well in Cambodia, agreeing with
Nixon that "the operation has given us greater confidence in the Vietnamization
program." Wanting to "keep the heat on so that the enemy doesn't assume that
Cambodia was our last gasp," the president directed the senior officers present to "clean out the sanctuaries" but also to focus on the "primary objective"
of securing South Vietnam. Looking to the future, Nixon ordered Abrams to
prepare plans for "offensive operations in Laos" and a "continuation of ARVN
ground and U.S. air operations in Cambodia." As the conversation wound down,
the secretary of defense, always with an eye toward the home front, cautioned
against overconfidence when assessing the South Vietnamese performance in
Cambodia. "My only problem," Laird noted, "is that they will get some setbacks.
We must not be too optimistic here at home."[92]

Laird's counsel suggested that any public assessment of the Cambodian incursion came with risks. Yet with the Joint Chiefs informing Abrams of the president's desire "to present the success of our operations in Cambodia in the most

favorable terms," reports emanated from Saigon highlighting the "vast amounts of weapons and tonnages of rice and ammunition" captured.[93] In July, Major General George W. Casey deemed Cambodia the "most successful operation in the history of the 1st Cavalry Division," while another senior officer believed it was "the toughest setback in twenty years" for the communists. Other MACV commanders sensed an "obvious pride" within the South Vietnamese army's ranks, a true "morale booster for all forces."[94]

The Cambodian incursion, however, proved a microcosm of the problems in balancing military operations with other aspects of strategy in Vietnam. Not only did the CIA call the figures of communist dead "highly suspect," but critics also wondered how the operation had truly affected Nixon's Vietnamization policy. While the ARVN had performed reasonably well, reports surfaced of "innumerable instances of looting" inside Cambodia and of South Vietnamese leaders unwilling to operate without "more and more B-52 strikes."[95] Jonathan Schell even questioned the motives of the cross-border operation. "If 'Vietnamization' of the war in South Vietnam is the ultimate aim of these moves," *The New Yorker* correspondent observed, "it is hardly well served by having South Vietnamese troops in Cambodia." Moreover, if the incursion was only a temporary sweep and disruption of the NVA's supply depots, then it hardly eliminated the communist threat so Vietnamization could proceed in a truly secure environment.[96]

Supporters argued the incursion bought the allies time to concentrate on not only Vietnamization but also pacification within South Vietnam. Yet according to Secretary Laird, results from the pacification program during the first six months of 1970, when MACV's attention was diverted by the Cambodian incursion, proved "spotty."[97] In truth, both quantitative and qualitative metrics told a discouraging story. Abrams reported an increase in refugees along the South Vietnam-Cambodia border. The number of terrorism incidents rose during the first half of 1970. And, in at least one province, Americans observed "a lack of resistance to night incursions of VC into rural hamlets and the withdrawal of officials, civilian cadre, and security force personnel." Laird even worried that the ARVN, "wandering all over Cambodia," was being sidetracked from the real mission of providing local security to the population.[98]

In fact, MACV only tangentially discussed the pacification effort throughout most of the Cambodian operation. Abrams hoped the campaign had taken pressure off the population, as the enemy concentrated on limiting the damage to his supply lines, but the addition of some 18,000 refugees only added to the allies' burdens. The general's messages throughout this period centered more on the military aspects of the fighting inside Cambodia. Throughout May, Abrams proposed continuing US air strikes in the border areas, "hitting the enemy the hardest blow possible in the time available," and keeping the "American troops in an offensive mood."[99] On occasion, MACV's commander reported on the status of

Regional and Popular Forces inside South Vietnam (desertions were still a problem) or on the need to "clean up" the base areas and "proceed on an expeditious basis with the pacification program." Yet for the most part, Abrams confined his analysis to first defeating the enemy threat in Cambodia before returning to the problems at hand in Vietnam. The "one war" approach remained a sequential as ever.[100]

By mid-June, senior Nixon officials were turning their gaze back to Saigon, hoping they might capitalize from what many hoped was a successful offensive into Cambodia. Conditions there, however, offered little cause for celebration. According to one August report, widespread inflation had "pushed the cost of living up 53 per cent over the last year." MACV considered the economic woes "a serious threat to the stability of the government." Even before the assault into Cambodia, Secretary Laird believed the GVN was "not well prepared" to meet the increasingly political nature of the struggle inside South Vietnam.[101] Assessments throughout the summer of 1970 supported such claims. Tensions between President Thieu and Vice President Ky were rising. Corruption was common. One pre-incursion report even suggested Thieu "had a 50-50 chance of survival" if the Nixon administration adhered to its troop redeployment timetable. The Cambodian offensive may have been a boon for the ARVN, but it did very little to ameliorate the political ailments afflicting the Saigon regime.[102]

In large sense, these longer-term implications of the incursion were hardly considered, either by the White House or inside MACV headquarters. Abrams and his staff merely presumed attacking the sanctuaries would foster a more liberal political environment necessary for successful negotiations. Kissinger later believed the administration faced "essentially a tactical choice" of neutralizing the sanctuaries or allowing the NVA to overrun Indochina. But it seemed the repercussions for grand strategy mattered most. The allied incursion inadvertently helped strengthen the Khmer Rouge, intensifying an already ongoing civil war inside Cambodia, while the violent social upheaval did nothing to secure a stable border with South Vietnam.[103] Saigon appeared to one reporter "a city under siege." In the countryside, US commanders witnessed "serious social problems to overcome: inflation, taxation, government responsiveness, corruption, and urban stagnation." At the international level, Beijing rebuffed White House attempts at direct communications over anger with the Cambodian raid. If Kissinger saw tactical gains from the attack, the strategic consequences, few of them positive, were already making themselves felt in the summer of 1970.[104]

The domestic shoe fell long before American forces returned from their Cambodian excursion that June. Nixon's decision to widen the war only furthered the distrust between Washington, DC, and the American public. As waves of student protests swept over the nation—Nixon suggested university activists were "bums"—the dam broke on 4 May 1970. At a Kent State University rally,

Ohio National Guardsmen shot and killed four unarmed students, wounding nine others. Two of the dead, Sandra Scheuer and William Knox Schroeder, were simply walking between classes and not involved in the demonstrations.[105]

Within days, protestors forced colleges and university presidents across the nation to suspend classes. At Seton Hall in New Jersey, about 180 policemen from five different communities were required to restore order. In Buffalo, State University students turned into "an angry mob," taunting police with cries of "Shoot me, shoot me," and "Remember Kent State." At the University of Texas in Austin, a throng of 2,000 threw rocks at police and stopped traffic in the downtown business district. Clashes across the city forced New York City mayor John Lindsay to issue a statement cautioning, "Violence in opposition to violence is not only wrong. It also defeats the cause of peace."[106] Ten days later, police shot two students and wounded twelve others at Mississippi's Jackson State College. As the *Boston Globe* reported the first week of May, Nixon's decision to march into Cambodia seemed an error of "epic proportions."[107]

The violence and social unrest on the nation's college campuses, in fact, underscored the interlocking nature of the war in Southeast Asia and the turbulent American home front in the late 1960s and early 1970s. Public outcry and the closing of nearly 450 colleges nationwide in Kent State's wake affected the president greatly. According to the White House chief of staff, Nixon felt "very concerned about campus revolt and basically helpless to deal with it." It seemed no coincidence that major newspapers reported "Nixon Vows Quick Cambodia Pullout" only two days after the Ohio shootings.[108]

Along with new legislative challenges—in May, Senators Frank Church and John Sherman Cooper introduced a bill to restrict US military operations in Cambodia—the student protests demonstrated the costs of expanding the war in hopes of shortening it. Even former veterans, like Philip Caputo, wondered if Nixon was truly fulfilling his campaign promise of seeking peace with honor. As the marine-turned-journalist recalled, "Almost two years later, we were still in Vietnam. True, American troops were being withdrawn, 'Vietnamization'... was still in progress, but the bombs continued to fall, the body bags were still coming home, if in diminishing numbers, and the draft continued to pluck young men out of small towns, neighborhoods, and farms."[109]

This growing popular discontent with the war affected not only the White House but also the US military command in South Vietnam. In the aftermath of Kent State, the Pentagon stressed that MACV keep American casualties low during the Cambodian operation, "the most important" concern according to Melvin Laird. Discouraged officers turned their ire on "vocal dissenters in and out of government" who were raising "doubts in servicemen's minds regarding the real value of what they are doing." A misguided press and anemic politicians only added to the discord. "Morale was not helped by news" from the United

States, noted one MACV report. One year after Kent State, the mood inside Abrams's headquarters had only soured further. In late May 1971, an enraged Abrams screamed at his staff that US senators "must be having champagne parties and celebrations—I don't know, *parades* over the *disarray* and the lack of political strength that there is in our country." Such were alarming, even dangerous, words from the top American general in Vietnam.[110]

Abrams's diatribe, however, missed a fundamental point. In reality, the Cambodian campaign's positive impact on Vietnamization was fleeting. As early as 17 May, less than three weeks after the incursion began, the 1st Cavalry Division's commanding general admitted that "the enemy has recovered his balance." By August, MACV staff officers already were reporting that Hanoi had "the capacity to continue its present annual rate of infiltration, and even to increase it."[111] Two months later, anti-government forces had attacked Cambodia's three major highways in an effort to strangle Phnom Penh. At year's end, MACV conceded that while the South Vietnam armed forces "demonstrated increased effectiveness, it could not meet the overall enemy threat" without US assistance. Abrams, reviewing the "developing picture" inside Cambodia in December, acknowledged that it painted "a very sobering picture."[112]

Arguably, the incursion had its most lasting impression on the Cambodian home front, contributing to a civil war that ultimately led to a genocidal campaign waged by the Khmer Rouge revolutionary leader Pol Pot. Nixon's decision to expand the war into Cambodia appeared the embodiment of unintended (and horrific) consequences.

Yet the fighting held import for American domestic policy as well. The anarchy spreading across America's campuses convinced the president that faltering public support could no longer sustain either a draft army or, more generally, US policy in Southeast Asia. The war, in short, was squandering the domestic consent Nixon needed to govern. In early June, the *New York Times* reported "widespread doubt among the most experienced American observers in South Vietnam that current United States policies will bring lasting peace."[113]

Not only was the president to blame. Halfway through the Cambodian incursion an unnamed "high-ranking civilian official" leaked to the press his doubts over MACV's handling of the war. "Abe just doesn't understand Vietnamization." In full public view, military strategy and presidential policy now seemed entirely out of balance. The story indicated that senior US military officers in Saigon were missing an essential point of Nixon's Vietnamization plan—"that South Vietnamese troops must take over from the Americans not when they are ready, but *ready or not*. Otherwise, the South Vietnamese will never be ready."[114]

Such skepticism alluded to a growing rift between the Nixon White House and Abram's headquarters in Saigon. Upon reflection, the split now appears somewhat ironic. For years, the American military brass had been lobbying hard to expand the war outside of South Vietnam. They argued that slackening the political leash would allow them to crush the enemy where it mattered, defeat the primary communist threat, and turn over the war to a South Vietnamese army capable of dealing with an ancillary internal rebellion. Instead, the Cambodian operation surfaced long-standing problems that many observers now concluded as insoluble. The ARVN, in fact, wasn't ready to assume the war on its own. Deep-seated political turmoil still plagued the Saigon government. South Vietnam's population continued to question the GVN's legitimacy. Hanoi's leaders remained implacable. And the American public no longer saw rewards to be reaped from the enduring sacrifices asked by a government still seeking an elusive peace with honor.

A War Already Won?

Despite the fact that the Cambodian incursion hardly proved the turning point anticipated by Nixon, it would still be invoked in later "better war" narratives. Thus, according to Lewis Sorley, in late 1970, "the war was won. The fighting wasn't over, but the war was won." Such a fanciful assessment rests on little, if any, credible evidence. Certainly, contemporaries did not feel they had won the war. That spring, MACV analysts surmised that the "enemy still retains a viable military and political apparatus throughout the Republic."[115] Of course, the Cambodian offensive scarcely affected the revolutionary units inside South Vietnam. One late summer investigation found the National Liberation Front "far from defeated." A candid Robert Komer, with an eye ever on Vietnam, reported to Kissinger a host of unresolved issues, from poor leadership in the ARVN to a "critical gap" in winning the political war against "the still strong VC shadow government."[116]

Other reports equally indicated the conflict far from over. In Binh Dinh province, the Vietcong gained a much-needed respite with the December withdrawal of the US 173rd Airborne Brigade, leading to "the virtual collapse of the pacification effort" there. The North Vietnamese army's fighting capacity also remained intact, as apparently did its supply base. According to the US ambassador to Laos, one Laotian general undertook the gruesome practice of "cutting open the stomachs of NVA casualties to see if they had been eating well, and found them still to be well fed."[117] Abrams's staff confessed the enemy simply had diverted its resupply efforts through Laos and that "no new, more effective and less costly formula to solve this logistics interdiction equation has been found." On the diplomatic front, Hanoi's envoys only toughened their stance after Cambodia. Rather than trumpet victory, Nixon and Kissinger were on the verge of settling for a major concession, a cease-fire in place, leaving thousands of NVA troops inside South Vietnam at war's end.[118]

The "better war" narrative thus underscores the colossal impropriety of attempting to parse apart the military from the political in any war, especially one so intricate as in Vietnam. French generals had been equally unpersuasive with similar arguments during the Algerian War. In that conflict, senior officers conspired against the French government, even organizing a failed putsch to establish a military junta, because of political negotiations with the Algerian nationalist Front de Libération Nationale (FLN). These generals had long been arguing they were "just at the moment of reaching their goal" before politicians ignobly settled for negotiations with the enemy.

Their American counterparts (and "better war" advocates) made similar claims about their own war in Vietnam. As one senior general alarmingly wrote of his service between 1970 and 1972, "My conviction is that our reluctance to use our power effectively unnecessarily lengthened the war, and cost us far more in the long run. War is too practical a manner to be turned over to the intellectuals." Thus, in this officer's view, the "early enthusiasm" for the war "gave way to the despair of the liberal community" because politicians and academics had improperly forayed into matters best managed by military professionals.[119]

Those professionals, however, had not won the war in the summer of 1970. Publicly, Nixon lauded allied forces for their conduct in the Cambodian campaign, calling it "the most successful operation of this long and very difficult war." In the first week of June, the president declared that "all of our major military objectives have been achieved" in Cambodia.[120] Behind the scenes, however, old problems endured. Security in South Vietnam's two northernmost corps tactical zones was "still threatened." Both the Joint Chiefs and Abrams's headquarters warned that an accelerated rate of redeployments would "impose imprudent risks to Vietnamization and U.S. objectives in South Vietnam." To Kissinger, though, the "greatest remaining problem" was "to convince the South Vietnamese people that the Viet Cong are really beaten and cannot come back."[121]

Nguyen Van Thieu ranked high among those needing convincing. South Vietnam's president watched the redeploying American GIs with dismay, ever more circumspect about taking US advice as his most important ally's troop withdrawals accelerated. The unfolding Cambodian campaign also left Thieu conflicted. Before the offensive, the president claimed he was "too weak to cooperate in an accommodation with the Communists." After the ARVN's solid performance outside of South Vietnam's borders, however, Thieu reversed course, saying he was now too strong to compromise with the enemy.[122] Still, the pace of US withdrawals worried Thieu. Few knew better the integral relationships among economic stability, social progress, and security. The GVN's leadership might minimize the revolutionary movement's control of the countryside, but senior officials understood full well that communist cadres still held influence among the rural population. The Cambodian incursion may have given "the cocky new ARVN" a morale boost, but President Thieu surely appreciated the longer-term implications of losing the stanchions of American military support, even if only to deal with a "residual level of violence."[123]

But the violence persisted, at much higher levels than optimistic officials anticipated. In early July, the US 101st Airborne Division, operating near the edges of the A Shau Valley, faced a renewed threat from the North Vietnamese Army. Having spent the spring establishing fire support bases east of the valley to blunt an expected enemy offensive, the Screaming Eagles were forced onto the defensive as the NVA relentlessly attacked American and South Vietnamese positions. One firebase off the valley's northeastern end, Ripcord, took the brunt of the communists' blow. For twenty-three days, the American defenders withstood a barrage of mortar and recoilless rifle fire as casualties mounted on both sides. In what would be the last major battle between US ground forces and the North Vietnamese Army, the 101st division commander ordered Ripcord evacuated. As one MACV report noted, "The cost and effort required for the defense of the firebase placed in grave jeopardy the successful accomplishment of other operations in the enemy's rear logistics area." American troopers, however, simply felt like bait. As one infantry grunt complained, "Nobody had a clear perception of the big picture, but the one thing many people were angry about was that they didn't feel that we had gotten the support from higher-higher that we should have."[124]

It appears few of the key leaders fighting the Vietnam War in 1970—Abrams among them—believed they had the support necessary to achieve victory. Certainly, Nixon's first full year in office left his foreign policy team disappointed. Though the president entered office aspiring to end the war quickly, by mid-1970, he was still speaking of the "search for lasting peace in Southeast Asia." An intransigent Hanoi Politburo, a plodding GVN, a seemingly unpatriotic American home front. In Nixon's mind, all were conspiring against a suitable end to a war no one any longer wanted.[125]

In addition, his senior military commander in Vietnam proved incapable of balancing a complex political-military strategy aimed at achieving peace with honor for the United States. It was not for lack of trying. Abrams worked to the point of physical exhaustion, suffering from ulcers, high blood pressure, pneumonia, and, in July, gall bladder surgery. Later that summer, the "absolutely exhausted" general collapsed at an Australian army ceremony in Vung Tau. Friends and critics alike wondered if Abrams ever fully recovered as the war dragged on into 1971.[126]

In one sense, MACV's commander mirrored the larger army he led in Vietnam. With the war persisting—one observer thought the conflict had "acquired an insane life of its own"—yet the withdrawal of American troops continuing, the US armed forces in Vietnam increasingly displayed symptoms of a grave illness. It seemed the imbalances between grand and military strategy were pulling at threads threatening to unravel the very fabric of Abrams's command. Leaders watched in alarm as racial clashes, incidents of "fragging," and military police apprehensions for drug abuse all increased as more and more troops withdrew. As one MACV report quizzically stated, the morale problems "paradoxically resulted from the success of Vietnamization." For those soldiers questioning the long-term prospects of South Vietnam, and dissenting from American policy sending them far from home, the irony could be found elsewhere. Why continue fighting and risk dying for a war clearly ending but not yet won?[127]

5

A Beleaguered Army at a Long War's End

"I killed 8 people that day. I shot a couple of old men who were running away. I also shot some women and children. I would shoot them as they ran out of huts or tried to hide." So testified Varnado Simpson, a US Army infantryman from Mississippi, in late 1969. Simpson had served with Charlie Company, 1st Battalion, 20th Infantry Division, then operating in South Vietnam's Quang Ngai province.[1] In March 1968, with the Tet offensive battles still raging, Charlie Company assaulted a small hamlet in Son My village. Though in country for just over three months, Simpson's unit already had lost men from sniper fire, booby traps, and minefields. Morale was flagging. Moreover, the tired and frustrated Americans saw the South Vietnamese people as "part of the problem." As one recalled, "You couldn't pinpoint who exactly was the enemy ... We were trying to work with these people, they were basically doing a number on us ... You didn't trust them anymore. You didn't trust anybody."[2]

Such were soldiers' attitudes as Charlie Company began its assault on 16 March into the hamlet designated as My Lai 4 on their tactical maps. Anticipating heavy resistance from enemy main force units, the Americans found only civilians. The lack of opposition mattered little. Throughout the morning, Charlie Company devolved into a killing machine that left My Lai in ruins and some 400 to 500 civilians dead. The Americans raped and murdered their way through the hamlet, at times under orders, at others to satisfy personal urges based on fear, retribution, or a misplaced sense of masculinity. As one radio operator surveying the devastation recalled, "I know for a fact they didn't hate to do it."[3]

As the slaughtering waned near noon, the reports from Charlie Company's chain of command recounted a successful operation in which the Americans killed 128 Vietcong. Missing from the official record were the courageous actions of one helicopter pilot, Hugh Thompson, who landed between the Vietnamese civilians and their executioners to halt the killing. Allegations of criminal misconduct, however, soon began to spread, enough so that "Americal" Division leaders opened an informal investigation. Despite confirmation from South Vietnamese sources, the official probe languished until Ronald Ridenhour, a young soldier recently returned stateside, sent a letter in March 1969 to more than thirty officials in Washington, DC, outlining the My Lai massacre. Though in "disbelief," Army Chief of Staff William Westmoreland ordered an inspector general inquiry that ultimately would result in one of the most infamous military trials of the twentieth century.[4]

Yet for well over a year, the butchery at My Lai remained concealed from the American public. Only in September 1969 did President Nixon receive a memo-randum from the deputy secretary of defense summarizing the "atrocity" against "unarmed, unresisting Vietnamese civilians." Noting that an investigation would determine whether charges should be referred to a court-martial hearing, Deputy Secretary David Packard advised that "such a trial could prove acutely embarrassing to the United States." Packard, however, mistimed the public rela-tions fiasco as journalist Seymour Hersh broke the story in mid-November.[5]

Focusing his piece on a young lieutenant, William L. Calley Jr., Hersh reported that the "mild-mannered, boyish-looking Vietnam combat veteran" was being charged by the army for "deliberately" murdering more than 100 Vietnamese civilians. In the weeks following Hersh's scoop, US newspapers realized Packard's worst fears. *The Washington Post*'s Peter Braestrup won-dered if antiwar critics were right in contending that "the Army and its con-duct of the Vietnam war will also be on trial."[6] In *The Christian Science Monitor*, Richard Strout opined that the My Lai story would probably shorten "the free time that President Nixon has to extricate United States troops" from Vietnam. In early December 1969, *The Washington Post* ran Murrey Marder's story predicting "a 'setback' to U.S. strategy in the Vietnamese war," in part because the massacre had given "the Communist side its greatest propaganda windfall of the war."[7]

Yet the increasing focus on Lieutenant Calley also brought to light funda-mental questions about those young Americans fighting an unpopular war far from home. Was Calley a cold-hearted executioner or a victim in an unjust war? Did the ghastly actions at My Lai result from command policy, from the "mili-tary's obsession" with the "grisly yardstick" of body counts? Or was the cause the "futility and uselessness" of the war itself?[8] While some argued the conflict dehumanized American soldiers, others, including three recent West Point grad-uates, accused senior leaders of creating a command climate that resulted in a "total disregard of Vietnamese lives." One My Lai defendant even alleged that General Abrams had personally witnessed prisoner torture but did nothing to stop it. Conservative commentator William F. Buckley Jr., however, counseled against blaming the war for the corruption of America's youth. "The danger," he warned, "is closer to home than Vietnam."[9]

Whether My Lai resulted from command policies, the "moral vacuum" of the war in Vietnam, or, in Buckley's words, from an American society devoted to "irresponsibility . . . and to an indifference to authority and the law," the massacre's aftermath left more than just William Calley on trial. By early 1970, critics on all sides were condemning the US Army. As one mother of a My Lai participant lamented, "I gave them a good boy and they sent me back a murderer." Veterans pointed to the "decline in the quality of officers," even as the Veterans of Foreign Wars' national commander denounced trying a soldier "for performing his duty."[10] Sensing the growing popular sympathy for Calley, Nixon, always with an eye on the public mood, intervened while the lieutenant appealed his court martial. In April 1971, the president ordered Calley released from the stockade and placed under house arrest while awaiting a final verdict. By the time of his ultimate parole in 1974, the lieutenant had become both the epitome of all that was evil in an immoral war and a Christ-like figure wrongly crucified for the sins of others. Even executioners could be fashioned as champions within the competing narratives of Vietnam.[11]

The contentious debate over My Lai quickly became embedded into the larger struggle over how best to tell the story of America's final years in Southeast Asia. If young men were "turning into animals" in the jungles of Vietnam, what did that mean for the soul of the nation? Did not the killing of civilians and destruction of rural hamlets undermine the original purpose of the war itself, to save the South Vietnamese people from a corrupt and dangerous ideology?[12] And if the US Army indeed was coming apart in Vietnam, did that reality not risk losing the larger global contest against Soviet-inspired communism? Veterans Administration psychiatrists might blame the excess killings on "the heavy use of superstrong Vietnamese marijuana," but clearly such charges missed a larger point. American soldiers were not fighting a "better war," but rather turning on themselves—and, in instances like My Lai, the Vietnamese population—during the final years of a conflict that no longer made sense to many of them.[13]

Moreover, the society sending its young draftees to war increasingly questioned the core assumptions that led the United States into what critics now saw only as a deadly quagmire. Senior officers, perhaps unsurprisingly, blamed the "permissiveness" of a post–World War II American society whose youth were suspect of governmental authority and willing to dissent from policymakers' decisions. Surely, these dissidents were making their way into the military ranks. As one senior officer observed, "With an increasing segment of the nation opposed to our Vietnam policies, it would be unusual if similar views were not held by many of our junior members."[14]

Yet while antiwar activism perceptibly found a voice among those being drafted, tales of an army collapsing during the war's final years now appear overblown. Without question, episodes of indiscipline rose under Abrams's command as soldiers doubted the merits of the war they were waging. But if racial unrest, drug use, and sagging morale chipped away at the army's institutional underpinnings, most soldiers, as one correspondent found, still took "perverse pride in doing the job they profess to hate."[15]

A wave of protest activism undoubtedly pervaded the ranks of the armed forces during the era of withdrawal. The "permissive" culture at home, however, neither caused the excessive use of force in Vietnam nor the "crisis" in which the military command found itself.[16] Rather, the inability to balance the aims of winning a war while departing from it—while simultaneously aspiring to achieve some sense of peace with honor—left both an American society and its soldiers in doubt as to why they were fighting at all.

A Long War Comes Home

By late 1969, the war in Southeast Asia had become fully entwined with American society. In journalist Michael Herr's estimation, the jungles of Vietnam and the streets of San Francisco were now simply one "extreme of the same theater." While disapproving pundits condemned the president for paying more attention to public opinion at home than to Vietnamese realities abroad, Nixon's first year in office clearly demonstrated the interrelationships between the two. Any continuing commitment to Saigon hinged on domestic support. Just as the draft army was "embedded" in American culture, so, too, was the American war in Vietnam rooted in the outlook of US policymakers and the people they represented. For Saigon leaders surveying the political landscape in the United States as the 1960s drew to a close, such truths produced a great deal of anxiety. Nixon might profess his unity with South Vietnam, but the mass public demonstrations and moratoria to end the war foretold a different outcome.[17]

Of course, the government of South Vietnam (GVN) bore witness to a long history of dissent within the United States, which took its most visible initial form after the assassination of President Ngo Dinh Diem. The same year of Diem's 1963 coup and murder, the War Resister's League organized its first protest against the war. A loose coalition of liberal and radical pacifists joined other rallies across the country, some dissenting against American nuclear policy and interventionism overseas, others questioning whether the Vietnamese could truly maintain the right of self-determination given US interference in what seemed a local issue. Over the next two years, antiwar activists slowly organized at the regional and national levels.[18]

While the civil rights movement captured much of the nation's attention in 1963 and 1964, college campuses became a central locale for consolidating dissent against the growing involvement in Vietnam. (Many antiwarriors would learn useful tactics from the civil rights struggle.) By 1965, the University of Michigan was holding its first "teach in" where students, faculty, and local activists came together to focus attention "on this war, its consequences and ways to stop it." A similar teach-in at the University of California, Berkeley, in May brought together over 20,000 people, many of whom were now protesting the US bombing campaign over North Vietnam.[19] That October, the Students for a Democratic Society (SDS) issued its "opposition to the war," declaring it "immoral" and encouraging "every member of our generation to object." In November, the Committee for Nonviolent Action sponsored a rally at which five young men publicly burned their draft cards. Though the self-described pacifists were heckled by many in the gathering crowd—some shouting "Burn yourselves, not your cards!"—a broader antiwar movement was plainly starting to coalesce.[20]

Two years later, the Johnson administration confronted a national undertaking aimed at ending the United States' participation in Vietnam. In 1967, the Spring National Mobilization Committee to End the War in Vietnam sponsored rallies in April that drew mammoth crowds from New York to San Francisco.[21] That month, famed civil rights activist Martin Luther King Jr. linked the war in Vietnam to the failures of LBJ's Great Society at home. The Nobel Peace Prize recipient proclaimed "the war was doing far more than devastating the hopes of the poor at home. It was sending their sons and their brothers and their husbands to die in extraordinarily high proportions relative to the rest of the population." Worse, the Vietnamese were suffering under the weight of American bombs. "Somehow this madness must cease," King exclaimed. "We must stop now."[22]

Johnson, as would his successor, persevered against the wave of public opposition, employing terms like "prestige" and "credibility" to justify America's commitment to South Vietnam. But those words increasingly rang hollow. By October 1967, demonstrators were marching on the Pentagon during Stop the Draft Week in Washington, DC. Protestors carried signs emblazoned with "LBJ The Butcher" and "Westmoreland: Supreme General of Genocide."[23] One year later, violent demonstrations rocked the 1968 Democratic National Convention in Chicago as Mayor William Daley mobilized some 25,000 police. News outlets emphasized the blood-soaked streets of "nightstick city," suggesting the nation, still reeling from the assassinations of Martin Luther King Jr. and Robert F. Kennedy earlier in the year, was tearing itself apart. Investigative journalist I. F. Stone insisted the brutality cut both ways. "The war is destroying our country as we are destroying Vietnam."[24]

To those senior military officers surveying the home front from their headquarters in South Vietnam, the violent antiwar demonstrations appeared misinformed at best, blatantly unpatriotic at worst. It seemed as if deluded activists had turned the entire aim of the war on its head. One student, for example, declared his opposition "to the United States Government's immoral, illegal and geno-cidal war against the Vietnamese people in their struggle for self-determination." Yet to officers in Vietnam, their mission sought that very objective. Worse, they argued, protestors only encouraged Hanoi to endure. Even in the years follow-ing Tet, at least some senior military leaders failed to appreciate why so many of America's youth were protesting the war's moral ambiguity.[25]

In part, the answer lay in a military strategy unable to reconnect the broken bonds between fraying public opinion and governmental policy. Even before Tet, a lack of discernible progress—in pacification, in Saigon's political stabil-ity, in subduing North Vietnam's will to endure—left an American home front increasingly questioning the costs of war. Westmoreland long had worried about a political war of attrition taking its toll on the patience of the American people. As he recalled in 1970 while still the army's chief of staff, "I had some concern as to whether or not our governmental structure, our body politic, was adaptable to the stresses and strains of a long commitment."[26] Henry Kissinger agreed. With the antiwar movement becoming mainstream, and Hanoi's diplomats engaging "in a campaign of psychological warfare," the national security advisor shared Westmoreland's concerns over the growing reservations held by more and more Americans.[27]

For many observers still on the fence, Tet proved a breaking point in terms of extending their support for a conflict riddled with doubt and uncertainty. The enemy offensive, outwardly taking MACV by surprise, gave credence to pro-testors' accusations that their government was lying about the progress being made in Vietnam. Some of the nation's religious leaders already had decreed the war as "dirty and inhumane," objecting to the treatment of prisoners, the "indis-criminate killing of civilians," and the "inadequacy of attempts to alleviate civil-ian hardships."[28] Now political leaders joined the chorus of dissenters. In March 1968, Senator Robert F. Kennedy expressed his concern that, "at the end of it all, there will only be more Americans killed; more of our treasure spilled out; and because of the bitterness and hatred on every side of this war, more hundreds of thousands of Vietnamese slaughtered."[29]

Despite the hopes sparked by a new military commander in Vietnam, public opinion on the war continued to sour. Senior leaders on the Joint Chiefs of Staff lamented the inability of those on the home front, including the political leader-ship, to appreciate the allied gains under Abrams. But as was too often the case, the military brass took a myopic view of the conflict inside Vietnam. They had difficulty acknowledging that Abrams's "better war" simply could not persuade the American people that a costly limited war still was one worth fighting.[30] As Kissinger's predecessor, Walt Rostow, saw it in late 1968, fewer at home saw any justification for the president's "unwillingness to agree to a cease-fire in place and our opposition to a coalition" government in South Vietnam. Over the next four years, little that Creighton Abrams achieved in theater did much to alter those views. In reality, public dissent only increased throughout the new MACV commander's tenure.[31]

The burgeoning antiwar movement's impact on military strategy and political decision-making remains a contested topic to this day. Yet there seems little doubt that those prosecuting the war in Vietnam felt constrained by home front dissidence. Abrams believed antiwar protests exerted "pressures on our own government" and increased "free world opposition." Wheeler's successor at the Joint Chiefs, Admiral Thomas Moorer, concurred. "The reaction of the noisy radical groups was considered all the time," the new chairman later noted. "And it served to inhibit and restrict the decision makers."[32] Other officers saw few partitions between the actions of stateside dissenters and those soldiers within their ranks who increasingly challenged the rationale for continued fighting and the discipline required to do so. As one army colonel recalled, "Dissent and dissenters inside America itself did much to discredit the war by spreading doubt and sowing despair."[33]

While dissidents surely did not stop the war on their own, it is plausible to argue they helped make stopping it more popular than continuing it. Without question, those in Nixon's "silent majority" persisted in supporting a foreign policy aimed at containing global communism. And the violence prosecuted by extremist groups like the Weather Underground surely provoked a backlash from many Americans alarmed by manifestos calling for an armed revolution at home. One army general, for instance, damned these "self-righteous . . . nihilists" who were determined to "destroy all of our existing moral standards." In the process, critics viewed mass demonstrations as self-defeating, in columnist James Reston's words, "not promoting peace but postponing it."[34]

Yet the antiwar movement also forced both the Johnson and the Nixon administrations to contemplate restraining the use of military force overseas. LBJ's decision to halt the bombing of North Vietnam and Nixon's check on the scope of the Cambodian incursion were informed by the prospects of domestic dissent. Though Abrams still prosecuted a violent campaign inside South Vietnam, in all likelihood, the antiwar movement helped reduce the extent of carnage triggered by the American war machine. At no time during Nixon's presidency did Abrams have a free hand in employing military force to its fullest extent. While officers maintained such restrictions prolonged the war, the political limitations established boundaries that, in fact, curbed the extent of killing. The incursion into Cambodia, as one example, lucidly revealed the consequences of expanding a war when not much thought was given to corollary outcomes.

The peace movement at home also could be seen as part of a larger global antiwar crusade. By the mid-1960s, international protests, often led by university students, increasingly challenged governments from Czechoslovakia to

Poland to Germany and France. This public opposition hardly limited itself to the Western world, rather comprising a "global disruption" that seemed only to further isolate policymakers in Washington, DC. Foreign policy consensus seemed to be slipping away.[35] While antiwar activists placed their opposition within a larger construct of transnational social justice, policy elite tended to view these resistance movements as linked to some nefarious, leftist global conspiracy. But if antiwar activity retained distinctive national qualities, the demonstrators' authenticity conformed across international borders. As Britain's daily national newspaper *The Guardian* found in late 1968, "the sincerity" of the antiwar protest was "real," even if the "shouts of 'Ho, Ho, Ho Chi Minh' echo without meaning."[36]

Though many protestors saw themselves as part of a larger global phenomenon, public awareness of the Vietnam War within the United States remained most sensitive to American casualties. Without question, the antiwar movement highlighted the devastation of the Vietnamese populations, both south and north. Activists traveled to North Vietnam, calling attention to the ravaging US bombing campaign. They charged that the United States was not winning in South Vietnam, only destroying a pre-industrial society that hardly threatened America's core interests. Critics argued the nation "must adopt as its working position that the lives of Vietnamese civilians are just as valuable as American lives."[37] But, as was the case in so many of America's wars, the public and its media more often than not focused on US dead and wounded. In losing the 1972 election to Nixon, a glum George McGovern conceded that his antiwar message no longer held resonance, in part, because of the Vietnamization program. "When the corpses changed colors," the South Dakota senator grumbled, "American interest diminished."[38]

If Americans were less attentive to the deaths of Southeast Asians, they were still fascinated by the "demo" culture at the center of the antiwar movement. Patriotic citizens might decry protestors' wanting allegiance while military officers denounced media outlets for the "undue attention paid to demonstrators," but youths flocked to the "hippie" counterculture expressed by those opposing the war. Musicians like Joan Baez and Bob Dylan, "yippies" like Abbie Hoffman and Jerry Rubin, and social critics like Timothy Leary all gained national attention by questioning the obvious hypocrisies in modern-day America.[39] It seemed not to matter that working-class families, whose attitudes the media dutifully covered, found the counterculture repulsive, unpatriotic, and fraying the bonds of national unity. Antiwar demonstrators were attractive. For many young Americans maturing into adulthood during the mid- to late 1960s, the war in Vietnam exposed the venality and hubris of a US foreign policy elite who seemingly cared little for the plight of the everyday citizen, not to mention that of the rural farmer in Vietnam.[40]

Of course, college students, the main foot soldiers of the antiwar movement, possessed both the time and the means to protest their government. These "casualties of our affluence," as Kissinger derisively called them, "had the leisure for self-pity, and the education enabling them to focus it in a fashionable critique of the 'system.'" But such aspersions undervalued the message of the antiwar crusade. Kissinger, Nixon, and the demonstrators all wanted the same thing—an end to the war in Vietnam.[41]

True, some protestors may have preferred that the war end in failure for the United States. And many of the movement's messengers, like those flocking to the Woodstock music festival in August 1969, often eclipsed the goal itself. Thus, the president could take aim at the "hippie college-types" and "peaceniks" while losing sight they were all working toward the same end. Certainly, Nixon accused the demonstrators of not seeing "anything wrong with abandoning the South Vietnamese people in order to end the war immediately." Such claims, though, undervalued the counterargument that continuing the war only furthered the suffering of the South Vietnamese while doing little to further American interests either at home or abroad. Moreover, as the antiwar movement expanded to returning Vietnam veterans, the working class found a growing voice in the larger protest society.[42]

By 1971, however, that protest society had peaked in terms of its support and its potential to influence US policy in Southeast Asia. Activist leaders, long frustrated by their inability to stop the war, turned to other pursuits. Perhaps a coalition that included so many competing voices—the clergy, civil rights leaders, students, veterans against the war, radical pacifists, and liberal-minded politicians—simply could not remain unified forever.[43] Or perhaps Nixon and Laird's policy of Vietnamizing the war, paired with revamping the nation's draft policies, took the wind out of many activists' sails. Even if two-thirds of polled Americans still considered the war in Vietnam a mistake in January 1971, the antiwar movement clearly had run its course. As *New York Times* correspondent Anthony Lewis reported that same month, "Vietnam does not dominate our consciousness as it did." To Lewis, even with "no real end" in sight, "the lower casualties and gradual American withdrawal" meant the war in Vietnam mattered less and less to most Americans.[44]

As the media gradually turned to other global matters in the early 1970s, the antiwar movement left behind a mixed legacy. It seems doubtful the mass demonstrations actually prolonged the war or alone proved to Hanoi's leaders they could outlast the United States in a protracted conflict. Yet the movement surely helped compel Nixon to disengage from Vietnam at a pace faster than his military commanders, and national security advisor, would have liked. If protestors did not alter the overriding objective in Southeast Asia, they did force changes to the ways in which Nixon's administration sought to achieve those aims.

Additionally, the "mindless rioters and professional malcontents" played on the president's worst character traits, fanning a paranoia that led to a domestic policy intent on silencing critics and restoring law and order to American streets.[45]

But perhaps most importantly for *how* the United States withdrew from Vietnam in the late 1960s and early 1970s, the antiwar movement helped change the relationship between American society and its draftee army. As the "demo" culture gained social credence in towns and cities across the nation, conscripted soldiers entering the ranks brought with them a new political consciousness, one that professional military officers deemed incompatible with the discipline needed for an army fighting a war against a stubborn enemy.[46]

Recruiting for an Unpopular War

Entering office in early 1969, Richard Nixon inherited a draft system long denounced as both inefficient and inequitable. Congress had passed legislation outlining the conscription of young American men for World War II in 1940. After the war, during which 10 million were inducted for service, the draft expired briefly before resuming in 1948, in part due to pleas for persistent military readiness during the burgeoning Cold War. Low draft calls after the Korean conflict meant few men were inducted, but conscription spiked in mid-1965 when President Johnson approved the deployment of US ground forces to South Vietnam. LBJ's decision not to mobilize the reserves—he deemed the political costs too high for a "limited" war like Vietnam—added further pressures to draft enough qualified men to fight in Southeast Asia while still maintaining the United States' global responsibilities. Yet deferments, often determined by white, middle-aged local draft board members, opened up the administration for criticism. The armed forces, it appeared, were preying on the less educated, poorer, and colored segments of American society.[47]

If Vietnam-era draft policies had their roots in the Korean conflict and the Cold War, so, too, did the decision to limit soldiers' combat tours to twelve months. Westmoreland opted to follow the precedent of the one-year tour established in Korea, believing it not only outweighed the alternative of rotating entire units but also helped maintain morale for what would likely be a long war. One senior officer, writing in mid-1969, agreed, arguing the individual soldier now had "a goal to which he can look forward."[48] Others, however, were less enthusiastic. Critics argued the one-year tour created "turbulence," so much so that units fluctuated between "order and chaos." A high rotation of soldiers undermined attempts at creating an institutional memory. Inexperienced leaders thus seemed to be the norm, every year learning similar lessons of those who came before them. Moreover, South Vietnamese army commanders ended the war having worked with some twenty to thirty US advisors. As one ARVN general recalled, "Every change of advisor disturbed the atmosphere of the unit."[49]

While military leaders did their best to compensate for the revolving door through which soldiers entered and departed their ranks, the draft and personnel rotation system illustrated the ways military strategy remained beholden to political decisions. Johnson's verdict not to call up the reserves meant both it and the National Guard became havens for those hoping to avoid service in Vietnam. In 1968, some 100,000 young men were on waiting lists for the National Guard alone.[50] Applications from sons in middle- and upper-class families tended to receive preferential treatment, making it politically risky for Johnson and Nixon to mobilize the nation's reserve forces. Additionally, at no time in the war did the percentage of African Americans in the Guard top 2 percent. In Mississippi, for example, only one black soldier was serving in the ranks of the more than 10,000 stateside guardsmen in 1969. The Dallas Cowboys football squad, in comparison, had ten players on the National Guard's rolls.[51]

Allegations of class warfare were soon in coming. If family affluence did not necessarily guarantee a draft deferral, enrolling in higher education, often inaccessible to those with low incomes, certainly did matter within the selective service system. Thus, those young men with the means (and apparent potential) to attend college were afforded opportunities unavailable to poorer Americans. While official conscription policies hardly intended to create divisions based

Figure 10 SWEATY BUSINESS. A weary soldier from the 9th Infantry Division exemplifies the hard fighting that endured during America's final years in Vietnam, 29 March 1969. (RG282S, Box 1, Kerwin Collection, MHI)

on class, perceptions of discrimination beleaguered local draft boards.[52] A sense of arrogance from those avoiding service did little to alleviate such concerns. As one Rhodes scholar callously observed, "There are certain people who can do more good in a lifetime in politics or academics or medicine than by getting killed in a trench." This contempt for lower-class "proles" only enflamed the grievances of working-class families who deemed, rightly or not, that they alone were bearing the burdens of an ugly war while Ivy Leaguers stayed safely at home to profit from the sacrifices of others.[53]

If more affluent communities suffered only marginally lower casualty rates in Vietnam than poorer American neighborhoods, what mattered more was the widespread impression of favoritism. With few means and thus often little inclination to avoid the draft, working-class sons believed they were shouldering the war effort. In the process, many of them felt increasingly isolated from the nation sending them off to Vietnam. Yet to view the conflict in such stark terms of class warfare tends to obscure the nuances of antiwar sentiments, even dissent, that were seeping into lower-income families during the late 1960s and early 1970s. A growing political consciousness, not just among college students, ensured that working-class enlistees often brought personal doubts of the war with them into the military's ranks. Far from a selective service system and antiwar movement pitting "hardhats" against "hippies," the ongoing draft for a stalemated war left many, if not most, families questioning the price of sending Uncle Sam their sons to fight in Vietnam.[54]

Of course, antiwar activists, aiming to promote their message within lower-income communities, tended to accentuate the evils of the impoverished fighting a rich man's war. Critics like Martin Luther King Jr. purposefully linked the plight of poor black families to the predatory nature of selective service. One antiwar poster, appealing directly to African Americans, broadcast a powerful slogan: "The only time we're in the front is when it's time to die."[55] If such race- and class-based arguments against the war relied more on an emotional appeal than on hard statistical analysis, they still seemed to have merit. When President Nixon declared in September 1969 a 50,000-man cut in draft calls, he acknowledged—with "unusual candor" according to the New York Times—that he was "simply buying time" to curb domestic dissent. To one news magazine, the president's new policy sought to "make the war less repugnant to critics at home." As the war endured, though, that repugnance was shared by more and more families across the socioeconomic spectrum of American society.[56]

Thus, by 1969, the antiwar movement gaining national attention at home seemed to be inexorably seeping into the armed forces with every new recruit. Even as troops started to withdraw from Vietnam, soldiers increasingly questioned the larger assumptions on the need for a continuing American presence in Southeast Asia. If South Vietnam fell, would US national security truly suffer?

Why, some asked, should I risk death if every "sign was that eventually there was going to be a peace agreement"?[57]

Media outlets soon began reporting on troubling signs within the military ranks. At Fort Belvoir, Virginia—an army post located on the outskirts of the nation's capital—GIs started an underground antiwar newspaper. In August, the *New York Times* ran a story under the byline "A Whiff of Mutiny in Vietnam." The following month *Newsweek* reported on a US infantry company in which soldiers refused orders to recover a downed helicopter in an area "honeycombed with enemy bunkers." The news journal painted a dire picture indeed. "As in no other modern U.S. war, there is a malaise among the troops in Vietnam. Hatred for the war runs deep, especially among the younger draftees."[58]

If such pronouncements exaggerated the impotence of Abrams's command, discontent among many soldiers still ran high, enough to make an impact on field operations. Even the Hanoi-based *Vietnam Courier* reported on GI resistance, citing fifteen examples of American soldiers defying orders in the first five months of 1969. By 1970, US commanders found themselves negotiating with their units, running "carrot-and-stick" operations and "combat consultations" to entice their men forward.[59] Yet the refusals continued. In May, soldiers manning Fire Base Washington rebuffed their leaders' orders to strike into Cambodia. As one private argued, "We have no business here. We have enough troubles in Vietnam." If acts of indiscipline proved outside the norm during the war's final years—most front-line units still performed competently—they nevertheless prompted officers to reconsider senior-subordinate relationships on which military command rested. As one company commander quipped in late 1970, "I've got 100 guys out here and 98 want to go home and two need psychiatric treatment."[60]

A *LIFE Magazine* special that year further detailed the challenges young officers faced in the field. "You Can't Just Hand Out Orders" related the story of Captain Brian Utermahlen, a West Point graduate commanding an infantry company in the 1st Cavalry Division near the Cambodian border. Utermahlen's longish hair, stubbly chin, and bedraggled uniform seemed at odds with the ideals of proper military discipline. The captain spoke honestly of his frustrations balancing the mission with the welfare of his unit, of soldiers not wanting to make contact with the enemy, and of his initial fears of being "fragged" by his own men. Yet Utermahlen clearly had won the respect of those men. He avoided unnecessary risks and cared less about his soldiers' appearance then how they performed their duties. A concerned Westmoreland, however, read the *LIFE* article and expressed worry over the captain's disheveled look and his soldiers' questioning of orders. Luckily for Utermahlen, a senior officer who knew the captain defended him to the army's chief of staff. Despite the verbal exchanges with his men, "there is never any doubt in anyone's mind as to who commands the company." Looks aside, "the discipline within the unit was strengthened" by the captain's relationship with his soldiers, by Utermahlen's willingness "to listen and to argue over tactics with his men."[61]

Westmoreland's concerns, shared by Abrams and his senior staff, were understandable given continued, and highly publicized, reports of indiscipline within MACV. In March 1971, fifty-three soldiers operating near Khe Sanh refused orders sending them into combat. Citing an "error in tactics," the brigade commander, Brigadier General John G. Hill, decided against disciplinary action. That same month, North Vietnamese regulars overran Firebase Mary Ann in Quang Tin province, killing thirty Americans and wounding eighty-two others. A MACV investigation found several factors contributing to the debacle: "attitudes of personnel involved; failure to follow established doctrine for defense; and lack of effective functioning of command within the brigade."[62] Then in September, soldiers at Firebase Pace, providing artillery support along South Vietnam's border, objected to being sent on a reconnaissance patrol. A signed letter from sixty-six soldiers soon followed, asking Senator Edward M. Kennedy to bring his "full weight of influence in the Senate . . . to enlighten public opinion on the fact that we ground troops still exist." Taped conversations from the defiant GIs included complaints that "they felt 'like meat' on an overexposed point with overwhelming North Vietnamese forces confronting them."[63]

Such acts of disobedience, even if sporadic, seemed inescapable as the American drawdown continued. Young leaders did their best to keep their soldiers motivated, to "give them a reason for risking their lives and for suffering the elements." Yet by 1970, they were fighting a steep uphill battle. Volney F. Warner, commanding a brigade in the 4th Infantry Division, found it tough to maintain a "keen combat edge" with the war winding down. "Problems associated with conflicting political goals and accompanying troop withdrawals," the colonel admitted, "make mission accomplishment most difficult."[64] Leaders in Abrams's headquarters might blame the "erosion of national will at home" for soldiers' flagging discipline, but clearly more was at play. Perhaps most importantly, those US troops still in Vietnam could no longer reconcile their personal sacrifices for a military strategy that, at best, ended in a negotiated settlement. Why, many soldiers asked, were they being asked to risk their well-being for a war no longer deemed essential for American security at home or abroad?[65]

While Abrams's "one war" articulation of strategy might have made sense for contemporary military commanders and later historians, soldiers on the ground could not resolve the fundamental inconsistencies with the application of that strategy. Leaders, quite simply, could not convince the troops their sacrifices were worth the attainment of some nebulous political goal. As one officer recalled, the "men were deeply affected by the lack of meaning of it all, given the risks they were called on to accept."[66] Another serving with the 173rd Airborne

Brigade concurred. "There is just not this spirit of going out and 'Making the World Safe for Democracy' or making the world safe for anything. It's just a floundering around through the same bushes, through the same towns, and they don't understand." Unit cohesion in the war's final years thus mostly rested on transactional relationships focused on maintaining personal safety and the care of comrades than on achieving MACV's strategic aims.[67]

Despite claims from on high that he was fighting a "better war" under Abrams, the average combat soldier found little to celebrate. The war had become, in one journalist's view, "a desultory struggle, punctuated by occasional explosions and tragedy, for the last Americans in combat in Vietnam."[68] For their leaders, there seemed few incentives to motivate men hoping to avoid an anonymous death in a fading war. Moreover, at least some young lieutenants and captains worried about the leverage they retained over GIs who already felt a sense of hopelessness. As one enlisted draftee observed, "You couldn't drop out in Nam, you were already dropped, and no matter what you dropped, you were already on the bottom."[69]

Army leaders, however, continued to fix blame for the disorder within their ranks on an unsympathetic, if not hostile, American home front. It appeared as if senior officers' love of service clouded any sense of empathy for their soldiers' contempt of the war. The decline in morale stupefied them. Many surely agreed with the May 1971 assessment of AP photographer, and former paratrooper, Rick Merron: "I just can't believe it. It's like we're drafting kids from a totally different country."[70]

In their search for answers, officers lashed out against a "hostile press" and the "lack of support for the war at home." Studies on drug use in theater highlighted that over 50 percent of soldiers had "used marijuana or drugs before coming to Vietnam." Even Abrams condemned a "certain amount of laxity" among his soldiers, due in part to rising domestic dissent. Such arguments would help establish an early foundation for the "better war" narrative in which the American armed forces had achieved outright success only to be forsaken by a faithless home front. The experiences of the US Army in Vietnam, though, told quite a different story.[71]

The Fall of an American Army?

On 29 March 1971, a court-martial jury at Fort Benning, Georgia, found Lieutenant William L. Calley Jr. guilty of murdering at least twenty-two Vietnamese civilians in My Lai hamlet back in March 1968. The life sentence of confinement to hard labor, fresh off the heels of a botched ARVN incursion into Laos, left President Nixon facing "still another Vietnam-related controversy."

Supporters of Calley tended to blame the war itself for turning young American boys into animals. One motel clerk just outside Fort Benning felt Calley deserved a medal. "They ought to give 'em all medals, God bless' em." Others, likening the proceedings to the post-World War II Nuremberg war crime trials, believed the US government was "picking on only the little fellows, as though looking for scapegoats." Why was Lyndon Johnson not on trial for deciding to go to war in Vietnam? Why not Richard Nixon for continuing it? Even those critics who thought Calley a war criminal, blindly following illegal orders, recognized the lieutenant had become a symbol of the larger war.[72]

That symbol depended largely on how one viewed the ongoing conflict. Calley was either a murdering scoundrel in a plainly immoral war or a loyal martyr defending the interests of freedom in an ugly yet necessary struggle against communism. The court-martial findings did little to quiet the debate. In fact, the My Lai proceedings appeared to put the entire nation on trial. Captain Ernest Medina, the company commander overseeing the assault on Son My, argued that "all Americans must share in the guilt of Lieutenant Calley." Peace advocate Jeremy Rifkin went further. "Individual soldiers should not be made scapegoats for Defense Department policy," Rifkin implored, because the My Lai massacre "was not an isolated incident."[73]

Claims that American soldiers engaged in savage acts as a consequence of official policy clearly put the Nixon administration, and MACV headquarters, on the defensive. Yet throughout the spring of 1970, with the massacre now exposed and allied forces driving into Cambodia, Abrams seemed most concerned with how public condemnation over My Lai was affecting troop morale. New recruits, according to MACV's commander, were more conscious of and curious about "war crimes." This left the individual soldier "more prone to question leader wisdom and judgment." And because the media was reporting the war "out of context," to Abrams there existed "some apprehension among officers that they may be unfairly blamed for operational incidents. This has resulted in lessened aggressiveness, particularly in aviation units." While the general reviewed MACV rules of engagement after the My Lai story broke, the attitude equating a massacre to an "operational incident" hardly convinced antiwar critics, or the Saigon government, that the US military was serious about limiting noncombatant casualties on a still violent battlefield.[74]

Even so, Abrams's trepidations over discord in the ranks seemed well placed. My Lai, according to one report, had "left deep scars within the military."[75] Yet if newly arrived soldiers to South Vietnam expressed reluctance in following orders because of the highly publicized murders, such misgivings paled in comparison to the unrest fueled by growing racial discord at home.

As antiwar critics condemned the Vietnam War for dehumanizing young American boys overseas, many African Americans witnessed a similar phenomenon in the United States. Despite recent gains in the civil rights movement, black communities still experienced widespread racism, all while watching family members drafted into a war that barely mattered to their own struggles for domestic advancement. Young blacks saw military service not as an opportunity but as more of a burden. Stokely Carmichael, chairman of the Student Nonviolent Coordinating Committee, contested arguments that the army provided youths in the ghetto or the rural South with a chance at upward mobility and a decent living. Speaking on NBC's *Meet the Press* in 1966, Carmichael questioned claims "saying to [the] black man that his only chance for a decent life is to become a hired killer because that's his sole function in the Army."[76]

More and more, politically conscious African American draftees ostensibly fighting for democracy abroad, but seeing little equality at home, doubted US policy in Southeast Asia. Many, like Lionel Anderson, felt "used," waging war on "oppressed people in Vietnam" while being "oppressed here in the States, discriminated against as individuals." Moreover, the military's attempts at turning diverse citizens into a uniform fighting force could only achieve so much. Private Allen E. Jones testified to these limitations in institutional standardization: "They say I am just a Marine, but how can I forget eighteen years of being black and all that being black means in this country?"[77]

Martin Luther King Jr.'s public stance against the war, and the dissolution of his message advocating peaceful protest after his death, only heightened African American resistance to the war in Vietnam. King's assassination seemed a tipping point. One returning veteran, watching the subsequent rioting and fires engulf Washington, DC, found an eerie scene in the nation's capital. "I left the battlefield in Vietnam. And now I find that my country is part of that battlefield."[78] Worse, leaders in the Black Panther movement, like Eldridge Cleaver, were now publicly advocating that African American veterans come home and use their military skills "to help us take our freedom and stop these racist pigs from committing genocide upon us, as they have been doing for the past 400 years."[79] King's message of peace apparently had its limits too.

This rise of black militancy clearly worried senior army officials. The "pervasive" racial unrest, they felt, was seeping through the porous boundaries between American society and the Vietnamese war. One lieutenant colonel, writing in *Military Review* in 1970, believed the "young black militant . . . brings into the Army an inbred distrust and dislike for the so-called 'white establishment'. . . and believes that racial equality can only be obtained by punishing those who commit discriminatory acts against any of his 'soul brothers.' "[80] Even Abrams worried, in less than artful language, "the racial unrest now exhibiting itself in our country could in some way infect our own men." That at least some military commanders viewed black activism as a contagion surely did little to promote racial harmony within the ranks.[81]

African American political action, however, seemed only to increase as the war in Vietnam drew down. In fact, even before Tet, black resistance to the war had gained a powerful voice other than King's when Muhammed Ali refused induction into the armed forces in April 1967. "I got no quarrel with them Vietcong," the boxing champion declared. Quickly stripped of his license, Ali received a five-year prison sentence and a $10,000 fine.[82] But his message resonated with black soldiers in Vietnam. One, Robert Sanders, recalled the incongruities of fighting for a country that did not fully embrace them. "We felt the American Dream didn't really serve us. What we experienced was the American Nightmare. . . . We felt that they put us in the front lines abroad and in the back lines at home."[83]

By mid-1969, the Black Power movement had become an integral part of the US military experience in Vietnam. African American soldiers increasingly questioned what they saw as discriminatory promotion policies, formed solidarity factions like the Black Liberation Front of the Armed Forces, and saluted each other with "the upraised clenched fist of Black Power."[84] They disputed Confederate flags hanging from barracks and joined discussion groups on the problems of race in America. Their activism not only gained national attention but also engendered fears of a coming race war at home. Media outlets warily reported on the possibility of young black soldiers, with "elaborate training in guerrilla warfare," returning home to become the "black urban commando[s] of the future."[85]

Without question, racial friction was less prevalent in combat outfits, where survival depended in large part on unit cohesion. Yet there also were more practical explanations for why rearward support bases experienced more racial tension than those troops on the front lines. As one black soldier in the 9th Infantry Division put it, "You know, when I am out in the bush carrying a grenade launcher, no white man is going to call me a nigger."[86]

Senior leaders did their best to address these racial tensions despite some officers' beliefs that "there's only one color here, and that's olive drab." Westmoreland ordered a mandatory race relations course for the Continental Army Command, while Abrams emphasized how race relations in the United States were part of the larger war effort.[87] Yet the Chicano Moratorium Against the War in Vietnam, held in East Los Angeles as the summer of 1970 drew to a close, suggested that not only African Americans felt disassociated from the society sending them off to Southeast Asia. Nor did rioting aboard the USS *Constellation* and *Kitty Hawk* in late 1972 indicate that racial unrest was confined to the ranks of the US Army.[88] If Nixon intended to withdraw from Vietnam as a matter of policy, demonstrating the strength of American democracy abroad, minority activists at home and overseas surely cast doubt on achieving such lofty ambitions.

So, too, did the steady stream of reports from Vietnam depicting Abrams's command as an organization riddled with drug problems. Press accounts told how drugs, "used by a majority of young soldiers in Vietnam" were "reducing the Army's effectiveness." One 1970 account spoke of "confused young men in combat turning to marijuana in sheer desperation."[89] That year, the Pentagon created a special task force to investigate the "alarming increase" of narcotics being used by troubled GIs. At year's end, MACV promulgated a directive creating Drug Abuse Suppression Councils down to the battalion level. The command also established education and rehabilitation programs, conducted search operations to "locate and destroy marijuana plants," and tightened customs security to reduce the flow of drugs coming into and leaving Vietnam.[90]

The media's conception of a troubled army, however, exaggerated the depths of MACV's drug problems. Without question, soldiers self-medicated to deal with the horrors of war. As one recalled, "We never smoked grass in combat but I do not think I could have made it without cracking if I had not used it in between patrols."[91] Others experimented with easily accessible opioids like heroin or smoked marijuana to rebel against the military establishment into which they were drafted. Many, perhaps most, relied instead on alcohol, a more socially acceptable form of drug within the military ranks. In fact, one Department of Defense study found that 88 percent of soldiers reported drinking while in Vietnam, often in "prodigious amounts."[92]

Such statistics, though, did not capture the nuances of drug use in Vietnam. One senior officer rightly noted that "young soldiers police themselves where they perceive themselves to be in danger, such as on patrol or on fire bases at which contact with the enemy is imminent." In general, drug abuse remained confined to rear areas where mistakes made by soldiers under the influence were less likely to be fatal. Moreover, while not solving the abuse problem, Abrams's decision to include education and rehabilitation into MACV's drug prevention program, along with mandatory urinalysis testing, made at least some inroads into limiting the effects of soldier misconduct.[93]

Still, Abrams had his hands full curtailing bad behavior among the withdrawing army's ranks. Few incidents better revealed the deep-seated frustrations carried by some soldiers than a phenomenon new to the military lexicon—fragging. The assassination of officers and senior NCOs by fragmentation grenades— "Grenades leave no fingerprints," recalled one helicopter pilot—added a further burden to young leaders carrying out Abrams's strategy in the war's final years. In 1970 alone, the army reported 271 fragging incidents resulting in 34 deaths.[94] One journalist called fragging a "macabre ritual" that had "ballooned into intra-Army guerrilla warfare." The practice sent a strong message to those leaders insensitive to their subordinates' dissatisfaction with the war. Perceived "ticket punchers," along with those officers intent on engaging in "crazy John Wayne tactics," were particularly targeted by disgruntled troops.[95]

As with drug use, though, fragging occurred more frequently in rear areas than on the front lines. Among the sprawling American bases sustaining the allied war effort, the material comforts often masked the frustrations held by many draftees who saw no purpose in their year-long deployment overseas. A visiting congressional panel found "the soldier in Vietnam has little or no way of dealing with his frustration in any constructive manner."[96] Resentment toward military life thus too often found deadly outlets. One private first class fragged his lieutenant for demanding the soldier have his hair cut. Another attempt on an NCO's life concerned the disbursement of cigarettes from sundry packs. Such incidents— one observer called the prevalence of fraggings a "grisly game of psychological warfare"—cast a pall over the senior-subordinate relationships so instrumental to military discipline.[97] The army, in short, appeared to be turning against itself.

Veteran soldiers accordingly believed fraggings were a product of the "new army." As one old-timer recounted, "The war between the men and the lifers, career soldiers, is more intense today than I've ever seen it." As with so many of the army's troubles, senior military leaders blamed society for draftees' contemptuous behavior. Abrams, indicative of his peers, believed acts of insubordination were akin to MACV's racial and drug problems "in that the men don't learn it here, they bring it with them."[98] As the war progressed, older officers, according to Newsweek, felt "increasingly alienated from the draftees of the Woodstock generation who thumb their noses at Army tradition." Morale sagged. One veteran officer serving at West Point in late 1970 lamented the public's indifference to those sacrificing for national security. The embittered lieutenant colonel simply could not understand those who laughed at the military academy's motto "Duty, Honor, Country." As he ruefully said, "Show me something better to live by."[99]

West Point's aspirational watchwords, however, offered little encouragement for young draftees questioning the motivation behind US foreign policy. Charles Strong, a machine gunner in the Americal Division, came from a migrant family background in South Carolina and hoped the war would pass him by. When it didn't, he saw nothing to convince him his service mattered. "The war in Vietnam," Strong recalled, "didn't do nothing but get a whole lot of guys fucked up for some money."[100]

This inability of professional officers and NCOs to motivate conscripts into embracing the larger aims of South Vietnamese independence suggested that by 1970 there essentially were two separate American armies now fighting in Vietnam. One, made up of reluctant draftees, fought simply to survive. "I think it's a disaster for the war to go on," said a veteran from Pennsylvania. Even short-term volunteers, like Tobias Wolff, thought the "war was something I had to get through." Career professionals filled the ranks of the other army. Committed to avoiding defeat, to maintaining their honor in a war gone bad, they fought not only the enemy inside South Vietnam, but also the disintegration that seemed to be eroding their institutional pillars. As one high-ranking officer at the Pentagon told the *New York Times*, "I'll take action against anybody that I'm convinced is working against the interests of the United States Government, because that's the oath I took—to defend our country against all enemies, foreign and domestic."[101]

While these divisions within the US Army aroused concern among senior officers and interest from the American press, cries that the army had been "sacrificed on the battlefield of Vietnam" now seem rather excessive. Contemporary reports, though, did paint a bleak picture. Near the end of 1970, public rumors circulated that "no unit commander" in Vietnam could "rely on any of his subordinates carrying out an order to engage the enemy."[102] The following year, two colonels—Robert D. Heinl Jr. and David H. Hackworth—levelled charges against the military establishment. Heinl's essay "The Collapse of the Armed Forces" became standard fare for those judging the army in Vietnam as filled with "murdering . . . drug-ridden . . . dispirited . . . near-mutinous" soldiers. Hackworth went further, blaming the losing war on unskilled military leaders who were "trained in management, not guerrilla warfare."[103] The public exposé did not end there. In September, *The Washington Post* ran a week-long series called "Army in Anguish." Even the US Army's professional journal *Military Review* featured a year-end essay from a British major general titled "An Army in Trouble," a clear sign that US allies were well aware of the Americans' difficulties in Vietnam.[104]

Yet if the US Army indeed was suffering from a "plague of disaffection and defiance within the ranks," senior officers were hardly idle. From combatting drug abuse to improving race relations, commanders pursued solutions to the myriad problems in South Vietnam and on army bases across the globe. During the last half of 1971, military lawyers in Vietnam worked on more than 275 bad-conduct special courts martial alone.[105] The year prior, US Army Chief of Staff Westmoreland commissioned a War College study of military professionalism. The survey of 450 officers found a "widespread feeling that the Army has generated an environment that rewards relatively insignificant, short-term indicators of success, and disregards or discourages the growth of the long-term qualities of moral and ethical strength on which the future of the Army depends." Worse, the study put into question whether problems at home were the causative factors of an organization many now saw as dysfunctional.[106]

If senior officers had few ready solutions to this toxic command climate— one that junior leaders believed the higher-ups had themselves created—the army in Vietnam pressed on in the war's final years. Without question, the unpopular, and still deadly, conflict placed immense pressures on the US

Figure 11 THE WAR COMES HOME. National Guard troops sitting on the floor against each side of a hallway in the Executive Office Building as demonstrators converged on Washington, DC, to protest the Cambodian incursion and Kent State shootings, 9 May 1970. (WHPO Master File #3494, RNL)

armed forces. To a close aide, a despondent Abrams confided, "I need to get this Army home to save it."[107] Yet other senior officers disagreed. Major General John H. Cushman, a senior advisor in the Mekong Delta region, believed the state of the army was bad, but "not disastrous." Diverging from the MACV commander, Cushman believed "the people who say the only way to solve the problem is to bring the boys home are just wrong. It would be disastrous for the Army's self-respect if people said we had to get out to save ourselves."[108] A growing fraternity of recently returned veterans, however, thought otherwise.

The Veterans' Turn

If the antiwar movement by 1971 had peaked in terms of its influence and enthusiasm, a seemingly unlikely source breathed new life into the protestors' cause that year. Since the spring of 1967, a small but flourishing group of Vietnam veterans had been marching in demonstrations, organizing speaking tours, and building local and regional support networks. By the following year, the Vietnam Veterans Against the War (VVAW) opened a national headquarters in New York City with state offices ranging from Massachusetts to California.[109]

The motivations for joining the VVAW varied. While one sociologist believed the combat soldier "often saw the peace movement as undercutting and demeaning the hardships endured by the American servicemen," there were good reasons to unite with antiwar activists. Some returning veterans wanted to highlight the racism or class divides seemingly endemic within the draft army in Vietnam. Others protested the dysfunctionality of that same army. Still other vets protested the war itself and the damage it was inflicting on American families.[110]

The appeal of the VVAW had considerable reach for such a new organization, threatening to aggravate an already serious morale problem inside South Vietnam. As one deployed soldier noted, "I just work hard at surviving so I can go home and protest all the killing." Protest they did. Over the 1970 Labor Day weekend, the VVAW planned a simulated "search-and-destroy" mission dubbed Operation Rapid American Withdrawal (RAW). The "guerrilla theater" was the organization's first national demonstration. Veterans in olive-drab fatigues, joined by other peace activists, marched from Morristown, New Jersey, to Valley Forge, Pennsylvania, reenacting village sweeps while "kidnapping" actors posing as Vietnamese civilians and demanding intelligence on the local community. They handed out fliers emblazoned with "A U.S. Infantry Company Just Came Through Here." World War II veterans lining the route of march heckled their ostensibly unpatriotic successors. But Operation RAW gained national media attention, setting the stage for even larger protests the following year.[111]

By 1971, frustration had seeped into the antiwar movement as Nixon refused to yield any political ground, at least publicly, to the protestors. With momentum from their Labor Day march, however, the VVAW forged ahead. Their next "demonstration" in late January took place in Detroit, specifically targeting the United States' "criminal policy" in Southeast Asia.[112] In a series of public hearings, labeled the Winter Soldier Investigation, VVAW organizers shared veteran testimony of atrocities committed by American soldiers in Vietnam. For three days, stories of torture and destruction followed one after another in a grisly procession. One veteran recounted "the burning of villages, the cutting off of ears, cutting off of heads, torturing of prisoners, calling in of artillery on villages for games, corpsmen killing wounded prisoners, napalm dropped on villages, women being raped, women and children being massacred." By such accounts, commonplace among the testimonies, it seemed as if the entire US Army in Vietnam had degenerated into a ruthless mob.[113]

Yet the Winter Soldier Investigation only set the stage for a much larger, week-long rally held in Washington, DC, that spring. Though Oregon Senator Mark Hatfield entered the entire Winter Soldier proceedings into the *Congressional Record*, VVAW organizers worried the larger antiwar message was making only a minor impression with the nation's policy elite. Nixon's support of the South Vietnamese incursion into Laos during February 1971 did little to mollify these fears. Thus, the VVAW set its sights on the capital. Planners intended Operation Dewey Canyon III—named after two previous US campaigns against NVA forces in Laos—to serve as a "limited incursion into the country of Congress." Veteran activists would march throughout Washington, DC, lobby congressional and senatorial leaders, and host antiwar speeches. The president might easily show contempt for those "spoiled children" within the peace movement, but attacking veterans surely came with a heavy dose of political risk.[114]

By 19 April, more than 1,000 veterans had descended on the nation's capital. Over the next four days, that number would more than double. On the 24th, some 500,000 demonstrators added their voice to the veterans' dissidence. Over the course of Dewey Canyon III, former soldiers—in Gloria Emerson's view, "an eccentric, a strange-looking army, wearing fatigues and field jackets, helmets and their old boonie hats"—declared their stance against the war. They marched to Arlington Cemetery, first turned away but later gaining access with a contingent of Gold Star mothers.[115] They conducted a sit-in at the Supreme Court, demanding the justices "rule on the constitutionality of the Vietnam War." They lobbied on Capitol Hill, one veteran, Larry Rottman, even presenting testimony to the Foreign Affairs Subcommittee. The messengers themselves seemed to make the antiwar message all the more significant. One member of the Daughters of the American Revolution confronted a protesting VVAW marcher with "Son, I don't think what you're doing is good for the troops." The veteran shot back, "Lady, we are the troops."[116]

The testimony of one veteran in particular gained national attention that Thursday. Before the Senate Committee on Foreign Relations, US Navy Lieutenant and VVAW spokesman John Kerry denounced the war and the psychological damage it was causing to fellow veterans. Kerry argued his country had "created a monster, a monster in the form of millions of men who have been taught to deal and trade in violence, and who are given the chance to die for the biggest nothing in history; men who have returned with a sense of anger and a sense of betrayal which no one has yet grasped." The Yale graduate, and skilled former debater, questioned the political justifications for continuing the "mystical war against communism" and argued that Americans had entered into a Vietnamese civil war where they did not belong. Worse, the nation's leaders had abandoned their veterans, evidenced by the poor treatment wounded soldiers were receiving in VA hospitals. Perhaps most importantly, Kerry maintained that "there is nothing in South Vietnam, nothing which could happen, that realistically threatens the United States of America." Indeed, to Kerry, the hypocrisy of justifications to continue the war helped explain why the country was tearing itself apart.[117]

The denouement of the week-long protest, though, came not from Kerry's highly publicized testimony. On Friday the 23rd, Dewey Canyon III concluded with a dramatic spectacle as veterans threw away their medals, ribbons, and awards citations on the steps of the US Capitol building. The protest came hard for some. As one VVAW member wrote, "My parents told me that if I turned in my medals that they never wanted anything more to do with me. That's not an easy thing to take," the vet shared. "I still love my parents."[118] Yet for hours, hundreds of anti-war veterans tossed away their medals. Some broke down crying, others angrily denouncing the war. One bearded vet declared into the staged microphone, "The bronze star, here, they gave it to me for killing fourteen people, man. It's not worth shit." By noon, discharge papers, Silver Stars, Purple Hearts, even Distinguished Service Crosses littered the Capitol grounds. The very symbols of warriors' service and sacrifice had been turned into an emblematic trash heap.[119]

Still, the veterans' antiwar movement was reinforced by one more act of rebellion that spring. Back in 1969, former marine lieutenant and current RAND analyst Daniel Ellsberg had made copies of a secret Defense Department study on US decision-making in Vietnam. Although Ellsberg himself had contributed to the project, commissioned in 1967 by then-Secretary of Defense Robert S. McNamara, reading through the full study two years later left an indelible mark. As he recalled, the "belief that we had *ever* had a right to try to 'win' in Vietnam, to impose our political preferences by military means, died for me in August and September 1969 as I read these volumes." A growing disillusionment with the war soon turned into motivation to end it. In Ellsberg's estimation, the "only way to change the course of the president's course was to bring pressure on him from outside, from Congress and the public."[120]

The release of the leaked study, dubbed *The Pentagon Papers*, by the *New York Times* on 13 June 1971 sent shockwaves through Washington, DC. Though the inquiry dealt with the period before Nixon entered the White House, the president's team railed against the "devastating security breach." Kissinger exploded that the leak would "destroy our ability to conduct foreign policy in confidence," while Nixon recalled the publication "was certain to hurt the whole Vietnam effort. Critics of the war would use them to attack my goals and my policies."[121] Thus, the White House immediately sought an injunction against the *New York Times* from publishing further excerpts of the papers. With uncommon speed, however, the Supreme Court ruled on 30 June that the administration had "not met the heavy burden of showing justification" for blocking the newspaper's further release of the papers. While Nixon turned his attention to destroying the career of the "despicable and contemptible" Ellsberg, the White House took an important lesson from the episode. Facing a hostile, even unpatriotic media, the administration would have to rely more and more on secret diplomacy to end the war in Vietnam.[122]

The uproar over *The Pentagon Papers* tended to overshadow the fact that the veterans' antiwar efforts, along with those of the larger protest movement, had reached their apex by mid-1971. Without question, the VVAW continued its service to the veteran community, working with local VA hospitals, assisting with therapy and rehabilitation programs, and volunteering in communities across the country.[123] But despite the national attention it received, the antiwar endeavor failed to persuade the Nixon White House to end the war on terms other than those of the president. The veterans surely gave credence to the movement. Who could contest, for instance, the right of a wounded warrior to throw his Purple Heart away in protest to an ugly war? Yet VVAW members could only watch in frustration as the conflict in South Vietnam raged on throughout 1971 and into 1972.

A Long War Goes On

By 1971, the United States Army in South Vietnam mirrored another military institution dealing with the stresses of a long war. The ARVN too had entered the new decade a battered, albeit resilient, organization. The US military command's evaluation painted a sobering picture. ARVN morale, while improved, "remained a problem." Desertion rates were higher in 1970 than in 1969. The rapid expansion of the South Vietnamese army resulted in an inadequate number of qualified leaders for the enlarged force. Lack of experience in the National Police equally plagued security efforts. According to one MACV report, "More than 25 percent of the force has less than 1 year of service; almost 60 percent has less than 4 years. The result is poor quality middle and low level leadership and lack of training and internal management." US advisor assessments of the ARVN spoke in similar terms. In January 1970, roughly 54 percent of South Vietnamese maneuver battalion commanders were captains, a billet normally filled by lieutenant colonels. Abrams clearly understood the relationship between effective ARVN leadership and the larger Vietnamization program, but cultivating quality officers took time.[124]

Yet the ARVN's leadership difficulties were just as much a social problem as a strictly military one. For years, common Vietnamese had watched their country serve as a bloody stage for warring armies. The consequences, many of them blamed on Americans, were as distressing as they were numerous: "the soaring cost of living, the increase of prostitution, family breakups because of wives leaving home to live with American soldiers, Vietnamese teens addicted to drugs, and traffic accidents caused by U.S. military vehicles."[125] Army pay failed to match rising inflation, leaving families victim to subsistence living and patrolling ARVN soldiers in search of food. And, of course, the National Liberation Front's relentless call for more taxes, more recruits, more sustenance exacerbated the problems of a population reeling from civil war. Hence, a divided society—by geography, by religion, by ethnic and political differences—regularly questioned the legitimacy of a South Vietnamese government that always seemed to be reacting to events rather than commanding them.[126]

In this sense, large segments of both American and South Vietnamese societies, and the armies they spawned, found the sacrifices of war no longer worth the costs. True, the national cause of South Vietnam's independence still mattered for many. But as a war without decision drew on, as casualties mounted, as soldiers felt increasingly disconnected from the government sending them into battle, the incentives to endure at all costs began to fade. Soldiers in both armies simply could not relate their daily activity to any strategic purpose.[127] As one American recalled of his unit in late 1969, "Our morale was pretty good, but not even our John Waynes talked about winning. We could see that the war was going on just like before we got there and was going to continue after we left. We just wanted to do our time and get the hell out." Such sentiments were more difficult to embrace for those South Vietnamese unable to escape after a year's tour. But by the early 1970s, many ARVN soldiers turned decidedly inward to concentrate on their individual and family survival.[128]

These interrelationships between war and society mattered as US forces continued their withdrawal from South Vietnam. In the end, Abrams's military strategy could not overcome the challenges posed by home front dissent spilling into the armed forces within South Vietnam. Neither the US Army nor the ARVN may have fully collapsed between 1969 and 1973, but the strains of a long war, both at home and on the battlefield, certainly had taken their toll. For many soldiers and civilians alike, the war, quite simply, had become meaningless. Thus, as the conflict moved fitfully toward the muddled endgame of a negotiated settlement, one central question remained. Had the Americans done just enough to leave behind a stable and independent South Vietnam?

6

From Victory to Defeat?

Abrams's Final Years

If American soldiers in Vietnam found little meaning from the ongoing war, Hanoi's general secretary of the Central Committee did not share their views. True, Le Duan faced a host of challenges in mid-1970. The Sino-Soviet split had damaged Hanoi's relationship with Beijing. Morale of the North Vietnamese population seemed to be slipping, requiring a police crackdown against any antiwar sentiment. Within the Politburo, Le Duan met with increased criticisms of his military policies. At the Central Committee's Eighteenth Plenum, held in January, delegates pushed through a final decree pronouncing that North Vietnam "must answer enemy attacks not only with war and political activity but also with diplomacy."[1] In a rebuff to Le Duan's aim of achieving a decisive battlefield victory, the declaration argued that terminating the American presence and support to the Saigon regime would come from more than just military action. The stalemated war had convinced Le Duan's opponents that diplomacy, backed by the use of force, offered the surest path to resolving the question of Vietnamese independence.[2]

Yet the war still mattered and thus still held meaning. Similar to Nixon's White House, the conflict had become for Hanoi a question of balancing the demands of the political and military struggle with the wrangling of high-level diplomacy. Le Duan might have his critics, but all senior North Vietnamese leaders agreed on the ultimate aim of national sovereignty and freedom from external influence.[3]

Of course, the American war had exacted a heavy price. Two years after its launch, the failed 1968 Tet offensive still cast a long shadow over the North Vietnamese Army (NVA) and, especially, the National Liberation Front (NLF). Le Duan poured resources and manpower into the military recovery effort, prompting opponents to charge he was setting back the DRV's own social revolution. Americans, for their part, claimed the 1970 Cambodian incursion had derailed Hanoi's plans for a summer offensive that year. Captured documents, however, indicated that North Vietnamese leaders held no such designs.[4] In fact, at the opening of 1971, Kissinger forwarded a report to the president highlighting "a major U.S. intelligence failure" in evaluating the value of Cambodian ports to the communist war effort. The enemy's logistics network had proved more extensive than previously assessed, a miscalculation resulting "from deficiencies in both intelligence collection and analysis." If the war had taken a toll on Hanoi, US analysts remained uncertain by how much.[5]

This ambiguity resulted, in part, from the changing nature of the communist threat after more than a decade of war. While Nixon and his advisors maintained watchful eyes on an enemy buildup in Laos at the end of 1970, US leaders in South Vietnam perceived a slackening of communist influence in the countryside, most notably in the Mekong River Delta region. Military correspondent William Beecher, though, questioned whether "this gain is real or illusory," and even optimists pointed out that the "current calm and unparalleled prosperity" did not "end the problem."[6] While the revolution waned in some areas of South Vietnam, NLF cadre remained committed to defeating the "American aggressors." Moreover, intelligence analysts still struggled to accurately assess the amount of political dissension within the local population, the damage being done by partisan bickering in Saigon, and the potential impacts of a negotiated cease-fire. Hanoi's decision to elevate the diplomatic struggle seemed only to further complicate an already convoluted political-military struggle.[7]

The ongoing US troop withdrawals undergirding Nixon's Vietnamization policy added yet another element to the dizzying array of factors swaying the course of the war. Creighton Abrams, for one, doubted whether the Saigon government could compensate for the diminishing American support. Near the end of 1970, the MACV commander expressed his private concerns over the loss of "adequate intelligence support" for the South Vietnamese armed forces. More importantly, the "acceleration of [the US] redeployment," Abrams cautioned Pacific Command's Admiral John S. McCain Jr., "provides the enemy increased freedom of movement and enhances his capabilities and opportunities to significantly interfere with and disrupt pacification and Vietnamization programs."[8]

Thus, with the United States committed—for most observers, irrevocably—to a withdrawal from Indochina, a major question arose. At what point would American military and civilian leaders fully lose their leverage over the course of events inside South Vietnam? The US nation-building effort had always been a bargaining process, a compromise between the Saigon policy elite and American advisors. By late 1970, however, it appeared as if Abrams and Ambassador Ellsworth Bunker were reacting to events more than commanding them. Even the early 1971 ARVN incursion into Laos suggested an uncomfortable loss of control on the military battlefield. Furthermore, as US ground troops continued their departure from the war-torn country, the threat of coercive airpower seemed, at best, a weak substitute for the prospects of nation building.[9]

The strategic guidance imparted by Secretary of Defense Melvin Laird highlighted the inherent problems with maintaining leverage as the American withdrawal progressed. Laird emphasized four goals for MACV in 1970: successful Vietnamization, reduction of US casualties, continued troop withdrawals, and stimulation of meaningful negotiations. Logically, Vietnamization meant strengthening the ARVN, thus accelerating progress in the war effort. In reality, none of these objectives facilitated the larger aims of defeating "externally directed and supported Communist subversion and aggression." Nor did they aid the South Vietnamese people in determining their future "without outside interference." Moreover, the 1971 Combined Campaign Plan changed the basic role of US forces. Instead of conducting operations, they would now "support and assist" their South Vietnamese counterparts.[10]

It seems plausible to argue, then, that by late 1970, Creighton Abrams no longer shaped the strategy of the war he was still waging in South Vietnam. His influence, both in Washington, DC, and in Saigon, was clearly waning. Increasingly over the next two years, the president and senior White House advisors would become "particularly critical" of Abrams, Nixon even complaining that the general did not "think creatively."[11] On two occasions, MACV's commander nearly lost his job. Meanwhile, South Vietnam's president sought to distance himself from the departing Americans even as he hoped to secure promises of continued aid for a struggle likely to endure after the last US troops went home.

If Abrams failed to command events on the ground in the war's final years, he should not bear sole responsibility for the allies' ultimate lack of success. Surely, the White House had given its principal military commander in Vietnam an unrealistic mission. As a staff study published by the Senate Foreign Relations Committee in 1970 illustratively concluded, "The assumptions on which American policy are based are ambiguous, confusing, and contradictory."[12] Additionally, Abrams came to realize a hard lesson discerned by previous US military leaders in Vietnam. There quite simply were limits to what American power could achieve in a war that preceded US intervention and would continue long after foreign troops withdrew.

Thus, it seems wrong to assume that Abrams truly fought a war any better than those commanders who came before him. It is even harder to conclude that a war already won in mid-1970 would now be lost by weak politicians at home with no stomach to see the conflict through to its rightful conclusion.

Congress Resurgent

Vietnam had long been an American war in which executive action trumped legislative influence. In fact, for most of the "small wars" fought by the United

States throughout the twentieth century, presidents rarely sought congressional approval. Rather, executive authority guided interventions in Panama, the Dominican Republic, the Philippines, and Lebanon to name but a few. Vietnam proved no different. Johnson's decision to enter into war, and Nixon's to sustain it, came with little input from lawmakers. Congress, of course, funded all these military enterprises and, in the process, seldom questioned the assertiveness of presidential foreign policy. In defending Pax Americana during the Cold War, legislators found few incentives to probe the deeper assumptions fostering an interventionist approach to world affairs.[13]

With the decision to escalate in Vietnam, congressional leaders had, on occasion, pushed back. As early as March 1965, Senator Mike Mansfield (D-Montana) wrote President Johnson that "our national interest lies in reducing, rather than in increasing, the unilateral role" the United States was playing in Southeast Asia. Most famously, Senator J. William Fulbright (D-Arkansas) publicly convened a series of Senate Foreign Relations Committee hearings in 1966 to "inform the American people, the members of the committee and Senate as fully as possible about the implications of the war in Vietnam."[14] One year later, national security advisor Walt Rostow shared with the president several senators' beliefs that the United States was "on a treadmill in Viet Nam." That August, the chairman of the Joints Chiefs cabled Westmoreland that senior policymakers were "becoming increasingly concerned with news media and congressional attitudes regarding the progress of the war."[15]

The Tet offensive provided further opportunity for those lawmakers seeking to question US policy in Vietnam. In March 1968, Senator Robert Kennedy (D-New York) declared "We are in the wrong place, and we are fighting the wrong kind of war." In the afterword to Kennedy's memoir *Thirteen Days*, published the following year, Richard E. Neustadt and Graham T. Allison argued that the expanding war had fueled "Congressional disillusion" and "a feeling of having been duped." The two political scientists, though, hit on an important point in assessing Johnson's wartime critics. "Attacks by congressmen," they maintained, "helped to legitimate dissent in the country, encouraging others, especially in universities and the media." Surely, criticism from a Democratic senator with such gravitas as Fulbright lent credibility to others viewing the war as detrimental to US national interests and inconsistent with American values.[16]

For the most part, however, congressional leaders gave the president and his advisors the benefit of the doubt to conduct foreign policy as they saw fit. At least initially. When Nixon took office, legislators understood that ending the war could not be accomplished overnight and thus gave the new administration time to implement a strategy aimed at disengaging the United States from Vietnam. As the president recalled of his first few months in office, "I still had a congressional majority on war-related votes and questions, but it was a bare one at best, and I could not be sure how long it would hold."[17] Nixon did his best to convince members of Congress, and the larger American public, that certain Cold War prescriptions still held sway. In February 1970, for instance, he argued that "Abandoning the South Vietnamese people . . . would jeopardize more than lives in South Vietnam. It would threaten our long-term hopes for peace in the world. A great nation cannot renege on its pledges. A great nation must be worthy of trust."[18]

By the spring of 1970, though, such soaring rhetoric had lost its power to persuade. Nixon later fumed at the senators and congressmen "swelling the ranks of the antiwar forces," but the incursion into Cambodia induced legislators to finally revolt against the president's Vietnam policy. In April, Senators Mark Hatfield (R-Oregon) and George McGovern (D-South Dakota) introduced an amendment to a military procurement bill calling for the withdrawal of all US troops from Cambodia within thirty days, the end of military operations in Laos by year's end, and the complete removal of American GIs from Vietnam by June 1971.[19] As the bill came up for debate in September, an emotional McGovern charged that "every Senator in this Chamber is partly responsible for sending 50,000 young Americans to an early grave. This Chamber reeks of blood." Though the "end the war" amendment failed to pass, the Senate sent a strong message to Nixon. Congressional support could no longer be taken for granted in what Senator Frank Church (D-Idaho) deemed a "war without end."[20]

The McGovern-Hatfield amendment's failure by a 55-39 margin not only portended impending problems with the legislative branch but also gave pause to Kissinger who was meeting with North Vietnamese diplomat Xuan Thuy in early September. Intent on moving into "substantive negotiations," the national security advisor reported back to Nixon that "Hanoi was prepared to wait a long time for unification of Vietnam." Yet talk from US senators of a "sharp downturn in support of the President's policies" threatened to undermine Kissinger's negotiating position in Paris. As he recalled in his memoirs, "The pattern was clear. Senate opponents of the war would introduce one amendment after another, forcing the Administration into unending rear guard actions to preserve a minimum of flexibility for negotiations. Hanoi could only be encouraged to stall, waiting to harvest the results of our domestic dissent."[21]

An energized legislature thus served as yet another reminder of the interrelationships between American society and the war in Vietnam. On two-year election cycles, congressional officials indeed were the ones most vulnerable to the rising antiwar sentiment within their local communities. Many were forced to consider their support of the war as they prepared for their re-election bids in 1970. Yet the public questioning, if not outright criticism, of Nixon's Vietnam policy rankled senior US officers in Saigon. As one general recalled, the bulk of military commanders in Vietnam "were able to hold their units together and carry out their mission right up to the very end, even though they knew the leaders back home, to include U.S. senators, were talking against them in the field, and they bitterly resented that." For those campaigning for re-election, however, the number of bitter soldiers in Vietnam had to be weighed against the number of disgruntled voters at home.[22]

Without question, some legislative officials turned against the war for more principled reasons. Senator Frank Church, for example, became convinced the struggle in Indochina was less a verdict on communism as it was on Vietnamese nationalism and anticolonial sentiment. Additionally, the prospects of executive overreach worried the Idaho senator. Allying with Republican colleague John Sherman Cooper of Kentucky in 1969, Church worked on bipartisan legislation to restrict the president's wartime powers. An amendment that year to restrict the use of American ground troops in Thailand and Laos without congressional approval easily passed in December. Yet Cooper and Church realized such limitations did little to curb the ongoing war inside South Vietnam. With Lon Nol's coup in 1970, however, the antiwar legislators decided to aim once more for legislation prohibiting US ground forces and advisors from operating inside Cambodia.[23]

The president, though, had stolen a march on Cooper and Church with his 30 April announcement on the Cambodian incursion. Less than two weeks later, the senators countered. Attaching an amendment to the Foreign Military Sales Act, the two sought to end all US support of the war outside the confines of South Vietnam. As Church explained, it was time "for the Congress to draw the line against an expanded American involvement" in a conflict needing to end. "If the Executive Branch will not take the initiative, the Congress and people must."[24] Nixon argued that his self-imposed 30 June deadline to have all Americans out of Cambodia made the amendment moot, but the senators persevered. At the end of June, the Senate passed the second Cooper-Church amendment. Debates in the House continued throughout the summer. Not until December did a modified version of the amendment pass both houses. *The Washington Post* declared it was "the first time in our history that Congress has attempted to limit the deployment of American troops abroad in the course of an ongoing war."[25]

Nixon's troubles with Congress, however, did not end there. In early January 1971, with Melvin Laird visiting South Vietnam—the defense secretary was "heartened" by the progress of Vietnamization—both houses voted to repeal the Tonkin Gulf resolution that gave President Johnson the initial authority to conduct military operations in Southeast Asia. Senator John Sparkman of Alabama believed the repeal would "help clear away some of the debris and controversy over executive-legislative branch powers and responsibilities that arose as a result of the war."[26] While largely symbolic, the move suggested a more

Figure 12 PONDERING AN EXIT FROM VIETNAM. President Nixon and Henry Kissinger talking in the Oval Office, just two days after the start of Lam Son 719, 10 February 1971. (WHPO Master File #5630, RNL)

assertive legislative branch on the horizon, further kindling the president's fears of losing his ability to shape the war's final outcome. Yet Nixon was not about to give up so easily. As he fumed to Kissinger during the opening round of the Cambodian incursion, "Those Senators think they can push me around, but I'll show them who's tough."[27]

An Expanding War Once More

A resurgent Congress disquieted senior military leaders just as much as, if not more so than, the president. At MACV headquarters, Creighton Abrams watched the unfolding political drama with visible unease. Back in 1968, not long after assuming command, the general had thundered to his staff that it was "really *shocking* how these politicos in the United States go *charging* around like a bull in a china shop saying what ought to be done out here *politically.* God Almighty!" The ongoing debates on Capitol Hill did little to soothe Abrams's temper. While the House considered the second Cooper-Church amendment, MACV's commander proposed expanding the war once more, this time with military action against suspected NVA anti-aircraft sites in Laos. The recommendation would prove a harbinger of the civil-military friction endemic in the final two years of the American war.[28]

To at least some observers, the stalemated conflict had also battered, if not nearly broken, the MACV commander. At fifty-six, Abrams had been in South Vietnam for more than four years by late 1970. His health had suffered. Hospitalized three times that year, once to remove his gall bladder, the general had lost weight and a supportive Laird quietly began lobbying for Abrams to replace Westmoreland upon his retirement as the army's chief of staff. When Frederick C. Weyand pinned on his fourth star in early November, speculation rose that MACV's deputy commander might take over the war as early as spring.[29]

Abrams, however, had his hands full and left such conjecturing to the press. As 1970 drew to a close, the MACV staff convened special meetings to discuss intelligence reports of a new North Vietnamese buildup in Laos. Though large-scale operations had decreased inside South Vietnam, MACV analysts noted "an increase in terrorism and small-unit harassing actions." More troubling, however, infiltration of major NVA units appeared along the Ho Chi Minh Trail, forcing Abrams to request a delay—leaked by "Pentagon sources"—in further troop withdrawals. The leak failed to impress the secretary of defense. Upon his return from Saigon in early 1971, Laird declared, according to the *New York Times,* that "South Vietnamese forces were improving so rapidly that 'additional thousands' of American troops could be withdrawn this year."[30]

The apparent contradictions between MACV estimates and Laird's optimism stemmed from the continuing inability of American analysts to accurately predict Hanoi's next strategic move. It made sense for North Vietnamese leaders to avoid expending scarce resources with approximately 50,000 US troops departing every six months. Some Politburo members even suggested that persistent military pressure might slow down rather than hasten American withdrawal timelines.[31] Still, Abrams's staff watched nervously as regiments from the North Vietnamese 312th Division returned to southern Laos after an apparent six-month absence. If Hanoi leaders had decided 1971 to be a year of transition rather than military offensives, the Laotian buildup, coupled with diplomatic intransigence in Paris, persuaded Abrams and his key subordinates of the need for preemptive action.[32]

Thus, while American warplanes continued their assault against the Ho Chi Minh Trail, MACV began advocating for a cross-border military operation into

Laos. Abrams had long been promoting such ideas. Westmoreland, responding to his West Point classmate's proposal for an assault into the Laotian panhandle back in 1965, had explained that an incursion "was not in the cards for the foreseeable future because of complex political and other considerations."[33] No doubt, both senior officers resented these political restrictions but Westmoreland knew his place. Moreover, Americans had been quietly operating inside Laos since the early 1960s, conducting "shallow penetration raids," probing operations, and air strikes. By 1968, US special operations teams were working inside the "neutral" country, hoping to develop a "native intelligence net" in the southern panhandle of Laos that had become "dominated by North Vietnamese forces."[34]

These initial forays into Laos only whetted the appetites of military brass who believed the success of Vietnamization depended on a "preemptive defensive raid" against NVA enclaves just outside of South Vietnam's borders. At the White House, Alexander Haig endorsed Abrams's proposal to employ two ARVN divisions to sever enemy lines of communication inside Laos, a "potentially decisive" operation according to MACV's chief.[35] Abrams also worked on winning over the Joint Chiefs. Not surprisingly, the service chiefs were an amenable crowd. At the Pentagon, Haig advocated on the MACV commander's behalf, recommending "authority to use the full range of US air support, to include tactical and strategic bombing, airlift and gunships." Congress may have prohibited the use of ground troops outside Vietnam, but Abrams still had a deadly arsenal to which he could turn.[36]

Thus, military leaders once more viewed an offensive outside South Vietnam's borders as a way to bolster Vietnamization. Chairman of the Joint Chiefs Thomas H. Moorer argued in late January 1971 that disruption of the NVA logistics hub at Tchepone in Laos would do more than simply increase the Lon Nol regime's chances of survival. The admiral claimed the operation would also "drastically delay the infiltration timetable for [enemy] personnel, facilitate Vietnamization in South Vietnam, and insure our ability to continue with a rapid rate of withdrawal of U.S. forces." Though Abrams confessed the South Vietnamese did not have the capacity to support themselves in Laos, Moorer believed US command of the air would more than compensate for the ARVN's deficiencies. "If the enemy fights, and it is likely that he will," the chairman declared, "U.S. air power and fire power should inflict heavy casualties which will be difficult to replace. The enemy's lack of mobility should enable us to isolate the battlefield and insure a South Vietnamese victory."[37] The coming weeks would prove Moorer an unreliable soothsayer.

The decision to support a Laotian operation, however, rested on more than proving the tenability of Vietnamization. For Nixon, a military offensive could demonstrate, in dramatic fashion, his continuing control over events. By giving "the NVN a bang," the president could advance his objective of "an enduring

Vietnam, namely, one that can stand up in the future." Moreover, the operation "provided insurance for next year when our force levels would be down."[38] Critics worried about "slipping into a wide-ranging air war that could last almost indefinitely," but Nixon thought the benefits far outweighed the risks. His cabinet even pointed to the Nixon Doctrine as a justification for widening the war once more. To the Senate Armed Services Committee in early February, Secretary of Defense Laird defended the use of "sea and air resources to supplement the efforts and the armed forces of our friends and allies who are determined to resist aggression, as the Cambodians are valiantly trying to do."[39]

Yet below the surface of Nixon's Laotian decision-making lurked crucial inconsistencies. With no guarantees of battlefield victory, a setback might very well undermine the goals of highlighting Vietnamization's progress and the president's leverage over Hanoi. The Laos proposal also disclosed that long-held assumptions on North Vietnam being the source of communist aggression still held sway over many military planners. For years, senior MACV officers campaigned for a cross-border offensive to slash the Ho Chi Minh Trail and isolate the South Vietnamese battlefield. Cut off from its external supply bases, they claimed, the insurgency would wither on the vine. Former congressman Walter Judd agreed, writing to Ambassador Bunker just as the operation commenced that if Hanoi failed to secure its logistical lines, "then it seems fairly clear that it will simply have to call off its aggression and return its forces to North Vietnam with real hope for a good future for Southeast Asia." Of course, the lines between northern aggression and southern revolution were never so neatly drawn.[40]

Furthermore, MACV's operational plans proved to be wholly transitory—hit the enemy, temporarily cut the Ho Chi Minh Trail, and depart. As one senior American official noted, a new incursion "should give the South Vietnamese another year's grace." This compared to Hanoi's more existential objective of remaining in Laos to safeguard their bases from which they could launch future military offensives aimed at terminating the South Vietnamese regime. MACV's logic thus entailed a crucial flaw. To prove Vietnamization's worth, overcome the insurgency inside South Vietnam, and build political bonds between Saigon and the rural population required more than just a brief raid into Laos. Neither Abrams nor his senior staff ever articulated how an improved ARVN, one capable of a fleeting cross-border incursion, would facilitate the growth of a southern political community that voluntarily supported Thieu's vision of the future. Secure borders might be a necessary component of building that community, but nowhere near sufficient alone for its inception and expansion.[41]

Thus, it seems most important to place the Laotian invasion of 1971 within the context of how well the government of South Vietnam, rather than the ARVN, was progressing. Some high-ranking officials did express concerns that the South Vietnamese armed forces needed additional time to mature. Army

Chief of Staff Westmoreland shared with Kissinger his support for an alternative plan in which the ARVN conducted smaller raids rather than a frontal assault into Laos. Admiral Moorer, though, affirmed the plan would proceed "exactly like Gen Abrams wants to do it and *no other way*." In April, after critics roundly denounced the miscarried operation, Kissinger quietly called Westmoreland to express his regret for not following the army chief of staff's advice.[42]

These discussions about the size of ARVN's planned raid concentrated more on the American withdrawal than on South Vietnamese political loyalties. Abrams called the Laos campaign "critical" to the US pullout, while Nixon publicly claimed its purpose to "save American lives, to guarantee the continued withdrawal of our own forces, and to increase the ability of the South Vietnamese to defend themselves without our help." In March, Kissinger told the president that "we've got to get enough time to get out" and ensure that North Vietnam did not "knock the whole place over." Even South Vietnamese generals, citing high morale after the prior year's Cambodian campaign, tended to think of a Laotian incursion in narrow terms of border security and cutting Hanoi's supply routes.[43] Without question, these were important objectives. But such failures in linking military operations to political progress would haunt MACV planners for the remainder of their war in Vietnam.

In the end, Nixon and Kissinger settled for a narrow military offensive to accomplish three primary objectives: to demonstrate the headway being made in Vietnamization, to limit domestic blowback against a widened war, and to buy time for the GVN. Behind closed doors, the president had already determined that US troop withdrawals would continue regardless of the ARVN's performance in Laos. In truth, then, the White House, not MACV headquarters, was now fully directing strategy inside South Vietnam. This civilian domination of military affairs certainly rankled professional officers who deemed Nixon's inner circle as far overstepping their bounds. As one senior US Army general recalled, the military assessments of Kissinger's NSC staff, in particular those of Alexander Haig, "were given more weight that the judgments of General Abrams, other responsible commanders in the field, and the Joint Chiefs of Staff."[44]

Of course, MACV still had a role to play. Abrams's planners rushed to conceive an operation that provided logistical and air support to the ARVN while achieving "maximum feasible disruption of the enemy timetable and destruction of stockpiles."[45] As with the Cambodian operation, though, top secret planning once more excluded the South Vietnamese until the last moment. And astoundingly, despite American officers' long-standing desire to expand the war into Laos, no detailed contingency plans had been developed by Abrams's planning staff. The first weeks of December 1970 thus became a flurry of activity inside MACV headquarters. On the 13th, Haig arrived in Saigon and, accompanied by Abrams and Ambassador Bunker, met with President Thieu and Chairman of the South Vietnamese Joint General Staff Cao Van Vien to present the outlines of what would soon be code-named Operation Lam Son 719.[46]

The primary objective of MACV's four-phased plan aimed to "cut and disrupt" the Ho Chi Minh Trail system in Laos. American forces would first secure lines of communication along the South Vietnamese-Laotian border while establishing logistical and fire support bases. Next, the ARVN 1st Division would attack into Tchepone, establish a base there, and in the third stage commence probes to cut the enemy's supply routes. The final phase, "dependent on developments," foresaw an optional attack southwest from Tchepone to clear out enemy base areas and supply caches.[47] A recently passed Cooper-Church Amendment forbade American ground troops from accompanying the ARVN outside of South Vietnam's borders. The South Vietnamese consequently would be on their own, save US air and artillery support, throughout much of the operation.[48]

Even before Lam Son 719 kicked off, however, signs appeared that trouble lay ahead. In late January 1971, MACV intelligence reported that the North Vietnamese army had been alerted to the impending offensive. CIA estimates that same week anticipated "that if the ARVN operation is marginally effective, it will encourage the Communists to continue their present course."[49] Senior US officials, with the benefit of hindsight, put into question why Lam Son 719 went forward in the first place. General Bruce Palmer Jr. recalled that "in cold objectivity, it did look very much like sending a boy to do a man's job in an extremely hostile environment." Kissinger, for his part, believed the operation "was a splendid project on paper. Its chief drawback, as events showed, was that it in no way accorded with Vietnamese realities."[50]

Despite the warning signs, Lam Son 719 proceeded as planned. On 30 January, US mechanized infantry units moved to secure the Khe Sanh area in preparation for the ARVN assault on 8 February. The shift of American forces into Quang Tri province, however, alerted the North Vietnamese, who quickly reinforced Tchepone. Already in these early stages, Abrams seemed off balance. Two days before the ARVN crossed into Laos, the general lamented that Washington officials did not understand that the outcome would be totally in his subordinates' hands. "There isn't anything I can tell them, or anybody else."[51] The NVA leadership, in comparison, apparently had no such management problems in reacting to the allied incursion. As MACV reported, "Communist resistance stiffened as ARVN forces penetrated deeper into Laos. Tanks often fought tanks, and hand-to-hand combat ensued. Communist AA [anti-aircraft] fire took its toll of helicopters and TACAIR. The enemy often organized coordinated counter-attacks, and in one instance completely overran an RVN support base."[52]

By mid-February, the shaky wheels of the Lam Son operation started to come loose. Lieutenant General Hoang Xuan Lam, commanding the South Vietnamese armed forces in Laos, had never led such a large-scale campaign. Throughout, he seemed incapable of managing the complexities of a major offensive in bad weather, the petty rivalries of his subordinate commanders, and the agile response from the defending communists. Worse, as Lam's forces clawed their way toward Tchepone, they presented "an excellent target for NVA gunners and 'human assault waves.'"[53] Despite encouraging reports from Abrams—ARVN performance was "very good and professional"—the White House worried Lam Son had bogged down in just under three weeks of fighting. To Admiral Moorer, Kissinger divulged that "I do not understand what Abrams is doing." Worse, the national security advisor failed to glimpse "anything aggressive" along Highway 9 on the route toward Tchepone. Lam Son 719 looked to be floundering.[54]

News from the front only worsened when the White House discovered that President Thieu had decided to abandon the operation and withdraw his forces from Laos earlier than expected. If highlighting ARVN fighting abilities interested Nixon most, the premature extraction of South Vietnamese troops threatened to publicly expose the deficiencies still attenuating Vietnamization. Thieu, though, saw little political gain by remaining in Laos as NVA reinforcements poured onto the scene. Abrams might view Lam Son 719 as "maybe the only decisive battle of the war," but South Vietnam's president thought otherwise.[55] The withdrawal decision threw White House leaders into a fit of rage. Kissinger shot off a message to Ambassador Bunker on 9 March, fuming that they had "not gone through all this agony just for the favorable headlines." Two days later, at a White House briefing, the national security advisor castigated the South Vietnamese as "sons of bitches" for "bugging out."[56]

The president's fury, however, soon turned on Abrams. As February drew to a close, Kissinger, already questioning whether MACV's commander understood the true objective of Lam Son 719, shared Nixon's dissatisfaction over the operation's progress with Ambassador Bunker. Reports that Abrams had failed to leave his headquarters during the campaign only heightened White House concerns. Frustrated, in Kissinger's words, by being "constantly outstripped by events," an enraged Nixon considered sending Haig to Saigon to replace the now embattled MACV commander.[57] Cooler heads—and Melvin Laird's faithful support of Abrams—prevailed. Nixon postponed a Haig-led fact-finding mission until mid-March. The damage to Abrams's reputation, however, had been done. H. R. Haldeman recorded on 23 March that both the president and Kissinger felt "they were misled by Abrams on the original evaluation of what might be accomplished" and "concluded they should pull Abrams out." With military operations in Laos winding down though, Nixon demurred, arguing it would not make much difference anyway.[58]

But the incursion had made a difference. Lam Son 719 shattered Nixon and Kissinger's faith in Creighton Abrams. In early June, Kissinger admitted to the president that he "wouldn't believe a word Abrams says anymore." Nixon concurred. "You've got to go to the local commanders from now on."[59] Then in September, after Abrams reportedly leaked to the press his reservations about the timetable for withdrawal of US troops, an infuriated Nixon once more considered "withdrawing the son-of-a-bitch." Kissinger agreed that Abrams was "no longer on top of this," prompting Nixon to insist on a deputy commander who would keep the senior general "from drinking too much and talking too much." The exchange over Abrams's alcohol problems would not be the last. Nor would the Laotian campaign be the low point of American civil-military relations in these final years.[60]

For the time being, Abrams's near relief remained private, but Nixon now had to confront the public assessments of Lam Son 719. Even before the ARVN's early departure from Laos, Nixon proclaimed success, arguing the offensive had "very seriously damaged" the communists' fighting capacity and that the US troop withdrawal schedule would "go forward at least at the present rate."[61] Abrams, even if out of favor at the White House, loyally supported his president's case to the press. At a 21 March press background briefing, the general predicted the ARVN would "come out of this with higher confidence." Though some weaker units withdrew in the face of enemy pressure, the majority "performed well and did not retreat." Most importantly, Abrams argued, "Lam Son 719 has succeeded in disrupting vital portions of the enemy's logistical system, capturing or destroying significant quantities of supplies and inflicting considerable damage on enemy units within the area of operation." By such accounts, the campaign looked to be the most decisive military engagement since Tet.[62]

Yet akin to the 1970 Cambodian incursion, assessments of Lam Son 719 varied widely. MACV reported the enemy lost some 13,000 dead, but the ARVN had equally suffered, losing 8,000 casualties—approximately 45 percent of the total forces earmarked for the campaign. In addition, the enemy downed more than 100 US helicopters supporting ARVN ground troops. Nor did Hanoi's supply problems seem all that grave. According to Haig, by 7 April, "American pilots reported that NVA truck traffic on the Ho Chi Minh Trail appeared to be back to normal."[63] One week later, Lieutenant General Michael S. Davison, the II Field Force commander, reported to Abrams that in Military Region 3 "the enemy continues to sustain himself without major reliance on external sources of supply." Kissinger hoped the disruption of the Ho Chi Minh Trail would aggravate Hanoi's supply shortages and limit enemy options in 1972, but evaluations of the North Vietnamese resupply system being "severely hurt" appeared optimistic given the temporary nature of the Laos raid.[64]

Such nuances tended to get lost in White House declarations of success. Still, talking points on enemy kill ratios, numbers of trucks destroyed, or individual weapons captured only persuaded so much. By late March and early April, journalists were writing of a new "credibility gap" and of an "ignominious and disorderly retreat" from Laos. According to the *New York Times*, Hanoi "won at least a propaganda victory" by blunting the South Vietnamese offensive.[65] Privately, Nixon grudgingly acquiesced to these views even as he lashed out against the press. On 21 April, the president told Kissinger that the war was presenting "a very serious problem. You see, the war has eroded America's confidence up to this point." Though he still believed that abandoning "our friends . . . would abandon ourselves," the president rearticulated the end-state of his Southeast Asian policy. As he imparted to Kissinger on the 23rd, "Winning the war simply means . . . letting South Vietnam survive. That's all."[66]

Six days later, the US 1st Cavalry Division, having served for more than five and half years in South Vietnam, wrapped up its guidons and headed home to Fort Hood, Texas. One officer, packing up the division's last items of gear, worried about getting mortared during the departure ceremonies. "We got hit a few days ago," he quipped, "and we thought they just might be zeroed in on our parade ground out there. That would have spoiled the party."[67]

The Tolls of War

For Americans serving a one-year tour in Vietnam, few appreciated fully that the army they were fighting with and the population they were fighting among had been at war for well over a decade. Even those who had been there longer described the South Vietnamese in paternalistic terms. Abrams spoke in July 1971 of providing "reinforcing support, largely psychological," to his Vietnamese allies. (This despite the general's earlier judgment that ARVN confidence had risen in the aftermath of Lam Son 719.) Senior MACV officers equally counseled that the armed forces had to "maintain a favorable image in the eyes of the people."[68] In Washington, policy assessments mirrored this tone. One National Intelligence Estimate, while positive in outlook for the remainder of 1971, hit on familiar problems within the South Vietnamese armed forces—serious personnel shortages, a lack of qualified leaders, low morale among the enlisted ranks, and high desertion rates. After nearly two years of Americans' prioritizing the Vietnamization effort, the RVNAF seemed as resistant as ever to organizational change.[69]

Perhaps more important than the ever-present gap between military allies, a chasm endured between Americans and the larger Vietnamese society. As critic William J. Lederer wrote, the "ugly and tragic fact is that in Vietnam the United States has no idea what is in the minds of the citizens." One US advisor in Hau Nghia province agreed: "Most Americans were not fully aware of what was going on around them."[70] Of course, some officers did appreciate a growing resentment among the population, indeed present if not well perceived by US troops.

By the late 1960s, South Vietnamese antiwar activists grew both in numbers and in influence. They worried that American political aims had "completely altered the nature of Vietnamese society" and that the "atrocious and endless" war was threatening the population with "total destruction." One ARVN officer, penning a "Letter to the People of the United States," even took aim at those US soldiers ostensibly there to help the Vietnamese. "You, my friends, have drunk the water of this tiny nation / But you have not yet understood the soul of the people."[71]

This opposition to the war, and to the Americans waging it, called into question claims of Vietnamization's progress. While Hanoi may have overstated the decisiveness of it military victory in Laos over the "Saigon puppet army," Abrams remained optimistic during the summer of 1971. Recent military operations had "produced maximum practical benefits," the general maintained, demonstrating the "success of the Vietnamization program."[72] But had they really? In Washington, senior officials were not so sure. While Kissinger complained of a "comprehensibility gap"—there remained a "great disparity" between the real situation in Vietnam and what Americans believed—Westmoreland broached the possibility of lowering the minimum age to 15 for induction into South Vietnam's Regional Forces. "It is absolutely essential," the army chief of staff claimed, "to have more strength on the ground." Yet such an expansion hardly guaranteed a viable ARVN once Americans departed. As one US major let slip to a journalist, "What we're likely to leave behind is a well-equipped military corpse."[73]

The varying assessments of Vietnamization resulted, in part, from depleting sources of intelligence. With fewer and fewer US advisors on the ground, MACV retained less capacity to evaluate South Vietnam's security apparatus and thus the country's chances to "hack it" in the future. Key questions lingered. How much progress had Vietnamization really made? Were South Vietnamese forces better equipped to counter the NLF or NVA threat? How would they contend with both once the Americans withdrew? Perhaps most importantly, if military progress was not being matched by political progress in Saigon or in the many provinces and districts throughout the countryside, did an improved ARVN matter? Surely, the increased size of the armed forces, preempting accessions into the labor force, held economic as well as political import. But as Abrams's command withered with every troop departure, so, too, did its influence, making it all the more difficult to answer these many unresolved issues still facing the Saigon government.[74]

Outside Saigon, the state of pacification proved just as mystifying. Seeking manpower spaces as US troop withdrawals continued, Abrams decided to stop allocating military personnel to the CORDS Phoenix program. With fewer advisors in the field, MACV surely lost some feel for pacification trends in the countryside. Thus, back in March, when *TIME* reported President Thieu's announcement that "99.8 percent of the population and 99.4 percent of the hamlets and villages were controlled by the government," Americans could do little more than shrug at such "unreliable—and often deliberately falsified—figures."[75]

Then, in early July 1971, William Colby gave up his duties as CORDS chief, returning home to help care for an ill daughter. In retrospect, the departure now seems fateful. Colby habitually told visitors that the war could not be won "unless the people participate." Yet in the aftermath of the Laos incursion, with no real end in sight for what was becoming a generational war for some Vietnamese, the population looked no more willing to fully support Saigon than they had been in years past. Less than one month after Colby departed, pacification reports noted "dangerous soft spots" cropping up in the countryside.[76] One US official believed the allies were holding their own against the NLF infrastructure. "But the other side is still better at improving and expanding it than our side is at whittling it down." By the time Nixon boasted in February 1972 that over 80 percent of the South Vietnamese population was "under effective Government control," such statistics of progress appeared as meaningless as they were untrustworthy.[77]

It seemed, then, that in the aftermath of Lam Son 719, senior US officials could only guess at how much headway their military and nonmilitary programs had made in strengthening the political foundations of South Vietnam. Nixon and Kissinger certainly worried how the recent offensives into Cambodia and Laos might hurt Thieu politically. During a July visit to Saigon, Kissinger covered a wide range of topics with the South Vietnamese president, foremost among them the continuing US pullout and the future of American military and economic aid.[78] But assessing the GVN's political endurance remained as cryptic as ever. Abrams hoped that by concentrating on security, MACV might help promote the "legal functioning of the constitutional process" during the upcoming national elections in October. The continuing US redeployments, however, left him with few resources, beyond the use of air power, to alter the military balance. As *Newsweek* reported in August, after years of dependence on the United States, "it was inevitable that South Vietnam would be racked by withdrawal pains."[79]

Thieu himself certainly realized the stakes and reemphasized the benefits of land reform in 1971 as a way to curry political favor with the rural population. Yet stubborn problems overshadowed any advances in agricultural production. Despite the Land-to-the-Tiller program, aimed partly at closing the inequality gap between landlords and tenant farmers, an enduring class divide left the popular masses resentful of those officials profiting from the war. Polls in late 1971 showed most South Vietnamese agreed that "the U.S. troops benefited a small number of people but had caused economic chaos and difficulties for the majority."[80] If Thieu still aimed at inspiring a "social revolution" in the countryside, the problems of corruption, a perceived lack of upward social mobility, and the president's own "strongman instinct" left a society guarded in its support of the Saigon regime. When Thieu—against US embassy advice—staged an uncontested election in October, the prospects of true political accommodation appeared dim. Disheartened American officials freely expressed their opinion that "South Vietnam's political generals were deliberately letting their country slide into political collapse."[81]

In one sense, this political bankruptcy mirrored the environmental consequences of fighting a long, destructive war across a rural countryside. The despoiling of the Vietnamese ecosystem not only slashed agricultural output, but also forced social dislocations that only further undermined the country's political community. By 1969, the US Air Force had sprayed chemical defoliants over 4 million acres of forests and almost 10 percent of South Vietnam's arable land. Though intended to deny insurgent access to strategic areas—"Only We Can Prevent Forests" read the Operation Ranch Hand motto—herbicide use came under increasing scrutiny by 1970.[82] Scientific investigations linked the chemicals to birth defects, while critics argued that chemical warfare violated the Geneva Protocol. MACV field commanders, however, endorsed crop destruction efforts, citing "widespread food shortages among enemy units with resulting lower morale, disruption of the logistic systems, and hampered combat operations." Laird, forever considering the adverse political costs of unpopular military operations, contested such views and, in late 1970, Abrams decided to phase out the use of herbicides.[83]

While civilian scientists and military staffs debated the long-term health consequences of MACV's defoliation program, specifically, the use of Agent Orange, the imposed redefinition of political and social spaces left local communities ill-equipped to fulfill Thieu's aims of political consolidation. Land reform efforts and the effects of an American-spawned ecocide disrupted hamlet and village life. In the process, rural farmers saw little gain in supporting a governmental bureaucracy that, regardless of Land-to-the-Tiller, still appeared to preference the elite. Changing land practices thus, by late 1971, had only made slight strides in building a broad political consensus at the national level. More importantly, however, the changing nature of the landscape itself exerted substantial influence over the rural population's dim views of the Saigon regime and its American benefactors.[84]

Perhaps unsurprisingly, attitudes among the South Vietnamese armed forces tended to emulate those of the larger population. One ARVN major general asked, in June 1971, "Why, after 15 years of continuous war in Vietnam, can we not see even a faint hope of peace?" That same month, Abrams sent a plea to his subordinate commanders asking for the names of ARVN colonels who might take over an ARVN division, a position normally reserved for major generals. Morale and leadership problems remained a mainstay in US evaluations. Four months later, *The Washington Post* reported that even pro-American Vietnamese were "utterly disillusioned" by the US troop departures.[85] In his headquarters, Abrams worried the Americans had "*retarded* the Vietnamese" by doing too much on their behalf. "*We* can't run this thing," the general exclaimed. "I'm absolutely convinced of that. *They've* got to run it." But as the summer wore on, US advisors fretted that without heavy air support, the ARVN would be challenged just to "muddle through" in those military regions hotly contested by enemy main force units.[86]

An "uneasy lull" in the summer of 1971 certainly offered the allies some breathing space as they recuperated from the hard fighting in Laos. The reasons behind this decline in enemy activity, though, once again eluded MACV. Surveying the southern provinces, Abrams curiously told his staff he would "be willing to bet a cigar or something that everybody's kind of happy out there in Long An and Hau Nghia because there isn't much going on." In Washington, senior officials proved far less sanguine. Admiral Moorer lightly admonished Abrams for not being kept "better informed" over enemy activity, while a White House senior review group concluded there were "no manpower constraints on the enemy's choice of strategies in 1971-72."[87] After a September trip to Vietnam, Haig reported to Kissinger that the continuing US redeployments could provide incentives for a North Vietnamese offensive. While Haig admitted having "practically no solid evidence on enemy intentions and capabilities," even without a full-blown military campaign, Hanoi "could set back the GVN's pacification effort" in a number of South Vietnamese provinces. The Americans appeared to be operating blind.[88]

Kissinger's negotiation efforts that summer, however, far overshadowed the battlefield lull. Back in May, the national security advisor had presented the North Vietnamese with an option that called for the release of all POWs and allowed for a fixed date to withdraw all US forces and a ceasefire-in-place under international supervision. (Such a cease-fire would allow NVA troops to remain inside South Vietnam proper.) In short, Nixon confirmed his willingness to forego a military victory and accept a negotiated settlement. The administration was also retreating from its earlier demands for a mutual troop withdrawal from South Vietnam. Then in July, on a secret trip to China, Kissinger scribbled in a briefing book the now infamous phrase, "We want a decent interval."[89] That same month, he reported to Nixon Hanoi's demand that the Americans replace Thieu and accept a coalition government in Saigon. In nearly all these discussions, the White House rarely consulted with Abrams who, Kissinger believed, had "just quit" and was not making any "extra-special effort."[90]

Kissinger's marginalia, though, should not be seen as conclusive evidence that Nixon cared only for an illusory peace. Beyond question, Kissinger did indeed use the term "decent interval" or some variation on several occasions. Special

Assistant to the National Security Advisor Winston Lord, though, recalled "no thought of a decent interval" in the White House and "no thinking . . . to work out a cynical deal which Kissinger and his associates didn't think would hold up."[91] Lord likely overstated his case, as Nixon and Kissinger indeed considered the possibility that South Vietnam might not endure after the Americans departed. Yet even as senior White House officials speculated that South Vietnam might have little prospect for long-term survival, they still worked tirelessly to give Saigon the best chance at lasting beyond a peace agreement.[92]

The president, in particular, saw a negotiated settlement as a harsh pill. Thus, he continued to view the threat of military action—"a big play" he called it—as a way to establish a foundation for some sense of political equilibrium between North and South Vietnam. Nixon hoped that the remaining US forces in Vietnam might put Hanoi at such a disadvantage militarily that there would at least be an interlude for the South Vietnamese political process to take hold. True, from a strict political sense, if the allies could forestall a communist victory militarily and politically, perhaps enough time would elapse between the final US withdrawal and the collapse of Saigon that critics would not see the relationship. In the end, it seems, talk of a "decent interval" was less a statement of policy than an admission of American limitations.[93]

The United States' willingness to make major diplomatic concessions in mid-1971, especially in the context of Sino-US negotiations, unquestionably stoked fears of abandonment among Saigon's political elite. How else could the GVN interpret Kissinger's stance of leaving the "future of South Vietnam to the historical process"?[94] Thus, with South Vietnam's presidential election on the horizon, Thieu decided to ensure his own political survival. US Embassy officials believed "it was absolutely essential that there be a contest." The State Department urged Thieu to reach out to the communists, even suggesting the benefits of a coalition government. In Kissinger's words, however, South Vietnam's president was convinced the country "could not afford a protracted period of ambiguous authority in the middle of a bitter war." When the final votes were tallied from the 3 October election, Thieu had received 94 percent of the vote.[95]

While the embassy judged the election's conduct "mechanically correct," critics decried the results. Congressman Abner Mikva (D-Illinois) called the political contest a "nonelection" and a "very big joke." Kissinger cabled Ambassador Bunker to remain vigilant against a possible coup. At MACV headquarters in early December, Deputy Ambassador Samuel D. Berger shared his concerns that Thieu's problem was "to create a political party to give constitutional support and continuity to the political system."[96]

Berger's worries, in particular, were well founded. Thieu's electoral landslide may have been a personal victory, but political stability and a sense of true nationhood remained elusive goals as 1971 drew to a close. Even if social energies fueled ongoing debates over what it meant to be South Vietnamese in a postconflict environment, by most, if not all, accounts, the Thieu regime still had a long road ahead in building a viable political community. Unfortunately, that community would soon be under assault from yet another North Vietnamese offensive hoping to give Hanoi a decisive military victory in 1972.

Victory through Airpower?

A flurry of activity marked the final months of 1971. In late October, Abrams announced the deactivation of one of the two US combat divisions still remaining in South Vietnam. On 12 November, Nixon publicized the withdrawal of an additional 45,000 US troops over the next two months. With some 175,000 Americans remaining in theater, the president promised another announcement in February.[97] Then, in late December, responding to enemy shelling of Saigon, Nixon authorized the resumption of bombing raids over North Vietnam. Abrams supported the decision, asserting the bombing would "help keep U.S. casualties low, safeguard the next troop withdrawal and blunt an offensive Hanoi appear[ed] to be planning against weak South Vietnamese forces in the Central Highlands." US Representative Robert Drinan (D-Massachusetts), a vocal critic of Nixon, however, called the five-day aerial campaign "indefensible and barbaric."[98] It would not be the last time critics denounced the White House for launching a brutal bombing offensive against the north.

Meanwhile, Abrams opened the new year determining how best to support a military transition in which MACV no longer played an operational role. (News reports leaked that the general would also soon be leaving Vietnam.)[99] The allies' combined campaign plan for 1972 thus reflected the Americans' narrowing advisory functions. According to their revised mission statement, the South Vietnamese armed and civil forces would "assure the security of the Vietnamese people throughout the RVN thus creating an environment in which Community Defense and Local Development Programs can be safely and successfully accomplished." Abrams's command would only "support" these objectives. Compared to the 1968 campaign plan of defeating VC/NVA forces and assisting the Saigon government to extend control throughout South Vietnam, the Americans clearly had lowered their expectations.[100]

Inside the Hanoi Politburo, however, Le Duan had come to a different conclusion. In the aftermath of Lam Son 719, the communists focused on conducting piecemeal attacks against allied troops and disrupting South Vietnam's pacification plans. Main force units spent time rebuilding their bases, while political cadre bolstered their proselytizing efforts. To make progress in negotiations, though, required a dramatic change to the "realities of the battlefield."[101] Thus, as he had done so often in the past, Le Duan conceived of a new military offensive to "defeat the American 'Vietnamization' policy, gain a decisive victory in 1972, and force the U.S. imperialists to negotiate an end to the war from a position of defeat." The ARVN's mixed performance in Laos, along with the continuing US troop withdrawals, surely helped the first secretary gain consensus in the Politburo for such a dramatic shift in the communists' military strategy.[102]

So too, though, did Nixon's February 1972 trip to China. The president hoped the historic visit, coupled with new bombing raids, would pressure North Vietnamese diplomats to put their shoulders into what he soon dubbed a "three-and-a-half year filibuster at the peace talks." The thawing of Sino-US relations certainly worried Hanoi. If China insisted that key sticking points be resolved in Paris, Le Duan might lose his independence in directing the path of negotiations. In fact, when informed of the Chinese decision to discuss the war during Nixon's visit, the North Vietnamese responded tersely: "Viet Nam is our country. You have no right to discuss with the United States the question of Viet Nam."[103]

Hanoi's spring offensive plans thus took into account the global shifts reforming larger Cold War relationships. Yet as conceived, the Nguyen Hue Offensive, named for the eighteenth-century Vietnamese ruler who defeated Chinese invading forces, also sought to influence the Paris peace talks. A general offensive aimed at territorial acquisitions would demonstrate the GVN's inability to provide countrywide security. Even if the South Vietnamese population did not rise up in support, the communists might revive the revolutionary movement in key areas like the Mekong Delta. Finally, provinces occupied by North Vietnamese forces could be used for leverage at the negotiating table.[104] Hanoi's military planners consequently designed a campaign envisioning three independent spearheads into South Vietnam—one across the DMZ into Quang Tri province, the second from Cambodia into Binh Long province toward Saigon, and the third cutting into the Central Highlands' Kontum province. Armor battalions, equipped with Soviet and Chinese tanks, would accompany the NVA divisions as they thrust into South Vietnam.[105]

As early as January 1972, MACV intelligence detected warning signs of a major enemy offensive. Senior US advisors reported tank sightings in western Kontum province that month. In February, Abrams voiced his concerns. "During the recent weeks the enemy threat has continued to increase," the general told his subordinate commanders. "I am convinced he now has sufficient major ground elements in position to launch his offensive."[106] Senior ARVN leaders came to similar conclusions, one projecting that the enemy had two chief goals: "a major military victory and the disruption of pacification." All the while, allied intelligence assets did their best to track movement along the Ho Chi Minh Trail, a perennial indicator of Hanoi's level of support to the southern revolution.

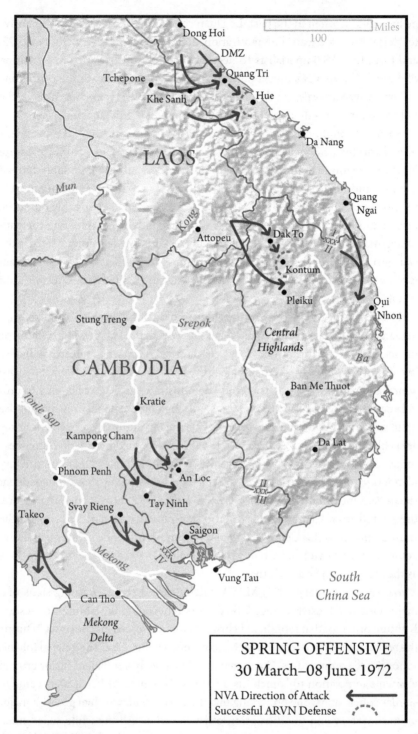

Map 3 Spring Offensive

Still, as during the 1968 Tet campaign, the timing and scope of the projected North Vietnamese offensive remained uncertain.[107]

Since Abrams believed a "major military effort" could begin "any day," he reflexively turned to his strategic air assets in hopes of blunting the imminent blow. "In searching for ways to inflict maximum damage on the enemy during his build up," MACV's commander unleashed the B-52s under his control on South Vietnam's border areas with Laos and Cambodia. Nixon, for the moment, concurred, telling Kissinger the "damned Air Force" offered the only cards he had left to play against an NVA tank assault.[108] At the Pentagon, Admiral Moorer asked for permission to strike high-value targets in North Vietnam and to "employ area denial munitions in the northern portion of the DMZ." By mid-February, the *Boston Globe* already was reporting that American air strikes in South Vietnam had "reached the highest level in 18 months as part of an effort to forestall a much-predicted Communist Tet lunar new year offensive."[109]

If both the *Globe* and MACV headquarters misread Hanoi's time schedule, their forecast of a major enemy offensive finally materialized in the early hours of 30 March. The defending ARVN, in some areas overstretched across wide-ranging outposts and firebases, crumpled under the weight of a multidivision assault. Some outposts received more than 2,000 rounds of artillery fire within the first eight hours of the attack alone.[110] Just south of the demilitarized zone, NVA armor "sent hundreds of government troops," according to one newspaper report, "retreating in disarray." In other areas, the ARVN fought tenaciously, disrupting the NVA advance and inflicting a heavy toll on the enemy assailants. Nixon later described the invasion as "a sign of desperation," but the White House and Pentagon clearly worried about the potential for upending the Vietnamization program and for the North Vietnamese "greatly enhancing their political and negotiating posture."[111]

Almost immediately, the president tore into his military leaders for not being more vigorous in counterattacking the North Vietnamese. He fumed to Kissinger to get the Air Force "off their ass and get them up there and hit everything that moves." In the aftermath of Lam Son 719, however, Nixon reserved his greatest scorn for the MACV commander. On 3 April, Moorer recorded that the president "was particularly critical of General Abrams and inquired as to where were General Abrams' recommendations for action. . . . He said he would take no excuses and he wanted forces augmented and action taken against the enemy without delay."[112] It did not help that despite Abrams cautioning for months of an impending invasion, both the general and Ambassador Bunker were out of the country visiting family when the North Vietnamese launched their assault. As *The Washington Post* dryly put it, the timing of the invasion "caught the American high command by surprise."[113]

As B-52s launched bombing runs against NVA troop formations and anti-aircraft sites, the South Vietnamese shouldered the brunt of the offensive on the ground. Nixon admonished the Joint Chiefs chairman to "hit the goddamn enemy," to keep American bombing "at the maximum." "I want to give it to them ten times right in the butt," he told Moorer in mid-April.[114] Far below the bombing runs, though, the ARVN struggled to parry the sweeping enemy attacks. Familiar problems once more reared their ugly heads. US advisors complained of command and control difficulties, the inability to counter NVA tanks, and the psychological setback caused by the invasion. Abrams reported to Laird the continuing ineffectiveness of Thieu's field commanders, while Haig recalled that an alarmed MACV chief thought the "South Vietnamese had lost their will to fight and that total capitulation might occur at any moment."[115]

While the North Vietnamese kept many ARVN units off balance throughout much of April and into May, South Vietnam's defenders extracted a heavy price from the invaders. In May alone, the NVA suffered more than 2,900 soldiers killed just in the fighting around Hue and lost more than sixty armored vehicles. With Vietnamization "under the gun," however, Nixon sought to put a positive spin on the general military situation.[116] In a report to the nation on 26 April, the president lashed out against a "clear case of naked and unprovoked aggression across an international border." He shared Abrams's evaluation that the South Vietnamese were "fighting courageously and well in their self-defense." Nixon then announced a decision that Hanoi's Politburo surely welcomed. "Vietnamization has proved itself sufficiently that we can continue our program of withdrawing American forces without detriment to our overall goal of ensuring South Vietnam's survival as an independent country." Moreover, the president directed the US delegation in Paris to return to the negotiating table. All the while, the American bombing campaign would continue to oppose "communist aggression" in South Vietnam.[117]

Nixon's remarks left little doubt of his intent to swing the focus of American foreign policy toward a rapprochement with China and the Soviet Union. The Moscow Summit scheduled for May 1972 demonstrated the president's desire to shift the national conversation to arms control, trade relations, and reducing tensions with the communist superpowers. Yet the war in Vietnam simply would not let go. With NVA forces now occupying South Vietnam's Quang Tri province, President Thieu declared martial law on 10 May. Abrams praised the ARVN's performance in "this battle to the death," but emphasized that American airpower alone could not contain the enemy's offensive.[118] From the US Embassy, Ambassador Bunker cabled the State Department with news of Thieu's decision to institute a comprehensive draft for all men between the ages of 17 and 43. As the *New York Times* reported in early May, the NVA offensive had brought the Saigon regime to a "perilous stage."[119]

At the White House, Nixon refused to yield. The day before Thieu declared martial law, the president ordered a new bombing campaign, Operation Linebacker, against North Vietnam. For months, Nixon had expressed his frustration over having "10 years of total *control* of the air in Laos and V. Nam," and yet the result had been "Zilch." He now demanded a widened bombing assault on North Vietnam that would restrict the flow of war material into the south while punishing Hanoi for its decision to invade. A "stepped-up destructor campaign" as one report called it.[120] By late May, Air Force and Navy jets were averaging more than 330 strikes a day. Air sorties hit military installations, transportation facilities, and even power plants. Senior MACV officials hoped the B-52 bombing runs might compensate for the ARVN's "inadequate leadership" and weaken the enemy's "staying power," but Nixon had higher goals, seeking an end to the war on his terms. "I cannot emphasize too strongly," he relayed to Kissinger, "that I have determined that we should go for broke."[121]

Once more, however, MACV's commander ran afoul of his commander in chief. Since early April, Abrams and Nixon had been clashing over where best to prioritize US air assets—against NVA forces inside South Vietnam as the general wished or against strategic targets in North Vietnam as Nixon ordered. Confident that Linebacker would not engender a Soviet response, the president fumed over Abrams's intransigence. Admiral Moorer conveyed to MACV that the president was "extremely out of patience" with the bombing campaign. Privately, the Joint Chiefs chairman recorded that Nixon did not "think Abe understands the real problem."[122] Thus, as he did after Lam Son 719, Nixon dispatched Haig to Saigon to stop Abrams from looking "inward" and confining his focus to the ground campaign inside South Vietnam. By May, the deteriorating relationship between the White House and MACV headquarters forced Kissinger to send an urgent message to Ambassador Bunker stating that the president was "nearing the end of his patience with General Abrams on the issue of air action against North Vietnam." The president had clearly lost confidence in his top field commander.[123]

While the debate over airpower raged, Abrams's stock fell even further with fresh complaints over his alcohol abuse. Not only was Nixon "disgusted with the consistent failure to carry out orders," but also with Abrams showing "no imagination" and "drinking too much." As the 1972 spring offensive appeared to catch MACV flat-footed, Kissinger advocated relieving the general. "We just cannot play these games with the supremacy of the field commander," he told Nixon. The president seemed to entertain the idea. "He's had it. Look, he's fat, he's drinking too much, and he's not able to do the job."[124] By early May, Kissinger, then en route to Paris, cabled Haig in Washington that he was "appalled" by a communiqué from MACV that the national security advisor found to be a "self-serving egg-sucking, panicky lecture by Abrams." For a second time, the president considered sacking the MACV commander, only to hold back yet again at the last moment. Still, Nixon thought he should "send someone over there as a cop to watch over that son-of-a-bitch Abrams." Though Laird continued to stick by the embattled general, there seemed little doubt that MACV headquarters no longer held any real influence over decision-making in the White House.[125]

As the civil-military relationship plunged to its nadir of the long American war, US planes continued to pound the enemy across Vietnam. Though Nixon fantasized leaving office "having destroyed North Vietnam's capability," the damage wrought to achieve those dreams underscored the unrelenting violence of the war's final years. Inside South Vietnam, one government official described the "cratered rice fields and defoliated forests, devastated by an alien air force that seems at war with the very land of Vietnam."[126] South Vietnamese refugees, some displaced for a second or third time from their homes, jammed into make-shift camps and urban areas seeking shelter from the bombing. In the process, the destruction caused by thousands of tons of bombs battered Saigon's hopes for pacifying the countryside. Relying on so much firepower to stem the enemy offensive had left behind a stunned civilian population. One Laotian, living under the onslaught of US bombers, illustrated the trauma shared by her South Vietnamese neighbors. "We didn't know which day we would die. Everyone just waited for the day of their death. All day and night the airplanes never stopped bombing."[127]

The impact of intensive bombing on Vietnamese society, however, mat-tered less to those in the White House and MACV headquarters who deemed it crucial to blunt what they called the "Easter Offensive" at all costs. Abrams recognized the level of "brutality"—"the highest it's ever been in the whole war," he reasoned—yet called increasingly for more air assets over South Vietnam. In Washington, Kissinger saw the "physical results of the fighting as a plus."[128] Nixon, though, continued to clash with MACV's commander over employing the air force's strategic bombers. "I don't want him to short-change our efforts to destroy North Vietnam," the president said of Abrams, "in order for a half-assed effort to do something in South Vietnam." Deriding the general for "thinking short-term," Nixon wanted more than just a "little pop" against Hanoi.[129]

On 8 May, the president upped the ante by ordering a blockade of North Vietnam and the mining of Haiphong harbor and other major ports. These actions would continue, Nixon warned, until Hanoi agreed to return American POWs and to "an internationally supervised cease-fire through-out Indochina."[130] With a Moscow summit on the near horizon, the escala-tion certainly came with political risks, both at home and abroad. Nixon, though, was willing to endure a new flurry of antiwar demonstrations and a slowdown in negotiations in order to blunt the enemy offensive. In fact, both sides believed they could gain more from battlefield successes than from the contentious peace talks in Paris, held only a week earlier, that Kissinger later described as "brutal." The day after the president's announcement, however, Thomas Oliphant, writing in the *Boston Globe*, questioned Nixon's logic on the expanded use of military force. "In claiming the actions he has ordered are the 'only way to stop the killing', the President implicitly confessed that the South Vietnamese would not be able to defend themselves against the current North Vietnamese offensive, even with the direct American air support and supporting bombing raids against North Vietnam."[131]

Nixon's escalation, though, did not end the fighting. Nowhere was that more evident than in An Loc, the capital of Binh Long province, only 65 miles northwest of Saigon. There, the full force of the North Vietnamese Easter Offensive took center stage as both Saigon leaders and the American press drew attention to the "heroic saga" of ARVN defenders shielding the provincial capital from assault. President Thieu, worried over losing face if An Loc fell, rushed reinforcements into the fray as Abrams directed strategic bombers toward the attacking NVA. According to one report, "In one 24-hour period, American B-52s dropped 2.6 million pounds of bombs around An Loc."[132] As civilian casualties mounted, province officials used bulldozers to dig mass graves. "The bodies were all over the streets," said one weary American advisor. By mid-June, when the siege was finally lifted, An Loc lay in ruins. The ARVN had suffered more than 5,000 casualties during the stand, the North Vietnamese five times that amount. Such devastation put into question South Vietnamese claims that while "An Loc may have been destroyed . . . when the fighting ended, the South Vietnamese troops still controlled the city." What good was it to "control" the remnants of a burned-out provincial capital that one observer described as "completely smashed, broken into pieces, reduced to rubble"?[133]

Such questions underscored the predictable competing assessments over who triumphed as the Nguyen Hue offensive sputtered to a close. While Abrams perceived a "noticeable improvement in the fighting spirit" of ARVN forces, he also acknowledged that, even in this late stage of the war, US advisors were "the glue that's held this whole thing together." Other evaluations, blaming Abrams for a "screwed up" ground war, credited the US Air Force for saving South Vietnam. Still others pointed to the enormous casualties suffered by the NVA as proof of meeting the "test" during a hard-fought battle.[134] Perhaps most accurately, Alexander Haig noted that "the reasons for optimism were limited. South Vietnam's two northern provinces remained under effective control of the tens of thousands of enemy troops who remained in the country." Haig then offered a laundry list of unresolved problems: army organizational issues, poor senior leadership, the strengthening of the Khmer Rouge in Cambodia, and Hanoi's insistence to overthrow Thieu's government.

In late June, the *Boston Globe* offered a bleak assessment. South Vietnam was "unable to stand alone."[135]

If the *Globe* presented a sobering assessment, the psychological effect of yet another countrywide assault, one leaving tens of thousands of NVA troops inside South Vietnam, left claims of Vietnamization's success in doubt. Thieu may have been given a "new lease on life," but few believed the 1972 spring offensive had settled the underlying political issues between north and south. For Creighton Abrams, however, his war was coming to an end. In late June, a reluctant Nixon nominated Abrams to succeed Westmoreland as the US Army chief of staff. Privately, the president, long soured on the general's performance, had called his "military leadership . . . a sad chapter in the proud military history of this country." Yet a faithful Laird continued to stand by the embattled MACV commander and urged Nixon to make the nomination. In late June, the general departed from South Vietnam with little fanfare and no public ceremonies. Like Westmoreland before him, Abrams was leaving behind a war not yet won.[136]

The war, though, was not done with Abrams. Back in March, an official investigation of Seventh Air Force Commander John D. Lavelle found the general had ordered unauthorized "protective reaction strikes" against North Vietnam. Additionally, Abrams's air deputy allegedly had falsified mission reports, leading to Senate hearings, a reduction in rank, and forced retirement. The affair quickly became entwined with Abrams's confirmation hearings, as Lavelle testified he had "discussed the bombings" with the former MACV commander.[137] The case, however, proved messier than what journalists described simply as an assault on civilian control over the military. Indeed, some pundits saw the Air Force general as an all too convenient scapegoat for Nixon's failed bombing policies. Without question, imprecise rules of engagement, coupled with operational requirements to ensure the safety of the US bomber fleet in South Vietnam, left Lavelle's decisions open to interpretation. If the White House had intimated that the Air Force approach the rules of engagement "liberally," for instance, was Lavelle being insubordinate or rather being cautious against the North Vietnamese air and anti-aircraft threats?[138]

The ongoing Senate inquiry left Abrams's confirmation uncertain. While Fred Weyand took charge of MACV, its former commander waited in uneasy limbo. In early July, Senator John C. Stennis (D-Mississippi) disclosed testimony linking Abrams to the unauthorized raids and to the false reporting system accounting for enemy action against US planes when there was none. If true, one commentary suggested, the general had been "insubordinate to the civilian authority whose orders he is sworn to obey."[139] For four months the hearings held up Abrams's confirmation. So contentious had the proceedings become that Senator Margaret Chase Smith (R-Maine) accused the general of "failing his duty." Despite Smith's dissent, the vote finally circulated to the Senate floor and Abrams's confirmation passed by a vote of 84 to 2 in mid-October. The drawn-out process, though, only further embittered Nixon who at year's end called the general "just a clod."[140]

The heated controversy over the Lavelle affair emphasized not only the sheer depths to which the civil-military relationship had sunk by 1972, but also the inability of military strategy to deliver on the president's most vital policy objectives. In short, Vietnamization was now largely irrelevant to how the administration ended the war through negotiated settlement. After years of trying to foster a stable Saigon government backed by a capable army, Nixon was no longer certain that South Vietnam could survive on its own.[141] Even in negotiations with Le Duc Tho at year's end, Kissinger accepted that the United States could "not give Saigon a guarantee of victory." "What we want," he told the North Vietnamese envoy, "is an agreement which gives the real political forces in Vietnam an opportunity over a period of time to develop, so that the Vietnamese people over a period of time can determine their destiny."[142]

By August, with his re-election looming, Nixon fretted that simply giving South Vietnam a chance, not a guarantee, to survive might not be enough to ensure American credibility overseas. In a conversation with his chief advisor, the president worried about having a viable foreign policy "if a year from now or two years from now, North Vietnam gobbles up South Vietnam." Kissinger believed they could, as long as Saigon's ruin appeared "the result of South Vietnamese incompetence." Thus, in a real sense, Vietnamization, as a policy, had become bankrupt. In the Americans' final summer of the war, Kissinger would negotiate only the most fundamental of military issues, leaving the Vietnamese to "settle their own affairs" after the institution of a cease-fire and the final withdrawal of US troops from Southeast Asia.[143]

The process of negotiations hence concentrated on preventing a near-term collapse of the South Vietnamese state, leaving behind the original aim of help-ing build a stable, noncommunist entity as a distant memory. Here, the dubi-ous results of the Easter Offensive mattered as both sides believed a diplomatic solution ripe given their own views of battlefield conditions. Thieu, however, saw the NVA troops remaining on South Vietnamese soil as a direct threat to his nation's survival, especially given the impending loss of US troop support.[144] Yet Kissinger's greatest concerns in Paris that summer focused on gaining a dip-lomatic end to the war before the November elections at home. During August and September, Le Duc Tho dropped his demands for Thieu's removal and for the formation of a coalition government in the south. Then, in early October, the envoys produced a draft agreement calling for an immediate cease-fire in place, a full US withdrawal, and the return of all POWs. No mention was made of the

North Vietnamese troops still occupying South Vietnam's northernmost provinces and other territory.[145]

The draft hardly provided a structure for achieving true stability inside South Vietnam and thus lasting peace. Indeed, John Negroponte, a member of the NSC staff, acknowledged this reality. In a private memorandum, he shared with Kissinger his belief that the Americans were "moving towards [a] framework of settlement which will enable us to disengage militarily, get our prisoners back and leave the Vietnamese to slug it out between themselves in a context of reduced main force violence but continued political struggle of intensive brutality."[146]

While Kissinger and Le Duc Tho haggled over provisions governing arms resupply to the competing factions inside South Vietnam, Thieu balked at a deal he saw as little more than a humiliating surrender. In Washington, a recently retired Westmoreland agreed, telling Nixon that "a ceasefire in place without [an NVA] withdrawal commitment . . . amounted to a de facto cessation by Thieu of sovereignty over substantial portions of South Vietnamese territories." Nixon, however, had already concluded the war must end. "We cannot go along with this sort of dreary business of hanging on for another four years. It's been too long."[147]

But Thieu did not want peace on the terms that Kissinger had negotiated. Too many concessions, he believed, put his nation at risk. Even a visit to Saigon by Abrams, sent by Nixon to "sell" the proposed agreement, made little impact. Consequently, when Kissinger declared "peace is at hand" on 26 October 1972, the South Vietnamese president seethed with anger. "I wanted to punch Kissinger in the mouth," Thieu recalled.[148]

If Nixon hoped to move forward alongside the Saigon government as a "willing partner," his desire for a swift peace agreement also impelled him to take a "hard line" with Thieu as much as with Hanoi's diplomats. The president clearly still hoped to "end the war with honor," yet Thieu balked at the Americans' political and military compromises. Negotiations quickly broke down in mutual recriminations. With Kissinger scrambling to pick up the pieces, and Hanoi blasting the Americans and South Vietnamese for reneging on the proposals to which Kissinger agreed, the South Vietnamese president remained adamant that he would not sell out his people.[149] Thieu objected to plans giving political voice to a "third force" inside South Vietnam, opposed any agreement mentioning the Provisional Revolutionary Government (PRG), and protested the lack of specificity on the status of the demilitarized zone between north and south. As one NSC staffer quipped, "After having said for years that the GVN was a sovereign, independent government, we now resented it acting that way by opposing what was from their point of view . . . a poor agreement."[150]

Figure 13 THE WAVES COME CRASHING IN. Political cartoonist Ranan R. Lurie's depiction of how the Easter Offensive was impacting Nixon's plans for Vietnamization, 2 May 1972. [*Ni@on Rated Cartoons*, rev. ed. (New York: Quadrangle, 1974), 100.]

Exit the Americans

By mid-December 1972, Richard Nixon's patience had run out. Thieu's intransigence, coupled with a diplomatic impasse in Paris, left a frustrated president turning once more to military force in hopes of achieving a political settlement. On the 12th, Nixon decided that if the diplomatic stalemate continued, "we're going to bomb the hell out of 'em." Two days later, the president dispatched an ultimatum to the North Vietnamese warning of grave consequences if serious negotiations did not resume within 72 hours.[151] As he recalled, "Only the strongest action would have any effect in convincing Hanoi that negotiating a fair settlement with us was a better option for them than continuing the war." The Joint Chiefs immediately began coordinating plans with CINCPAC and Weyand's air deputy for a "massive three-day strike up North which would envision using as many B52s as possible." Naval forces would also reseed the mines in Haiphong harbor. In short, the White House was seeking to make "a tremendous psychological blow."[152]

Aiming directly to influence the North's will, hundreds of American B-52 sorties began pounding strategic targets around Hanoi and Haiphong beginning on 18 December. For the next eleven days, US planes dropped over 42,000 bombs on North Vietnam. Hanoi Radio called the raids "devastating." To Nixon and Kissinger, though, the breakdown in negotiations left them little choice but to unleash the only remaining weapons in their military arsenal. As the national security advisor argued just before Operation Linebacker II kicked off, if the White House accepted a modified peace agreement simply based on Hanoi's diplomatic rebuff, it "would make us look impotent." A massive bombing campaign, however, while causing the North to "scream for a few weeks," would more importantly "make the agreement enforceable." Such assumptions, however, overlooked the certainty of NVA troops remaining inside South Vietnam even after arranging a final settlement. The bombing might induce Hanoi back to the negotiating table, but it did not necessarily mean Le Duc Tho would concede to all of Thieu or Kissinger's demands.[153]

As Nixon expected, the public outcry to Linebacker II was swift and condemnatory. Senator George McGovern, fresh off his loss in the recent presidential election, argued, "It defies all reason to suggest that the North Vietnamese will abandon their cause now—after a generation of struggle—simply because we are bombing the North once again." Writing in *The Christian Science Monitor*, Robert R. Bowie, head of policy planning in the State Department during the Eisenhower administration, called the around-the-clock bombing "heartrending," while the British tabloid *Daily Mirror* labeled the campaign "Nixon's Christmas deluge of death."[154] Nor did the bombing dispel Thieu's fears that his allies were about to forsake him. As he told Haig in late December, "It is very clear to me that there will be no peace as a result of this agreement." Cao Van Vien, chairman of the South Vietnamese Joint General Staff, went further. The final months of 1972, the general surmised, had exposed the ugly truth that "U.S. policy had shifted toward appeasement and accommodation with the Communists even at the price of reneging on a commitment to help an ally maintain independence."[155]

By month's end, however, Hanoi agreed to return to the negotiating table. With the loss of fifteen B-52s in less than two weeks of bombing, Nixon welcomed an end to Linebacker II and the possibility of sealing a final settlement. As Haig warned Thieu, though, "Under no circumstances will President Nixon accept a veto from Saigon in regard to a peace agreement." Airpower advocates quickly extolled the bombing campaign's virtues, one even arguing the war had been won because of it. "Unfortunately," lamented Admiral U. S. Grant Sharp, "we failed to press home our advantage."[156] Such arguments rested on scant evidence. A comparison of the October draft agreement and the final peace settlement yields few, if any, major differences. Moreover, by mid-March 1973, the North Vietnamese had resumed their "heavy rate of personnel infiltration and logistics movements through Southern Laos into Cambodia and South Vietnam." If the final US bombing campaign had won the war, neither Hanoi's diplomats nor the North Vietnamese Army seemed to have taken notice.[157]

In the end, no amount of American military muscle, bombing or otherwise, could resolve the fundamental issue of whether South Vietnam was a viable nation capable of effective governance. Nixon certainly aspired to give Saigon a fighting chance at survival once the last American troops departed, to secure an "honorable peace" that he and his administration "could live with."[158] Yet as the weary combatants edged toward a final peace agreement, it seemed clear to many observers that despite its preponderance of power, the United States had been unable to stabilize a weak ally for the long-term political struggle just beyond the horizon. As one ARVN general noted, "Self-salvation cannot be achieved simply by efforts to put an end to the military aspects of the hostilities." Securing final victory thus rested on a still unresolved question despite decades of brutal war. What was the South Vietnamese political corollary to the United States' immense advantages in military power?[159]

Epilogue and Conclusions

Questioning "Victory" in an American War

On Tuesday morning, 23 January 1973, Richard Nixon held a "pro forma" cabinet meeting to discuss the end of America's war in Vietnam. White House Chief of Staff H. R. Haldeman, in attendance on what he felt was a "historic day," noted in his diary the president's optimism. "We have peace with honor," Nixon declared, "the POW's are back, the supervised cease-fire, and the right of South Vietnam to determine their own future." In the president's view, a responsible American nation had persevered and, in fact, had saved an ally's freedom. Four days later, delegates from North and South Vietnam, the southern Provisional Revolutionary Government, and the United States signed the Paris Agreement on Ending the War and Restoring Peace in Vietnam. As Nixon later claimed, "We had won the war."[1]

Such reminiscences, however, obscured a far murkier ending to the United States' crusade in Southeast Asia. Nixon may have believed he had won the war, only for others to "lose the peace," but such neat assessments were hardly shared at the time. The day after the Paris signing, Frances FitzGerald, writing in *The Washington Post*, asked questions that surely were on the minds of many Americans. "Is the Vietnam war over, and if so, who has won it?" In public, Kissinger stated, in admittedly ambiguous language, that the agreement had to be judged "in terms of the evolution that it starts."[2] In private, he conceded to Alexander Haig that "we know the goddamned agreement will probably not work, but we've got to be in the position where if it doesn't work it will be the result of the other side." Yet only three days after the signing, the *New York Times* reported that both sides had continued fighting, each accusing the other "of scores of additional cease-fire violations." Perhaps the agreement had not restored peace.[3]

True, Hanoi released American prisoners of war while the Saigon government "engaged in intense political organization activity" as the agreement went into effect. But North Vietnam had not abandoned its goal of gaining control of the south. In the first six months of 1973 alone, some 65,000 NVA recruits poured into South Vietnam, all while Hanoi stockpiled tanks, artillery, and anti-aircraft weapons for a future offensive. By late March, as the last MACV soldiers departed from Vietnam, it seemed clear the war had ended only for the Americans. As one US advisor noted, there "was a growing sense that one was sitting on a time bomb and that the North Vietnamese were adding new sticks of dynamite to that bomb every day."[4] On the 29th, Fred Weyand, MACV's last commander, retired his unit's colors. Despite great sacrifice, Weyand declared, the allies had prevented "an all-out attempt by an aggressor to impose its will through raw military force." As the general concluded before boarding a plane to depart Vietnam, "Our mission has been accomplished."[5]

Nowhere in these public pronouncements of success did senior US officials use the word "victory." Perhaps it no longer mattered, at least for the moment. As the *Boston Globe* reckoned, the United States was simply giving "a painful, unfinished war back to the Vietnamese." Americans just wanted to move on. Still, the Nixon administration looked to bolster what it left behind. Back in October 1972, not long after Kissinger declared peace was at hand, the Defense Department embarked on a resupply program to deliver the South Vietnamese armed forces much-needed weapons, ammunition, fuel, and other war-related equipment.[6] Dubbed Operations Enhance and Enhance Plus, the effort proved to be the final exclamation point on Nixon's Vietnamization policy. The US government spent more than $750 million to help the ARVN combat both NVA forces that had remained in South Vietnam and a reviving local insurgency that belied claims the National Liberation Front had been destroyed during the 1968 Tet offensive. By September 1973, *The Washington Post* was reporting that government forces were "waging a sustained campaign to wrest land and people from Communist control in . . . [some] of the most important areas of the country."[7]

Nixon, however, who was waging his own battles at home, increasingly lost interest in South Vietnam's affairs. In late 1973, Congress passed a joint resolution curbing the president's power to commit US forces to military action without consent of the legislative branch. Moreover, domestic economic woes, spurred by a global recession, hinted at a decline in future military aid to South Vietnam. But for the president, the political crisis caused by the illegal break-in at the Democratic National Committee headquarters in Washington, DC, mattered most. Watergate would consume Nixon for the remainder of his time in office, leading to his resignation in August 1974 and the inauguration of a new president with little appetite to recommit the nation to an ongoing civil war in Vietnam.[8]

With little risk of direct American involvement, Le Duan moved to consolidate his gains and prepare North Vietnam's military forces "to seize the strategic opportunity" against the embattled south. Throughout 1973, the communists mobilized their manpower, assailed remote ARVN outposts and bases, and attacked the GVN's pacification programs. As these attacks continued during the following year, Le Duan concluded the time was ripe to unleash a new, country-wide offensive in 1975. The military onslaught of South Vietnam would either force a surrender or compel Nguyen Van Thieu to accept a coalition government in Saigon.[9] Most Politburo members, to include Le Duan, expected to achieve total victory in 1976. Only then would the Party finally "liberate South Vietnam, complete the people's national democratic revolution in the whole country and proceed to reunify our homeland."[10]

The general secretary, however, had overestimated the resistance South Vietnam could muster in the fateful spring of 1975. True, the ARVN had fought tenaciously in late 1974 and into the new year, parrying communist offensives in all four of South Vietnam's corps areas. Yet without the backing of American firepower, and lacking a coordinated response from its Joint General Staff, the South Vietnamese armed forces inexorably lost ground. With the invaders seizing more and more territory, the RVNAF abandoned crucial equipment as deserting soldiers turned to protect their families rather than the nation itself. When Hanoi launched its final assault on 26 April 1975, dubbed the Ho Chi Minh Campaign, the outcome seemed little in doubt. Four days later, NVA tanks broke through the gates of Independence Palace in Saigon. The Republic of Vietnam was no more.[11]

Saigon's fall exposed the reality that the end of Vietnam's civil war could not be compromised, at least for Le Duan and the Hanoi Politburo. The north's definition of victory demanded a purging of the south's political society. In truth, all sides understood the Paris peace agreement would not stand, only that the United States would withdraw unilaterally. A long-lasting political compromise simply was unacceptable to Hanoi, for it undermined the ultimate aims of unification and true Vietnamese independence.[12] As General Cao Van Vien recalled, the agreement "did not terminate the conflict . . . but established a state of 'half war-half peace' in which political activities would take precedence over military operations." That may have been true in the near term, but both sides realized that hard fighting lay ahead. Thus, even in 1973, before the peace accord's ink was dry, South Vietnamese children were preparing for a "war from which they saw no exit."[13]

Of course, the Americans had exited, provoking the wrath of their erstwhile partner Nguyen Van Thieu. In a fiery speech as he resigned his presidency in April 1975, Thieu denounced the United States for allowing "our combatants to die under the hail of shells. This is an inhumane act by an inhumane ally."[14] Unsurprisingly, at least some Americans came to a vastly different conclusion. They pointed to the Norwegian Nobel Committee jointly awarding Henry Kissinger and Le Duc Tho the 1973 Peace Prize as proof that US diplomats had maintained the nation's credibility while withdrawing from Vietnam. While Le Duc Tho declined the honor, Kissinger accepted with the observation that "certain war has yielded to an uncertain peace in Vietnam." But the fall of Saigon less than eighteen months later put into question whether the ideal of peace—"our common destiny," Kissinger proclaimed—was, in experience, "our common practice."[15]

Reinventing Success after a Lost War

Kissinger's acceptance speech might now be seen as an opening salvo in a prolonged contest over who would command the postwar narrative of an already hotly debated conflict. Questions abounded. Did the United States win or lose in Vietnam? Had "peace with honor" been achieved? If the United States did lose, who was to blame? Certainly, Nixon and his senior advisors maintained they had given the Saigon government every opportunity to succeed on its own. The Americans' departure, they argued, demonstrated that larger political aims, in fact, had been achieved. As early as 1971, Nixon had declared publicly that from "the outset our constant primary goal has been a negotiated end to the war for all participants." Never mind that Thieu clung to his own policy of "four no's" to the brutal end: "no negotiations with the communists, no surrender of territory, no coalition government, and no communist political activity."[16]

If the peace indeed had been lost, neither Nixon nor Kissinger were prepared to accept responsibility. The former shared with a confidante that by 1973 "we had achieved our political objective: South Vietnam's independence had been secured. But by 1975," Nixon continued, "the Congress destroyed our ability to enforce the Paris agreement and left our allies vulnerable to Hanoi's invading forces."[17] Kissinger, for his part, offered his thoughts to the new president, Gerald R. Ford. In a wide-ranging memorandum, he discussed the problems of domestic support, of "liberal Democrats" unable to support a war against a revolutionary movement, of the media's "fascination with issues that were, at best, peripheral," of the US armed forces "not suited to this kind of war," and of diplomatic efforts being undermined by politics at home. Kissinger hoped to avoid public "self-flagellation," arguing that "we should not characterize our role in the conflict as a disgraceful disaster."[18] Yet in the aftermath of Saigon's fall, few Americans were prepared to look back on their experiences in Southeast Asia with much pride.

Thus set in motion a series of rationalizations, justifications, and denunciations from key participants about why the United States had seemingly come up short in Vietnam. (Creighton Abrams's death in September 1974 from lung cancer ensured he would play no role in this final "battle" of the American War.) Senior uniformed leaders decried "civilian, political decision makers who chose out of flagrant arrogance or naïve wishful thinking to ignore the sound, time-vindicated principles of military strategy."[19] Westmoreland, speaking in 1978 to students at the US Army's Command and General Staff College, observed that "the handling of the Vietnam affair was a shameful national blunder." Others blamed Congress for reducing crucial funding to the GVN, while still others believed their "principal vulnerability was the weakness inherent in democracy itself." Soldiers meanwhile blamed "gutless politicians and, worse yet, gutless general officers." It seemed no one or no institution was safe from condemnation.[20]

While officers steadfastly maintained—"truthfully" from their perspective—that they "were not allowed to fight to win," such arguments, at least in the mid- to late 1970s, failed to resonate with the larger American public. Rather, it seemed, Vietnam had unceremoniously exposed the limits of US power abroad. No "peace dividend" followed the Paris agreement, as weary Americans, so long at war with each other over the Vietnam conflict, now endured both political and economic crises at home in the aftermath of Watergate and the 1973 oil shock.[21] Surely, some veterans met with hostility upon returning home. One, for instance, felt "all I got from people around me was that Vietnam veterans were drug addicts, murderers, freaked-out criminals." By and large, however, most Americans looked to move beyond the whole unpleasant experience. If former Secretary of State Dean Rusk was correct in deeming the war's end a "surrender," such assessments did not fit easily into the preferred national narrative of the world's righteous superpower defending liberty and freedom abroad.[22]

Little during the Ford and Jimmy Carter administrations gave Americans much evidence to challenge such dour conceptions of the United States' place in the world. Concerned army officers in the mid-1970s spoke of a "current malaise" and of a "general confusion in America." Carter's spotlight on international human rights apparently offered no comfort. Such an ideological shift in US foreign policy seemed ill-suited to those in uniform already worried about rebuilding after Vietnam "to defend the national interests lest some aggressor decide to exploit our perceived weakness."[23] When Carter delivered his now famous "crisis of confidence" speech in July 1979, all indicators suggested the United States had sunk to new lows after its unsuccessful war in Southeast Asia. The president lamented "the growing doubt about the meaning of our own lives and in the loss of a unity of purpose for our nation." Worse, this erosion of confidence threatened "to destroy the social and the political fabric of America."[24]

Yet, in a way, the fall of Saigon would help Ronald Reagan re-envision the war as a "noble cause" in the early 1980s. By appropriating veterans' arguments that they had been stabbed in the back by feckless politicians, the new president could advocate on the behalf of those who "fought as well and as bravely as any Americans have ever fought in any war." The antidote to Carter's crisis of confidence? For Reagan, a commitment that no peace would be a "peace of humiliation and gradual surrender." Rather, peace would be "best served by strength not bluster." By rehabilitating the veteran, Reagan aimed to rejuvenate the nation. These honorable warriors had fought a moral and just war, helping a small country, "newly free from colonial rule," establish self-rule and defend against "a totalitarian neighbor bent of conquest." In Reagan's telling, no moral confusion clouded why the United States went to war in Vietnam.[25]

By ushering in an American *dolchstoß* ("stab-in-the-back") story, blame for a lost war could be parceled out in such a way that the original cause remained true. Thus, Americans still had a role to play in world affairs. Reagan consequently lambasted critics stricken by the "Vietnam Syndrome," political shorthand for "an unwillingness to commit [U.S. troops] to an unwinnable conflict." No, the president countered, the war in Vietnam had been winnable. Had Congress not acted "with unprecedented irresponsibility," the United States would have maintained its pledge to South Vietnam and the young nation's survival ensured.[26] Unsurprisingly, Richard Nixon, writing in 1985, agreed with Reagan. The same year *Rambo: First Blood Part II* hit theaters, the former president attacked the symptoms of the Vietnam Syndrome. While Rambo rescued fictional POWs still being held captive in Vietnam, Nixon attacked real-life propagandists who made "Americans ashamed of their power, guilty about being strong, and forgetful about the need to be willing to use their power to protect their freedom and the freedom of others."[27]

In the process of defending what Reagan and his supporters now saw as an honorable cause, veterans could receive a long-overdue welcome home. Commemorations could become therapeutic, not just for the soldier but for the nation. Even debate over the Vietnam Veterans Memorial Wall, finished in 1982, revolved around whether the gabbro panels properly honored veterans' sacrifices. While one veteran described it as a "black gash of shame," designer Maya Lin hoped instead that the Wall would symbolize a recovery of sorts. "I had the impulse to cut open the earth ... an initial violence that in time would heal. The grass would grow back, but the cut would remain."[28] Adopted properly—at least in political terms—the memorial could also exhibit a renewed sense of patriotism. Thus, when President Reagan spoke at the Wall on Veterans Day in 1988, he called on the country to "remember the devotion and gallantry with which all [Vietnam War veterans] ennobled their nation as they became champions of a noble cause."[29]

Subsequently, the Vietnam War could still be useful in this new American reckoning. If the war had been fought bravely by gallant soldiers defending freedom abroad, then the United States could "win" in future conflicts by not taking counsel of irresolute policymakers' fears. The nation could thus "stand tall" again, proud in new military actions aimed at spreading US influence abroad, upholding democratic values against communism, and, perhaps most importantly, demonstrating the renewed vigor of the American people. The lesson of Vietnam, according to MACV's former pacification chief William Colby, was "not that the United States should avoid involvement in revolutionary situations," but rather "come to terms with the question of how to express, and use, its superpower."[30]

It is here, then, that the "better war" narrative reemerged as a convenient storyline for those revisionists looking to exploit a usable past. Not only was the cause just, but the war had been won. By the end of Reagan's presidency, veterans were proudly pointing out that the US Army had "brought the enemy to its knees by the end of 1972." When MACV folded its colors for the final time, they argued, South Vietnam's government was "standing firmly on its own feet." State Department Foreign Service Officer Norman B. Hannah echoed these sentiments. "The United States did not lose a war in Indochina," Hannah maintained. "American forces consistently defeated North Vietnamese forces in South Vietnam. Our forces withdrew in an orderly planned process, completed two years before Hanoi launched its final aggression in 1975."[31] In short, Creighton Abrams had helped lead the allies to military victory.

The Limits of a "Better" War

Despite the congenial nature of such arguments, embraced by military officers who desperately wanted to believe they had won their war, the American experience in Vietnam more aptly demonstrated the problems of defining "victory" in a nuclear age. When noted political scientist Robert Osgood revisited the topic of "limited war" in 1979, he questioned whether any use of military force could have "stopped the guerrilla warfare or enabled the GVN to overcome political weaknesses that enabled such warfare to continue." To Osgood, the "national interests at stake were not sufficiently compelling to Americans to have justified a scale and duration of combat necessary to win the war." Within this interpretation, the boundary lines between political aims and military means were not as defined as those advocating a "better war" narrative may have liked. Osgood was proposing, quite correctly, that there were problems in arguing military officers had won in Vietnam, only to be undercut by irresponsible politicians.[32]

In reality, US military strategy under Abrams could not transcend declining support for a war that no longer mattered, at least existentially, either to the Nixon administration or to the American people. The lack of tangible progress surely aided in such assessments. In the aftermath of the 1968 Tet offensive, the allies simply had not demonstrated clearly enough that they were winning. Both Vietnamization and pacification remained fitful processes. Incursions into Cambodia and Laos had only temporarily wounded the enemy. The National Liberation Front, while damaged, retained its presence in the countryside. Political and economic problems continued to undermine the Saigon government's legitimacy. Hanoi's will had not been broken, as evidenced by the 1972 spring offensive. Thus, while US army officers long had claimed that American prestige relied on preserving South Vietnam's independence, they could not overcome the unremitting local problems that proved stubbornly resistant to outside influence.[33]

These officers clearly were fighting an uphill battle. By 1969, senior policymakers in the White House no longer deemed national security at stake in Southeast Asia. The Vietnamese conflict consequently became of peripheral concern within the larger Cold War context. True, South Vietnam continued to represent a "symbolic test of intentions, wills and strength" as one lieutenant colonel had noted back in 1962. But, in the greater scheme of US global affairs, the conflict became an unpleasant affair to be concluded rather than won.[34]

By differentiating the vital from the peripheral, the Nixon White House left Abrams's command struggling to make armed force in Vietnam purposeful. Throughout the war's final years, the president intended American power to "create conditions which can lead to peace." Yet Abrams could never quite match that power to such ambitious aims. Of course, the political environment of South Vietnam mattered. Not long after Abrams took command, one American officer highlighted the "realities of a people's war" in which US troops had long been immersed. "A political revolution is something quite different from a conventional military campaign," he noted, "and yet we persist in viewing Vietnam as a war which will be won when we bring enough power and force to bear." Granted, most all MACV officers realized they were fighting more than just a conventional campaign. Abrams's "one war" depiction spoke to that reality. Yet the American command also retained its faith, even after most US troops had departed Vietnam, in military power sustaining the Saigon regime throughout a protracted political civil war.[35]

This faith proved groundless, in part, because of the changing geopolitical context of the late 1960s and early 1970s. Likely no military strategy crafted inside Vietnam could overcome the realities of a US foreign policy aimed more and more at promoting and maintaining improved relations with China and the Soviet Union. As Nixon saw it, the majority of Americans were "sick of the war" in Southeast Asia and wanted to move on from it. Global commitments, other than to South Vietnam, demanded attention elsewhere. Thus, within the larger framework of détente and the opening to China, the Vietnamese civil war mattered only in how it might impact the prestige of the United States as it withdrew from a muddled conflict.[36]

Perhaps just as importantly, the strategic dialogue between the White House and MACV headquarters had degenerated to the point of dysfunctionality. The toxic relationship shared by the administration and Abrams's command left little room for harmonizing grand and military strategies. Surely, Nixon's unrealistic expectations of what MACV could accomplish in balancing the myriad elements of the allies' campaign plans—Vietnamization, pacification, and combat to name but a few—left Abrams in a difficult spot. The general, however, more often than not seemed out of step with his commander in chief. Not only did the White House question Abrams's leadership in the aftermath of the 1971 Laotian incursion and the 1972 North Vietnamese spring offensive, but his character as well. The MACV commander, for his part, consistently saw policymakers as out of touch, hindering progress inside South Vietnam rather than listening to professional military advice. Thus, the "better war" narrative required the propagation of a central allegation: unwise civilians, inexperienced in the art of strategy, had yanked defeat from the jaws of victory.

Such constructions, though, rested far more on myth than evidence. In the aftermath of Tet in 1968, many journalists, and Americans, wanted to believe a new commander with a new strategy could turn the war around. Yet this "Abe Abrams cult" embarrassed even the general himself. Senior military officers from Saigon to the Pentagon knew the allied approach changed only in small details after Abrams took command of MACV. And as early as 1969, at least some journalists began questioning their earlier faith in fresh leadership. In September, *Newsweek* asserted that Nixon, attempting "to reconcile a policy of withdrawal with pressures for outright victory," appeared to be "succeeding at neither."[37] The following year, one colonel argued the US Army ultimately had to be judged on what it left "behind in the way of a functioning social order, viable government, and military establishment capable of sustaining both against attack." An "infinite number of military victories," he declared, would "still fall short of political success." Yet under Creighton Abrams, the allies had achieved neither military victory nor political success. By one account, only "mutual exhaustion had paved the way for peace."[38]

Contesting the "better war" myth thus has merit, for false perceptions of the past matter in the present. In large sense, the "surge" narrative of the Iraq War would build on what seemed to be a useful historical precedence. The "deeply conventional" General George Casey could conveniently play the role of William Westmoreland with David Petraeus performing as the new Abrams. Just as counterinsurgency commanders under Abrams had "improved dramatically in every way," so, too, could the US Army do "practically everything differently under Petraeus."[39] And yet the purported seismic strategic shift in Iraq (and to a lesser extent Afghanistan) has left behind a contested record rivalling that of the American saga in Vietnam. In short, pundits in the mid-2000s were selling a theoretically war-winning strategy based on an overly simplistic, if not completely erroneous, reading of history.[40]

A more careful investigation of Abrams's tenure in Vietnam might have uncovered the far less agreeable perspective that the "one war" approach had, in fact, only partially fulfilled Nixon's political goals. True, the US withdrawal advanced as a matter of policy rather than collapse. Yet judged on what it left behind, one seems hard pressed to argue MACV "won" its war. Even in late 1971, Abrams admitted to his staff that he had failed to find "the right balance" in coordinating so many aspects of a complex political-military conflict. One year later, as the Vietnamese combatants staggered back to their feet after the NVA's costly spring offensive, journalist Peter Arnett wrote of the last American infantrymen departing with "pride worn thin." To Arnett, US strategy had "failed," illustrated by the war in the countryside "being fought at a much more furious pace than when the first American ground troops came in." Those troops might be leaving, but the war was "still on for the Vietnamese."[41]

Arnett hit on an essential critique of the "better war" myth. A key deficiency in the Abrams-centric tale is how devoid the story is of Vietnamese voices. By arguing "that the root cause of South Vietnam's defeat was the slashing of assistance by the U.S. Congress in 1974," scholars could insinuate that Americans had achieved, at very least, a military victory.[42] But the betrayal narrative leaves out the numerous Vietnamese, north and south alike, who doubted the war was won during Abrams's tenure. Nor did civilians living in the south's crowded urban areas or war-torn countryside deem a "better war" had been fought on their behalf. In fact, even MACV's command historians noted in their review of 1972 the numerous issues "yet to be successfully addressed." Major problems included "pervasive corruption, inexperienced leadership in the RVNAF, lack of middle management expertise, a fragmented body politic, and an over-reliance on the military to govern." It seemed the assumptions on which American strategy were based, that US forces could transform Vietnamese society, had proved ill-founded.[43]

Such criticisms of the "better war" narrative should not simply shift blame from the American Congress to the Saigon regime. Reductive arguments seeking a single point of failure in a complicated revolutionary war hardly further our understanding of Vietnam's long political-military struggle. The point, rather, is that military strategy, even an inclusive one reflecting a conflict's political nature, may not always attain its objectives, especially in a war over ideas. Despite the comprehensiveness of the "one war" approach, it was still, at its base, a military strategy. Pacification, for instance, remained an inherently violent affair under Abrams. Vietnamization too often concentrated on ARVN's capacity to wage battle. Moreover, while the insurgency may have faced "great difficulties" in 1969 and 1970, the Saigon government never fully took advantage of the NLF's struggles in the countryside. Rather than sharing in a political vision of the future, the bulk of the southern population continued to debate the meaning of what its society should represent in a postwar environment.[44]

Thus, Abrams faced a dual problem neither he nor his predecessor ever resolved. Through a broad military strategy, MACV had to overcome thorny political-military obstacles inside South Vietnam while, at the same time,

proving the United States' geopolitical credibility by prevailing in a local war
with seemingly global implications. In waging war, Abrams had to demonstrate
not only the legitimacy of the Saigon regime but also the primacy of US grand
strategy in Southeast Asia. Thus, as early as Abrams's deputy commander stint
at MACV headquarters, American officers were speaking in ambitious terms of
"restructuring . . . the Vietnamese society" in ways that would be "truly revolutionary." Such aspirations, however, never accorded with local realities. In truth,
only the Vietnamese could fashion the political and social revolutions determining national identity in the postcolonial era.[45]

It seems beneficial then to reconsider the Abrams years not as a "better
war," but rather as a case study in the limits of US power abroad. The war's
outcome never lay entirely in American hands. As much as US officials in
South Vietnam aimed for what CORDS chief William Colby dubbed the
"three selfs"—self-defense, self-government, and self-development—they too
often found Saigon leaders moving in an opposite direction that seemed to
undermine such goals. As one late 1969 report noted, the "lesson seems to be
that although the U.S. retains the power of persuasion Thieu retains freedom
of action, even after he has been persuaded."[46] This lack of leverage over host
nation institutions and leaders had bedeviled frustrated American advisors for
years. Yet the phenomenon should not be surprising. Throughout the long war
in Vietnam, even during the Abrams era, US officials could not fully manip-
ulate South Vietnamese leaders who held their own visions of the future.
Americans might be persuasive given their economic and military advantages,
but they were never omnipotent.[47]

In fact, a misplaced hope in Abrams's "new" strategy to influence the GVN,
and thus shape the war's outcome, may actually have done more harm than
good simply by prolonging the conflict. False expectations of what MACV's
new commander could deliver after the 1968 Tet offensive provided Nixon
with the political cover to carry on despite deep-seated questions over whether
he actually could achieve "victory." In the process, the South Vietnamese
nation shuddered under the weight of fresh military campaigns, B-52 bombing runs, and shocks to its economic system. So, too, did its Cambodian and
Laotian neighbors suffer from the ongoing war. These "disruptive effects," as
RAND anthropologist Gerald C. Hickey called them, not only "restructured
Vietnamese society" for the worse but also, in the process, tended to reduce the
already tentative political support Thieu's regime enjoyed in the countryside.
As war correspondent Jonathan Schell quipped, "The more we won, the more
we lost."[48]

Schell, however, proved only partially correct. As the war raged on after
1968, it was the Vietnamese, not the Americans, who lost the most. True, more
than 20,000 US servicemen and women died during the lethal years after Tet.

Yet Vietnamese, on both sides of the demilitarized zone, suffered far more. By one account, some 598,500 combatants were killed or wounded in the final four years of American involvement. (Such a figure excludes civilian casualties, which proved far higher.)[49] Placed within the context of a negotiated settlement secured in Paris, one must question whether another four years of war warranted these grave human costs. Did a "better war" truly offer any meaning to these deaths? Had expanded fighting into Cambodia and Laos, and extended bombing runs over North Vietnam, left South Vietnam any more stable than in the months just after Tet? It seems doubtful. In reality, given that a stalemate was the best Abrams could produce over four years of fighting, that a client regime was really no better prepared for the contested peace to follow, perhaps there were, in fact, substitutes to military "victory."

The Limits of an American War

Nearly fifty years after the fall of Saigon, the time is ripe to reconsider the Vietnam War as many Vietnamese see it—the American War. This is more than just linguistic deconstruction or a convenient way to place blame for failure on South Vietnam's government, armed forces, or people. Rather, and perhaps counterintuitively, such a reevaluation places the Americans in a subordinate role when taking an extended view of the struggle for Vietnamese unification and independence. The American War, quite simply, was only one phase in a much longer conflict. The contest between social orders over political legitimacy had less to do with the leverage US civilian and military leaders could wield in Southeast Asia than in choices Vietnamese themselves were making throughout a long and brutal conflict. The American War may not have been "irrelevant to the Vietnamese wars," as one historian has argued, but it clearly represented only one part of a much larger whole.[50]

A reconsideration of the American War also emphasizes the fundamental aspects of a struggle long preceded by any US advisors or soldiers' arrival in Indochina. The emergence of a Vietnamese nationalism in the early 1900s not only defined the boundary lines of political discord among competing factions but also confirmed that a local issue would only be decided by local actors. None of these underlying questions about what Vietnamese nationalism meant in the modern era could be resolved by US military might. Perhaps that is why, even after Saigon's fall, senior policymakers like Alexander Haig continued to believe that the "source of the war in Vietnam was Moscow, just like the source of the war in Korea was Moscow." By focusing on the external threat, Americans could more easily come to grips with the unpleasant outcomes inside South Vietnam.[51]

Yet the internal questions of GVN legitimacy both predated and persisted after the Americans' arrival. If political legitimacy might be characterized as investing "power with authority," then any outcome of the struggle between Hanoi and Saigon ultimately depended on "the evolution of *internal* politics" within the latter regime.[52] International politics, and US involvement, surely mattered. But choices made by the GVN and South Vietnamese people in allowing for political competiveness within state borders remained the underlying issue. To be sure, this competition was always more than just an anticommunist struggle. Nor was it simply an American effort, as Westmoreland put it back in 1965, "to bring the population around to our point of view and separate them emotionally and then later politically from the Viet Cong." Rather, the contest, at its core, centered on how South Vietnam, as an "imagined political community," chose to establish and organize the fundamental relationships between people and government.[53]

These choices included complex deliberations over GVN corruption, NLF repression and violence, the United States' military intervention, and political loyalties not just of the rural population but of the urban one as well. In the process, as one observer noted in 1973, a "political settlement and an end to the war depend[ed] upon the creation of a political community between the nationalists and the communists in South Vietnam."[54] And yet the lines between these two groups were never so neatly drawn. Thus, the matter of self-determination involved multifaceted questions not just over South Vietnamese identity, but over *Vietnamese* identity as well. Many southerners therefore could easily view American involvement as a "rootless foreign movement," even as Thieu hoped to employ US resources in his quest to mobilize the population and pacify the countryside. In this important sense, the negotiated settlement resulting in America's withdrawal from Southeast Asia never settled the crucial issue of political belonging inside South Vietnam.[55]

The controversial ending to the American War thus has far less to do with Abrams's strategy or congressional funding or domestic opposition than with South Vietnam's inability to develop a peacetime national identity in a time of war. Without pause, the destructive conflict that raged across South Vietnamese society left little opportunity to build a broad alliance among disparate political, social, and religious groups. Every year the war continued, that society became more and more fragmented. As much as Americans craved to reform governmental processes within South Vietnam, the unremitting war offered no respite to weary nation-builders seeking to build something viable for the future.[56]

Thus, while the GVN exercised only limited influence outside of Saigon, in large part because the countryside remained a hotly contested battlefield, American strategists toiled in vain to translate military power into political progress. In contrast to the "better war" myth, they never succeeded. Saigon's elites and many among the population may have thought of themselves as distinctly South Vietnamese, yet, as one ARVN general noted, "contradictions" in the state's social arrangements endured.[57] For far too many South Vietnamese then, the possibility of enduring war after 1973 left them unwilling to voluntarily bestow their political loyalties to a government of questionable legitimacy. If Thieu's regime could not cajole or coerce or inspire the popular majority to share in its vision of a separate South Vietnamese identity, that identity ultimately could not create a foundation strong enough to sustain a new nation.

Granted, this is a difficult proposition given the sacrifices of so many who gave their lives to construct a new Republic of Vietnam. But perhaps such lines of inquiry into the Vietnamese War, not just the American one, can impart much needed perspective when US policymakers consider intervening into countries already engaged in long civil wars. War curbs popular participation in shared, albeit contested, forms of governance. Local governments seeking legitimacy tend to atrophy as their populations focus on survival. Even in fragmented societies, the local population too often sees outsiders, especially those in military uniform, as occupying forces rather than as allies helping to build a new political community. War is not without its consequences.

America's final years in Vietnam remain a contested battlefield, a landscape of residue minefields from the past, because of war's long reach. But we can only profit from its study when we set aside long-held tropes about savior generals who swoop in after calamity, rescue a losing war thanks to a new and better strategy, only to have their triumphs forsaken by civilians back at home. The final Americans who withdrew from Vietnam did so not as victors, but as participants in a stalemated conflict. Abrams's "one war" approach may have been necessary to maintain that military impasse, but it alone proved far from sufficient in erecting an integrated South Vietnamese political community, built on voluntary participation from the masses, capable of standing on its own.[58]

At very best, Abrams's signal accomplishment was to alter, if only temporarily and reluctantly, the US military culture from one captivated by visions of traditional battlefield "victory" to one accepting the obligations of a political alternative in Vietnam. Without question, the general helped oversee a broad military effort that took into account the political realities that made Vietnamization necessary. He never relented in helping ensure the United States' strategic withdrawal from Southeast Asia worked as best it could. Yet arguments that Abrams made the war in Vietnam any "better" appear far less convincing when we view the conflict from mid-1968 to early 1973 as a brief, yet violent, American episode in a much longer Vietnamese saga.

NOTES

Introduction

1. John F. Kennedy, "Remarks at West Point to the Graduating Class of the U.S. Military Academy," 6 June 1962. Gerhard Peters and John T. Woolley, *The American Presidency Project*, http://www.presidency.ucsb.edu/ws/?pid=8695. Three years later, US Army officers were still discussing how the late president's remarks related to counterinsurgency operations. See Lt. Col. Gustav J. Gillert Jr., "Counterinsurgency," *Military Review* 45, no. 4 (April 1965): 25–26. On Kennedy's approach to Vietnam in 1961 and 1962, see John M. Newman, "The Kennedy-Johnson Transition: The Case for Policy Reversal," in *Vietnam: The Early Decisions*, eds. Lloyd C. Gardner and Ted Gittinger (Austin: University of Texas Press, 1997), 158–162.
2. Richard Nixon, "Remarks to the Corps of Cadets at the United States Military Academy in West Point, New York," 29 May 1971. Gerhard Peters and John T. Woolley, *The American Presidency Project*, http://www.presidency.ucsb.edu/ws/?pid=3029.
3. Of course, policymakers and pundits during the Kennedy and early Johnson administrations saw much to decry in Southeast Asia. Harry McPherson recalled of this time that "the United States had to prevent the Communists from controlling South Vietnam because . . . all of Asia . . . would otherwise be threatened . . . [and] our defeat would give the Communists . . . a worldwide advantage." *A Political Education: A Washington Memoir* (Boston: Houghton Mifflin, 1988), 388. Nixon, himself, spoke using similar tones in a 1964 *Reader's Digest* article, warning of dire consequences if the United States failed in Southeast Asia. See David F. Schmitz, *Richard Nixon and the Vietnam War: The End of the American Century* (Lanham, MD: Rowman & Littlefield, 2014), 12–13.
4. Charles DeBenedetti with Charles Chatfield, *An American Ordeal: The Antiwar Movement of the Vietnam Era* (Syracuse, NY: Syracuse University Press, 1990), 380. David S. Broder, " 'Going It Alone,' " *The Washington Post*, 23 March 1975.
5. Chester L. Cooper, *The Lost Crusade: America in Vietnam* (New York: Dodd, Mead, 1970), 408.
6. Dave Richard Palmer, *Summons of the Trumpet: U.S.-Vietnam in Perspective* (San Rafael, CA: Presidio Press, 1978), xii. On the price of war to Americans, see George Donelson Moss, *Vietnam: An American Ordeal*, 5th ed. (Upper Saddle River, NJ: Pearson Prentice Hill, 1990, 2006), 428–429. On demoralization, see Michael H. Hunt and Steven I. Levine, *Arc of Empire: America's Wars in Asia from the Philippines to Vietnam* (Chapel Hill: University of North Carolina Press, 2012), 239.
7. On competing interpretations of the postwar assessments, see David L. Anderson, "One Vietnam War Should Be Enough and Other Reflections on Diplomatic History and the Making of Foreign Policy," *Diplomatic History* 30, no. 1 (January 2006): 1–21.

8. "Westmoreland Calls 1967 Year of Progress," *Los Angeles Times*, 27 December 1967. For similar reports, see Carroll Kilpatrick, "Gains Gradual in Pacification, Komer Reports," *The Washington Post*, 22 November 1967; George C. Wilson, "War's End in View—Westmoreland," *The Washington Post*, 22 November 1967; and James Reston, "Washington: Why Westmoreland and Bunker Are Optimistic," *New York Times*, 22 November 1967. The MACV prognosis at the end of 1967 was, for the most part, optimistic. See USMACV Quarterly Evaluation Report, December 1967, MHI, pp. 4–6. So, too, was the US Army Chief of Staff Harold K. Johnson. See "Vietnam—Progress or Stalemate?," *Army Digest* 22, no. 12 (December 1967): 6–7. For an overview of LBJ's salesmanship campaign, see Gregory A. Daddis, "Choosing Progress: Evaluating the 'Salesmanship' Campaign of the Vietnam War in 1967," in *Assessing War: The Challenge of Measuring Success and Failure*, eds. Leo J. Blanken, Hy Rothstein, and Jason J. Lepore (Washington, DC: Georgetown University Press, 2015), 173–196.

9. Clark Clifford quoted in Notes of Meeting, 4 March 1968, *FRUS, 1964–1968*: VI: 318. "More Than a Diversion," *New York Times*, 2 February 1968. Affidavit of David Halberstam, William C. Westmoreland against CBS Inc., 20 April 1984, Folder 42, Box 1, Larry Berman Collection (*Westmoreland vs. CBS*), TTUVA, p. B-224. On claims of media bias during Tet, David F. Schmitz, *The Tet Offensive: Politics, War, and Public Opinion* (Lanham, MD: Rowman & Littlefield, 2005), xv.

10. Telegram from the Embassy in Vietnam to the Department of State, 15 February 1968, *FRUS, 1964–1968*: VI: 216. The *Wall Street Journal* quoted in W. W. Rostow, *The Diffusion of Power: An Essay in Recent History* (New York: Macmillan, 1972), 519. On editors' preferences for American-centric stories, see Peter Braestrup, *Big Story: How the American Press and Television Reported and Interpreted the Crisis of Tet 1968 in Vietnam and Washington*, Vol. 1 (Boulder, CO: Westview Press, 1977), 450. See also Clarence R. Wyatt, *Paper Soldiers: The American Press and the Vietnam War* (New York: W.W. Norton, 1993), 184.

11. "The War in Vietnam," *Newsweek*, 19 February 1968, 30.

12. Westmoreland in Michael Charlton and Anthony Moncrieff, *Many Reasons Why: The American Involvement in Vietnam* (New York: Hill and Wang, 1978), 146. Bunker agreed that the "Tet attacks were a failure within Viet-Nam, and a brilliant success in America." Telegram from the Embassy in Vietnam to the Department of State, 16 January 1969, *FRUS, 1964–1968*: VII: 823. For a counterargument to this rationale, see D.W. Beveridge, "The Ground War in Vietnam, a Strategy of Tactics: US Operational Concepts Under Westmoreland," *Defence Force Journal*, no. 76 (May/June 1989): 42.

13. Hedrick Smith and Neil Sheehan, "Westmoreland Requests 206,000 More Men, Stirring Debate in Administration," *New York Times*, 10 March 1968. Gene Roberts, "Saigon General Says Foe Has Replaced His Losses," *New York Times*, 10 March 1968. The *Washington Post* quoted in Braestrup, *Big Story*, 161. A 24 January 1969 CIA report called Tet a "low point" in the larger allied military picture. "The Situation in Vietnam: Overview and Outlook," Folder 1, Box 63, NSC Files, Vietnam Subject Files, RNL, p. 2.

14. Aggressive will in David W. P. Elliott, "Hanoi's Strategy in the Second Indochina War," in *The Vietnam War: Vietnamese and American Perspectives*, eds. Jayne S. Werner and Luu Doan Huynh (Armonk, NY: M.E. Sharpe, 1993), 88. On the American-centric views of war reporting in 1968, see George Bailey, "Television War: Trends in Network Coverage of Vietnam 1965–1970," *Journal of Broadcasting* 20, no. 2 (Spring 1976): 155. Only 1 percent of news stories read by anchormen covered the South Vietnamese government. For conclusions on Tet from Hanoi's perspective, see Merle L. Pribbenow II, "General Võ Nguyên Giáp and the Mysterious Evolution of the Plan for the 1968 Tết Offensive," *Journal of Vietnamese Studies* 3, no. 2 (Summer 2008): 24–26; and Gabriel Kolko, *Anatomy of a War: Vietnam, the United States, and the Modern Historical Experience* (New York: Pantheon Books, 1985), 327–328. It is important to note that historians equally dismissed the difficulties faced by the South Vietnamese. Anthony James Joes, for instance, argues that the "years after the Tet Offensive of 1968 had been good ones for South Viet Nam." *The War for South Viet Nam, 1954–1975*, rev. ed. (Westport, CT: Praeger, 2001), 108.

15. Julian J. Ewell, interview by Ted Gittinger, 7 November 1985, Oral History Collection, LBJL, p. I-5. On popular dissatisfaction in the United States, see Robert R. Tomes, *Apocalypse Then: American Intellectuals and the Vietnam War, 1954–1975* (New York: New York University Press, 1998), 171.

16. Palmer, *Summons of the Trumpet*, 201. Phillip B. Davidson agreed that the news media distorted the "Tet offensive as an American defeat." *Vietnam at War, The History: 1946–1975* (Novato, CA: Presidio Press, 1988), 441.

17. Such questions were raised in Cincinnatus, *Self-Destruction: The Disintegration and Decay of the United States Army During the Vietnam Era* (New York: W.W. Norton, 1981), 9–10. See also Jerry Lembcke, *The Spitting Image: Myth, Memory, and the Legacy of Vietnam* (New York: New York University Press, 1998), 136–139. Journalist Don Oberdorfer, however, argued that no one won during Tet. "Everybody lost. The North Vietnamese and Viet Cong lost a battle. The United States Government lost something even more important—the confidence of its people at home." *Tet!* (Garden City, NY: Doubleday, 1971), 329.

18. Beverly Deepe, "Viet Drives: U.S. Regains Strategic Momentum on Battlefield," *The Christian Science Monitor*, 12 April 1968. On the differences between Westmoreland and Abrams, see David Halberstam, *The Best and the Brightest* (New York: Random House, 1969), 559–560; and Gen. Walter T. Kerwin, interview by Albin Wheeler and Ronald Craven, 9 April 1976, Senior Officers Debriefing Program, Box A, Creighton Abrams Story, MHI, p. 14. According to Kerwin, while Westmoreland "looked the part of a soldier," Abrams "was the type of man that if you look around twice, if he was in civilian clothes, and say, 'Christ, is he a general?'"

19. "General With a Flair: Creighton William Abrams, Jr.," *New York Times*, 7 April 1967. Kevin Buckley, "General Abrams Deserves a Better War," *New York Times*, 5 October 1969. "A 'Different' War Now, With Abrams in Command," *U.S. News & World Report*, 26 August 1968, p. 12.

20. "Westmoreland's Strategy: Will It Pass the Acid Test?," *U.S. News & World Report*, 12 February 1968.

21. Henry Kissinger, *Ending the Vietnam War: A History of America's Involvement in and Extrication from the Vietnam War* (New York: Simon & Schuster, 2003), 8. For a full expression of this thesis, see Lewis Sorley, *A Better War: The Unexamined Victories and Final Tragedy of America's Last Years in Vietnam* (New York: Harcourt Brace, 1999).

22. Nixon quoted in Cooper, *The Lost Crusade*, 444. Loren Baritz argues that like their predecessors, Nixon and Kissinger "misrepresented the relevance of Vietnam to our security." *Backfire: A History of How American Culture Led Us into Vietnam and Made Us Fight the Way We Did* (New York: William Morrow, 1985), 229.

23. Sir Robert Thompson, *No Exit from Vietnam* (New York: David McKay, 1969), 142. After Tet, Secretary of Defense Clark Clifford intimated that Hanoi held the strategic initiative because "the enemy can control his casualty rate." In Thomas C. Thayer, *War without Fronts: The American Experience in Vietnam* (Annapolis, MD: Naval Institute Press, 1985, 2016), 91.

24. On an "alternate strategy," see Joes, *The War for South Viet Nam*, 122. "Smoldering stalemate" in Telegram from the Embassy in Vietnam to the Department of State, 12 January 1966, *FRUS, 1964–1968: IV*: 53. It is important to note that as early as January 1966, senior US officials already worried about being mired in a stalemate.

25. Costs of war in US Office of Information, General, MACV 1968 Summary, 1 March 1969, Folder 01, Box 00, Bud Harton Collection, TTUVA. On inaccuracy of media coverage on strategic issues, see James Landers, *The Weekly War: Newsmagazines and Vietnam* (Columbia: University of Missouri Press, 2004), 145–146.

26. Letter from the Commander of the Fleet Marine Force, Pacific (Krulak) to Secretary of Defense McNamara, 4 January 1967, *FRUS, 1964–1968: V*: 21. On translating a moral commitment, see Address by Gen. W. C. Westmoreland to the Opening Session of the Annual Convention, American Association of School Administrators, 15 February 1969, Speech File Service, Office of the Chief of Information, Department of the Army, OSDHO, p. 8. *The Hartford Courant* correctly reported that "Westmoreland was expected to beat back the North Vietnamese, overcome the Viet Cong and, in effect, win the war. But Abrams's mission has been quite different—his responsibility is to wind down U.S. fighting and to withdraw American forces gradually." "Gen. Abrams Expected to Stay Through Year," 17 January 1971. On the "subjectivity of the victory," see Robert Mandel, *The Meaning of Military Victory* (Boulder, CO, and London: Lynne Rienner, 2006), 9.

27. On turmoil at home, see Robert J. McMahon, "Turning Point: The Vietnam War's Pivotal Year, November 1967—November 1968," in *The Columbia History of the Vietnam War*, ed.

David L. Anderson (New York: Columbia University Press, 2011), 203. A 1980 survey found that more than one-third of polled Americans did not believe the war was winnable under any circumstances. Gerard J. DeGroot, *A Noble Cause? America and the Vietnam War* (Harlow, Essex, UK: Longman, 2000), 267.

28. Michael Lind argues the United States would have suffered a significant geopolitical loss if it did not contest communist expansion in Southeast Asia. *Vietnam: The Necessary War* (New York: The Free Press, 1999), 256, 270. On the damage Tet caused to the credibility of American strategy in Vietnam, see Halberstam, William C. Westmoreland against CBS Inc., TTUVA, B-225.

29. Robert M. Cassidy, "Winning the War of the Flea: Lessons from Guerrilla Warfare," *Military Review* Special Edition, Counterinsurgency Reader (October 2006): 5. Austin Long, *Doctrine of Eternal Recurrence: The U.S. Military and Counterinsurgency Doctrine, 1960–1970 and 2003–2006* (Santa Monica, CA: RAND Corporation, 2008), 17. For supposed historical credence to such arguments, writers could turn to Lewis Sorley who argued that under "Abrams the strategy, tactics, and concept of the war all changed, with the previous emphasis on body count as the measure of merit now shifting to population security." *Vietnam Chronicles: The Abrams Tapes, 1968–1972* (Lubbock: Texas Tech University Press, 2004), 3.

30. Victor Davis Hanson, *The Savior Generals: How Five Great Commanders Saved Wars That Were Lost—from Ancient Greece to Iraq* (New York: Bloomsbury Press, 2013), 3–4, 191. For a counterargument to Hanson, see Gian P. Gentile, "A (Slightly) Better War: A Narrative and Its Defects," *World Affairs* (Summer 2008): 57–64; and Hannah Gurman, ed., *Hearts and Minds: A People's History of Counterinsurgency* (New York: The New Press, 2013), 3, 96.

31. As an example, see Douglas Brinkley and Luke A. Nichter, eds., *The Nixon Tapes* (Boston: Houghton Mifflin Harcourt, 2014). In over 700 pages of text, Abrams appears only once in the weighty tome, Robert Mann, *A Grand Delusion: America's Descent into Vietnam* (New York: Basic Books, 2001). For an overview of the period from an operational military history perspective, see James H. Willbanks, *Abandoning Vietnam: How America Left and South Vietnam Lost Its War* (Lawrence: University Press of Kansas, 2004). For new scholarship on the antiwar movement, see Penny Lewis, *Hardhats, Hippies, and Hawks: The Vietnam Antiwar Movement as Myth and Memory* (Ithaca, NY: Cornell University Press, 2013).

32. For instance, see Frank Boccia, *The Crouching Beast: A United States Army Lieutenant's Account of the Battle for Hamburger Hill, May 1969* (Jefferson, NC: McFarland, 2013). George Lepre, *Fragging: Why U.S. Soldiers Assaulted Their Officers in Vietnam* (Lubbock: Texas Tech University Press, 2011). James J. Wirtz contends the failure at Tet "set the stage for changes in U.S. strategy," yet his analysis focused mostly on the Johnson administration. *The Tet Offensive: Intelligence Failure in War* (Ithaca, NY: Cornell University Press, 1991), 3.

33. Gregory A. Daddis, *Westmoreland's War: Reassessing American Strategy in Vietnam* (New York: Oxford University Press, 2014), 171. For a pithier version of this argument, see Gregory A. Daddis, "The Myth of an American Attrition Strategy in the Vietnam War," in *The Routledge Handbook of American and Diplomatic History: 1865 to the Present*, eds. Antonio S. Thompson and Christos G. Frentzos (New York: Routledge, 2013), 242–251.

34. See Paul M. Kattenburg, *The Vietnam Trauma in American Foreign Policy, 1945–75* (New Brunswick, NJ: Transaction, 1992), 203–204; Mark Atwood Lawrence, *The Vietnam War: A Concise International History* (New York: Oxford University Press, 2008), 132; and Scott Sigmund Gartner, *Strategic Assessment in War* (New Haven, CT: Yale University Press, 1997), 130. Herbert Y. Schandler argues that after July 1965 "the American response in Vietnam was a conventional military one." "America and Vietnam: The Failure of Strategy," in *Regular Armies and Insurgency*, ed. Ronald Haycock (London: Croom Helm, 1979), 91.

35. Thomas E. Ricks, *The Generals: American Military Command from World War II to Today* (New York: Penguin Press, 2012), 319–320. John A. Nagl, *Learning to Eat Soup with a Knife: Counterinsurgency Lessons from Malaya and Vietnam* (Chicago and London: University of Chicago Press, 2002), 171, 173.

36. On Vietnam being tangential to US national security, see James S. Olson and Randy Roberts, *Where the Domino Fell: America and Vietnam, 1945–2010*, 6th ed. (West Sussex, UK: Wiley Blackwell, 2014), 195. This compared to Secretary of State Dean Rusk's testimony in April 1966. "Vietnam Policy—Testimony at the Committee Hearings," *Congressional Digest* 45, no. 4

(April 1966): 114. On stalemate leading to regionalization of conflict, see Lien-Hang T. Nguyen, "Cold War Contradictions: Toward an International History of the Second Indochina War, 1969–1973," in *Making Sense of the Vietnam Wars: Local, National, and Transnational Perspectives*, eds. Mark Philip Bradley and Marilyn B. Young (New York: Oxford University Press, 2008), 220. On links between détente and Vietnam, see Min Chen, "Myth and Reality of Triangulations: A Study of American Withdrawal from Vietnam 1972–75," *Asian Profile* 18, no. 6 (December 1990): 525–526. Abrams did adapt to change, which makes sense given that "strategy is a process, a constant adaptation to shifting conditions and circumstances." Williamson Murray and Mark Grimsley, "Introduction: On Strategy," in *The Making of Strategy: Rules, States, and War*, eds. Williamson Murray, Macgregor Knox, and Alvin Bernstein (New York: Cambridge University Press, 1994), 1. Finally, Harry G. Summers Jr. placed much blame for the strategic mess in Vietnam on the "failure to invoke the national will." *On Strategy: A Critical Analysis of the Vietnam War* (Novato, CA: Presidio Press, 1982), 19.

37. Troop figures in Ronald H. Spector, *After Tet: The Bloodiest Year in Vietnam* (New York: The Free Press, 1993), 26. Lt. Col. Don H. Payne argued not long after Tet that the "solution for the Vietnam War should be consistent with what we expect and want to happen after that war." "What Happens After Vietnam?," *Military Review* 48, no. 9 (September 1968): 42. Lewis Sorley argues, without much evidence, that Abrams oversaw a "thoroughgoing revision of the whole approach to the war." *Thunderbolt: General Creighton Abrams and the Army of His Times* (New York: Simon & Schuster, 1992), 233. For critiques on the "better war" thesis, see Dale Andradé, "Rethinking the Years After Tet," *Joint Forces Quarterly*, no. 23 (Autumn/ Winter 1999-2000): 107–108; and David Hunt, "Dirty Wars: Counterinsurgency in Vietnam and Today," *Politics & Society* 38, no. 1 (2010): 64. For an example of debates within the field, see Phillip E. Catton, "Refighting Vietnam in the History Books: The Historiography of the War," *OAH Magazine of History* (October 2004): 7–11.

38. National Security Meeting, 8 May 1972, *FRUS, 1969–1976*, VIII: 495. It is important to note that civilian policymakers did not dispute MACV's approach, especially in terms of pacification, under either Westmoreland or Abrams. See James McAllister, "Who Lost Vietnam? Soldiers, Civilians, and U.S. Military Strategy," *International Security* 35, no. 3 (Winter 2010/11): 100.

39. Department of the Army, *Field Manual 100-5, Operations of Army Forces in the Field* (Washington, DC: Headquarters, Department of the Army, September 1968), 1–2.

40. Hal Brands, *What Good Is Grand Strategy? Power and Purpose in American Statecraft from Harry S. Truman to George W. Bush* (Ithaca, NY: Cornell University Press, 2014), 1. See also Colin S. Gray, *The Strategy Bridge: Theory for Practice* (New York: Oxford University Press, 2010), 18, 28–29; and Colin S. Gray, *Modern Strategy* (New York: Oxford University Press, 1999), 54, 163–163. For a historical review of these delineations, see Beatrice Heuser, *The Evolution of Strategy: Thinking War from Antiquity to the Present* (New York: Cambridge University Press, 2010), 16.

41. John M. Collins, *Grand Strategy: Principles and Practices* (Annapolis, MD: Naval Institute Press, 1973), 14–15.

42. Richard M. Nixon, *The Real War* (New York: Warner Books, 1980), 106. The US Embassy in Vietnam, before Nixon's inauguration, spoke in similarly broad terms when laying out the "fundamental objectives" in South Vietnam. See "Objectives and Courses of Action of the United States in South Viet-Nam," n.d., *FRUS, 1964–1968*: VII: 719.

43. Abrams to Cushman, Peers, Kerwin, and Eckhardt, 7 September 1968, Abrams Messages #1290, CMH.

44. The "basic elements of Vietnam policy" were laid out in Henry Kissinger, "Vietnam Options," 11 September 1969, Folder 2, Box 91, NSC Files, Vietnam Subject Files, RNL. John Dumbrell has argued that part of the problem in integrating grand and military strategies stemmed from the fact that the "attention of Nixon and Kissinger was constantly shifting between the conflict in Vietnam, the onrush global détente, and the threat of disorder on the streets of America." *Rethinking the Vietnam War* (New York: Palgrave Macmillan, 2012), 120.

45. Purpose of grand strategy in Brands, *What Good Is Grand Strategy?*, 2. Hopeful assumptions in Joseph Alsop, "Nixon Gives Abrams a Manageable Task," *The Hartford Courant*, 25 April 1970. On the necessity for a plausible grand strategy, see Gray, *Modern Strategy*, 58.

46. Arthur Schlesinger, "Topics: Dissent and the Vietnam War," *New York Times*, 6 May 1967.

47. Kissinger, 12 October 1972, *FRUS*, 1969–1976, IX: 123. Henry Kissinger, "Alternative Vietnam Strategies," 20 July 1970, Folder 4, Box 91, NSC Files, Vietnam Subject Files, RNL.

48. Editor's Note in John T. Wheeler, "Pentagon Agrees: No More Vietnams," *The Hartford Courant*, 7 December 1969. Interestingly, a year earlier, *U.S. News & World Report* quoted one US diplomat saying: "It would be a tragedy for our nation if war weariness at home—and anxiety for peace at any price—forced us to give away now what seems almost in our grasp." "Victory 'Almost in Our Grasp,' " 11 November 1968, p. 36.

49. As the 1971 Combined Campaign Plan noted, "The people are the greatest asset to the GVN [Government of South Vietnam], and gaining their active commitment is the GVN goal." Combined Campaign Plan, 1971, Historians Files, CMH, p. 12.

50. Special National Intelligence Estimate, Short-Term Prospects in South Vietnam, 4 February 1965, *FRUS*, 1964–1968: II: 144.

51. LTG William McCaffrey, interview by Center of Military History, 12 April 1972, VNIT Folder 1048, CMH, pp. 57–58. On the competing definitions of Vietnamese identity, see Nu-Anh Tran, "South Vietnamese Identity, American Intervention, and the Newspaper *Chính Luận* [Political Discussion], 1965-1969," *Journal of Vietnamese Studies* 1. no. 1–2 (February/ August 2006): 180, 185. On fears of declining popular will inside South Vietnam, see memorandum from Kissinger to Nixon, 6 March 1969, *FRUS*, 1969–1976, VI: 87.

52. Richard Nixon, *No More Vietnams* (New York: Arbor House: 1985), 15. Lewis Sorley echoed this point, for it supported his thesis that Abrams had turned around the war effort after Tet. "Even as the cumulative effect of the 'one war' approach was reaching a peak, influences were at work that would eventually undermine much of what had been accomplished." *A Better War*, 228. On the role of dissent, see Andrew Z. Katz, "Public Opinion and Foreign Policy: The Nixon Administration and the Pursuit of Peace With Honor in Vietnam," *Presidential Studies Quarterly* 27, no. 3 (Summer 1997): 496–513.

53. On legitimacy and violence, see Christian Olsson, " 'Legitimate Violence' in the Prose of Counterinsurgency: An Impossible Necessity?," *Alternatives: Global, Local, Political* 38. no. 2 (2013): 156. Holy Grail in *The Pentagon Papers: The Defense Department History of United States Decisionmaking on Vietnam* [The Sen. Gravel Edition, 5 vols.], Vol. II (Boston: Beacon Press, 1971–1972), 278. Lawrence W. Serewicz sees Kissinger's approach to foreign policy as an attempt to bring the "external realm . . . into balance with the domestic realm through an approach focused on the limits to America's power and the need for the nation to act as an ordinary country." *America at the Brink of Empire: Rusk, Kissinger, and the Vietnam War* (Baton Rouge: Louisiana State University Press, 2007), 10.

54. "Puppets" in Lawrence E. Grinter, "Bargaining between Saigon and Washington: Dilemmas of Linkage Politics during War," *Orbis* 18, no. 3 (Fall 1974): 841. Social disorder in Gerald C. Hickey, *U.S. Strategy in South Vietnam: Extrication and Equilibrium* (Santa Monica, CA: RAND Corporation, 1969), 2.

55. Incapacity in R. W. Komer, *Bureaucracy Does Its Thing: Institutional Constraints on U.S.-GVN Performance in Vietnam* (Santa Monica, CA: RAND Corporation, 1972), 10. Social revolution in Nguyen Cao Ky, *Twenty Years and Twenty Days* (New York: Stein and Day, 1976), 136–137. On contesting the narrative of the passive farmer, see Thomas L. Ahern Jr., *Vietnam Declassified: The CIA and Counterinsurgency* (Lexington: University Press of Kentucky, 2010), 361–362; and Tran, "South Vietnamese Identity, American Intervention, and the Newspaper *Chính Luận*," 175. Charles A. Joiner, however, posited that South Vietnam's "unhappy 'constituents' can vote, realistically, only for a choice of horrors." *The Politics of Massacre: Political Processes in South Vietnam* (Philadelphia: Temple University Press, 1974), 4. In tracking the war's progress, Ward Just asked, "What is the quantitative measurement of passive resistance?" *To What End: Report From Vietnam* (Boston: Houghton Mifflin, 1968; New York: Public Affairs, 2000), 68.

56. Jeffrey Record, *The Wrong War: Why We Lost in Vietnam* (Annapolis, MD: Naval Institute Press, 1998), 95. For a more persuasive counterargument, see Douglas Porch, *Counterinsurgency: Exposing the Myths of the New Way of War* (New York: Cambridge University Press, 2013), 216. The best review of the historiographical debate on this topic can be found in Gary R. Hess, *Vietnam: Explaining America's Lost War* (Malden, MA: Blackwell, 2009), 91–98.

57. Abrams quoted in John Prados, *Vietnam: The History of an Unwinnable War, 1945–1975* (Lawrence: University Press of Kansas, 2009), 308.

58. For the argument of MACV officers exhibiting "little appreciation for the multidimensional nature of people's war," see Andrew F. Krepinevich, "Vietnam: Evaluating the Ground War, 1965–1968," in *An American Dilemma: Vietnam, 1964–1973*, eds. Dennis E. Showalter and John G. Albert (Chicago: Imprint Publications, 1993), 91. More appropriately, the authors of *The Pentagon Papers* maintained that "by the summer of 1967, pacification had become a major ingredient of American strategy in Vietnam, growing steadily in importance and the amount of resources devoted to it." *The Pentagon Papers*, Vol. II, 515.

59. The interrelationships between the military and the political are discussed in Jeffery Clarke, "On Strategy and the Vietnam War," in *Assessing the Vietnam War: A Collection from the Journal of the U.S. Army War College*, eds. Lloyd J. Matthews and Dale E. Brown (Washington, DC: Pergamon-Brassey's International Defense Publishers, 1987), 75; Gray, *The Strategy Bridge*, 7; and Charles A. Stevenson, *Warriors and Politicians: US Civil-Military Relations under Stress* (London and New York: Routledge, 2006), 195. As an earlier example of US leaders thinking about more than just military campaigns in South Vietnam, see Hobart Rowen, "U.S. Mapping an Attack on Viet Inflation," *The Washington Post*, 12 August 1966.

60. On the irrelevance of US military power to the war's political realities, see Christian Appy, *American Reckoning: The Vietnam War and Our National Identity* (New York: Viking Press, 2015), 177. Ronald Spector argues that the "costly struggles of 1968 . . . were a political success for the Communists." *After Tet*, 312.

61. Donn Starry, interview by John Collison and Bill Burleson, 14 December 1976, Senior Officers Debriefing Program, Box B, Creighton Abrams Story, MHI, p. 36.

62. John H. Hay, interview by James Thomas, 1981, Senior Officer Oral History Program, MHI, p. 84. On the air campaign and reserve call-up, see Lawrence J. Korb, *The Joint Chiefs of Staff: The First Twenty-Five Years* (Bloomington: Indiana University Press, 1976), 167. Even during the war, one MACV staff report argued, "There is little doubt that given a free hand the US has had, all along, the resources necessary to pursue the conflict to a conclusion consistent with our objective." Headquarters, USMACV, "One War," MACV Command Overview, 1968–1972, Historians Files, CMH, p. 15. For a counterargument to the stab in the back theory, see Roy K. Flint, "Army Professionalism for the Future," *Military Review* 51, no. 4 (April 1971): 4–5. There remains a persistent myth in the literature. Veterans and historians alike argue that with the destruction of the National Liberation Front after Tet, the war became a strictly conventional conflict. Thus, with similarities between Korea and Vietnam, the US armed forces had the opportunity to play to their strengths and win the war, only to have policymakers withdraw them at the most inauspicious time. As an example of this (substantially false) contention, see Robert Thompson, "Revolutionary War in Southeast Asia," in *All Quiet on the Eastern Front: The Death of South Vietnam*, ed. Anthony T. Bouscaren (Old Greenwich, CT: Devin-Adair, 1977), 116.

63. Senior Officer Debriefing Report, COL Gus S. Peters, Box 14, HQ USARV Command History Senior Officer Debriefing Reports, RG 472, NARA, p. 4.

64. "Special Report from Vietnam," *Army* 18, no. 5 (May 1968): 18. Zais to Abrams, 1 October 1969, Melvin Zais Papers, MHI, p. 2. Nixon quoted in William M. Hammond, *Reporting Vietnam: Media and Military at War* (Lawrence: University Press of Kansas, 1998), 293. The president also argued later that "this was the first war in our history during which our media were more friendly to our enemies than our allies." Nixon, *The Real War*, 115.

65. Daniel C. Hallin, "The Media, the War in Vietnam, and Political Support: A Critique of the Thesis of an Oppositional Media," *Journal of Politics* 46, no. 1 (February 1984): 11. See also William M. Hammond, "The Press in Vietnam as Agent of Defeat: A Critical Examination," *Reviews in American History* 17, no. 2 (June 1989): 312–323.

66. For an overview of the revisionist case for the "lost victory," see Hess, *Vietnam*, 185–191. See also Jeffrey Kimball, "Debunking Nixon's Myths of Vietnam," *New England Journal of History* 56, nos. 2–3 (Winter 1999–Spring 2000): 33–40. Nixon, *No More Vietnams*, 165. On Westmoreland squandering public support, see Lewis Sorley, *Westmoreland: The General Who Lost Vietnam* (Boston: Houghton Mifflin Harcourt, 2011), 107.

67. Nixon, *The Real War*, 114. Schmitz, *Richard Nixon and the Vietnam War*, xiii. Christian Appy correctly notes that "prolonging the war did not preserve American credibility; it only did further damage to the nation's reputation." *American Reckoning*, xvi.

68. Howell Raines, "Reagan Calls Arms Race Essential to Avoid a 'Surrender' of 'Defeat,'" *New York Times*, 19 August 1980. On the making of this myth, see Charles Mohr, "Once Again—Did the Press Lose Vietnam?," in *The American Experience in Vietnam: A Reader*, ed. Grace Sevy (Norman: University of Oklahoma Press, 1989), 147; and Tarak Barkawi, *Globalization and War* (Lanham, MD: Rowman & Littlefield Publishers, 2006), 111. On the malleability of the Vietnam analogy, see Mark Atwood Lawrence, "Policymaking and the Uses of the Vietnam War," in *The Power of the Past: History and Statecraft* (Washington, DC: Brookings Institution Press, 2016), 50–51.

69. William E. DePuy, *Changing an Army: An Oral History of General William E. DePuy, USA Retired* (Carlisle Barracks, PA: US Military History Institute, 1988), 125. For an example of how officers saw the enemy's sanctuaries in Cambodia and Laos, see Peers to Abrams, 17 August 1968, Abrams Messages #1121, CMH. Nixon assured that the "Vietnam War was not unwinnable." *No More Vietnams*, 18.

70. No intention from Herbert Y. Schandler, *America in Vietnam: The War That Couldn't Be Won* (Lanham, MD: Rowman & Littlefield, 2009), 157. Abrams, of course, hoped to overpower NVA troops inside South Vietnam, but never gained permission to defeat North Vietnam proper by attacking across the DMZ. Acceptance of defeat in Russell F. Rhyne, "Victory in Vietnam," *Military Review* 50, no. 2 (February 1970): 38.

71. Julian Paget, *Counter-Insurgency Operations: Techniques of Guerrilla Warfare* (New York: Walker, 1967), 158.

72. On the need to recognize the limits of strategy, see Lawrence Freeman, *Strategy: A History* (New York: Oxford University Press, 2013), 610. Issues affecting American policy in *The Pentagon Papers*, Vol. II, 19–23.

73. Nixon quoted in DeGroot, *A Noble Cause?*, 206–207.

74. William R. Corson, *Consequences of Failure* (New York: W.W. Norton, 1974), 17. On change in political objectives, see H. R. McMaster, *Dereliction of Duty: Lyndon Johnson, Robert McNamara, the Joint Chiefs of Staff, and the Lies That Led to Vietnam* (New York: Harper Perennial, 1997), 332.

75. On military capabilities not being relevant to Saigon's survival, see William S. Turley, *The Second Indochina War: A Concise Political and Military History*, 2nd ed. (Lanham, MD: Rowman & Littlefield, 1986, 2009), 241. On the relationships between "salvation and destruction," see Ferdinand Eberstadt, "The Failure of Force," in *Who We Are: An Atlantic Chronicle of the United States and Vietnam*, eds. Robert Manning and Michael Janeway (Boston: Little, Brown, 1969), 248. Military occupation in Frances FitzGerald, *Fire in the Lake: The Vietnamese and the Americans in Vietnam* (Boston: Little, Brown, 1972), 407. On the relationships between social structures and military power, see Stephen Peter Rosen, "Military Effectiveness: Why Society Matters," *International Security* 19, no. 4 (Spring 1995): 5–31. As an example of a "lost war" narrative, Henry Kissinger impugned the home front turmoil of the late 1960s, believing the "consensus that had sustained our postwar foreign policy had evaporated." *White House Years* (Boston: Little, Brown, 1979), 56.

Chapter 1

1. Colin Leinster, "The Two Wars of General Lew Walt," *LIFE*, 26 May 1967, 83. "Marineland," in William Tuohy, "Downgrading of Top Marines Seen in Viet Command Shifts," *Los Angeles Times*, 3 March 1968. Allan R. Millet correctly notes that "much of III MAF's 1967 campaign plan focused on stopping NVA incursions across the border." *Semper Fidelis: The History of the United States Marine Corps* (New York: Macmillan, 1980), 588.

2. NVA divisions in Millett, ibid. I Corps data from "A Marine's Guide to the Republic of Vietnam," Folder 09, Box 01, Peter Swartz Collection, TTUVA, pp. 12–19.

3. Gen. Walter T. Kerwin, interview by Albin Wheeler and Ronald Craven, 9 April 1976, Senior Officers Debriefing Program, Box A, Creighton Abrams Story, MHI, p. 18. See also James Carafano, "Tet Offensive: Inside MACV Headquarters," *Vietnam*, June 2006. Lewis Sorley

argues that the "decision probably came as no surprise to Abrams, who had recently experienced his own frustrations in trying to deal with some of the senior Marine commanders while on a projected visit to Khe Sanh." *Thunderbolt: General Creighton Abrams and the Army of His Times* (New York: Simon & Schuster, 1992), 213.

4. Westmoreland to Wheeler, 10 December 1967, Folder 06, Box 1, Veteran Members of the 109th Quartermaster Company Collection, TTUVA.

5. On credibility of a countrywide assault, see Editorial Note, *FRUS, 1964–1968,* VI: 73; James J. Wirtz, *The Tet Offensive: Intelligence Failure in War* (Ithaca, NY: Cornell University Press, 1991), 83, 139; and Ronnie E. Ford, *Tet 1968: Understanding the Surprise* (London: Frank Cass, 1995), 4. On Westmoreland's views of Khe Sanh, see Phillip B. Davidson, *Vietnam at War, The History: 1946–1975* (Novato, CA: Presidio Press, 1988), 496–499.

6. Truncation of ceasefire in Graham A. Cosmas, *MACV: The Joint Command in the Years of Withdrawal, 1968–1973* (Washington, DC: Center of Military History, 2007), 51.

7. John Prados argues that Westmoreland *"wanted* to fight a battle along the border." *The Blood Road: The Ho Chi Minh Trail and the Vietnam War* (New York: John Wiley & Sons, 1999), 243. For an overview of the fighting in I Corps during the Tet offensive, see Willard Pearson, *The War in the Northern Provinces, 1966–1968* (Washington, DC: US Government Printing Office, 1975), chapters 4 and 5.

8. "Running the Show," in Cosmas, *MACV,* 75. George C. Herring, *America's Longest War: The United States and Vietnam, 1950–1975,* 4th ed. (New York: McGraw-Hill, 1979, 2002), 227–234.

9. William Tuohy, "Marine Leaders Criticized as Unimaginative," *The Washington Post,* 3 March 1968. Tuohy, "Downgrading of Top Marines Seen in Viet Command Shifts." Ted Sell, "Marine View of Command Shifts in Vietnam," *Los Angeles Times,* 7 April 1968. Jonathan Schell noted in late 1969 that the "striking fact about the siege of Khe Sanh is that the position held there by the Marines had no strategic importance." In *Observing the Nixon Years* (New York: Pantheon Books, 1989), 10.

10. Millet notes that the marines, in fact, were asking this fundamental question. *Semper Fidelis,* 591. For a differing view, see John Southard, *Defend and Befriend: The U.S. Marine Corps and Combined Action Platoons in Vietnam* (Lexington: University Press of Kentucky, 2014), 140–141.

11. A key argument within the historiography rests on the claim that Abrams discounted the use of the "body count" to measure progress in the war. Yet a review of metrics used by MACV in early 1970—the status of enemy activity, the operational effectiveness of local forces, the level of South Vietnamese security—suggests few if any changes in the ways that MACV operated before Abrams took over. MACV, in truth, still used "body counts" and "kills" to "report the results of operations." See MACV Chief of Staff Action Memorandum No. 70–11, "Indicators to Supplant 'Body Count' as a Measure of Progress," 26 January 1970, Body Counts File, Safe 78/1, Histories Division, CMH.

12. Robert Komer quoted in Davidson, *Vietnam at War,* 512. Francis "Bing" West quoted in James William Gibson, *The Perfect War: The War We Couldn't Lose and How We Did* (New York: Vintage Books, 1986), 174.

13. Correspondents falsely inferring a change in strategy in Guenter Lewy, *America in Vietnam* (New York: Oxford University Press, 1978), 134. There is an element of irony here, as Abrams distrusted the media and "politicos" in the United States who appeared uninformed of the political situation inside South Vietnam yet charged "around like a bull in a china shop saying what out to be done out here politically." In Lewis Sorley, ed., *Vietnam Chronicles: The Abrams Tapes, 1968–1972* (Lubbock: Texas Tech University Press, 2004), 26.

14. Noted of President's Meeting with Wheeler and Abrams, 26 March 1968, *FRUS, 1964–1968,* VI: 459–465; Editorial Note, 477–479. See also Edward J. Drea, *McNamara, Clifford, and the Burdens of Vietnam, 1965–1969* (Washington, DC: Office of the Secretary of Defense Historical Office, 2011), 189–190. Of note, the mission for MACV remained relatively unchanged since 1962: "to assist and support the Government of Vietnam in its efforts to provide for its internal security, defeat communist insurgency, and resist overt aggression." Felt to McGarr, 8 February 1962, *FRUS, 1961–1963,* II: 112.

15. Ellsworth Bunker, interview by Michael L. Gillette, 12 December 1980, Oral History Collection, LBJL, p. II-10. "The Army Chief of Staff on Military Strategy in Vietnam," *Army Digest* (April 1968): 6–9. L. F. Chapman Jr., Memorandum for the President, 2 February 1968, Folder 3, Box 76, Series I, Official Correspondence, Harold K. Johnson Collection, MHI.

16. Herman Kahn, "On the Possibilities for Victory or Defeat," in Frank E. Armbruster, Raymond D. Gastil, Herman Kahn, William Pfaff, and Edmund Stillman, *Can We Win in Vietnam?* (New York: Frederick A. Praeger, 1968), 179. Population data from Sharpe to Morrick, Population of Vietnam, 1 November 1966, Folder 24, Box 15, Douglas Pike Collection, Unit 06: Democratic Republic of Vietnam, TTUVA. District and province numbers in Robert W. Komer, "Pacification: A Look Back . . . And Ahead," *Army* 20, no. 6 (June 1970): 24. Border and topography in T. T. Connors, M. G. Weiner, and J. A. Wilson, *The Land Border of South Vietnam: Some Physical and Cultural Characteristics* (Santa Monica, CA: RAND Corporation, 1970), 1, 7–11.

17. Lewis W. Walt, interview, 24 January 1969, Oral History Collection, LBJL, p. 4.

18. Wallace M. Greene, "Vietnam: The Issue and the Response," *Vital Speeches of the Day* 33, no. 16 (1 June 1967): 510. On "balanced approach," see Michael A. Hennessy, *Strategy in Vietnam: The Marines and Revolutionary Warfare in I Corps, 1965–1972* (Westport, CT: Praeger, 1997), 77–78. See also Southard, *Defend and Befriend*, 130; and Ward Just, "It's a 3-Front War in I Corps Area as Marines Fight for Pacification," *The Washington Post*, 13 April 1967. As Hennessy argues, the marines "found themselves primarily attempting to 'isolate' the battlefield, and were compelled to fight conventional North Vietnamese troops" (p. 7).

19. Krulak quoted in William Conrad Gibbons, *The U.S. Government and the Vietnam War: Executive and Legislative Roles and Relationships, Part IV: July 1965–January 1968* (Washington, DC: US Government Printing Office, 1994), 198. Yet the general also described the "balanced approach" in his memoirs. Victor H. Krulak, *First to Fight: An Inside View of the U.S. Marine Corps* (Annapolis, MD: Naval Institute Press, 1984), 183.

20. Edward F. Palm, "Tiger Papa Three: The Fire Next Time," *Marine Corps Gazette* (February 1988): 76. On inability to "push a strong population control strategy," see the official USMC History, Jack Shulimson, Leonard A. Blasiol, Charles R. Smith, and David A. Dawson, *U.S. Marines in Vietnam: The Defining Year, 1968* (Washington, DC: History and Museums Division, US Marine Corps, 1997), 608.

21. Senior Officer Debriefing Report, Col. Gus S. Peters, 6 June 1968, Box 14, HQ USARV Command History Senior Officer Debriefing Reports, RG 472, NARA. See also "War Take-Over by South Vietnam—When?," *U.S. News & World Report*, 13 May 1968, pp. 58–59. For similar condemnations, a full year earlier, see NARA 9–34. Col. Arndt L. Mueller, 15 July 1967, Box 12, Senior Officer Debriefing Reports, RG 472, NARA.

22. Kelly Orr, "South Vietnam Army Good—But Still No. 2 to Ho's," *Boston Globe*, 15 May 1968. "Thieu Signs S. Viet Mobilization Law," *The Washington Post*, 20 June 1968.

23. Peters Debriefing Report, NARA. After a July 1968 trip to Vietnam, Secretary of Defense Clark Clifford wrote to the president that the "major problem we face here is that of putting the ARVN and the other South Vietnamese forces in a position to take over more of the war. Despite all the talk over the years, they still are badly in need of a better leadership, better training, additional equipment and an improvement of living conditions for themselves and their families." Clifford to Johnson, 18 July 1968, *FRUS, 1964–1968*, VI: 876.

24. Nhã Ca, *Mourning Headband for Hue* (Bloomington: Indiana University Press, 2014), xxvi-xxviii, 21, 93, 129. For an American perspective, see Charles A. Krohn, *The Lost Battalion of Tet: Breakout of the 2/12th Cavalry at Hue* (Annapolis, MD: Naval Institute Press, 2008), 127 and the larger work, John Laurence, *The Cat from Hué: A Vietnam War Story* (New York: Public Affairs, 2002).

25. Westmoreland to Wheeler and Sharp, 2 January 1967, *FRUS, 1964–1968*, V: 5.

26. David Halberstam, "Return to Vietnam," *Harper's* 235, no. 1411 (December 1967): 49. Komer, then head of the US pacification effort, report in MACV Commanders Conference, 19 May 1968, Pacification Overview, Conclusions Folder, Historians Files, CMH, p. 2.

27. Farmer quoted in James Walker Trullinger Jr., *Village at War: An Account of Revolution in Vietnam* (New York: Longman, 1980), 129.

28. William Thomas Allison, *Military Justice in Vietnam: The Rule of Law in an American War* (Lawrence: University Press of Kansas, 2007), 121. Douglas S. Blaufarb, *The Counterinsurgency Era: U.S. Doctrine and Performance, 1950 to the Present* (New York: The Free Press, 1977), 263.

29. Telegram from the Embassy in Vietnam to the Department of State, 6 January 1965, *FRUS, 1964–1968*, II: 13. Six months later, Westmoreland reported that the "fabric of GVN civil

functions and services" had been rendered "ineffective and listless by successive coups and changes" and the military arm was in "need of revitalization." Westmoreland to Wheeler, 24 June 1965, *FRUS, 1964–1968*, III: 42. Komer quoted in Notes of Meeting, 12 July 1967, *FRUS, 1964–1968*, V: 606.

30. Bunker, interview, LBJL, I-13. See also Sorley, *Vietnam Chronicles*, 146. "The Situation in Vietnam: Overview and Outlook," 24 January 1969, Folder 1, Box 63, NSC Files, Vietnam Subject Files, RNL, p. 4.

31. Bui Diem with David Chanoff, *In the Jaws of History* (Bloomington: Indiana University Press, 1999), 277. Lam Quang Thi, *The Twenty-Five Year Century: A South Vietnamese General Remembers the Indochina War to the Fall of Saigon* (Denton: University of North Texas Press, 2001), 321. On traditional social norms, see Neil L. Jamieson, *Understanding Vietnam* (Berkeley: University of California Press, 1993), chapter 1.

32. Nguyen Cao Ky, *Twenty Years and Twenty Days* (New York: Stein and Day, 1976), 122. Col. Edwin W. Chamberlain Jr., Senior Officer Debriefing Report, 10 March 1973, Digital Archive Collection, USAAWCL, p. 8. Douglas S. Blaufarb and George K. Tanham argue that governments gain popular support either through persuasion or coercion. Thus, it seems useful to consider graft and corruption in wartime South Vietnam as a tool of persuasion for at least some government officials. *Who Will Win? A Key to the Puzzle of Revolutionary War* (New York: Crane Russak, 1989), 18.

33. James H. Willbanks notes that Hanoi sent 80,000 to 90,000 replacements into South Vietnam between the early Tet fighting and the end of April. *The Tet Offensive: A Concise History* (New York: Columbia University Press, 2007), 66. Enemy's military weaknesses in HQ, USMACV, Command History, 1968, Vol. I, Entry MACJ03, RG 472, NARA, p. 39. Le Duan's full title was general secretary of the Central Committee of the Vietnam Workers' Party.

34. Department of the Army Pamphlet 525-2, *Lessons Learned: Vietnam Primer* (Washington, DC: Headquarters, Department of the Army, 1967), 53. On Le Duan's tactical changes, see Lien-Hang T. Nguyen, *Hanoi's War: An International History of the War for Peace in Vietnam* (Chapel Hill: University of North Carolina Press, 2012), 114–115.

35. Wheeler in *Vietnam: A History in Documents*, ed. Gareth Porter (New York: New American Library, 1981), 358. Cronkite in Peter Braestrup, *Big Story: How the American Press and Television Reported and Interpreted the Crisis of Tet 1968 in Vietnam and Washington*, Vol. 2 (Boulder, CO: Westview Press, 1977), 189. On the political fallout from Cronkite's speech, see Willbanks, *The Tet Offensive*, 68–69.

36. Townsend Hoopes to the Secretary of Defense, "The Infeasibility of Military Victory in Vietnam," 14 March 1968, Folder 1, Box 11, Larry Berman Collection (Presidential Archives Research), TTUVA. Komer blamed "official Washington" that had "totally misread the real situation here. Washington has focused on our own losses, not on the enemy's." In Cosmas, *MACV*, 88.

37. R. W. Apple Jr., "Gen. Abrams Due for Vietnam Post," *New York Times*, 27 March 1967.

38. Roy Reed, "Gen. Abrams Gets Post in Vietnam," *New York Times*, 1 April 1967. "Abrams May Replace Westmoreland," *Boston Globe*, 2 April 1967.

39. Biography, Gen. Creighton W. Abrams, Box 55, Creighton W. Abrams Papers, MHI. On Abrams's hometown background, see Robert Anglin, "In Agawam, He's 'Toots,'" *Boston Globe*, 7 April 1967. Vance quoted in Davidson, *Vietnam at War*, 519.

40. Davidson, ibid. Ronald H. Spector, *After Tet: The Bloodiest Year in Vietnam* (New York: The Free Press, 1993), 213. "General With a Flair: Creighton Williams Abrams, Jr.," *New York Times*, 7 April 1967. On respect within army, see S. L. A. Marshall, "Naming of Top Tactician to Vietnam a Wise Move," *Los Angeles Times*, 21 April 1967.

41. Bruce Palmer Jr., *The 25-Year War: America's Military Role in Vietnam* (Lexington: University Press of Kentucky, 1984), 26.

42. Lt. Gen. John H. Hay, interview by James Thomas, 1981, Senior Officer Oral History Program, MHI, p. 83.

43. Apple, "Gen. Abrams Due for Vietnam Post." On constraints of a conventional past, see Larry E. Cable, *Conflict of Myths: The Development of American Counterinsurgency Doctrine and the Vietnam War* (New York: New York University Press, 1986), 282; Richard Lock-Pullan, *US Intervention Policy and Army Innovation* (London and New York: Routledge, 2006), 18; and

Peter H. Wilson, "Defining Military Culture," *Journal of Military History* 72, no. 1 (January 2008): 21. Graham Cosmas argues Abrams's concept was based on not only his own experiences but also the policies he inherited from Westmoreland. *MACV*, 128.

44. Komer to Vance, 7 April 1967, *FRUS, 1964–1968*, V: 311. Heintges to Westmoreland, 21 April 1967, Policy/Strategy 21-31 April 1967 Folder, Box 6, Paul L. Miles Papers, MHI. Rowland Evans and Robert Novak, "Inside Report . . . LBJ's War Frustration," *The Washington Post*, 27 March 1967.

45. Wheeler to Westmoreland, 31 October 1967, Folder 9, Box 6, Series I, Official Correspondence, WC Westmoreland Collection, MHI. On ARVN's problems, see Robert Buzzanco, *Masters of War: Military Dissent and Politics in the Vietnam Era* (New York: Cambridge University Press, 1996), 321; and Palmer, *The 25-Year War*, 72.

46. William Tuohy, "No. 2 Military Man in Vietnam Gets Around," *Los Angeles Times*, 14 September 1967. Kerwin, interview, Senior Officers Debriefing Program, MHI, 11. On evaluating the RVNAF, see MACV Directive 18-3, "Army Information and Data Systems Program Review and Analysis for RVNAF Progress," 13 January 1968, MHI; and USMACV, Program Review and Analysis for RVNAF Progress, 31 August 1968, MHI.

47. Abrams quoted in Sorley, *Thunderbolt*, 201. Westmoreland to Abrams, 25 November 1967, *FRUS, 1964–1968*, V: 1071. MACV reorganization in Jeffrey J. Clarke, *Advice and Support: The Final Years, 1965–1973* (Washington, DC: Center of Military History, 1988), 209; and David T. Zabecki, *Chief of Staff: The Principal Officers behind History's Great Commanders*, Vol. 2 (Annapolis, MD: Naval Institute Press, 2008), 212–213.

48. Dong Van Khuyen, "The RVNAF," in *The Vietnam War: An Assessment by South Vietnam's Generals*, ed. Lewis Sorley (Lubbock: Texas Tech University Press, 2010), 60–61. For an argument castigating MACV over the M-16 issue, see Lewis Sorley, "Reassessing ARVN," Lecture, Vietnam Center, Texas Tech University, Lubbock, TX, 17 March 2006, pp. 3–5. Gene Roberts, "Clifford Pledges More Firepower to Saigon Forces," *New York Times*, 15 July 1968.

49. Languished in Lewis Sorley, *Westmoreland: The General Who Lost Vietnam* (Boston and New York: Houghton Mifflin Harcourt, 2011), 151. Kerwin, interview, MHI, 14. See also Thomas Noel, interview by Steve Glick, Senior Officers Debriefing Program, Creighton Abrams Story, MHI, 4. Conrad Crane recommended how historians should reconsider arguments that Abrams kept his "brilliance under a bushel" in email with the author, 21 July 2014. In fact, during Abrams's transition, most all senior policymakers in Washington agreed with Westmoreland's approach. Walt Rostow, for instance, laid out for LBJ a list of unresolved problems in early 1967 yet noted "Westy's vision of 1967 is basically cheering." Rostow to Johnson, 26 January 1967, *FRUS, 1964–1968*, V: 62.

50. Palmer, *The 25-Year War*, 63. On Abrams sharing Westmoreland's views, see Dale Andrade, "Westmoreland Was Right: Learning the Wrong Lessons from the Vietnam War," *Small Wars & Insurgencies* 19, no. 2 (June 2008): 164; and Cosmas, *MACV*, 129. No doubt, Abrams was aware of contemporary criticism, such as the well-publicized work James M. Gavin, *Crisis Now* (New York: Random House, 1968).

51. John M. Carland, "Winning the Vietnam War: Westmoreland's Approach in Two Documents," *Journal of Military History* 68, no. 2 (April 2004): 557–559. For Westmoreland's own views on how he developed his strategy, see William C. Westmoreland, *A Soldier Reports* (Garden City, NY: Doubleday, 1976), chapter 8.

52. USMACV, Command History, 1967, Vol. I, Entry MACJ03, RG 472, NARA, pp. 326–327. Emphasis added. In reviewing the nonmilitary aspects of the war, National Security Advisor McGeorge Bundy wrote to the president in mid-February 1966 that "Westmoreland has never neglected the critically important task of persistent effort to strengthen the forces of the GVN." *FRUS, 1964–1968*, IV: 231. In a July 1967 meeting with the Secretary of Defense Robert McNamara, Abrams also agreed with Westmoreland's assessment on the necessary number of troops in Vietnam. Drea, *McNamara, Clifford, and the Burdens of Vietnam*, 141.

53. Combined Campaign Plan, 1968, Historians Files, CMH, pp. 2–4. Andrew J. Birtle, *U.S. Army Counterinsurgency and Contingency Operations Doctrine, 1942–1976* (Washington, DC: Center of Military History, 2006), 371.

54. Historical Division, Joint Chiefs of Staff, "The Joint Chiefs of Staff and the War in Vietnam, 1960–1968," Part III, JCSHO, p. 51-1. See also U.S. Grant Sharp and William C. Westmoreland, *Report on the War in Vietnam* (Washington, DC: US Government Printing Office, 1969), 157; and Gregory A. Daddis, *Westmoreland's War: Reassessing American Strategy in Vietnam* (New York: Oxford University Press, 2014), 89.

55. Mission Council Action Memorandum No. 191, 8 May 1967, National Security File, Vietnam Country File, Box 43, Vol. 70, Memos (A), LBJL. See also MACV Commanders' Conference, 21 May 1967, Box 5, Paul L. Miles Papers, MHI; and William B. Rosson, "Four Periods of American Involvement in Vietnam: Development and Implementation of Policy, Strategy and Programs, Described and Analyzed on the Basis of Experience at Progressively Senior Levels" (Ph.D. diss., University of Oxford, 1979), 241. The South Vietnamese ambassador to the United States, Bùi Diễm, described Bunker as a "professional diplomat" who "harbored a deep sympathy for the Vietnamese people." *In the Jaws of History*, 247. As an example of the language Bunker disliked, see Beverly Deepe, " 'Other War' Stalls: South Vietnam Pacification Program Seen Tottering on Brink of Collapse," *The Christian Science Monitor*, 6 May 1967.

56. Komer to Johnson, 27 April 1967, *FRUS*, 1964–1968, V: 353. Bunker to Johnson, 21 June 1967, Folder 23, Box 1, Veteran Members of the 109th Quartermaster Company Collection, TTUVA.

57. James J. Wirtz, "Intelligence to Please? The Order of Battle Controversy during the Vietnam War," *Political Science Quarterly* 106, no. 2 (Summer 1991): 242–253. George W. Allen, *None So Blind: A Personal Account of the Intelligence Failure in Vietnam* (Chicago: Ivan R. Dee, 2001), 250–251. On Westmoreland wanting to lower the figures for political reasons, see Affidavit of David Halberstam, William C. Westmoreland against CBS Inc., 20 April 1984, Folder 42, Box 1, Larry Berman Collection (*Westmoreland v. CBS*), TTUVA, p. B-228. On the libel suit, Don Kowet and Sally Bedell, "Anatomy of a Smear: How CBS Broke the Rules and 'Got' Gen. Westmoreland," *TV Guide*, 29 May 1982; and Stephen B. Young, "*Westmoreland v. CBS*: The Law of War and the Order of Battle Controversy," *Parameters* (Winter 1991–1992): 74–94.

58. Samuel A. Adams, interview by Ted Gittinger, 20 September 1984, Oral History Collection, LBJL, pp. I-3 to I-5. Daniel O. Graham, *Confessions of a Cold Warrior* (Fairfax, VA: Preview Press, 1995), 51–62.

59. Simply defining the enemy proved a practical problem for soldiers as well. As one recalled, the "VC would be the farmer you waved to from your jeep in the day who would be the guy with the gun out looking for you at night." Al Santoli, *Everything We Had: An Oral History of the Vietnam War by Thirty-three American Soldiers Who Fought It* (New York: Random House, 1981), 49. Marine Francis J. West Jr. noted that families of known Vietcong, sympathetic to the cause, "might be called passive supporters of the enemy." *The Pragmatists: A Combined Action Platoon in I Corps* (Santa Monica, CA: RAND Corporation, 1968), 43. See also "How Big Is the Enemy?," *Chicago Tribune*, 23 December 1967.

60. Sam Adams, "Vietnam Cover-Up: Playing War with Numbers," *Harper's* 250, no. 1500 (May 1975): 41–44, 62–73. Sam Adams, *War of Numbers: An Intelligence Memoir* (South Royalton, VT: Steerforth Press, 1994), 83. Ellsworth Bunker, interview by Michael L. Gillette, 12 October 1983, Oral History Collection, LBJL, p. III-1. Abrams to Wheeler, Sharp, and Westmoreland, 20 August 1967, Folder 3, Box 6, Series I, Official Correspondence, WC Westmoreland Collection, MHI.

61. Carver to Helms, 13 September 1967, *FRUS*, 1964–1968, V: 799–801. The 1968 combined campaign plan, written as the order of battle controversy was being settled, listed the estimated VC/NVA strength in South Vietnam as some 299,000 to 334,000 personnel. Combined Campaign Plan, 1968, Historians Files, CMH, p. A-1. For definitions of enemy forces included in the order of battle, see *Southeast Asia Analysis Report*, December 1967, MHI, p. 7.

62. Julian Paget, *Counter-Insurgency Operations: Techniques of Guerrilla Warfare* (New York: Walker, 1967), 157. See also J. Bowyer Bell, *The Myth of the Guerrilla: Revolutionary Theory and Malpractice* (New York: Alfred A. Knopf, 1971), 22. One writer in *Military Review* exclaimed that "war can never be separated from political intercourse." William D. Franklin, "Clausewitz on Limited War," *Military Review* 47, no. 6 (June 1967): 24.

63. Westmoreland's operational concepts in Birtle, *U.S. Army Counterinsurgency and Contingency Operations Doctrine*, 368–369. Internal defense and development in Robert Duncan Downie, *Learning from Conflict: The U.S. Military in Vietnam, El Salvador, and the Drug War* (Westport, CT: Praeger, 1998), 55–57.

64. Westmoreland to Wheeler, 30 October 1967, Policy/Strategy 21–31 October 1967 Folder, Box 6, Paul L. Miles Papers, MHI, pp. 2–3. Westmoreland was fairly consistent in his strategic approach. See Concept of Military Operations in SVN, 26 August 1966, Policy/Strategy 21–30 August 1966 Folder, Box 6, Paul L. Miles Papers, MHI.

65. Westmoreland to Wheeler, 30 October 1967, MHI, 10. See also *The Pentagon Papers: The Defense Department History of United States Decisionmaking on Vietnam* [The Sen. Gravel Edition, 5 vols.], Vol. IV (Boston: Beacon Press, 1971–1972), 350–351. Ambassador at Large Henry Cabot Lodge Jr. noted in late August 1967 that pacification was receiving "the highest priority which it has ever had—making it, in effect, the main purpose of all our activities."

66. Joint Chiefs of Staff to McNamara, 27 August 1965, *FRUS, 1964–1968*, III: 361. North Vietnam as the "source" of the war in Harry G. Summers Jr., *On Strategy: A Critical Analysis of the Vietnam War* (Novato, CA: Presidio Press, 1982), 88. See also Tarak Barkawi, *Globalization and War* (Lanham, MD: Rowman & Littlefield, 2006), 112; and Sandra Scanlon, *The Prowar Movement: Domestic Support for the Vietnam War and the Making of Modern American Conservatism* (Amherst: University of Massachusetts Press, 2013), 165. *U.S. News & World Report* seemed to agree, calling the "civil war" in Vietnam a "façade." "One War That's Being Won in South Vietnam," 12 August 1968.

67. Peers to Abrams, 16 November 1968, Abrams Messages #1825, CMH. MG George I. Forsythe, 14 April 1969, Senior Officer Debriefing Reports, CMH. On hungry Chinamen, see F. K. Mearns, 9 April 1969, Senior Officer Debriefing Reports, CMH.

68. Abrams to Wheeler and Sharp, 21 November 1967, Abrams Messages #191, CMH.

69. Abrams to Westmoreland, 18 November 1967, Abrams Messages #185, CMH. Operation Arc Light was the deployment of B-52 strategic bombers in a close air support role inside South Vietnam. See Carl Berger, ed., *The United States Air Force in Southeast Asia* (Washington, DC: Office of Air Force History, 1977), 149–168. Tac air was shorthand for tactical air support.

70. Ward Just, "Guerrillas Wreck Pacification Plan," *The Washington Post*, 4 February 1968. Tom Buckley, "Offensive Is Said to Pinpoint Enemy's Strengths," *New York Times*, 2 February 1968. Jack Gould, "U.S. Is Losing War in Vietnam, N.B.C. Declares," *New York Times*, 11 March 1968. Still, as David F. Schmitz argues, the offensive "did not produce a dramatic swing in popular opinion." *The Tet Offensive: Politics, War, and Public Opinion* (Lanham, MD: Rowman & Littlefield, 2005), 158.

71. On this point, see Cosmas, *MACV*, 219 and William M. Hammond, *Public Affairs: The Military and the Media, 1968–1973* (Washington, DC: Center of Military History, 1996), 33.

72. Westmoreland to Wheeler, Johnson, and Sharp, 2 August 1967, Folder 29, Box 1, Veteran Members of the 109th Quartermaster Company Collection, TTUVA. Robert Elegant believed "US public-relations policies made the press and the authorities not merely adversaries, but enemies." "How to Lose a War: Reflections from a Foreign Correspondent," *Encounter* 57, no. 2 (August 1981): 86.

73. Neil Sheehan, *A Bright Shining Lie: John Paul Vann and America in Vietnam* (New York: Random House, 1988), 728. James B. Sterba, "G.I.'s Outburst Widens Censorship Issue," *New York Times*, 5 January 1970. "Newsman Suspended by Army," *The Washington Post*, 5 January 1970. "Newsmen Hit Military's 'Lid' on Viet Battlefield Information," *The Hartford Courant*, 23 January 1971. A frustrated Abrams once even lost his temper and shouted, "You people won't believe me whatever I say." George McArthur, "Secrecy Issue an Old Tale to War Reporters," *Los Angeles Times*, 15 July 1971.

74. Area in John Paxton, ed., *The Statesman's Year-Book: Statistical and Historical Annual of the States of the World for the Year 1972–1973* (New York: Macmillan, 1972), 1477. On winning the war on many levels, see Orrin Schwab, *A Clash of Cultures: Civil-Military Relations during the Vietnam War* (Westport, CT: Praeger Security International, 2006), 77. Abrams's experience fit within more general observations on strategy as a function of "multiple independent variables" and as an environment in which the enemy continually compensates for its weaknesses. See Beatrice Heuser, *The Evolution of Strategy: Thinking War from Antiquity to the*

Present (New York: Cambridge University Press, 2010), 18; and Colin S. Gray, "Why Strategy Is Difficult," *Joint Forces Quarterly* (Summer 1999): 10.

75. Abrams quoted in Buzzanco, *Masters of War*, citing message to Wheeler, Westmoreland, and Sharp, 22 March 1968, 334. Abrams also called the war a "bottomless pit." In Martin van Creveld, *Command in War* (Cambridge, MA: Harvard University Press, 1985), 258.

76. On labor force supporting the trail, see John Prados, "The Road South: The Ho Chi Minh Trail," in *Rolling Thunder in a Gentle Land: The Vietnam War Revisited*, ed. Andrew Wiest (New York: Osprey, 2006), 83. In mid-1969, Abrams was still discussing the problems of enemy infiltration into South Vietnam. See Abrams to McConnell, 29 June 1969, Folder 6, Box 65, NSC Files, Vietnam Subject Files, RNL. While concerned about a superpower confrontation, LBJ also feared the repercussions inside Laos and Cambodia if the war expanded.

77. Westmoreland quoted in Prados, *The Blood Road*, 141.

78. Gravely damaging the war effort in Sorley, *Westmoreland*, 199. Though resting on scant evidence, such an argument was congenial to the author for it helped feed into his better war thesis. For a counter to this claim, see John M. Shaw, *The Cambodian Campaign: The 1970 Offensive and America's Vietnam War* (Lawrence: University Press of Kansas, 2005), 7; and Ngo Quang Truong, "RVNAF and US Operational Cooperation and Coordination," in Sorley, *The Vietnam War*, 173, which notes that "the introduction of US combat forces in early 1965 saved the Republic of Vietnam from military defeat and helped it restore stability and consolidate a more viable regime." On institutional constraints, see R. W. Komer, *Bureaucracy Does Its Thing: Institutional Constraints on U.S.-GVN Performance in Vietnam* (Santa Monica, CA: RAND Corporation, 1972), 14–16.

79. Walter T. Kerwin Jr. quoted in Zabecki, *Chief of Staff*, 215. On Westmoreland's plans for operations into Laos, see Prados, *The Blood Road*, 206–207.

80. Ellsworth Bunker, interview, 12 December 1980, LBJL, p. II-8. On bigger problems exposed by Tet, and Westmoreland's request for additional troops, see Robert Dallek, *Flawed Giant: Lyndon Johnson and His Times, 1961–1973* (New York: Oxford University Press, 1998), 508.

81. Combat Operations After Action Report, CG II Field Force Vietnam, HQ, Box 33, USARV Command Historian After Action Reports, NARA, p. 27. PSDF in Dale Andradé, *Ashes to Ashes: The Phoenix Program and the Vietnam War* (Lexington, MA: Lexington Books, 1990) 81. One contemporary document argued "the populace was passive because they had not been politically motivated and organized." Quoted in Westmoreland to Wheeler, Sharp, Bunker, and Abrams, 13 February 1968, Abrams Messages #286, CMH. Yet at least some MACV officers argued the "non-committed attitude was due primarily to the fact that the people were still subjected to the influence of both the VC and the GVN." Press Briefing, 1968 Tet Offensive in II CTZ, 17 April 1968, Folder 1, Bud Harton Collection, TTUVA, p. 7.

82. Bunker to Johnson, 15 February 1968, *FRUS, 1964–1968*, VI: 215. USMACV Quarterly Evaluation Report, January-March 1968, MHI, p. 2.

83. BG John W. Barnes, Deputy Senior Advisor, II Corps Tactical Zone, 15 December 1968, Box 1, Senior Officer Debriefing Reports, RG 472, NARA, p. 1. Westmoreland to Sharp, 26 February 1968, Abrams Messages #339, CMH. Peter R. Kann, "Saigon Takes Stock," *The Wall Street Journal*, 7 February 1968. Thi, *The Twenty-Five Year Century*, 212. As a counter to these assumptions, see Ngo Vinh Long, "The Tet Offensive and Its Aftermath" in *The Tet Offensive*, eds. Marc Jason Gilbert and William Head (Westport, CT: Praeger, 1996), 101.

84. Westmoreland to Wheeler, 12 February 1968, in William Thomas Allison, *The Tet Offensive: A Brief History with Documents* (New York: Routledge, 2008), 178. Attacking base areas in Combat Operations After Action Report, Army 1968, II Field Force Vietnam, Tet Offensive Part I, n.d., Folder 01, Bud Harton Collection, TTUVA. On pacification program, see Bunker to Johnson, 8 February 1968, *FRUS, 1964–1968*, VI: 152. In March 1969, Abrams estimated pacification had been set back "3 to 6 months in 19 provinces" during 1968. COMUSMACV to CINPAC, 4 March 1969, Folder 3, Box 62, NSC Files, Vietnam Subject Files, RNL, p. 3. Regaining the tactical initiative in Micheal Clodfelter, *Vietnam in Military Statistics: A History of the Indochina Wars 1772–1991* (Jefferson, NC: McFarland, 1995), 135.

85. Clark Clifford, interview by Paige Mulhollan, 14 July 1969, Oral History Collection, LBJL, p. III-10. Hedrick Smith and Neil Sheehan, "Westmoreland Requests 206,000 More Men, Stirring Debate in Administration," *New York Times*, 10 March 1968. On the debate over

the troop request, and Wheeler's attempts to force the president to call up the reserves, see Davidson, *Vietnam at War*, 448–459; and John B. Henry II, "February, 1968," *Foreign Policy*, no. 4 (Autumn 1971): 3–33.

86. COMUSMACV to American Embassy, Paris, France, 27 May 1968, Historians Files, US Strategy, Vietnam 1965–1975, CMH. Westmoreland also noted that "Pacification operations are inseparable from the main offensive." Tran Ngoc Chau with Ken Fermoyle, *Vietnam Labyrinth: Allies, Enemies, and Why the U.S. Lost in Vietnam* (Lubbock: Texas Tech University Press, 2012), 321. One ARVN general, writing on the pacification program, recalled that after Tet the "countryside was once again left open to enemy control." Tran Dinh Tho, "Pacification," in Sorley, *The Vietnam War*, 224.

87. LBJ quoted in Michael D. Pearlman, *Warmaking and American Democracy: The Struggle over Military Strategy, 1700 to the Present* (Lawrence: University Press of Kansas, 1999), 371. "How Goes Thieu's Government?," *TIME*, 16 August 1968. Robert W. Komer, *Organization and Management of the "New Model" Pacification Program—1966–1969* (Santa Monica, CA: RAND Corporation, 1970), 80. Samuel P. Huntington, "The Bases of Accommodation," *Foreign Affairs* 46, no. 4 (July 1968): 649.

88. War of words in Merle L. Pribbenow II, "General Võ Nguyên Giáp and the Mysterious Evolution of the Plan for the 1968 Tết Offensive," *Journal of Vietnamese Studies* 3, no. 2 (Summer 2008): 11. On the internal debate, see Lien-Hang T. Nguyen, "The War Politburo: North Vietnam's Diplomatic and Political Road to the Tết Offensive," *Journal of Vietnamese Studies* 1, nos. 1–2 (2006): 10–11.

89. 1967 report in *Victory in Vietnam: The Official History of the People's Army of Vietnam, 1954–1975*, trans. Merle L. Pribbenow (Lawrence: University Press of Kansas, 2002), 214–215. The background of this strategic thinking can be found in Robert K. Brigham, *Guerrilla Diplomacy: The NLF's Foreign Relations and the Viet Nam War* (Ithaca, NY: Cornell University Press, 1999), 8–11; K.W. Taylor, *A History of the Vietnamese* (New York: Cambridge University Press, 2013), 601–605; and Pierre Asselin, *Hanoi's Road to the Vietnam War, 1954–1965* (Berkeley: University of California Press, 2013), 209–210.

90. Outcomes of the Tet offensive from Hanoi's perspective in Nguyen Vu Tung, "Coping with the United States: Hanoi's Search for an Effective Strategy," in *The Vietnam War*, ed. Peter Lowe (New York: St. Martin's Press, 1998), 48–49; Porter, *Vietnam: A History in Documents*, 362–363; and War Experiences Recapitulation Committee of the High-Level Military Institute, *The Anti-U.S. Resistance War for National Salvation 1954–1975: Military Events* (Hanoi: People's Army Publishing House, 1980), 110.

91. Diem, *In the Jaws of History*, 228. On Le Duan's view of negotiations, see Nguyen, *Hanoi's War*, 115–120.

92. Quoted in Charles E. Neu, *America's Lost War, Vietnam: 1945–1975* (Wheeling, IL: Harlan Davidson, 2005), 169. It is important to note that while "the communists were severely mauled by the military campaigns in 1968, they were not completely destroyed." Ang Cheng Guan, *Ending the Vietnam War: The Vietnamese Communists' Perspective* (London and New York: Routledge Curzon, 2004), 17.

93. Robert Barkdoll, "Abrams to Succeed Gen. Westmoreland," *Los Angeles Times*, 11 April 1968. Max Frankel, "Gen. Abrams Gets Top Vietnam Post; Deputy Is Named," *New York Times*, 11 April 1968. Gene Roberts, "Each Side in War Claiming Big Gains as Parley Opens," *New York Times*, 13 May 1968. On the political environment at home after Tet, see Lyndon Baines Johnson, *The Vantage Point: Perspectives of the Presidency, 1963–1969* (New York: Holt, Rinehart and Winston, 1971), 384.

94. George Ashworth, "Command Change: New Path?," *The Christian Science Monitor*, 25 March 1968.

95. Abrams to McCain, 1 October 1968, Abrams Messages #1554, CMH. On Abrams talking about the "system," see Sorley, *Thunderbolt*, 238.

96. On language and strategic theories, see J. Boone Bartholomees Jr., ed., *U.S. Army War College Guide to National Security Policy and Strategy* (Carlisle, PA: Strategic Studies Institute, 2006), 79–84, 103.

97. William Tuohy, "Reward or Kick? Westmoreland's Transfer Weighed," *Los Angeles Times,* 24 March 1968. "General Westmoreland Criticized, Defended," *Boston Globe,* 16 February 1968. On talk of Westmoreland being kicked upstairs, Phillip Davidson, MACV's chief intelligence officer under both Westmoreland and Abrams, stated, "Nothing could be less factual." *Vietnam at War,* 479.

98. Analyst and Abrams both quoted in Hammond, *Public Affairs,* 24. Ambassador Lodge agreed, reporting after Tet that "it will be necessary, for a number of reasons, to continue to conduct offensive operations in Vietnam." Lodge quoted in Wheeler to Johnson, 11 March 1968, *FRUS,* 1964–1968, VI: 367.

99. Ted Sell, "Shift in Vietnam: Westmoreland to Get U.S. Post," *Los Angeles Times,* 23 March 1968.

100. The counterfactual outlined here arose from a conversation with Professor Marilyn Young, New York University. Murrey Marder, "Abrams Sees LBJ," *Boston Globe,* 27 March 1968. Hanoi's post-Tet evaluation can be found in *Victory in Vietnam,* 223–224. See also Melvin Small, *At the Water's Edge: American Politics and the Vietnam War* (Chicago: Ivan R. Dee, 2005), 109.

101. On official dates of Abrams's promotions, see Johnson to Lemnitzer et al., 11 April 1968, Abrams Messages #443, CMH; and Kerwin to Abrams, 2 June 1972, Abrams Messages, CMH. On "no formal order or directive mandating his new approach," see Richard A. Hunt, *Pacification: The American Struggle for Vietnam's Hearts and Minds* (Boulder, CO: Westview Press, 1995), 221.Westmoreland's final advice in *FRUS,* 1964–1968, VI: 720. As early as June 1968, Abrams was forecasting that future operations would include the marines continuing to "find and destroy enemy forces" and the allies conducting security, combat sweep, and multibattalion size operations. Abrams to Wheeler, Sharp, 24 June 1968, Abrams Messages #766, CMH. The MACV command history for 1968 erroneously reported that US forces were no longer "regularly engaged in large, multi-battalion operations." USMACV, Command History, 1968, Vol. I, NARA, 2.

102. COMUSMACV, Operational Guidance, 27 July 1968, MHI. COMUSMACV, Operational Guidance, 18 August 1968, MHI. J3 Inputs to Report of the MACV Effort, 1968–1970, Filing Cabinet B9, Box 3, MACV Command Historian's Collection, MHI, pp. I-2 to I-6. Anticipating the enemy had also been Westmoreland's policy.

103. Difficulties maintaining contact in Gen. William E. DePuy, interview by Bill Mullen and Les Brownlee, 26 March 1979, Box 1, William E. DePuy Papers, MHI, tape 3, interview 2, p. 3. COMUSMACV, Operational Guidance, 4th Quarter CY 68, 28 September 1968.

104. Equal emphasis in Cosmas, *MACV,* 135. COMUSMACV, Operational Guidance No. 5, 5 April 1969, MHI. As Abrams commanded earlier, "All types of operations are to proceed simultaneously, aggressively, persistently, and intelligently—plan solidly and execute vigorously, never letting the momentum subside." COMUSMACV, Operational Guidance, 13 October 1968, MHI. See also Sorley, *Vietnam Chronicles,* 45.

105. Komer quoted in *The Lessons of Vietnam,* eds. W. Scott Thompson and Donaldson D. Frizzell (New York: Crane, Russak, 1977), 79. Peter Braestrup, "Few U.S. Officers Back Idea for a 'New' War Strategy," *The Washington Post,* 28 March 1968. Hanson W. Baldwin, "Vietnam: In the Field, More of the Same 'Gradualism,'" *New York Times,* 31 March 1968. On the "one war" idea not being new, see Headquarters, USMACV, "One War," MACV Command Overview, 1968–1972, Historians Files, CMH, p. 13. The document, however, argued that "only after Tet 68 did the 'one war' concept become a direction." On the decentralization of US tactics, see MG Glenn D. Walker, 30 June 1970, Box 17, HQ USARV Command History, Senior Officer Debriefing Reports, RG 472, NARA, p. 2. Shelby L. Stanton suggests the one war plan actually "limited American military participation to a mobile defensive stance while preparing the South Vietnamese forces to take over their areas of responsibility." *The Rise and Fall of an American Army: U.S. Ground Forces in Vietnam, 1965–1973* (Novato, CA: Presidio Press, 1985), 284.

106. Drea, *McNamara, Clifford, and the Burdens of Vietnam,* 196–198. Peter Braestrup, "Ground Action Remains Slack as Reds Regroup," *Los Angeles Times,* 8 July 1968. Officers working closely with Abrams did "not foresee any basic changes in the way the war is being conducted." Gene Roberts, "Abrams Is Expected to Carry on Westmoreland's Basic War Policies," *New York Times,* 15 April 1968. One officer said that Abrams "was as committed to search-and-destroy operations as his predecessor and, if anything, would wage them more aggressively."

107. William Tuohy, "U.S. Officials Disagree on Defense of Saigon," *Los Angeles Times*, 12 June 1968. Fifteen minutes in Lewis Sorley, *A Better War: The Unexamined Victories and Final Tragedy of America's Last Years in Vietnam* (New York: Harcourt Brace, 1999), 17. Abandoning Khe Sanh in Robert B. Asprey, *War in the Shadows: The Guerrilla in History* (Garden City, NY: Doubleday, 1975), 1238; and John Prados, *Vietnam: The History of an Unwinnable War, 1945–1975* (Lawrence: University Press of Kansas, 2009), 317. Wheeler to Abrams, 5 June 1968, Abrams Messages #573, CMH. See also Sharp to Wheeler, 14 June 1968, Abrams Messages #647, CMH.

108. George McArthur, interview by Larry Engelmann, Summer 1985, transcript in author's possession. Hay, interview by Thomas, MHI, p. 85. Gene Roberts, "For Gen. Abrams, Defense of Saigon Rates Top Priority," *New York Times*, 14 August 1968. Cosmas, *MACV*, 115. In early June, Abrams intended to "develop counter measures to defeat the enemy while reducing to a minimum both casualties to non-combatants and destruction of civilian property." Abrams to Wheeler, 5 June 1968, Box 66, Creighton W. Abrams Papers, MHI. See also Abrams to Sharp, 9 June 1968, Abrams Messages #603, CMH.

109. Senior Officer Debriefing Program Report of LTG Fred C. Weyand, 4 October 1968, MHI, p. 4. At a public appearance in October 1968, Weyand noted that "the strategy I was directed to pursue during the past two and a half years incorporated every type of military operation I had ever heard of and some I hadn't heard of." Address by LTG Frederick L. Weyand to the National Guard Association of the United States, 10 October 1968, Folder 73, Box 3, Westmoreland Personal Papers, RG 319, NARA. On the problematic language within the better war myth, see the BDM Corporation, "A Study of Strategic Lessons Learned in Vietnam," Vol. VI, Conduct of the War, General Holdings, MHI, pp. 3–75.

110. Kerwin, interview by Wheeler and Craven, MHI, p. 21. Abrams to Wheeler, 26 June 1968, Abrams Messages #786, CMH. One officer recalled that the changes Abrams made resulted in US forces "adhering to a defensive concept that could be likened to a series of rings around Saigon." Col. Marvin D. Fuller, VNIT 277, CMH, 3.

111. "The Situation in the Countryside," n.d., Folder 6, Box 117, NSC Files, Vietnam Subject Files, RNL, p. 12. A combined strategic review on 15 June 1968 led to no addenda to the 1968 combined campaign plan. Combined Campaign Plan, 1968, Historians Files, CMH, p. 27. To Clark Clifford, Abrams reported in mid-July that the "present and programmed U.S./Free World Forces are adequate to cope with the enemy forces in South Vietnam and those known to be infiltrating." Clifford to Johnson, 18 July 1968, *FRUS, 1964–1968*, VI: 878.

112. Sheehan, *A Bright Shining Lie*, 741–742. Tasks in USMACV, "One War," MACV Command Overview, CMH, p. 30. See also Andrew J. Goodpaster, interview with William D. Johnson and James C. Ferguson, AY 1976, Senior Officers Debriefing Program, MHI, p. 41. F. J. West Jr. noted, however, that the allies could not "minimize the challenge the NVA and the VC main forces offer to any security attempt in Vietnam." *Area Security* (Santa Monica, CA: RAND Corporation, 1969), 10.

113. Zeb B. Bradford, "With Creighton Abrams during Tet," *Vietnam* (February 1998): 45. For an example of the multiple missions being conducted by US units, see LTG W. R. Peers, Senior Officer Debriefing Report, 23 June 1969, General Holdings, MHI. On Westmoreland setting the strategic foundation for the American effort, see Clarke, *Advice and Support*, 505.

114. Officer quoted in the ironically titled report by Bernard Weinraub, "Abrams for Westmoreland—A Sharp Contrast," *New York Times*, 16 June 1968. See also Spector, *After Tet*, 216; and Buzzanco, *Masters of War*, 337.

115. Impacts of mini-Tet in USMACV Quarterly Evaluation Report, 1 April–30 June 1968, MHI, pp. 2–3; Operational Report—Lessons Learned, Headquarters, 101st Airborne Division, Period Ending 31 July 1968, MHI; Willbanks, *The Tet Offensive*, 67; and Spector, *After Tet*, 158–159. Westmoreland's account can be found in *Report on the War in Vietnam*, 167. Joseph B. Treaster, "Heaviest Fighting in Months Erupts in South Vietnam," *New York Times*, 19 August 1968. Spoiling operations in Editorial Note, *FRUS, 1964–1968*, VI: 978.

116. Businessman quoted in Beverly Deepe, "Rocketing of Saigon Shatters Viet Lull," *The Christian Science Monitor*, 24 August 1968. For a similar take, see Hoang Ngoc Lung, "The

General Offensives of 1968–1969," in Sorley, *The Vietnam War*, 486. Abrams to Sharp, 19 June 1968, Abrams Messages #714, CMH.

117. Abrams to Wheeler, 28 July 1968, Abrams Messages #969, CMH. LTG Julian Ewell, interview, 15 October 1991, Historians Files, CMH, p. 11. Ground assaults in Thomas C. Thayer, *War Without Fronts: The American Experience in Vietnam* (Annapolis, MD: Naval Institute Press, 1985, 2016), 46.

118. F. J. West Jr. and Charles Benoit, "A Brief Report from Rural Vietnam," 31 October 1968, Folder 24, Strategy File #1, Thayer Papers, CMH, p. 2. One official report rationalized of the pacification efforts that "shortfalls in attainment could not be viewed as failures but rather as indicators of change and the need for readjustment." USMACV, "One War," MACV Command Overview, CMH, 34. On Project Recovery, see Hunt, *Pacification*, 144–145; John Prados, *Lost Crusader: The Secret Wars of CIA Director William Colby* (New York: Oxford University Press, 2003), 203; and Komer, *Organization and Management of the "New Model" Pacification Program*, 83.

119. Abrams to Wheeler and Sharp, 5 June 1968, Abrams Messages #563, CMH. Abrams to Wheeler and Sharp, 17 June 1968, Abrams Messages #680, CMH.

120. American Embassy Saigon to Secretary of State, 25 February 1969, Folder 1, Box 63, NSC Files, Vietnam Subject Files, RNL. J3 Inputs to Report of the MACV Effort, MHI, p. I-5. Operation days in Laird to Nixon, "Possible Responses to Enemy Activity in South Vietnam," 4 March 1969, Folder 19, Box 64, NSC Files, Vietnam Subject Files, RNL. For similar language prior to Tet on the need for aggressive action, see Headquarters, US Army Vietnam, "Battlefield Reports: A Summary of Lessons Learned," Vol. 3, May 1967, p. 2; and Department of the Army Pamphlet No. 350-15-9, *Training, Operations—Lessons Learned*, 1 April 1968, MHI, p. 32.

121. Nguyễn Công Luận, *Nationalist in the Viet Nam Wars: Memoirs of a Victim Turned Soldier* (Bloomington: Indiana University Press, 2012), 330. MACV officer quoted in Cosmas, *MACV*, 244. As a result, "North Vietnamese regular forces increasingly took over the brunt of the heavy fighting." David W. P. Elliott, *The Vietnamese War: Revolution and Social Change in the Mekong Delta, 1930–1975*, concise ed. (Armonk, NY: M.E. Sharpe, 2003, 2007), 328.

122. "The War: A Time of Uncertainty," *TIME*, 20 September 1968. "New Sweep Launched in Ashau Valley," *The Washington Post*, 9 August 1968. As a comparison to how little had changed, see Lessons Learned, Headquarters, 101st Airborne Division, 24 May 1968, Digital Archive Collection, USAAWCL. Of note, smaller "roving" operations were not always productive. As one veteran recalled, "We didn't like to be out there in such small groups. We'd all leave the perimeter the way we were ordered to . . . [but] once we got out of sight, we'd circle around, meet up at a prearranged location, and then go together to a spot where we'd all set up . . . Safety in numbers." Michael Takiff, *Brave Men, Gentle Heroes: American Fathers and Sons in World War II and Vietnam* (New York: William Morrow, 2003), 400.

123. Beverly Deepe, "U.S. Deals from Strength," *The Christian Science Monitor*, 23 October 1968. Beverly Deepe, "Abrams Sees Chink in Viet Cong Armor," *The Christian Science Monitor*, 24 October 1968. "Pile on" in Bernard Weinraub, "Enemy Strategy in Vietnam at Puzzle," *New York Times*, 23 September 1968; and Operational Report of Headquarters, II Field Force Vietnam for Period Ending 31 October 1968, Box 18, USARV Command History OR/LL, RG472, NARA. Robert J. Graham, "Vietnam: An Infantryman's View of Our Failure," *Military Affairs* 48, no. 3 (July 1984): 135. Kill ratios in Moor to Kissinger, "MACV Assessment of Current Communist Strategy and Tactics in South Vietnam," 8 April 1969, Folder 6, Box 65, NSC Files, Vietnam Subject Files, RNL. On the JCS chairman suggesting "search-and-destroy" be "stricken from the lexicon of military terminology employed in South Vietnam," see Wheeler to Laird, 21 July 1969, *FRUS*, 1969–1976, VI: 313. However, one senior officer in the 4th Infantry Division reported as late as February 1971 that search-and-destroy operations were "habitually employed" even if they were "essentially unproductive." MG William A. Burke, 18 February 1971, Senior Officer Debriefing Reports, CMH, p. 17.

124. Abrams to Wheeler, 26 May 1968, Abrams Messages #520, CMH. Abrams to Wheeler and McCain, 6 March 1969, Folder 9, Box 67, NSC Files, Vietnam Subject Files, RNL. July staff meeting in Sorley, *Vietnam Chronicles*, 12.

125. John M. Hawkins, "The Costs of Artillery: Eliminating Harassment and Interdiction Fire during the Vietnam War," *Journal of Military History* 70 (January 2006): 112–113. LTG A. S. Collins Jr., 7 January 1971, Senior Officer Debriefing Reports, CMH, pp. 15–16. On command emphasis to limit "unnecessary casualties," see Kerwin to Abrams, 12 September 1968, Abrams Messages #1329, CMH. Andrew Birtle found that efforts to "reduce the volume of H&I fire were only modestly successful." *U.S. Army Counterinsurgency and Contingency Operations Doctrine*, 382. One artillery captain noted that in the summer and fall of 1968, "friendly fire incidents were causing as many casualties as the NVA/VC." CPT Bery, letter to MAJ Torrence, n.d., Adventure Board, Torrence Collection, WPSC.

126. Col. George S. Patton, 7 April 1969, Senior Officer Debriefing Reports, CMH. Operational Report of 11th Armored Cavalry Regiment for Period Ending 31 October 1968, 10 November 1968, Box 2, Operations Report—Lessons Learned, 11th Armored Cavalry Regiment, MACV Command Historian's Collection, MHI. Reports for Periods Ending 31 January and 18 August 1969 in ibid.

127. Gordon Livingston, "Letter from a Vietnam Veteran," *The Saturday Review*, 20 September 1969, 23.

128. Reserve in Sorley, *Vietnam Chronicles*, 113. Sorties in J3 Inputs to Report of the MACV Effort, MHI, p. I-10. Tonnage in The Committee of Concerned Asian Scholars, *The Indochina Story: A Fully Documented Account* (New York: Pantheon Books, 1970), 97. Joseph Alsop, "The B-52s over Vietnam—Death Out of the Empty Air," *Los Angeles Times*, 6 December 1968. Joseph Alsop, "Viet Reds Open Major Drive; B-52 Bomb Bays Hold Answer," *Los Angeles Times*, 14 February 1969. Matthew Adam Kocher, Thomas B. Pepinsky, and Stathis N. Kalyvas found that "indiscriminate violence through bombing remained common" during the Abrams years. "Aerial Bombing and Counterinsurgency in the Vietnam War," *American Journal of Political Science* 55, no. 2 (April 2011): 216.

129. Officer quoted in "Role of B-52's Is Shifting," *New York Times*, 5 October 1968. On disrupting infiltration, see Notes of the President's Meeting with Foreign Policy Advisers, 30 July 1968, *FRUS, 1964–1968*, VI: 921. On Abrams's views of bombing halts, see Notes of Meeting, 6 September 1968, *FRUS, 1964–1968*, VII: 15; and Haig to Kissinger, 8 April 1970, Folder 1, Box 1009, NSC Files, Alexander M. Haig Special File, RNL. One captured NVA lieutenant argued that the US reliance on airpower and artillery fire showed that "American Infantry units are weak." Quoted in Malcolm A. Danner and Billy J. Biberstein, "A View from the Enemy's Side: Thoughts of a Captured NVA Lieutenant," in *A Distant Challenge: The U.S. Infantryman in Vietnam, 1967–1972*, ed. Infantry Magazine (Nashville, TN: Battery Press, 1983), 104.

130. USMACV, Command History, 1968, Vol. I, NARA, p. 33. Abrams called the NLF infrastructure "the guts of their effort." "Notes from a Conversation with General Abrams and Lt. General Ewell," 18 January 1970, Folder 3, Box 1009, NSC Files, Alexander M. Haig Special File, RNL, p. 2. A "Village Defense Study" seemed to support Abrams's approach, noting there was "no *single* operational threat." Advanced Research Projects Agency, "Village Defense Study—Vietnam," CORDS Historical Working Group Files, 1967–1973, Box 3, RG 472, NARA, p. 8. Andrew F. Krepinevich Jr., however, argues that in late 1968 and into 1969 the "kill VC" syndrome "remained *the* primary method of evaluating commanders." *The Army and Vietnam* (Baltimore and London: Johns Hopkins University Press, 1986), 254.

131. Abrams to Wheeler, 28 September 1968, Abrams Messages #1454, CMH. Bunker quoted in Howard B. Schaffer, *Ellsworth Bunker: Global Troubleshooter, Vietnam Hawk* (Chapel Hill: University of North Carolina Press, 2003), 207.

132. Combined Campaign Plan, 1968, Historians Files, CMH, pp. 2–5. Combined Campaign Plan, 1969, Historians Files, CMH, pp. 2–7. J3 Inputs to Report of the MACV Effort, MHI, p. II-1. On the comparison between the two plans, see Cosmas, *MACV*, 130–131, and James H. Willbanks, *Abandoning Vietnam: How America Left and South Vietnam Lost Its War* (Lawrence: University Press of Kansas, 2004), 50–51. The 1969 MACV command history noted that "the 1969 operational guidance emphasized the spirit of the offensive and relentless attacks against the enemy." It also added that the assumptions for the 1969 campaign plan "were basically unchanged from 1968." HQ, USMACV, Command History, 1969, Vol.

I, Entry MACJ03, RG 472, NARA, pp. II-5, II-20. See also USMACV Quarterly Evaluation Report, 1 July–30 September 1968, MHI, p. 4.

133. Combined Campaign Plan, 1969, CMH, 8. A late November 1970 report found "so little change" in what had "been recommended again and again over the past years." Brian M. Jenkins, *The Unchangeable War*, RM-6278-ARPA, November 1970, CMH Library. See also Cincinnatus, *Self-Destruction: The Disintegration and Decay of the United States Army during the Vietnam Era* (New York: W.W. Norton, 1981), 125.

134. Wheeler quoted in Notes of the President's Meeting, 14 October 1968, *FRUS*, 1964–1968, VII: 189. On the final phase of the Tet offensives, see Nguyen, *Hanoi's War*, 122–123. Peter Braestrup noted that "Westmoreland bequeathed to Abrams an apparently weakened foe, a vast logistics network to give U.S. forces mobility and firepower, and a growing South Vietnamese Army which, to the private surprise of its own leaders, had held up rather well at Tet." "The Abrams Strategy in Vietnam," *The New Leader*, 9 June 1969, 4.

135. "The 'War without a Goal': Mood of Americans in Vietnam," *U.S. News & World Report*, 24 June 1968, 31. "U.S. Vietnam Deaths Top 30,000," *Boston Globe*, 11 December 1968.

136. Graham Cosmas convincingly argues that "Abrams's approach to the war was an evolutionary expansion upon that of his predecessors." *MACV*, 139.

Chapter 2

1. Clark Clifford with Richard Holbrooke, *Counsel to the President: A Memoir* (New York: Random House, 1991), 542–544. John Prados argues that Abrams "would have gotten nowhere without Clifford's political savvy, his influence on Johnson, and his steady hand in dealing with the Joint Chiefs of Staff." *Vietnam: The History of an Unwinnable War, 1945–1975* (Lawrence: University Press of Kansas, 2009), 261.

2. Edward J. Drea, *McNamara, Clifford, and the Burdens of Vietnam, 1965-1969* (Washington, DC: Office of the Secretary of Defense Historical Office, 2011), 195. Clifford to Johnson, 18 July 1968, *FRUS*, 1964–1968, VI: 876.

3. Clifford quoted in Drea, 536. Abrams quoted in Lewis Sorley, *A Better War: The Unexamined Victories and Final Tragedy of America's Last Years in Vietnam* (New York: Harcourt Brace, 1999), 56. On the lack of trust the Nixon White House had in Abrams, see Dale Andrade, "Westmoreland Was Right: Learning Wrong Lessons from the Vietnam War," *Small Wars & Insurgencies* 19, no. 2 (June 2008): 173.

4. Robert B. Semple Jr. "Nixon and Vietnam," *New York Times*, 14 September 1969. "Gen. Abrams Says Resignation Bunk," *The Hartford Courant*, 13 September 1969.

5. H. R. Haldeman, *The Haldeman Diaries: Inside the Nixon White House* (New York: G.P. Putnam's Sons, 1994), 436–437.

6. Hal Brands, *What Good Is Grand Strategy? Power and Purpose in American Statecraft from Harry S. Truman to George W. Bush* (Ithaca, NY: Cornell University Press, 2014), 3. On the relationships between policy and strategy, see Beatrice Heuser, *The Evolution of Strategy: Thinking War from Antiquity to the Present* (New York: Cambridge University Press, 2010), 27; Hew Strachan, "The Lost Meaning of Strategy," in *Strategic Studies: A Reader*, 2nd ed., eds. Thomas G Mahnken and Joseph A. Maiolo (New York: Routledge, 2014), 430; and Hy Rothstein, "Civil-Military Relations and Assessments," in *Assessing War: The Challenge of Measuring Success and Failure*, eds. Leo J. Blanken, Hy Rothstein, and Jason J. Lepore (Washington, DC: Georgetown University Press, 2015), 22.

7. Department of the Army, *Field Manual 100–5, Operations of Army Forces in the Field* (Washington, DC: Headquarters, Department of the Army, September 1968), 1–2. Colin S. Gray, *Modern Strategy* (New York: Oxford University Press, 1999), 55. On the comprehensiveness of a grand strategy, see Paul Kennedy, "Grand Strategy in War and Peace: Toward a Broader Definition," in *Grand Strategies in War and Peace*, ed. Paul Kennedy (New Haven, CT: Yale University Press, 1991), 5. On relationships between strategic theory and practice, see Hew Strachan, *The Direction of War: Contemporary Strategy in Historical Perspective* (New York: Cambridge University Press, 2013), 105; and Antulio J. Echevarria II, *Towards an American Way of War* (Carlisle, PA: US Army War College Strategic Studies Institute, 2004), 12.

8. Abrams to Wheeler, 6 January 1968, Abrams Messages #2161, CMH. Abrams to Wheeler, 27 November 1968, Abrams Messages #1901, CMH.

9. Memorandum of Conversation with President-Elect Nixon, 19 January 1969, *FRUS, 1969–1976*, VI: 2. "GIs' Vietnam Deaths Pass 25,000 Mark," *The Washington Post*, 21 June 1968.

10. On the disconnects between policy and strategy, and the role home front dissent played, see Charles DeBenedetti with Charles Chatfield, *An American Ordeal: The Antiwar Movement of the Vietnam Era* (Syracuse, NY: Syracuse University Press, 1990), 235. Ken Hughes argues that "Nixon did not treat Vietnamization as a serious strategy. Instead, he used it to justify the actions he deemed politically expedient." *Fatal Politics: The Nixon Tapes, the Vietnam War, and the Casualties of Reelection* (Charlottesville: University of Virginia Press, 2015), 15.

11. Abrams to Wheeler, 2 June 1969, Abrams Messages #3303, CMH.

12. Westmoreland quoted in William Thomas Allison, *The Tet Offensive: A Brief History with Documents* (New York: Routledge, 2008), 109. On the long road to US withdrawal, see Ronald H. Spector, "The First Vietnamization: U.S. Advisors in Vietnam, 1956–60," Folder 02, Box 01, Douglas Pike Collection: Unit 02-Military Operations, TTUVA; Larry A. Niksch, "Vietnamization: The Program and Its Problems," Congressional Research Service, 5 January 1972, Folder 01, Box 19, ibid., p. CRS-5; The Committee of Concerned Asian Scholars, *The Indochina Story: A Fully Documented Account* (New York: Pantheon Books, 1970), 132; and John J. Tolson, *Airmobility, 1961–1971* (Washington, DC: US Government Printing Office, 1973), 214. Clark Clifford, though, noted in April 1968 that the Johnson administration was "embarked upon a new policy of gradually turning over the war effort to the South Vietnamese armed forces." Peter Braestrup, "U.S. Troop Relief by Saigon Held Unlikely," *Los Angeles Times*, 15 April 1968.

13. On defining victory, see Herman Kahn, "On Establishing a Context for Debate," in *Can We Win in Vietnam?*, eds. Frank E. Armbruster, Raymond D. Gastil, Herman Kahn, William Pfaff, and Edmund Stillman (New York: Frederick A. Praeger, 1968), 23. "Barely concealed surrender" in Joseph Alsop, "Nixon Told War Can Be Won If U.S. Maintains Pressure," *The Washington Post*, 30 December 1968. James Reston opined that at "some point, the President is going to have to recognize that there is a fundamental difference between his policy of withdrawing gracefully from the war, and ending the war." "A Whiff of Mutiny in Vietnam," *New York Times*, 27 August 1969.

14. Notes of President's Meeting, 29 October 1968, *FRUS, 1964–1968*, VII: 399–416. Notes on Tuesday Luncheon, ibid.: 428–433.

15. Notes of President's Meeting, ibid., 404. On aspects not being hierarchical, see Colin S. Gray, *Fighting Talk: Forty Maxims on War, Peace, and Strategy* (Westport, CT: Praeger Security International, 2007), 54.

16. Clifford, *Counsel to the President*, 564–565.

17. Abrams quoted by Congressman Hale Boggs in "Abrams Note Read, Before Vote on Plank," *Boston Globe*, 29 August 1968. Richard Bergholz, "Delegates Reject Peace Plank in Victory for Johnson Policies," *Los Angeles Times*, 29 August 1968. Of note, Abrams spoke rather contemptuously of what was happening at the Democratic Convention. "One of the interesting things to me in that—part of that plank was to *abolish* search and destroy operations, but when you think of a serious proposal in the Democratic platform to *prescribe* the *tactics* of the field commander on the battlefield, it's really quite an amazing development." In Lewis Sorley, ed., *Vietnam Chronicles: The Abrams Tapes, 1968–1972* (Lubbock: Texas Tech University Press, 2004), 42.

18. "U.S. Staff Officers in Vietnam Praise Plank on the War," *New York Times*, 30 August 1968. Graham A. Cosmas, *MACV: The Joint Command in the Years of Withdrawal, 1968–1973* (Washington, DC: Center of Military History, 2007), 126–127.

19. Johnson quoted in George C. Herring, *America's Longest War: The United States and Vietnam, 1950–1975*, 4th ed. (New York: McGraw-Hill, 1979, 2002), 266. See also Larry Berman, *No Peace, No Honor: Nixon, Kissinger, and Betrayal in Vietnam* (New York: The Free Press, 2001), 31. On LBJ's expectations for the halt, see Richard H. Immerman, "'A Time in the Tide of Men's Affairs': Lyndon Johnson and Vietnam," in *Lyndon Johnson Confronts the World: American Foreign Policy, 1963–1968*, eds. Warren I. Cohen and Nancy Bernkopf Tucker

(New York: Cambridge University Press, 1994), 88. Regarding Humphrey, see Don Fulsom, *Treason: Nixon and the 1968 Election* (Gretna, LA: Pelican, 2015), 38.

20. War Experiences Recapitulation Committee of the High-Level Military Institute, *The Anti-U.S. Resistance War for National Salvation 1954–1975: Military Events* (Hanoi: People's Army Publishing House, 1980), 112. On Hanoi's views, see Pierre Asselin, *A Bitter Peace: Washington, Hanoi, and the Making of the Paris Agreement* (Chapel Hill: University of North Carolina Press, 2002), 10. "Shocked and angry" in William M. Hammond, *Public Affairs: The Military and the Media, 1968–1973* (Washington, DC: Center of Military History, 1996), 49. Clifford, *Counsel to the President*, 587. Robert K. Brigham, *Guerrilla Diplomacy: The NLF's Foreign Relations and the Viet Nam War* (Ithaca, NY: Cornell University Press, 1999), 82.

21. LBJ quoted in Evan Thomas, *Being Nixon: A Man Divided* (New York: Random House, 2015), 178. Nixon's intermediary was Anna Chennault, a Washington socialite and right-wing lobbyist. See Jeffrey Kimball, *Nixon's Vietnam War* (Lawrence: University Press of Kansas, 1998), 56–57; and Fulsom, *Treason*, 40.

22. On politicization of the bombing halt, see David F. Schmitz, *Richard Nixon and the Vietnam War: The End of the American Century* (Lanham, MD: Rowman & Littlefield, 2014), 36–37. GVN reactions in Brigham, *Guerrilla Diplomacy*, 83; Howard B. Schaffer, *Ellsworth Bunker: Global Troubleshooter, Vietnam Hawk* (Chapel Hill: University of North Carolina Press, 2003), 214; and US Embassy in Vietnam to the Department of State, 6 November 1968, *FRUS, 1964–1968*, VII: 572–577. For an excellent overview of this episode, see Ken Hughes, *Chasing Shadows: The Nixon Tapes, the Chennault Affair, and the Origins of Watergate* (Charlottesville: University of Virginia Press, 2014), 19–56.

23. Nixon quoted in "U.S.: Rising Voice of the War Critics," *U.S. News & World Report*, 18 March 1968; and Robert Mann, *A Grand Delusion: America's Descent into Vietnam* (New York: Basic Books, 2001), 615. Nixon's speechwriter William Safire noted that Nixon was "hamstrung" on foreign policy. He could "criticize the conduct of the war, but not the war itself." *Before the Fall: An Inside View of the Pre-Watergate White House* (Garden City, NY: Doubleday, 1975), 34. For Nixon's earlier views on Vietnam, see Andrew L. Johns, "A Voice from the Wilderness: Richard Nixon and the Vietnam War, 1964–1966," *Presidential Studies Quarterly* 20, no. 2 (June 1999): 317–335; and Richard M. Nixon, "Asia After Viet Nam," *Foreign Affairs* 46, no. 1 (October 1967): 111–125. "Honorable end" in Asselin, *A Bitter Peace*, 13.

24. South Vietnamese Ambassador to the United States Bùi Diễm believed "Nixon's so-called secret plan to end the war was a fiction, created out of whole cloth to enhance his candidacy." With David Chanoff, *In the Jaws of History* (Bloomington: Indiana University Press, 1999), 248. On differing definitions of the war's "successful conclusion," see David L. Anderson, *The Vietnam War* (New York: Palgrave Macmillan, 2005), 84; and Schmitz, *Richard Nixon and the Vietnam War*, 33. My thanks to Ed Moise for assistance with this paragraph.

25. Henry Kissinger, *White House Years* (Boston: Little, Brown, 1979), 227. Norman A. Graebner, "The Scholar's View of Vietnam, 1964–1992," in *An American Dilemma: Vietnam, 1964–1973*, eds. Dennis E. Showalter and John G. Albert (Chicago: Imprint Publications, 1993), 30. On a "strategic trap," see Harriet B. Kurtz, "The Collapse of US Global Strategy," *Military Review* 49, no. 5 (May 1969): 44. For an outline of what Nixon inherited, see Walter Isaacson, *Kissinger: A Biography* (New York: Simon & Schuster, 1992), 158–159; and Jeremi Suri, *Henry Kissinger and the American Century* (Cambridge, MA: Belknap Press of Harvard University Press, 2007), 211.

26. Aide quoted in Allan E. Goodman, *The Lost Peace: America's Search for a Negotiated Settlement of the Vietnam War* (Stanford, CA: Hoover Institution Press, 1978), 107. The statement about fewer troops, though, was false. The maximum number of US troops in Vietnam was attained in April 1969 under Nixon, not under Johnson. Of note, positive reporting emanated from Saigon at the time of Nixon's inauguration. See Charles Mohr, "Optimism Emerges in Saigon as Allies Make Major Gains," *New York Times*, 3 January 1969.

27. Richard M. Nixon, *RN: The Memoirs of Richard Nixon* (New York: Grosset & Dunlap, 1978), 349. Counter-inaugural in Melvin Small, *At the Water's Edge: American Politics and the Vietnam War* (Chicago: Ivan R. Dee, 2005), 125. Jessica M. Chapman notes that Washington was determined "to fit Vietnam's complicated internal struggle for independence into its Cold War paradigm." Nixon, though, aspired to change that paradigm and thus the United States'

relationship with South Vietnam. *Cauldron of Resistance: Ngo Dinh Diem, the United States, and 1950s Southern Vietnam* (Ithaca, NY: Cornell University Press, 2013), 201.

28. The full text of Nixon's address can be found in "Nixon: 'I Shall Consecrate . . . My Energies . . . to Peace,'" *The Washington Post*, 21 January 1969. For analysis, see Jeremi Suri, *Power and Protest: Global Revolution and the Rise of Détente* (Cambridge, MA: Harvard University Press, 2003), 233.

29. On continuity of war managers, see William Bundy, *A Tangled Web: The Making of Foreign Policy in the Nixon Presidency* (New York: Hill and Wang, 1998), 54.

30. Special White House consultant Leonard Garment quoted in William Burr and Jeffrey Kimball, *Nixon's Nuclear Specter: The Secret Alert of 1969, Madman Diplomacy, and the Vietnam War* (Lawrence: University Press of Kansas, 2015), 54. On linkages to Korea, see Berman, *No Peace, No Honor*, 45.

31. This argument is made in William Burr and Jeffrey Kimball, "Nixon's Nuclear Ploy," *Bulletin of Atomic Scientists* (January/February 2003): 31; and Jeffrey Kimball, "Vietnam War Nixonography," *Passport: The Society for Historians of American Foreign Relations Review* 43, no. 3 (January 2013): 27–28. For a larger overview of this thesis, see chapter 2 in *Nixon's Nuclear Specter*. It is important to note that the "madman theory" did not posit that Nixon *was* a madman, only that Nixon sometimes chose to *seem* so.

32. Pierre Asselin questions the "madman theory" in "Feature Review: Kimball's Vietnam War," *Diplomatic History* 30, no. 1 (January 2006): 164. On Nixon's makeup, see Kenneth Payne, *The Psychology of Strategy: Exploring Rationality in the Vietnam War* (New York: Oxford University Press, 2015), 114–115. On being surrounded by enemies, see Thomas, *Being Nixon*, xiii.

33. Kissinger quoted in David L. Prentice, "Choosing 'the Long Road': Henry Kissinger, Melvin Laird, Vietnamization, and the War over Nixon's Vietnam Strategy," *Diplomatic History* (2015): 19. Duck Hook planning in Richard A. Hunt, *Melvin Laird and the Foundation of the Post-Vietnam Military, 1969–1973* (Washington, DC: Office of the Secretary of Defense Historical Office, 2015), 119–120; and Schmitz, *Richard Nixon and the Vietnam War*, 58, 64. Kissinger wrote that the primary objective was "to give Hanoi incentive to negotiate a compromise settlement through a series of military blows."

34. Nixon quoted in Herring, *America's Longest War*, 280. On the summer period and the Duck Hook plan, see Burr and Kimball, *Nixon's Nuclear Specter*, 178–190.

35. Kissinger's exchange with Dobrynin and administration dissent of Duck Hook in Isaacson, *Kissinger*, 246–248. See also Suri, *Henry Kissinger and the American Century*, 218.

36. Lien-Hang T. Nguyen, "Waging War on All Fronts: Nixon, Kissinger and the Vietnam War, 1969–1972," in *Nixon in the World: American Foreign Relations, 1969–1977*, eds. Fredrik Logevall and Andrew Preston (New York: Oxford University Press, 2008), 191. Jeffrey Kimball, *The Vietnam War Files: Uncovering the Secret History of Nixon-Era Strategy* (Lawrence: University Press of Kansas, 2004), 22–23.

37. Kissinger, *White House Years*, 436. See also Harriman to Rogers, 31 January 1969, *FRUS, 1969–1976*, VI: 47. A top-level meeting in late February focused on "working out a program of potential military actions which might jar the North Vietnamese into being more forthcoming at the Paris talks." Kimball, *The Vietnam War Files*, 60. Henry Kissinger also noted that "Hanoi bargained only when it was under severe pressure," *Diplomacy* (New York: Simon & Schuster, 1994), 684.

38. Kissinger quoted in Marilyn B. Young, *The Vietnam Wars, 1945–1990* (New York: HarperCollins, 1991), 239. Nixon in *Vietnam and America: A Documented History*, eds. Marvin E. Gettleman, Jane Franklin, Marilyn Young, and H. Bruce Franklin (New York: Grove Press, 1985), 425. Mark Atwood Lawrence, *The Vietnam War: A Concise International History* (New York: Oxford University Press, 2008), 145.

39. Official quoted in Peter Braestrup, "Viet Pressure Keeps Up," *The Washington Post*, 5 January 1969. Nixon believed it "vitally important" to keep pressing the enemy. Hunt, *Melvin Laird and the Foundation of the Post-Vietnam Military*, 96. See also Gideon Rose, *How Wars End: Why We Always Fight the Last Battle* (New York: Simon & Schuster, 2010), 162; and Schmitz, xv.

40. On fears of looking weak, see Kimball, *Nixon's Vietnam War*, 13. On links to larger Cold War, see Lloyd Gardner, "The Last Casualty? Richard Nixon and the End of the Vietnam War,

1969–1975," in *A Companion to the Vietnam War*, eds. Marilyn B. Young and Robert Buzzanco (Malden, MA: Blackwell, 2002), 230. Mann, *A Grand Delusion*, 616. Paul M. Kattenburg, *The Vietnam Trauma in American Foreign Policy, 1945–75* (New Brunswick, NJ: Transaction, 1992), 166.

41. HQ USMACV, Command History, 1968, Vol. I, Entry MACJ03, RG 472, NARA, pp. II-5 to II-9. Combined Campaign Plan, 1968, Historians Files, CMH, p. 4. Jeffrey J. Clarke, *Advice and Support: The Final Years, 1965–1973* (Washington, DC: Center of Military History, 1988), 391.

42. Julian J. Ewell, interview by Robert Crowley and Norman M. Bissell, Senior Officers Debriefing Program, Transcripts of Debriefing, Box 1, Julian J. Ewell Papers, MHI, p. 82. Some argue that Abrams tried to implement a new strategy that de-emphasized large-scale conventional operations but could not convince traditional-minded officers to follow suit. See Carter Malkasian, *A History of Modern Wars of Attrition* (Westport, CT: Praeger, 2002), 197; and Douglas S. Blaufarb, *The Counterinsurgency Era: U.S. Doctrine and Performance, 1950 to the Present* (New York: The Free Press, 1977), 269.

43. Combat After Action Report of Operation Speedy Express, 14 June 1969, Historians Files, CMH. Dale Andradé, "Presidential Unit Citation for 9th Infantry Division," 27 July 1993, Historians Files, CMH. On realization of impending redeployments, see Donn Starry, interview by Jim Bergen, John Collison, and Bill Burleson, Senior Officers Debriefing Program, Box B, Creighton Abrams Story, MHI, p. 33.

44. David H. Hackworth and Eilhys England, *Steel My Soldiers' Hearts: The Hopeless to Hardcore Transformation of 4th Battalion, 39th Infantry, United States Army, Vietnam* (New York: Simon & Schuster, 2002), 100. Ewell quoted in Andrew J. Birtle, *U.S. Army Counterinsurgency and Contingency Operations Doctrine, 1942–1976* (Washington, DC: Center of Military History, 2006), 368. Despite Ewell's claims, military operations did not appear to greatly improve population security and pacification plans. See Andrew F. Krepinevich Jr., *The Army and Vietnam* (Baltimore and London: Johns Hopkins University Press, 1986), 255.

45. Sidle to Bolton, "Speedy Express," 17 January 1972, Historians Files, CMH. "Pacification's Deadly Price," *Newsweek*, 19 June 1972, 43. For an official response to the *Newsweek* article— "the rules of engagement in effect during the operation included appropriate restrictions"— see Doolin to Porter, 8 August 1972, Historians Files, CMH. Yet one soldier recalled that his battalion commander told him his unit "would not be extracted from the field until we had gotten him a body count." Combat After Action Interviews, 4/47th Infantry, 4 May 1969, VNIT Folder 377, CMH, p. 12.

46. Ira A. Hunt Jr., *The 9th Infantry Division in Vietnam: Unparalleled and Unequaled* (Lexington: University Press of Kentucky, 2010), 143. Admin CINCPAC to CINCPAC, Enemy Body Count, 31 January 1970, Body Count Folder, Box 369, OSDHO. Abrams quoted in *Newsweek*, "Pacification's Deadly Price, 43."

47. J3 Inputs to Report of the MACV Effort, 1968–1970, Filing Cabinet B9, Box 3, MACV Command Historian's Collection, MHI, pp. 7–12. Robert D. Sander, *Invasion of Laos, 1971: Lam Son 719* (Norman: University of Oklahoma Press, 2014), 53–54.

48. Abrams to Sullivan, 6 March 1969, Abrams Messages #2621, CMH. MACV Quarterly Evaluation Report, 1 January–1 March 1969, MHI, p. 3. Sorley, *Vietnam Chronicles*, 156. A. J. Langguth, *Our Vietnam: The War, 1954–1975* (New York: Simon & Schuster, 2000), 542. Oddly, Langguth argues that Abrams "concentrated on controlling the South Vietnamese population" yet details the general's request to invade Cambodia. For an exceedingly rosy evaluation of Dewy Canyon, see Mark W. Woodruff, *Unheralded Victory: The Defeat of the Viet Cong and the North Vietnamese Army, 1961–1973* (Arlington, VA: Vandamere Press, 1999), 159.

49. Officer quoted in Joseph B. Treaster, "Enemy Bombards Cities and Bases in South Vietnam," *New York Times*, 23 February 1969. Casualties in Alexander M. Haig Jr., with Charles McCarry, *Inner Circles: How America Changed the World, a Memoir* (New York: Warner Books, 1992), 225. See also James S. Olson and Randy Roberts, *Where The Domino Fell: America and Vietnam, 1945–2010*, 6th ed. (West Sussex, UK: Wiley Blackwell, 2014), 198. According to Phillip B. Davidson, enemy directives noted that the offensive's primary target "would be United States forces and installations, with secondary priority going to destruction of lines of

communication and attacks against the snowballing pacification program." *Vietnam at War, the History: 1946–1975* (Novato, CA: Presidio Press, 1988), 532. See also Shelby L. Stanton, *The Rise and Fall of an American Army: U.S. Ground Forces in Vietnam, 1965–1973* (Novato, CA: Presidio Press, 1985), 287–288.

50. Kissinger in Berman, *No Peace, No Honor*, 57. Abrams's request in Hammond, *Public Affairs*, 66. Nixon in Langguth, *Our Vietnam*, 544. Cosmas, *MACV*, 286–287.

51. Power base in Dale Van Atta, *With Honor: Melvin Laird in War, Peace, and Politics* (Madison: University of Wisconsin Press, 2008), 153. Joan Hoff, "A Revisionist View of Nixon's Foreign Policy," *Presidential Studies Quarterly* 26, no. 1 (Winter 1996): 110. On influence of US Embassy and JCS, see Schaffer, *Ellsworth Bunker*, 219; John P. Leacacos, "Kissinger's Apparat," *Foreign Policy*, no. 5 (Winter 1971–1972): 4; and Dale R. Herspring, *The Pentagon and the Presidency: Civil-Military Relations from FDR to George W. Bush* (Lawrence: University Press of Kansas, 2005), 186.

52. Kissinger quoted in Dorothy C. Donnelly, "A Settlement of Sorts: Henry Kissinger's Negotiations and America's Extrication from Vietnam," *Peace & Change* 9, no. 2/3 (Summer 1983): 63. Institutional power in Seymour M. Hersh, *The Price of Power: Kissinger in the Nixon White House* (New York: Summit Books, 1983), 25. See also Isaacson, *Kissinger*, 170. To maintain a certain freedom of action, Kissinger (and Nixon) believed diplomacy was best served by withholding information from as many policy advisors as possible. See P. Edward Haley, *Congress and the Fall of South Vietnam and Cambodia* (East Brunswick, NJ: Fairleigh Dickinson University Press, 1982), 28; and Suri, *Henry Kissinger and the American Century*, 222.

53. Memorandum of Conversation, 2 August 1966, *FRUS, 1964–1968*, IV: 543–547. Henry A. Kissinger, "The Viet Nam Negotiations," *Foreign Affairs* 47, no. 2 (January 1969): 234. Kissinger, *White House Years*, 234. Prentice, "Choosing 'the Long Road,'" 3.

54. On Kissinger's views of the international system, see Lawrence W. Serewicz, *America at the Brink of Empire: Rusk, Kissinger, and the Vietnam War* (Baton Rouge: Louisiana State University Press, 2007), 89–97. On linkages to Vietnam, see Suri, *Henry Kissinger and the American Century*, 212. Seymour Hersh believed Kissinger "came into the Nixon White House profoundly skeptical about the Vietnam War." *The Price of Power*, 46.

55. Henry Kissinger, *Nuclear Weapons and Foreign Policy* (New York: Harper & Brothers, 1957), 7. Hersh, *The Price of Power*, 26–27.

56. Robert E. Osgood, *Limited War: The Challenge to American Security* (Chicago: University of Chicago Press, 1957), 7. Greg Grandin, *Kissinger's Shadow: The Long Reach of America's Most Controversial Statesman* (New York: Metropolitan Books, 2015), 26–27. On limited war theory, see Christopher M. Gacek, *The Logic of Force: The Dilemma of Limited War in American Foreign Policy* (New York: Columbia University Press, 1994), 134–135; Thomas C. Schelling, *The Strategy of Conflict* (Cambridge, MA: Harvard University Press, 1960), 188–189; and Stephen Peter Rosen, "Vietnam and the American Theory of Limited War," *International Security* 7, no. 2 (Fall 1982): 83–113.

57. Nixon, *RN*, 380. Schmitz, *Richard Nixon and the Vietnam War*, 50. Robert Dallek argues Nixon "spent close to a month agonizing over how to respond." *Nixon and Kissinger: Partners in Power* (New York: HarperCollins, 2007), 117. Kissinger wanted to sequence the bombing, and thus link it to diplomacy, by hitting the communists first and then asking for private talks. Editorial Note, *FRUS, 1969–1976*, VI: 96.

58. Richard Nixon, *No More Vietnams* (New York: Arbor House: 1985), 108. John Dumbrell, *Rethinking the Vietnam War* (New York: Palgrave Macmillan, 2012), 110. On COSVN, see Carolyn Eisenberg, "Remembering Nixon's War," in Young and Buzzanco, 262; and Van Atta, *With Honor*, 180. On multiple objectives, see Earl H. Tilford Jr., "Bombing Our Way Back Home: The Commando Hunt and Menu Campaigns of 1969–1973," in *Looking Back on the Vietnam War: A 1990s Perspective on the Decisions, Combat, and Legacies*, eds. William Head and Lawrence E. Grinter (Westport, CT: Greenwood Press, 1993), 129. Secrecy in Nancy Zaroulis and Gerald Sullivan, *Who Spoke Up? American Protest against the War in Vietnam, 1963–1975* (Garden City, NY: Doubleday, 1984), 218. On coercive diplomacy, see Thomas C. Schelling, "Arms and Influence," in Mahnken and Maiolo, 123.

59. Kissinger to Nixon, 11 September 1969, Folder 2, Box 91, NSC Files, Vietnam Subject Files, RNL. Kissinger to Nixon, 5 September 1969; Lynn to Kissinger, 16 September 1969;

Vietnam Special Studies Group Memorandum, 13 October 1969; and Lynn to Kissinger, 18 November1969 in Richard Hunt VSSG Folder, OSDHO. On Ellsberg, see Isaacson, *Kissinger*, 162–163; Hersh, *The Price of Power*, 48–49; and Bundy, *A Tangled Web*, 159–160.

60. NSSM 1 questions in *FRUS*, 1969–1976, VI: 5–10. William Beecher, "Diverse Plans Offered," *New York Times*, 12 January 1969. Alexander Haig recalled that this "concentration of foreign policy in the White House represented a conscious effort on Nixon's part to avoid the groupthink of the Kennedy administration and the consensus of the Johnson administration that had led the country, among other costly mistakes, into the impasse of Vietnam." *Inner Circles*, 203.

61. MACV omitting criticisms in James H. Willbanks, *Abandoning Vietnam: How America Left and South Vietnam Lost Its War* (Lawrence: University Press of Kansas, 2004), 11–12. On disagreements, see Willard J. Webb, *The Joint Chiefs of Staff and the War in Vietnam, 1969–1970* (Washington, DC: Office of Joint History, 2002), 8–9; Bundy, 62–63; and Jeffrey J. Clarke, "Vietnamization: The War to Groom an Ally," in Showalter and Albert, *An American Dilemma*, 161.

62. Abrams quoted in Sorley, *Vietnam Chronicles*, 305. Kissinger quoted in Burr and Kimball, *Nixon's Nuclear Specter*, 73. Order of battle controversy in Phillip B. Davidson, *Secrets of the Vietnam War* (Novato, CA: Presidio Press, 1990), 52–58. Abrams complained in November 1969 that he still couldn't "make any sense out of what we carry as [enemy] strength."

63. "Vietnam Policy Alternatives" in *FRUS*, 1969–1976, VI: 18–22. Abrams quoted in Haig to Kissinger, 6 March 1969, Folder 9, Box 67, NSC Files, Vietnam Subject Files, RNL. See also Abrams to Wheeler and McCain, 25 March 1969, Abrams Messages #2783, CMH. For a counterargument strongly urging Nixon to refrain from retaliation, see Sneider to Kissinger, 6 March 1969, Folder 9, Box 67, NSC Files, Vietnam Subject Files, RNL. A February assessment from Abrams noted the "overall deployment of [allied] forces remains sound." In Haig to Eagleburger for Kissinger, 26 February 1969, Folder 8, Box 62, NSC Files, Vietnam Subject Files, RNL. A summary of the NSSM 1 responses can be found in *FRUS*, 1969–1976, VI: 129–152.

64. Kiss quoted in Suri, *Henry Kissinger and the American Century*, 213. Jeffrey Kimball, "'Peace with Honor': Richard Nixon and the Diplomacy of Threat and Symbolism," in *Shadow on the White House: Presidents and the Vietnam War, 1945–1975*, ed. David L. Anderson (Lawrence: University Press of Kansas, 1993), 157.

65. Jonathan Schell, *Observing the Nixon Years* (New York: Pantheon Books, 1989), 63–64. Joseph A. Fry notes that the influential Sen. J. William Fulbright acknowledged there was no "satisfactory way of ending the war." *Debating Vietnam: Fulbright, Stennis, and Their Senate Hearings* (Lanham, MD: Rowman & Littlefield, 2006), 158.

66. Nixon in Hersh, *The Price of Power*, 119; and *No More Vietnams*, 114. On use of the term "decent interval," see Isaacson, *Kissinger*, 485–486; Burr and Kimball, *Nixon's Nuclear Specter*, 74. Kimball believes Nixon came into office intending to "win" in Vietnam yet only later came to accept the decent-interval solution. *Nixon's Vietnam War*, xii. For counterarguments to Kimball's, see Pierre Asselin, H-Diplo FRUS Reviews, No. 21, 17 April 2013, 5; Asseslin, "Feature Review," 165–166; and John M. Carland, *Passport: The Society for Historians of American Foreign Relations Review* 43, no. 3 (January 2013): 23. Johannes Kadura posits that Nixon and Kissinger "sought to gain time, make the North turn inward, and create a perpetual equilibrium." *The War after the War: The Struggle for Credibility during America's Exit from Vietnam* (Ithaca, NY: Cornell University Press, 2016), 4.

67. Kissinger, "The Viet Nam Negotiations," 233–34. In his own defense, see Henry Kissinger, *Ending the Vietnam War: A History of America's Involvement in and Extrication from the Vietnam War* (New York: Simon & Schuster, 2003), 338. Alexander Haig argued that "there wasn't anybody, from the president to Kissinger to anybody else, that intentionally double-crossed Saigon." In Christian G. Appy, *Patriots: The Vietnam War Remembered from All Sides* (New York: Viking Press, 2003), 401.

68. Kissinger to Nixon, 11 September 1969, *FRUS*, 1969–1976, VI: 381. Frances FitzGerald, *Fire in the Lake: The Vietnamese and the Americans in Vietnam* (Boston: Little, Brown, 1972), 404. On the majority of Americans believing communism should "be feared at all times," see Walter Goldstein, "The American Political System and the Next Vietnam," in *Revolutionary*

War: Western Response, eds. David S. Sullivan and Martin J. Sattler (New York: Columbia University Press, 1971), 97–98. Yet Gil Merom argues, "American ground forces were pulled out of Vietnam largely because of domestic, and in particular, campus pressure." *How Democracies Lose Small Wars: State, Society, and the Failures of France in Algeria, Israel in Lebanon, and the United States in Vietnam* (New York: Cambridge University Press, 2003), 237.

69. Ward S. Just, "Notes on a Losing War," *The Atlantic* 223, no. 1 (January 1969): 44.

70. Kissinger, *White House Years*, 228. Betrayal in Haldeman, *The Haldeman Diaries*, 65. On concepts of credibility, see Jeffrey P. Kimball, "Richard M. Nixon and the Vietnam War: The Paradox of Disengagement with Escalation," in *The Columbia History of the Vietnam War*, ed. David L. Anderson (New York: Columbia University Press, 2011), 218.

71. Arnold Isaacs, "The Limits of Credibility," in *Major Problems in the History of the Vietnam War*, 2nd ed., ed. Robert J. McMahon (Lexington, MA: D.C. Heath, 1995), 446. For a counterargument to the "prestige" claim, see Townsend Hoopes, *The Limits of Intervention: An Inside Account of How the Johnson Policy of Escalation in Vietnam Was Reversed* (New York: David McKay, 1969), 238–240.

72. Kissinger quoted in Young and Buzzanco, *A Companion to the Vietnam War*, 242. Murrey Marder, "Fulbright Asks New Viet Policy," *The Washington Post*, 22 March 1969. On squandering Congress's original goodwill, see Robert D. Schulzinger, "Richard Nixon, Congress, and the War in Vietnam, 1969–1972," in *Vietnam and the American Political Tradition: The Politics of Dissent*, ed. Randall B. Woods (New York: Cambridge University Press, 2003), 300. Of course, lawmakers had been criticizing the war effort long before Nixon took office. As an example, see Tom Wicker, "Kennedy Asserts U.S. Cannot Win," *New York Times*, 9 February 1968.

73. Hedrick Smith, "Harriman Calls on U.S. to Lead in Reduction of Vietnam Combat," *New York Times*, 25 May 1969. Robert J. Donovan, "Quit Ground War by 1971—Clifford," *Los Angeles Times*, 19 June 1969. Godfrey Sperling Jr., "McGovern Calls for 30-day Vietnam Standstill," *The Christian Science Monitor*, 5 July 1969.

74. Laird to Nixon, 4 September 1969, *FRUS, 1969–1976*, VI: 360. On challenges from legislative branch, see Haley, *Congress and the Fall of South Vietnam and Cambodia*, 19–20. Rather than fear the national security bureaucracy, as opposed to Congress, Nixon and Kissinger loathed it. See Rose, *How Wars End*, 175.

75. Bruce K. Chapman, "Rep. Laird's Platform Device Called Springboard to Power," *The Milwaukee Journal*, 3 April 1966. Steven Casey, *When Soldiers Fall: How Americans Have Confronted Combat Losses from World War I to Afghanistan* (New York: Oxford University Press, 2014), 181.

76. Haig, *Inner Circles*, 227. One Laird associate noted "he wants to get out of Vietnam . . . so much he can taste it." In Gabriel Kolko, *Anatomy of a War: Vietnam, the United States, and the Modern Historical Experience* (New York: Pantheon Books, 1985), 356. Laird quoted in Isaacson, *Kissinger*, 237.

77. Laird quoted in Van Atta, *With Honor*, 176; and Sorley, *Vietnam Chronicles*, 141. Hunt, *Melvin Laird*, 99. Terence Smith, "Laird to Ask More Funds to Bolster Saigon's Army," *New York Times*, 10 March 1969.

78. "What Secretary Laird Learned in Vietnam," *U.S. News & World Report*, 24 March 1969, 27.

79. Laird report to the President, 13 March 1969, Folder 13, Box 70, NSC Files, Vietnam Subject Files, RNL.

80. "Abrams Opposes Early Cutback in Viet Troops," *Los Angeles Times*, 14 January 1969. B. Drummond Ayres Jr., "U.S. Officers in Saigon Cool to G.I. Pullout Soon," *New York Times*, 15 January 1969. On Abrams requesting B-52 attacks against the Cambodian sanctuaries, see Hunt, *Melvin Laird*, 144–145.

81. Wheeler to Laird, 12 March 1969, *FRUS, 1969–1976*, VI: 107. According to Walter Isaacson, "the U.S. military was appalled by the notion of Vietnamization because they considered it tantamount to a slow surrender." *Kissinger*, 235. See also James H. Willbanks, *A Raid Too Far: Operation Lam Son 719 and Vietnamization in Laos* (College Station: Texas A&M University Press, 2014), 10.

82. Prentice, "Choosing 'the Long Road,'" 15. Schmitz, *Richard Nixon and the Vietnam War*, 56. Nixon, *RN*, 392.

83. Niksch, "Vietnamization," TTUVA, p. CRS-4. By 10 April 1969, Nixon had already "directed the preparation of a specific timetable for Vietnamizing the war." NSSM 36, *FRUS, 1969–1976*, VI: 195–196. On the multiple aspects of Vietnamization's military component, see Laird to Nixon, 4 September 1969, *FRUS, 1969-1976*, VI: 361.

84. Bunker in Sorley, *Vietnam Chronicles*, 143. Hughes, *Fatal Politics*, ix. James Farmer argued in late 1964 that the two criteria for "winning" were security and the creation of a viable government. *Counterinsurgency: Principles and Practices in Viet-Nam* (Santa Monica, CA: RAND Corporation, 1964), 2. Kissinger laid out the objectives for negotiations to Nixon on 3 April 1969. They included mutual withdrawal of all external forces, a cease-fire, agreement that there would be a separate and independent South Vietnam for at least five years, and a mechanism for supervising the settlement. *FRUS, 1969–1976*, VI: 183.

85. My sincere thanks to Edwin Moise, Clemson University, for helping me work through and articulate the thoughts in the preceding two paragraphs. Email to author, 21 December 2016.

86. Tran Von Don, *Our Endless War: Inside Vietnam* (San Rafael, CA: Presidio Press, 1978), 183. Marc B. Adin, "Vietnam: Involvement and Vietnamization, an Odyssey of Deceit," *Viet Nam Generation* 7, no. 1–2 (1996): 21. "Officials See Hope of Winning War," *The Washington Post*, 14 October 1969.

87. "Transcript of President Nixon's Address to the Nation on the War in Vietnam," *New York Times*, 15 May 1969. Stuart H. Loory, "Nixon Blueprint: Pullout in Year by Both Sides," *Los Angeles Times*, 15 May 1969. Kent S. Sieg argues that Nixon downgraded the 1969 Paris peace talks as an avenue toward a final peace settlement. "The Lodge Peace Mission of 1969 and Nixon's Vietnam Policy," *Diplomacy and Statecraft* 7, no. 1 (March 1996): 175. On escalation during this period, see Schmitz, *Richard Nixon and the Vietnam War*, 147. On implications to military strategy and JCS concerns, see Webb, *The Joint Chiefs of Staff and the War in Vietnam*, 52.

88. Nixon, *No More Vietnams*, 104–107. Kimball, *Nixon's Vietnam War*, 98. As *The Washington Post* reported, the president "was careful not to commit himself to a timetable for his passing of the torch." George C. Wilson, "Vietnamese Army Faces Sink-or-Swim Situation," 15 May 1969.

89. Wheeler to McCain and Abrams, 28 March 1969, Abrams Messages #2809, CMH. Abrams to Wheeler and McCain, 30 March 1969, Abrams Messages #2833, CMH. Abrams to McConnell and McCain, 11 May 1969, Abrams Messages #3125, CMH.

90. Abrams to reporter in Cosmas, *MACV*, 134. Bombing in Robert B. Asprey, *War in the Shadows: The Guerrilla in History* (Garden City, NY: Doubleday, 1975), 1303. Abrams to Wheeler and McCain, 27 March 1969, Abrams Messages #2802, CMH.

91. War Experiences Recapitulation Committee, *The Anti-U.S. Resistance War*, 122. On dilemmas Abrams faced, see Van Atta, *With Honor*, 203; and Hammond, *Public Affairs*, 82.

92. Officer quoted in Philip Fradkin, "U.S. War Strategy Same Under Nixon," *The Washington Post*, 13 May 1969. Kill ratios in Jack Walsh, "ARVN—Bigger, Better, Bolder Than Year Ago," *Pacific Stars & Stripes*, 22 March 1969. Abrams in Cosmas, *MACV*, 147. According to the MACV Command History, Abrams announced a three-faceted goal for 1969: "combat operations to defeat the enemy and promote security, increased effort to improve and modernize the RVN's Armed Forces (RVNAF), and a further emphasis on pacification and building the inchoate republic into a viable state." USMACV, Command History, 1969, Vol. I, NARA, p. 1.

93. "U.S. Paratroopers Driving Into Reds' Valley Stronghold," *Los Angeles Times*, 24 March 1969. Maximum pressure in Wheeler to Laird, 21 May 1969, Folder 6, Box 67, NSC Files, Vietnam Subject Files, RNL. See also Andrew Wiest, *Vietnam's Forgotten Army: Heroism and Betrayal in the ARVN* (New York: New York University Press, 2008), 157.

94. Melvin Zais, interview by William L. Golden and Richard C. Rice, Senior Officers Oral History Program, Melvin Zais Papers, MHI, p. 581. Senior Officer Debriefing Report: LTG Melvin Zais, CG, XXIV Corps, 20 August 1970, MHI, pp. 2, 10.

95. Wheeler to Laird, 21 May 1969, Folder 6, Box 67, NSC Files, Vietnam Subject Files, RNL, p. 2. Frank Boccia, *The Crouching Beast: A United States Army Lieutenant's Account of the Battle for Hamburger Hill, May 1969* (Jefferson, NC: McFarland, 2013), 2. Samuel Zaffiri, *Hamburger Hill: May 11–20, 1969* (Novato, CA: Presidio Press, 1988), 16.

96. "Summary of Action and Results," 24 May 1969, Folder 01, Bud Harton Collection, TTUVA. Boccia, 396. See also, Wiest, *Vietnam's Forgotten Army*, 158–164.

97. Honeycutt quoted in "Woe to the Victors," *Newsweek*, 2 June 1969, 42. "The Battle for Hamburger Hill," *TIME*, 30 May 1969, 27–28.

98. Jay Sharbutt, "U.S. Assault on Viet Mountain Continues, Despite Heavy Toll," *The Washington Post*, 20 May 1969. Honeycutt quoted in *Newsweek*, 2 June 1969, 42.

99. Robert G. Kaiser, "Commanders Say Tactics Save Lives," *The Washington Post*, 8 June 1969. "General Hails Fight for Hamburger Hill," *Chicago Tribune*, 23 May 1969. "Action at Apbia," *New York Times*, 22 May 1969. MACV contended the "objectives of Apache Snow were successfully carried out." J3 Inputs to Report of the MACV Effort, MHI, p. II-28. Casualty figures in Zaffiri, *Hamburger Hill*, 244. "Summary of Action and Results," 24 May 1969, TTUVA. Repetition in Daniel C. Hallin, *The "Uncensored War" The Media and Vietnam* (New York: Oxford University Press, 1986), 176. The Joint Chiefs also contended that a defensive strategy would hurt the allies' morale. Webb, *The Joint Chiefs of Staff and The War in Vietnam*, 52.

100. Abrams in Sorley, *Vietnam Chronicles*, 259. Explaining Hamburger Hill requires a bit of intellectual gymnastics for "better war" proponents. As an example, Lewis Sorley contends enemy KIA and WIA figures at Ap Bia "were not the real measure of success. Rather, it was disruption of the enemy system, which prevented him from laying the groundwork for operations in the populated areas to the east." However, under Westmoreland, similar operations are labeled a myopic infatuation with attrition. *A Better War*, 141.

101. "Teddy Blasts Assault But Not Its Leader," *Chicago Tribune*, 25 May 1969. "Teddy on the Stump," *Newsweek*, 2 June 1969, 33. Zaffiri, 246–257. B. Drummond Ayres Jr., "U.S. Aides Defend Apbia Peak Battle," *New York Times*, 22 May 1969. Zais quoted in J3 Inputs to Report of the MACV Effort, MHI, p. II-35. In the battle's aftermath, Abrams responded to colleagues, "If they would let me know where they would like me to fight the next battle, I would be glad to do it there." Lewis Sorley, *Thunderbolt: General Creighton Abrams and the Army of His Times* (New York: Simon & Schuster, 1992), 261.

102. Stanton, *The Rise and Fall of an American Army*, 301. Neil Sheehan, "Letters from Hamburger Hill," *Harper's Magazine*, 1 November 1969, 41. Ward Just, "The Reality of War on Hamburger Hill," *The Washington Post*, 21 May 1969. On seeing "the purpose for which a war is fought *as part of war itself*," see Echevarria, *Towards an American Way of War*, 18.

103. Allan E. Goodman, "South Vietnam: Neither War Nor Peace," *Asian Survey* 10, no. 2 (February 1970): 112. On opposition groups, see "Vietnam: December 1969," a Staff Report Prepared for the Use of the Committee on Foreign Relations, United States Senate, 2 February 1970, Folder 06, Box 07, Douglas Pike Collection: Unit 11-Monographs, TTUVA, p. 13; and Charles A. Joiner, *The Politics of Massacre: Political Processes in South Vietnam* (Philadelphia: Temple University Press, 1974), 17, 27. On the ARVN, see B. Drummond Ayres Jr., "South Vietnamese Troops Showing Uneven Progress," *New York Times*, 2 June 1969; "The Laird Plan," *Newsweek*, 2 June 1969, 44; and "Can U.S. Get Out of the War Now?," *U.S. News & World Report*, 5 May 1969, 34–35.

104. Vietnamese leader quoted in Allan E. Goodman, *Politics in War: The Bases of Political Community in South Vietnam* (Cambridge, MA: Harvard University Press, 1973), 3. Tom Wicker, "Can Saigon Face Political Competition?," *New York Times*, 20 May 1969.

105. On Thieu's address to the National Assembly and his six points for a "constructive solution," see McMahon, *Major Problems in the History of the Vietnam War*, 396–397. Moor to Kissinger, 1 July 1969, *FRUS, 1969–1976*, VI: 282–283. RAND analysts also brought attention to the economic problems. See Gerald C. Hickey, *U.S. Strategy in South Vietnam: Extrication and Equilibrium* (Santa Monica, CA: RAND Corporation, 1969), 7; and Timothy Hallinan, *Economic Prospects of the Republic of Vietnam* (Santa Monica, CA: RAND Corporation, 1969), 19.

106. Elizabeth Pond, "Aid 'Too Little, Too Late'?," *The Christian Science Monitor*, 4 June 1969. As reported to Abrams the following year, measures taken in the allied pacification effort were "not enough to constitute a viable socio-economic development program commensurate with what has been achieved in the field of territorial security and political development." Zais to Abrams, 12 June 1970, Melvin Zais Papers, MHI.

107. Jeffrey Race, *War Comes to Long An: Revolutionary Conflict in a Vietnamese Province* (Berkeley: University of California Press, 1972), 163. Robert L. Sansom, *The Economics of Insurgency in the Mekong Delta of Vietnam* (Cambridge, MA: MIT Press, 1970), 56–65. Thomas C. Thayer, *War without Fronts: The American Experience in Vietnam* (Annapolis, MD: Naval Institute Press, 1985, 2016), 238–239.

108. Abrams to Wheeler, 28 January 1970, Abrams Messages #5141, CMH. Liberated areas in Hannah Gurman, "Vietnam—Uprooting the Revolution: Counterinsurgency in Vietnam," in *Hearts and Minds: A People's History of Counterinsurgency*, ed. Hannah Gurman (New York: The New Press, 2013), 101. For a South Vietnamese perspective, which outlines the need to import rice, see Sorley, *Vietnam Chronicles*, 246. See also Mark Philip Bradley, *Vietnam at War* (New York: Oxford University Press, 2009), 118.

109. Arthur M. Cox, "Real Bar to Peace Is Found in Thieu," *The Washington Post*, 14 September 1969. Terence Smith, "Thieu's Disappointing New Cabinet," *New York Times*, 7 September 1969. Abrams to McCain and Wheeler, 19 October 1969, Abrams Messages #4483, CMH. USMACV, Command History, 1969, Vol. I, NARA, p. II-27. Hickey, *U.S. Strategy in South Vietnam*, 6.

110. Truong Nhu Tang with David Chanoff and Doan Van Toai, *A Vietcong Memoir: An Inside Account of the Vietnam War and Its Aftermath* (New York: Harcourt Brace Jovanovich, 1985), 147. USMACV, Command History, 1969, pp. II-40, III-29. James P. Harrison, *The Endless War: Vietnam's Struggle for Independence* (New York: Columbia University Press, 1989), 277–268.

111. John R. Galvin, *Fighting the Cold War: A Soldier's Memoir* (Lexington: University Press of Kentucky, 2015), 154. Robert H. Johnson, "Vietnamization: Can It Work?," *Foreign Affairs* 48, no. 4 (July 1970): 643. Goodman details the intricacies of the political competition in "South Vietnam: Neither War Nor Peace," 114–122. Of course, violence and terrorism were integral parts of this competition. See Asprey, *War in the Shadows*, 1323.

112. Factionalism in Hickey, 4. Militarization in Goodman, *Politics in War*, 5.

113. Abrams to Westmoreland, 25 February 1968, Abrams Messages #333, CMH. As an example of media reports, see Joseph Kraft, "The True Failure in Saigon—South Vietnam's Fighting Force," *Los Angeles Times*, 3 May 1967.

114. Kissinger to Nixon, 11 September 1969, Folder 2, Box 91, NSC Files, Vietnam Subject Files, RNL, p. 6. On inconsistent reporting, see Wheeler to Laird, 21 July 1969, *FRUS, 1969–1976*, VI: 310–311; and Clarke, *Advice and Support*, 331. Bunker in Sorley, *Vietnam Chronicles*, 99. On ineffective leadership, see Peers to Abrams, 5 June 1968, Abrams Messages #575, CMH.

115. Expansion in Thayer, *War without Fronts*, 61. The RVNAF increased from 825,000 in 1969 to over 1 million by 1972. Willbanks, *Abandoning Vietnam*, 2. Body counts in Abrams to Wheeler and McCain, 7 October 1968, Abrams Messages #1507, CMH. Abrams not over-emphasizing ARVN improvements in Clifford to Johnson, 18 July 1968, *FRUS, 1964–1968*, VI: 881.

116. Low level of competence in Holdridge to Kissinger, 22 December 1969, Folder 1, Box 1010, NSC Files, Vietnam Subject Files, RNL. No new mechanisms in Ronald H. Spector, *After Tet: The Bloodiest Year in Vietnam* (New York: The Free Press, 1993), 116. Kissinger to Nixon, 23 June 1969, Folder 2, Box 74, NSC Files, Vietnam Subject Files, RNL.

117. BG Richard J. Allen, "Combat Operations in Built-Up Areas," 9 October 1968, VNIT Folder 151, CMH. On mobility, see Abrams to Wheeler, 28 April 1969, Abrams Messages #3036, CMH. On how MACV rated the RF/PFs, see Territorial Forces Evaluation System (TFES) Handbook, November 1969, Folder 10, Box 43, Douglas Pike Collection: Unit 03-Statistical Data, TTUVA. One report noted the "RF/PF relation with ARVN is still inadequate." Holdridge to Kissinger, RNL, p. 2.

118. Senior Officer Debriefing Program: Report of Col. C. E. Jordan Jr., 4 February 1969, CMH, p. 9. "Notes from a Conversation with General Abrams and Lt. General Ewell," 18 January 1970, Folder 3, Box 1009, NSC Files, Alexander M. Haig Special File, RNL. Offensive spirit in Senior Officer Debriefing Program, BG Donald D. Dunlop, 30 April 1969, Folder 01, Bud Harton Collection, TTUVA, p. IV-7. On linkages to pacification program, see Robert D. Ramsey III, *Advising Indigenous Forces: American Advisors in Korea, Vietnam, and El Salvador* (Fort Leavenworth, KS: Combat Studies Institute Press, 2006), 56.

119. Insular cohesion in F. J. West Jr., *Area Security* (Santa Monica, CA: RAND Corporation, 1969), 13. US mission assessment of combat loads in Kissinger to Nixon, 30 October 1969, *FRUS, 1969–1976*, VI: 474. See also Headquarters, United States Military Assistance Command, Vietnam, "MACV Combat Experiences 5–69," 6 January 1970, MHI, p. 5.

120. Kissinger to Nixon, 12 December 1969, Folder 4, Box 91, NSC Files, Vietnam Subject Files, RNL. Nixon's handwritten comments are in the margins. See also Kissinger to Nixon, 23 June 1969, Folder 2, Box 74, ibid.; and Kissinger to Nixon, 5 September 1969, Folder 1, Box 91, ibid. On multiple missions for the RVNAF, see S. Canby, B. Jenkins, and R. B. Rainey, *A Ground Force Structure and Strategy for Vietnam in the 1970s* (Santa Monica, CA: RAND Corporation, 1970), 6. On the ARVN relying too heavily on US firepower, see Robert H. Scales Jr., *Firepower in Limited War*, rev. ed. (Novato, CA: Presidio Press, 1995), 149.

121. Robert M. Montague Jr., "Pacification: The Overall Strategy in South Vietnam," Student Essay, US Army War College, 22 April 1966, Box 1, Robert M. Montague Papers, MHI, p. 2. Westmoreland quoted in Embassy to Department of State, 11 January 1965, *FRUS, 1964–1968*, II: 47. According to George C. Herring, the South Vietnamese resisted a combined command, "perceiving it as a form of neocolonialism. " 'Peoples Quite Apart': Americans, South Vietnamese, and the War in Vietnam," *Diplomatic History* 14, no. 1 (Winter 1990): 6.

122. Superficial combined operations in Senior Officer Debriefing Program: Report of MG Charles P. Brown, 14 May 1971, CMH, 2. See also Douglas Kinnard, *The War Managers: American Generals Reflect on Vietnam* (New York: DaCapo Press, 1977, 1991), 92. One ARVN colonel also noted that the "RVNAF made no adjustments in doctrine, organization or training to compensate for the departure of American troops or firepower." In Allan E. Goodman, "The Dual-Track Strategy of Vietnamization and Negotiation," in *The Second Indochina War: Proceedings of a Symposium Held at Airlie, Virginia, 7–9 November 1984*, ed. John Schlight (Washington, DC: Center of Military History, 1986), 149.

123. A. S. Collins Jr., "Ideas on Vietnam," Fall 1970, Box 7, A. S. Collins Papers, MHI. CPT Edward J. Haydash to MAJ Torrence, 9 April 1969, Adventure Board, Box 2, Torrence Collection, WPSC. Abrams quoted in Sorley, *Vietnam Chronicles*, 355, 624. See also Clarke, *Advice and Support*, 392. Desertions in Headquarters, USMACV, "One War," MACV Command Overview, 1968–1972, Historians Files, CMH, p. VII-18. US advisors also contended with ARVN leader involvement in drug trafficking. Spector, *After Tet*, 103.

124. Laird to Nixon, 4 September 1969, Folder 3, Box 91, NSC Files, Vietnam Subject Files, RNL, p. 4. For a military perspective of this problem, see Rosson to Moorer and McCain, 29 July 1970, Folder 1, Box 92, ibid.

125. Hackworth, *Steel My Soldiers' Hearts*, 131. Zais, interview by Golden and Rice, MHI, 478. Philip Beidler, "The Invisible ARVN: The South Vietnamese Soldier in American Representations of the Vietnam War," *War, Literature & the Arts* 19, no. 1/2 (2007): 307.

126. Maturity in USMACV, "One War," MACV Command Overview, CMH, p. VII-44. Survey in Kinnard, *The War Managers*, 87. Combined operations in MACV Quarterly Evaluation Report, 1 April–30 June 1969, MHI, p. 6; and Eric M. Bergerud, *The Dynamics of Defeat: The Vietnam War in Hau Nghia Province* (Boulder, CO: Westview Press, 1991), 226.

127. Jonathan Randal, "Vietnam's Army: Sometimes It Only Seems to Fight," *New York Times*, 11 June 1967. "Baby-Sitting with ARVN," *Newsweek*, 10 November 1969, 61. Abrams to Wheeler and McCain, 8 August 1969, Abrams Messages #3791, CMH.

128. Nguyen Cao Ky, *Twenty Years and Twenty Days* (New York: Stein and Day, 1976), 125. On assessing Vietnamization, see Richard H. Shultz Jr., "The Vietnamization-Pacification Strategy of 1969–1972: A Quantitative and Qualitative Analysis," in *Lessons from an Unconventional War: Reassessing U.S. Strategies for Future Conflicts*, eds. Richard A. Hunt and Richard H. Shultz Jr. (New York: Pergamon Press, 1982), 63; and Charles E. Neu, *America's Lost War, Vietnam: 1945–1975* (Wheeling, IL: Harlan Davidson, 2005), 146.

129. Meaningful victory in Clark M. Clifford, "A Viet Nam Reappraisal," *Foreign Affairs* 47, no. 4 (July 1969): 622. Kissinger, *White House Years*, 57, 191–192. Calming public opinion in USMACV, Command History, 1969, Vol. I, NARA, p. III-14. "Can Vietnamization Work?," *TIME*, 26 September 1969, 25–26.

130. Abrams in *The Joint Chiefs of Staff and The War in Vietnam*, 57. On interests driving commitments, see Leon J. Perkowski, "Deterrence vs. Disentanglement: Military Resistance to Nixon's Troop Withdrawal from South Korea, 1969–1971," paper presented at the Society for Military History conference, Montgomery, AL, 11 April 2015, pp. 11–12. See also Donald Kelly Jones, "Commitment, Disengagement and the Nixon Doctrine," *Military Review* 52, no. 12 (December 1973). Clark Clifford argued that "we had fulfilled our obligations to the South Vietnamese many times over." *Counsel to the President*, 568. On NATO, see David L. Prentice, "J. William Fulbright and the Retreat of American Power: Anglo-Australian Views of Fulbright and U.S. Neo-Isolationism, 1965–1970," paper presented at the "J. William Fulbright in the International Perspective: Liberal Internationalism and U.S. Global Influence" conference, Fayetteville, AS, September 2015.

131. Color of bodies in Jerry M. Tinker, "Vietnam: The Human Costs," in *Why Are We Still in Vietnam?*, eds. Sam Brown and Len Ackland (New York: Random House, 1970), 85. Making war "usable" in Hew Strachan, "The Lost Meaning of Strategy," *Survival* 47, no. 3 (Autumn 2005): 49. William Beecher, "Vietnam: The Problem Is How to Disengage without Causing a Collapse," *New York Times*, 22 June 1969. According to the 1969 MACV Command History, the "President regarded 'Vietnamization' as both a goal and a program to achieve that goal at the earliest practical time." Vol. I, NARA, p. 3.

132. Abrams quoted in Starry, interview by Bergen, Collison, and Burleson, MHI, p. 35. On gaps between policy and execution, see R. W. Komer, *Bureaucracy Does Its Thing: Institutional Constraints on U.S. -GVN Performance in Vietnam* (Santa Monica, CA: RAND Corporation, 1972), 7.

133. Joint Statement of Nixon and Thieu, Folder 4, Box 72, NSC Files, Vietnam Subject Files, RNL. "Text of Communique by Nixon and Thieu After the Midway Talks," *New York Times*, 9 June 1969. "The Situation in Vietnam: Overview and Outlook," 24 January 1969, Folder 1, Box 63, NSC Files, Vietnam Subject Files, RNL, p. 4. Carroll Kilpatrick, "Nixon and Thieu Seek Solidarity at Midway Today," *The Washington Post*, 8 June 1969. Hedrick Smith, "Nixon Off to Meet With Thieu Today on Course of War," *New York Times*, 8 June 1969.

134. Diem, *In the Jaws of History*, 259. On the PRG being established the same week as Midway, see Brigham, *Guerrilla Diplomacy*, 87. Thieu's consent in "Vietnam: Potentially a Turning Point," *Los Angeles Times*, 8 June 1969.

135. Hedrick Smith, "Nixon to Reduce Vietnam Force, Pulling Out 25,000 G.I.'s by Aug. 31," *New York Times*, 9 June 1969. Stuart H. Loory, "Vietnam Cutback: 25,000 Troops to Be Pulled Out," *Los Angeles Times*, 9 June 1969.

136. Wheeler quoted in Van Atta, *With Honor*, 236. Kissinger also worried the unilateral withdrawal would be "irreversible." *Ending the Vietnam War*, 84. On opposition to the policy, see Stephen E. Ambrose, "Richard Nixon: A Belligerent Dove," in *Commanders in Chief: Presidential Leadership in Modern Wars*, ed. Joseph G. Dawson III (Lawrence: University Press of Kansas, 1993), 150. Of note, the US withdrawal caused the RVN minister of national defense to request an accelerated activation of territorial forces. Army Activities Report: SE Asia, 3 December 1069, MHI, p. 37

137. Joseph Alsop, "How Long Does Nixon Have?," *Los Angeles Times*, 12 June 69. Joseph Kraft, "Token Withdrawals: Presidential Push on Troop Cutbacks Is Needed to Avert Foot-Dragging," *The Washington Post*, 24 August 1969.

138. Wheeler quoted in Sorley, *Vietnam Chronicles*, 269. Joseph Alsop, "Nixon Would Be Wise to Heed Abrams' Call for Pullout Pause," *The Washington Post*, 30 March 1970.

139. Richard Nixon, "Informal Remarks in Guam with Newsmen," 25 July 1969. Gerhard Peters and John T. Woolley, *The American Presidency Project*, http://www.presidency.ucsb.edu/ws/?pid=2140. Don Oberdorfer, "U.S. Bars New Asia War Role," *The Washington Post*, 26 July 1969. According to Dale Van Atta, the announcement "caught Kissinger by complete surprise." *With Honor*, 221.

140. Richard M. Jennings, "The Thrust of the Nixon Doctrine," *Military Review* 52, no. 2 (February 1972): 7. On limits, see Serewicz, *America at the Brink of Empire*, 86. The Chinese media cast the doctrine as a ploy to "slyly" use "Asians to fight Asians." Chris Tudda, *A Cold War Turning Point: Nixon and China, 1969–1972* (Baton Rouge: Louisiana State University Press, 2012), 24.

141. On his doctrine being misinterpreted as a total withdrawal from Asia, see Nixon, *RN*, 395. Local self-sufficiency in Hoff, "A Revisionist View of Nixon's Foreign Policy," 112. Achieving limited success in Brian M. Jenkins, *The Unchangeable War*, RM-6278-ARPA, November 1970, CMH Library, p. v. Scott Sigmund Gartner, "Differing Evaluations of Vietnamization," *Journal of Interdisciplinary History* 29, no. 2 (Autumn 1998): 258.

142. Bardshar, J3 OJCS, to Wheeler, 25 September 1969, Box 11, Creighton W. Abrams Papers, 1969-1970, MHI. See also Hunt, *Melvin Laird*, 113–114. On mission change, see Willbanks, *Abandoning Vietnam*, 17, 49; Cosmas, *MACV*, 250–251; and Kimball, *Nixon's Vietnam War*, 151. In one sense, senior policymakers hoped that a victory achieved by the RVNAF actually would serve US interests better, since a South Vietnamese victory would be more likely to be a stable and lasting one.

143. USMACV, Command History, 1969, Vol. I, NARA, pp. II-3 to II-4. Charles A. Stevenson, *Warriors and Politicians: US Civil-Military Relations under Stress* (London and New York: Routledge, 2006), 66. For a media reaction, see "Expected War Instructions to Abrams: New Words for an Old Time," *The Hartford Courant*, 27 July 1969; and James P. Sterba, "Vietnam: The Strategy Is Still 'Maximum Pressure' on the Enemy," *New York Times*, 29 June 1969.

144. "Memorial Day," *The Washington Post*, 30 May 1969. For a discussion on the US withdrawal not ending the war, see Brian M. Jenkins, "A People's Army for South Vietnam: A Vietnamese Solution," November 1971, Folder 05, Box 04, Douglas Pike Collection: Unit 11-Monographs, TTUVA, p. 3. On Abrams's limited influence, see Cosmas, *MACV*, 180.

Chapter 3

1. As an example, see Roger Trinquier, *Modern Warfare: A French View of Counterinsurgency* (Westport, CT: Praeger Security International, 1964, 2006). Of note, Trinquier echoed Galula in arguing that any counterinsurgency campaign must be "organized methodically" (p. 54).

2. David Galula, *Pacification in Algeria, 1956-1958* (Santa Monica, CA: RAND Corporation, 1963, 2006), 246–247.

3. Servan-Schreiber quoted in Grégor Mathias, *Galula in Algeria: Counterinsurgency Practice versus Theory*, trans. Neal Durando (Santa Barbara, CA: Praeger, 2011), 26. For a deeper analysis, see Jean-Jacques Servan-Schreiber, *Lieutenant in Algeria*, trans. Ronald Matthews (New York: Alfred A. Knopf, 1957). On issues with Galula's claims, see Mathias, xi, 14, 46, 66, and 93; and Lawrence Freedman, *Strategy: A History* (New York: Oxford University Press, 2013), 189.

4. David Galula, *Counterinsurgency Warfare: Theory and Practice* (New York: Frederick A. Praeger, 1964, 2005), 136. Pedagogical approach in Mathias, 58. For an overview of the French officer, see Ann Marlowe, *David Galula: His Life and Intellectual Context* (Carlisle, PA: Strategic Studies Institute, 2010).

5. "Handbook for Military Support of Pacification," February 1968, Folder 14, Box 5, United States Armed Forces Manual Collection, TTUVA, p. 1. See also J3 Inputs to Report of the MACV Effort, 1968-1970, which noted that the "ultimate objective of Allied combat operations in Vietnam was security for the population so that pacification and development could progress." Filing Cabinet B9, Box 3, MACV Command Historian's Collection, MHI, p. III-16. An 8 November 1967 NSC meeting noted that "we should stop using the word 'pacification' since it connotes a peaceful operation—exactly the opposite of what is really involved." *FRUS*, 1964-1968, V: 998. For an earlier view of the topic, see Lt. Col. Robert L. Bullard, "Military Pacification," *Journal of the Military Service Institution of the United States* XLVI, no. CLXIII (January-February 1910): 1–24.

6. Minutes of National Security Meeting, 12 September 1969, *FRUS*, 1969-1976, VI: 400. On Abrams being more restrained, see Lewis Sorley, *A Better War: The Unexamined Victories and Final Tragedy of America's Last Years in Vietnam* (New York: Harcourt Brace, 1999), 124. Counterarguments to this claim appear in David W. P. Elliott, *The Vietnamese War: Revolution and Social Change in the Mekong Delta, 1930-1975*, concise ed. (Armonk, NY: M.E. Sharpe, 2003, 2007), 330; and Gabriel Kolko, *Anatomy of a War: Vietnam, the United States, and the Modern Historical Experience* (New York: Pantheon Books, 1985), 358.

7. Department of the Army, *Field Manual 100-5, Operations of Army Forces in the Field* (Washington, DC: Headquarters, Department of the Army, September 1968), 1–6. See also Walter E. Kretchik, *U.S. Army Doctrine: From the American Revolution to the War on Terror* (Lawrence: University Press of Kansas, 2011), 190–191. Still, one officer lamented that "no *comprehensive or systematic* campaign ever developed to formulate or promote a corresponding new professional concept." Peter M. Dawkins, "The United States Army and the 'Other' War in Vietnam: A Study of the Complexity of Implementing Organizational Change" (Ph.D. diss., Princeton University, 1979), 268.

8. Col. Irving Heymont, "Armed Force and National Development," *Military Review* 49, no. 11 (December 1969): 50. Lt. Col. Garold L. Tippin, "The Army as a Nationbuilder," *Military Review* 50, no. 10. (October 1970): 11–12. Col. Lawrence E. Van Buskirk, "Maintenance Personnel in Nationbuilding," *Military Review* 49, no. 11 (November 1969): 10–17. See also Col. Maurice D. Roush, "Master Plans for Nationbuilding," *Military Review* 49, no. 2 (February 1969): 77–85.

9. James M. Carter, *Inventing Vietnam: The United States and State Building, 1954–1968* (New York: Cambridge University Press, 2008), 245. Richard A. Hunt, *Melvin Laird and the Foundation of the Post-Vietnam Military, 1969–1973* (Washington, DC: Office of the Secretary of Defense Historical Office, 2015), 468.

10. Frances FitzGerald, *Fire in the Lake: The Vietnamese and the Americans in Vietnam* (Boston: Little, Brown, 1972), 414. Hedrick Smith, "Nixon's Asian Moves," *New York Times*, 23 August 1969.

11. Stagnant and backward societies in Michael E. Latham, "Redirecting the Revolution? The USA and the failure of nation-building in South Vietnam," *Third World Quarterly* 27, no. 1 (2006): 32. See also Michael E. Latham, *Modernization as Ideology: American Social Science and "Nation Building" in the Kennedy Era* (Chapel Hill: University of North Carolina Press, 2000), 62, 67. Instability and anticommunism in Dean C. Tipps, "Modernization Theory and the Comparative Study of Societies: A Critical Perspective," *Comparative Studies in Society and History* 15, no. 2 (March 1973): 210. The United States as the model in Mark T. Berger, "Decolinisation, Modernisation and Nation-Building: Political Development Theory and the Appeal of Communism in Southeast Asia, 1945–1975," *Journal of Southeast Asian Studies* 34, no. 3 (October 2003): 429. Collapse of colonialism in Carter, *Inventing Vietnam*, 25.

12. Kenneth W. Kennedy, "Civic Action as a Cold War Weapon" (student thesis, US Army War College, MHI, 9 March 1962), 15. On this point, see also Joseph G. Clemons Jr., "The Dilemma of the Vietnam Enclaves" (student essay, US Army War College, MHI, 13 January 1967), 6; and Austin Long, *On "Other War:" Lessons from Five Decades of RAND Counterinsurgency Research* (Santa Monica, CA: RAND Corporation, 2006), 22. Christopher Fisher, "The Illusion of Progress: CORDS and the Crisis of Modernization in South Vietnam, 1965–1968," *Pacific Historical Review* 75, no. 1 (February 2006): 41.

13. Edward Miller, *Misalliance: Ngo Dinh Diem, the United States, and the Fate of South Vietnam* (Cambridge, MA: Harvard University Press, 2013), 13, 56, 66–68.

14. Lansdale to Gilpatric, 22 March 1962, *FRUS, 1961-1963*, II: 256–257. See also John O'Donnell, "Life and Times of a USOM Prov Rep," in *Prelude to Tragedy: Vietnam, 1960–1965*, eds. Harvey Neese and John O'Donnell (Annapolis, MD: Naval Institute Press, 2001), 222–223. FM 31–15 defined civic action as "any action performed by the military force utilizing military manpower and material resources in cooperation with civil authorities, agencies, groups, which is designed to secure the economic or social betterment of the civilian community." Department of the Army, *Field Manual 31–15, Operations against Irregular Forces*, May 1961, 18. For a South Vietnamese perspective, see Nguyen Duc Cuong, "Building a Market Economy during Wartime," in *Voices from the Second Republic of South Vietnam (1967–1975)*, ed. K. W. Taylor (Ithaca, NY: Cornell Southeast Asia Program Publications, 2014), 90–114.

15. Rostow quoted in Latham, *Modernization as Ideology*, 56. Milton C. Taylor, "South Viet-Nam: Lavish Aid, Limited Progress," *Pacific Affairs* 34, no. 3 (Autumn 1961): 243.

16. Charles Wolf Jr., *Insurgency and Counterinsurgency: New Myths and Old Realities* (Santa Monica, CA: RAND Corporation, 1965), 2. Col. Edwin F. Black, "'Dragon's Teeth' of Freedom," *Military Review* 44, no. 8 (August 1964): 22. Such assumptions undergirded the

strategic hamlet program. See, for example, Maj. William A. Smith Jr., "The Strategic Hamlet Program in Vietnam," *Military Review* 44, no. 5 (May 1964): 17–23.

17. On strategy, popular will, and nationalism, see Gary W. Gallagher, *The Confederate War* (Cambridge, MA: Harvard University Press, 1997), 111. On government programs, see Record of Meeting with Prime Minister, 31 May 1968, *FRUS, 1964–1968*, VI: 740; James R. Bullington and James D. Rosenthal, "The South Vietnamese Countryside: Non-Communist Political Perceptions," *Asian Survey* 10, no. 8 (August 1970): 653; and Gerald C. Hickey, *Accommodation and Coalition in South Vietnam* (Santa Monica, CA: RAND Corporation, 1970), 8. Pride, loyalty, and endurance in Larry Burrows, "Vietnam: 'A Degree of Disillusion,' " *Life*, 19 September 1969, 67. Control efforts in Martin G. Clemis, "The Control War: Communist Revolutionary Warfare, Pacification, and the Struggle for South Vietnam, 1968–1975" (Ph.D. diss., Temple University, 2015), 24.

18. Jonathan Schell, *Observing the Nixon Years* (New York: Pantheon Books, 1989), 4. Samuel L. Popkin, "Pacification: Politics and the Village," *Asian Survey* 10, no. 8 (August 1970): 68. Carter, *Inventing Vietnam*, 7.

19. Maj. Harry G. Summers Jr., "Politics and Culture in Southeast Asia," *Military Review* 50, no. 6 (June 1970): 34. Americans tended to compare these GVN faults to the NLF that "regarded the armed struggle as secondary to the political struggle." Douglas Pike, *Viet Cong: The Organization and Techniques of the National Liberation Front of South Vietnam* (Cambridge, MA: M.I.T. Press, 1966), 232.

20. Kolko, *Anatomy of a War*, 381. Mark Philip Bradley, *Vietnam at War* (New York: Oxford University Press, 2009), 86. Way of life in Richard A. Hunt, *Pacification: The American Struggle for Vietnam's Hearts and Minds* (Boulder, CO: Westview Press, 1995), 28. On soldiers not understanding the GVN's political vision, see Robert K. Brigham, *ARVN: Life and Death in the South Vietnamese Army* (Lawrence: University Press of Kansas, 2006), 40.

21. Stuart A. Herrington, *Silence Was a Weapon: The Vietnam War in the Villages* (Novato, CA: Presidio Press, 1982), 38. Otto Heilbrunn, "When Counterinsurgents Cannot Win," *Military Review* 49, no. 10 (October 1969): 43. William J. Duiker argues, "To the end, the only real source of Saigon's authority was the U.S. military presence." *The Communist Road to Power*, 2nd ed. (Boulder, CO: Westview Press, 1981, 1996), 353.

22. Allan E. Goodman, "The End of the War as a Setting for the Future Development of South Vietnam," *Asian Survey* 11, no. 4 (April 1971): 341. Bradley, *Vietnam at War*, 3. For an earlier view of this issue, see R. Michael Pearce, *Evolution of a Vietnamese Village—Part I: The Present, After Eight Months of Pacification* (Santa Monica, CA: RAND Corporation, 1965), 55, 62.

23. Objectives Plan in HQ USMACV, Command History, 1971, Vol. I, Entry MACJ03, RG 472, NARA, p. II-7. Similar language was used in the 1970 Command History, Vol. I, NARA, p. I-1. Le Ly Hayslip and Dien Pham, "Caught in the Crossfire: The Civilian Experience," in *Rolling Thunder in a Gentle Land: The Vietnam War Revisited*, ed. Andrew Wiest (New York: Osprey, 2006), 153. Dual aspects of pacification in Hunt, *Pacification*, 1. Tendency to view peasants as "totally passive" in Thomas L. Ahern Jr., *Vietnam Declassified: The CIA and Counterinsurgency* (Lexington: University Press of Kentucky, 2010), 362.

24. Jeffrey J. Clarke, *Advice and Support: The Final Years, 1965–1973* (Washington, DC: Center of Military History, 1988), 521. Organization and leadership in Sir Robert Thompson, *No Exit from Vietnam* (New York: David McKay, 1969), 147. Strong political structure in Paul M. Kattenburg, *The Vietnam Trauma in American Foreign Policy, 1945–75* (New Brunswick, NJ: Transaction, 1992), 203. Political potential of the countryside in Bullington and Rosenthal, "The South Vietnamese Countryside," 655. See also Tran Dinh Tho, "Pacification," in *The Vietnam War: An Assessment by South Vietnam's Generals*, ed. Lewis Sorley (Lubbock: Texas Tech University Press, 2010), 244.

25. Embassy in Vietnam to Department of State, 14 August 1961, *FRUS, 1961–1963*, I: 276. As an example of the "better war" thesis as it relates to pacification, see Lewis Sorley, "To Change a War: General Harold K. Johnson and the PROVN Study," *Parameters* 28, no. 1 (Spring 1998): 93–109. For a much more persuasive counterargument, see Andrew J. Birtle, "PROVN, Westmoreland, and the Historians: A Reappraisal," *Journal of Military History* 72, no. 4 (October 2008): 1213–1247.

26. Pearce, *Evolution of a Vietnamese Village*, x. See also John C. Donnell and Charles A. Joiner, "South Vietnam: 'Struggle' Politics and the Bigger War," *Asian Survey* 7, no. 1 (January 1967): 53.

27. Williams, 28 December 1955, *FRUS*, 1955–1957, I: 608. Williams's successor, Lt. Gen. Lionel C. McGarr, took a similar approach in the introduction of his "Tactics & Techniques of Counter-Insurgent Operations," MAAG-Vietnam, 10 February 1962, General Historians Files, CMH, p. 2. See also William Rosenau, *US Internal Security Assistance to South Vietnam: Insurgency, Subversion and Public Order* (New York: Routledge, 2005), 105–107.

28. Allen B. Jennings, ed., *Readings in Counterinsurgency* (West Point, NY: Department of Social Sciences, 1962), 131. Paucity of talent in Edward Geary Lansdale, *In the Midst of Wars: An American's Mission to Southeast Asia* (New York: Harper & Row, 1972), 229. Civil Guard in McGarr to Nguyen Dinh Thuan, 28 October 1960, Folder 14, Box 2, Douglas Pike Collection, Unit 01: Assessment and Strategy, TTUVA, p. 2; Briefing Charts, Personal Use of Lt. Gen. S. T. Williams, 31 May 1957, Conversations with President Diem Folder, Box 3, Samuel T. Williams Papers, MHI, p. 14; and Rufus Phillips, "A Report on Counter-Insurgency in Vietnam," 31 August 1962, Folder 4, Box 1, Earl R. Rhine Collection, TTUVA, p. 4. See also Larry E. Cable, *Conflict of Myths: The Development of American Counterinsurgency Doctrine and the Vietnam War* (New York: New York University Press, 1986), 187.

29. Basic Counterinsurgency Plan for Viet-Nam in *FRUS*, 1961–1963, I: 1–3. *The Pentagon Papers: The Defense Department History of United States Decisionmaking on Vietnam* [The Sen. Gravel Edition, 5 vols.], Vol. II (Boston: Beacon Press, 1971–1972), 25. On politicians echoing the need for more than just a military answer to fighting insurgencies, see Arthur M. Schlesinger, *Robert Kennedy and His Times* (Boston: Houghton Mifflin, 1978), 463.

30. Outline Plan of Counterinsurgency Operations, 10 January 1962, *FRUS*, 1961–1963, II: 17–19. Focusing on military operations in Christopher K. Ives, *US Special Forces and Counterinsurgency in Vietnam: Military Innovation and Institutional Failure, 1961–1963* (London and New York: Routledge, 2007), 81.

31. Psychological Requirements of Hop Tac, 13 July 1965, Folder 6, Box 13, Douglas Pike Collection, Unit 03: Insurgency Warfare, TTUVA. The BDM Corporation, "A Study of Strategic Lessons Learned in Vietnam," Vol. V, Planning the War, General Holdings, MHI, p. 5–34. For precedents of the clear and hold approach, see CINCPAC-COMUSMACV Conference Agenda Items, 30 October 1963, Historian's Background Material Files, Box 16, RG 472, NARA; and National Campaign Plan, Phase II, 22 June 1963, Part I, Historian's Background Material Files, 206–202, Box 1, RG 472, NARA.

32. Thomson and Ropa to Bundy, 7 January 1966, *FRUS*, 1964–1968, IV: 28–29. Hunt, *Pacification*, 25–27. Guenter Lewy, *America in Vietnam* (New York: Oxford University Press, 1978), 88.

33. Ambassador Lodge quoted in *FRUS*, 1964–1968, IV: 609. On evolution of the pacification program, see John Prados, *Lost Crusader: The Secret Wars of CIA Director William Colby* (New York: Oxford University Press, 2003), 183–188.

34. NSAM 362, 9 May 1967, *FRUS*, 1964–1968, V: 398–399. MACV Monthly Evaluation Report, May 1967, MHI, p. 8. Robert Thompson, Report on National Police, 1 April 1971, Folder 5, Box 92, NSC Files, Vietnam Subject Files, RNL.

35. Organizations and Functions for Civil Operations and Revolutionary Development Support, 28 May 1967, Folder 3, Box 1, John B. O'Donnell Collection, TTUVA. Jonathan Randal, "The Shake-up in Saigon," *New York Times*, 13 May 1967.

36. Combined Campaign Plan, 1968, Historians Files, CMH, p. B-2. Some officers worried, however, that coordinating RVNAF activities raised questions as to "how deeply do we want to become involved in the internal workings of the host society." Senior Officer Debriefing Program Report of LTG Fred C. Weyand, 4 October 1968, MHI, p. 7.

37. "Handbook for Military Support of Pacification," TTUVA, p. 1. U.S. Grant Sharp and William C. Westmoreland, *Report on the War in Vietnam* (Washington, DC: U.S. Government Printing Office, 1969), 229. On difficulties with implementation, see Tho, "Pacification," in Sorley, *The Vietnam War*, 215. Ambassador Ellsworth Bunker believed "hamlet and village security . . . was the primary objective." Interview by Michael L. Gillette, 9 December 1980, Oral History Collection, LBJL, p. I-18.

38. "Handbook for Military Support of Pacification," TTUVA, p. 56. "A Program Against the VC Infrastructure," 27 July 1967, Box 4, Richard M. Lee Papers, MHI, p. 9. MACV, Blueprint for Vietnam, 1967, General Holdings, MHI, pp.1725, 1727. RVNAF responsibility for pacification in HQ, USMACV, Command History, 1968, Vol. I, Entry MACJ03, RG 472, NARA, p. 14. On the composition and missions of the MATs, see Terry T. Turner, "Mobile Advisory Teams in Vietnam: A Legacy Remembered," *On Point: The Journal of Army History* 16, no. 4 (Spring 2011): 34–41.

39. Operational Report—Lessons Learned, 1st Cavalry Division, 28 November 1966, Box 1, 1st Cavalry Division OR/LL, MACV Command Historian's Collection, MHI. After Action Report, James Bond, 2nd Brigade, 1st Cavalry Division, 11 July 1966, Historians Files, CMH.

40. "Important Pacification Accomplishments in 1967," Box 7, Robert M. Montague Papers, MHI. William Leonhart, Updating Supplement to "The Other War in Vietnam—A Progress Report," Box 7, Robert M. Montague Papers, MHI. Unified direction in James Dobbins, Michele A. Poole, Austin Long, and Benjamin Runkle, *After the War: Nation-Building from FDR to George W. Bush* (Santa Monica, CA.: RAND Corporation, 2008), 135.

41. Headquarters, USMACV, Combat Experiences 3–69, MHI, p. 18. John C. Donnell, "Expanding Political Participation—The Long Haul from Villagism to Nationalism," *Asian Survey* 10, no. 8 (August 1970): 692.

42. Leaflets in Jonathan Schell, *The Military Half: An Account of Destruction in Quang Ngai and Quang Tin* (New York: Alfred A. Knopf, 1968), 22–23.

43. Resiliency in Burrows, "Vietnam: 'A Degree of Disillusion,'" 71. The ARVN was also pulled in multiple directions in synchronizing combat missions with territorial security and pacification efforts. See Tran Von Don, *Our Endless War: Inside Vietnam* (San Rafael, CA: Presidio Press, 1978), 219.

44. Ward Just, *To What End: Report From Vietnam* (Boston: Houghton Mifflin, 1968; New York: Public Affairs, 2000), 165. Social engineering in report by Sen. Mike Mansfield, 18 December 1962, in *Vietnam: A History in Documents*, ed. Gareth Porter (New York: New American Library, 1981), 235; and Andrew J. Birtle, *U.S. Army Counterinsurgency and Contingency Operations Doctrine, 1942–1976* (Washington, DC: Center of Military History, 2006), 389. See also Harry G. Summers Jr., *On Strategy: A Critical Analysis of the Vietnam War* (Novato, CA: Presidio Press, 1982), 44. One critic questioned whether it made "sense to give military forces nation-building tasks that are essentially civilian in nature." James L. Trainor, "What Business Does the Military Have in Pacification/Nation-Buidling?," *Armed Forces Management* (August 1967): 32.

45. "Behavior of Certain U.S. Advisors in Kien Hoa Province," 27 March 1970, CORDS Historical Working Group Files, 1967–1973, Box 24, HQ USMACV, RG 472, NARA. David Donovan, *Once a Warrior King: Memoirs of an Officer in Vietnam* (New York: McGraw-Hill, 1985), 95. Sgt. Paul Kelly quoted in *Dear America: Letters Home from Vietnam*, ed. Bernard Edelman (New York: Pocket Books, 1986), 109–110. See also Eric M. Bergerud, *Red Thunder, Tropic Lightning: The World of a Combat Division in Vietnam* (Boulder, CO: Westview Press, 1993), 224.

46. James R. Lay, "How Tactical Units of the US Army in Vietnam Can Get the Most Out of Civic Action with the Minimum Cost and Expenditure of Resources"(student essay, US Army War College, MHI, 17 January 1968), p. 11. Nguyễn Công Luận, *Nationalist in the Viet Nam Wars: Memoirs of a Victim Turned Soldier* (Bloomington: Indiana University Press, 2012), 358. John C. "Doc" Bahnsen Jr. recalled that most pacification efforts in the 11th Cavalry Regiment "were one- or two-day affairs." *American Warrior: A Combat Memoir of Vietnam* (New York: Citadel Press, 2007), 306.

47. Department of the Army, Operations Report—Lessons Learned 6–67— "Observations of a Brigade Commander," 27 December 1967, 32–33. Soldier quoted in Mark Baker, *Nam: The Vietnam War in the Words of the Men and Women Who Fought There* (New York: William Morrow, 1981), 164. Gordon Livingston noted "the evident fact that at an operational level most Americans simply do not care about the Vietnamese." "Letter from a Vietnam Veteran," *The Saturday Review*, 20 September 1969, 22.

48. Robert M. Montague Jr., "Pacification: The Overall Strategy in South Vietnam" (student essay, US Army War College, Box 1, Robert M. Montague Papers, MHI, 22 April 1966), p. 6.

49. On army doctrine, see Birtle, *U.S. Army Counterinsurgency and Contingency Operations Doctrine*, 366, 388. System in Nathan Leites and Charles Wolf Jr., *Rebellion and Authority: An Analytic Essay on Insurgent Conflicts* (Chicago: Markham, 1970), 32–34. Triple dislocation in Eqbal Ahmad, "Revolutionary War and Counter-Insurgency," in *Revolutionary War: Western Response*, eds. David S. Sullivan and Martin J. Sattler (New York: Columbia University Press, 1971), 6.

50. John J. McCuen, *The Art of Counter-Revolutionary War: The Strategy of Counterinsurgency* (St. Petersburg, FL: Hailer, 1966, 2005), 152. See also William Colby with James McCargar, *Lost Victory: A Firsthand Account of America's Sixteen-Year Involvement in Vietnam* (Chicago: Contemporary Books, 1989), 240; and Carter, *Inventing Vietnam*, 214.

51. On counterinsurgency falling out of favor, see David Fitzgerald, *Learning to Forget: US Army Counterinsurgency Doctrine and Practice from Vietnam to Iraq* (Stanford, CA: Stanford Security Studies, 2013), 37; and Loren Baritz, *Backfire: A History of How American Culture Led Us into Vietnam and Made Us Fight the Way We Did* (New York: William Morrow, 1985), 279. On continuing faith in pacification, see Ahern, *Vietnam Declassified*, 372; and Elliott, *The Vietnamese War*, 383. Problems with modernization theory in Tipps, "Modernization Theory and the Comparative Study of Societies," 206; and Fisher, "The Illusion of Progress," 50.

52. USMC colonel quoted in James Walker Trullinger Jr., *Village at War: An Account of Revolution in Vietnam* (New York: Longman, 1980), 150. On control still being a necessity, see S. Canby, B. Jenkins, and R. B. Rainey, *A Ground Force Structure and Strategy for Vietnam in the 1970s* (Santa Monica, CA: RAND Corporation, 1970), 11.

53. Officer quoted in Donovan, *Once a Warrior King*, 41. On paucity of leadership at the district and provincial levels, see Hunt, *Pacification*, 131.

54. Clifford to Johnson, 18 July 1968, *FRUS, 1964–1968*, VI: 876.

55. Komer to Johnson, 4 October 1967, *FRUS, 1964–1968*, V: 864. On Komer's relationship with Abrams, see Graham A. Cosmas, *MACV: The Joint Command in the Years of Withdrawal, 1968–1973* (Washington, DC: Center of Military History, 2007), 187; and Frank L. Jones, *Blowtorch: Robert Komer, Vietnam, and American Cold War Strategy* (Annapolis, MD: Naval Institute Press, 2013), 169. A sense of Komer's optimism can be found in Komer to Johnson, 28 February 1967, *FRUS, 1964–1968*, V: 208–209; and R. W. Komer, *Impact of Pacification on Insurgency in Vietnam* (Santa Monica, CA: RAND Corporation, 1970), 7.

56. Walter Kerwin quoted in David T. Zabecki, *Chief of Staff: The Principal Officers Behind History's Great Commanders*, Vol. 2 (Annapolis, MD: Naval Institute Press, 2008), 214. See also Gen. Walter T. Kerwin, interview by Albin Wheeler and Ronald Craven, 9 April 1976, Senior Officers Debriefing Program, Box A, Creighton Abrams Story, MHI, p. 12.

57. Aide quoted in Jones, *Blowtorch*, 199. Gene Roberts, "Komer Optimistic Over Pacification Despite Foe's Drive," *New York Times*, 19 April 1968. Peter Braestrup, "Pacification 'Back on Track,'" *The Washington Post*, 19 April 1968.

58. Warner to Komer, 10 July 1968, Box 1, Volney F. Warner Papers, MHI. Multiple issues related to pacification in USMACV, Command History, 1968, Vol. I, NARA, p. 519; and Chester L. Cooper et al., "The American Experience with Pacification in Vietnam, Vol. III: History of Pacification," March 1972, Folder 65, U.S. Marine Corps History Division, Vietnam War Documents Collection, TTUVA, pp. 290–292. For an assessment of these efforts, see Dale Andrade and James H. Willbanks, "CORDS/Phoenix: Counterinsurgency Lessons from Vietnam for the Future," *Military Review* 86, no. 2 (March–April 2006): 16–17. A less sanguine evaluation is Frank L. Jones, "Blowtorch: Robert Komer and the Making of Vietnam Pacification Policy," *Parameters* 35, no. 3 (Autumn 2005): 116.

59. On Komer's departure, see Jones, *Blowtorch*, 205–206; and Thomas W. Scoville, *Reorganizing for Pacification Support* (Washington, DC: US Army Center of Military History, 1999), 82–83. Komer summed up his philosophy on pacification in Robert W. Komer, *Organization and Management of the "New Model" Pacification Program—1966–1969* (Santa Monica, CA: RAND Corporation, 1970), 237–240.

60. David Hoffman, "Pacification Changes Hinted by New Chief," *The Washington Post*, 18 November 1968. "Soft Spoke Pacification Chief," *New York Times*, 14 February 1969. Marquis Childs, "Vietnam Pacification Drive Takes a More Realistic Turn," *The Washington*

Post, 28 March 1969. On Colby's earlier career in Vietnam, see Prados, *Lost Crusader*, 159–188; and chapter 9 in Randall B. Woods, *Shadow Warrior: William Egan Colby and the CIA* (New York: Basic Books, 2013).

61. Tad Szulc, "Pacification, Amid Gains, Is Said to Face Hard Road," *New York Times*, 14 February 1970.

62. Cooper et al., "The American Experience with Pacification in Vietnam," TTUVA, p. 301. For enduring problems, see Col. C. E. Jordan Jr., CORDS MACV, 10 November 1968, Box 8, Senior Officer Debriefing Reports, RG 472, NARA. As an example, even with the new focus at the village level, "all province and district chiefs are still military officers." "Vietnam: December 1969," Folder 06, Box 07, Douglas Pike Collection: Unit 11-Monographs, TTUVA, p. 6. The training of CORDS officials suggested continuity as well. See Maj. Lawrence D. Silvan, "Handout Material Collected at the MACV/CORDS Advisor Orientation Course," 2 December 1969, VNIT Folder 558, CMH.

63. HQ, USMACV, Command History, 1969, Vol. I, Entry MACJ03, RG 472, NARA, pp. II-4 to II-5. Combined Campaign Plan, 1969, Historians Files, CMH, pp. B-1-1 to B-1-3. Nor did Colby's 9 December 1968 meeting with President Johnson suggest any major changes to the pacification program. *FRUS, 1964–1968*, VII: 737–741.

64. W. E. Colby, 1969 Accelerated Pacification Campaign, July–October 1969, 28 June 1969, CORDS Historical Working Group Files, 1967-1973, Box 6, RG 472, NARA. COMUSMACV to CINCPAC, 1969 Pacification Planning, 2 April 1969, Folder 65, US Marine Corps History Division Vietnam War Documents Collection, TTUVA. Guidelines, Pacification Campaign, 1969, Historians Files, CMH. Woods, *Shadow Warrior*, 298.

65. W. E. Colby, Implementation of the 1969 PD Plan, 21 February 1969, Folder 3, Box 62, NSC Files, Vietnam Subject Files, RNL. 9th Infantry Division 1969 Pacification and Development Plan, 12 May 1969, Historians Files, CMH. Abrams argued that attacking the enemy's political cadre would facilitate building bonds between the people and the government. See Lewis Sorley, ed., *Vietnam Chronicles: The Abrams Tapes, 1968–1972* (Lubbock: Texas Tech University Press, 2004), 63.

66. Abrams in Headquarters, USMACV, "One War," MACV Command Overview, 1968–1972, Historians Files, CMH, p. 30. See also James H. Willbanks, *Abandoning Vietnam: How America Left and South Vietnam Lost Its War* (Lawrence: University Press of Kansas, 2004), 57, and Duiker, *The Communist Road to Power*, 303. Woods, *Shadow Warrior*, 290. Komer argued that "Tet made Vietnamization feasible." *Organization and Management of the "New Model" Pacification Program*, 81.

67. Popkin, "Pacification," 664. Advisor quoted in William Tuohy, "Pacification Is Tied to Security," *The Washington Post*, 27 June 1968.

68. Special National Intelligence Estimate, 6 June 1968, *FRUS, 1964–1968*, VI: 763. Bunker to Johnson, 19 December 1968, *FRUS, 1964-1968*, VII: 769. CIA in Prados, *Lost Crusader*, 213. On Abrams and the links between military operations and pacification, see A. J. Langguth, *Our Vietnam: The War, 1954–1975* (New York: Simon & Schuster, 2000), 575; and Sorley, *Vietnam Chronicles*, 105.

69. Farmer quoted in Trullinger, *Village at War*, 142. Speedy Express in Philip Knightley, "Vietnam 1954–1975," in *The American Experience in Vietnam: A Reader*, ed. Grace Sevy (Norman: University of Oklahoma Press, 1989), 135.

70. RD cadre issues in Initiation of Interagency Coordinating Group for Vietnamization of Intelligence, 5 May 1970, Folder 16, Box 15, Douglas Pike Collection: Unit 01-Military Operations, TTUVA, p. B-19. Risking death in F. J. West Jr., *Area Security* (Santa Monica, CA: RAND Corporation, 1969), 6. Intimidation in Michael Lee Lanning and Dan Cragg, *Inside the VC and the NVA: The Real Story of North Vietnam's Armed Forces* (New York: Fawcett Columbine, 1992), 186–187. Planting agents in Ngo Quang Truong, "Territorial Forces," in Sorley, *The Vietnam War*, 208. On these being long-standing issues, see DePuy to Goodpaster, 18 April 1967, *FRUS, 1964–1968*, V: 321–325.

71. John L. Cook, *The Advisor* (Philadelphia: Dorrance, 1973), 93. See also House Committee on Armed Services, *Progress of the Pacification Program* (Washington, DC: US Government Printing Office, 1970), 5418. Colby's focus on security in Sorley, *Vietnam Chronicles*, 60. Coercion in Pike, *Viet Cong*, 240–241. Allies' indiscriminate use of firepower in Louis

A. Wiesner, *Victims and Survivors: Displaced Persons and Other War Victims in Viet-Nam, 1954–1975* (Westport, CT: Greenwood Press, 1988), 32.

72. Colby quoted in Cooper et al., "The American Experience with Pacification in Vietnam," TTUVA, 295. Komer, *Organization and Management of the "New Model" Pacification Program*, 88. Project Takeoff Summary, Folder 65, US Marine Corps History Division Vietnam War Documents Collection, TTUVA; Hunt, *Pacification*, 99–100. Komer was speaking of "accelerated pacification" as early as 1966. See Draft Paper (with Rostow), 20 September 1966, *FRUS, 1964–1968*, IV: 650–651.

73. APC goals in USMACV, Command History, 1968, Vol. I, NARA, p. 522. Robert W. Komer, "Clear, Hold and Rebuild," *Army* 20, no. 5 (May 1970): 22. Woods, *Shadow Warrior*, 297. Jones, *Blowtorch*, 201.

74. COMUSMACV to CINCPAC, 14 February 1969, Folder 3, Box 62, NSC Files, Vietnam Subject Files, RNL. For an example of different performance indicators, see MACV SEER Report, 4th Quarter, CY69, Digital Archive Collection, USAAWCL.

75. *St. Louis Post-Dispatch* quoted in Seymour Melman, ed., *In the Name of America: The Conduct of the War in Vietnam by the Armed Forces of the United States as Shown by Published Reports* (New York: Clergy and Laymen Concerned about Vietnam, 1968), 145. Numbers in Operational Report—Lessons Learned, Headquarters, 1st Infantry Division, Period Ending 31 January 1969, 21 May 1969, Digital Archive Collection, USAAWCL. "Softness" in Moor to Haig, 30 January 1969, Folder 3, Box 62, NSC Files, Vietnam Subject Files, RNL. HES statistics of 1.7 million in Hunt, *Pacification*, 197. On problems with statistics, see p. 206. "Fast-and-thin" (a term coined by John Paul Vann) in Clemis, "The Control War," 316. Officials in Saigon could never rule out the possibility that an agreement for a cease-fire might emerge at any time, locking into place existing battle lines. This uncertainty, and the desire to claim as much territory as possible before talks reached some kind of agreement, were factors that drove the "fast-and-thin" approach.

76. Tran Quang Minh, "A Decade of Public Service: Nation-Building during the Interregnum and Second Republic (1964–76)," in Taylor, *Voices from the Second Republic of South Vietnam*, 51. Roy L. Prosterman, "Land-to-the-Tiller in South Vietnam: The Tables Turn," *Asian Survey* 10, no. 8 (August 1970): 751–752, 764. For an overview of the Land-to-the-Tiller program, see MacDonald Salter, "The Broadening Base of Land Reform in South Vietnam," *Asian Survey* 10, no. 8 (August 1970): 724–737. On land reform being an NLF tactic, see William R. Andrews, *The Village War: Vietnamese Communist Revolutionary Activities in Dinh Tuong Province, 1960–1964* (Columbia: University of Missouri Press, 1973), 64–65; and Robert K. Brigham, "Ho Chi Minh, Confucianism, and Marxism," in *The War That Never Ends: New Perspectives on the Vietnam War*, eds. David L. Anderson and John Ernst (Lexington: University Press of Kentucky, 2007), 116–117.

77. Luận, *Nationalist in the Viet Nam Wars*, 380. On land reform's impact, see Jeffrey Race, "How They Won," *Asian Survey* 10, no. 8 (August 1970): 640; and David Biggs, *Quagmire: Nation-Building and Nature in the Mekong Delta* (Seattle: University of Washington Press, 2010), 217.

78. Bunker to Johnson, 2 October 1968, *FRUS, 1964–1968*, VII: 115. On increases to the National Police and RF/RFs, see Abrams to Wheeler, 4 February 1969, Abrams Messages #2352, CMH; Lt. Col. Dave E. Sheperd Jr., "Republic of Vietnam's National Police," *Military Review* 51, no. 6 (June 1971): 69–74; and Thomas C. Thayer, *War Without Fronts: The American Experience in Vietnam* (Annapolis, MD: Naval Institute Press, 1985, 2016), 157. Abrams's support in Sorley, *A Better War*, 69. Abolishing village elections in Woods, *Shadow Warrior*, 295.

79. Richard Nixon, *No More Vietnams* (New York: Arbor House: 1985), 132–133. Douglas S. Blaufarb and George K. Tanham, *Who Will Win? A Key to the Puzzle of Revolutionary War* (New York: Crane Russak, 1989), 87. Dale Andradé, *Ashes to Ashes: The Phoenix Program and the Vietnam War* (Lexington, MA: Lexington Books, 1990) 82–83. On Thieu's consolidating his own power, see Tom Buckley, "The ARVN Is Bigger and Better, But—," *New York Times*, 12 October 1969.

80. The Vietnamese Village, Handbook for Advisors, Folder 02, Box 01, Ronald Tausch Collection, TTUVA, p. 4. Robert G. Kaiser, "Saigon Generals Make Up Strong 'New Class,'" *Los Angeles Times*, 23 November 1969. One veteran, commenting on the quality of local

leadership, noted that the "closer you were to North Vietnamese troops, the tougher it was to have development." Al Santoli, *To Bear Any Burden: The Vietnam War and Its Aftermath in the Words of Americans and Southeast Asians* (Bloomington: Indiana University Press, 1999), 212.

81. Erwin R. Brigham, "Pacification Measurement," *Military Review* 50, no. 5 (May 1970): 51. On doubts of data in Washington, see Ahern, *Vietnam Declassified*, 306.

82. Pacification Data Bank—November 1969, Folder 10, Box 43, Douglas Pike Collection: Unit 03-Statistical Data, TTUVA. One report also suggested that "continuing progress in pacification appears to depend, too, on maintaining a large American advisory infrastructure." "Vietnam: December 1969," TTUVA, 7.

83. Komer in USMACV, "One War," MACV Command Overview, CMH, p. 26. Montague in Komer, *Organization and Management of the "New Model" Pacification Program*, 87. Arthur J. Dommen, "Viet Cong: Now Fish in a Hostile Sea," *Los Angeles Times*, 2 March 1969. 1969 offensive in USMACV Quarterly Evaluation Report, January–March 1969, MHI, pp. 5–6.

84. Rowland Evans and Robert Novak, "Pacification Impossible in Vietnam While the Vietcong's VCI Survives," *The Washington Post*, 20 April 1970. On this being a longstanding problem, see Westmoreland to Wheeler, 28 August 1965—"The vast majority of the VC live in hamlets and villages which at one time were probably loyal to the government"— Box 5, Paul L. Miles Papers, MHI; and Notes of Meeting, 12 July 1967, *FRUS*, 1964–1968, V: 603.

85. Lt. Gen. Arthur S. Collins Jr., 7 January 1971, Senior Officer Debriefing Reports, CMH, pp. 24–25. On earlier evaluations of the population, see Durbrow to Herter, 7 March 1960, in Porter, *Vietnam*, 199; and Kirkpatrick and de Silva to McCone, 10 February 1964, *FRUS*, 1964–1968, I: 65. "Politically inert" in McPherson to Johnson, 13 June 1967, *FRUS*, 1964–1968, V: 494.

86. Col. Jerry F. Dunn, "A New Look at Pacification," *Military Review* 50, no. 1 (January 1970): 86. See also Blaufarb and Tanham, *Who Will Win?*, 25. The communists too had to deal with popular "ambivalence." See Andrew Wiest, "The 'Other' Vietnam War," in *America and the Vietnam War: Re-examining the Culture and History of a Generation*, eds. Andrew Wiest, Mary Kathryn Barbier, and Glenn Robins (New York: Routledge, 2010), 63.

87. On Abrams believing he had to deal with the enemy's "major formations" first before moving on to pacification, see Sorley, *Vietnam Chronicles*, 16. NSC study group in Andrew J. Birtle, "Persuasion and Coercion in Counterinsurgency Warfare," *Military Review* 88, no. 4 (July–August 2008): 50. Little had changed since 1965 in the "sequence of steps" required in pacification. See W. E. DePuy, The Techniques of Pacification, 22 September 1965, Pacification 1965–1975 Folder, Historians Files, CMH. In fact, see similar language on the enemy as a system in David W. P. Elliott and W. A. Steward, *Pacification and the Viet Cong System in Dinh Tuong: 1966–1967* (Santa Monica, CA: RAND Corporation, 1969).

88. Kissinger to Nixon, 16 November 1970, *FRUS*, 1969–1976, VII: 168. The Situation in the Countryside, Folder 1, Box 118, NSC Files, Vietnam Subject Files, RNL, p. 2. Tasks in USMACV, Command History, 1969, Vol. I, NARA, pp. II-5 to II-6.

89. Abrams in USMACV, "One War," MACV Command Overview, CMH, pp. 25, 52. Control as an element of security in MACV Long Range Planning Task Group, Area Security Principles and Application, Area Security Concept, 1969–1970, Historians Files, CMH, p. 5.

90. Elliott, *The Vietnamese War*, 333. See also Mai Elliott, *RAND in Southeast Asia: A History of the Vietnam War Era* (Santa Monica, CA: RAND Corporation, 2010), 300. APC in Eric M. Bergerud, *The Dynamics of Defeat: The Vietnam War in Hau Nghia Province* (Boulder, CO: Westview Press, 1991), 224. On pacification under Abrams being violent, see Clemis, "The Control War," 224–225.

91. Bunker to Nixon, 16 July 1969, Folder 10, Box 75, NSC Files, Vietnam Subject Files, RNL. Michael Herr, *Dispatches* (New York: Alfred A. Knopf, 1968, 1978), 44. Levels of force in IDA Study S-316, "The Productivity of Major Military Forces in Vietnam: A Statistical Analysis of Three Years of War," Box 2, Donn A. Starry Papers, MHI. Security not substituting for pacification in John Prados, *The Hidden History of the Vietnam War* (Chicago: Ivan R. Dee, 1995), 220. On this point, see also George R. Vickers, "U.S. Military Strategy and the Vietnam War," in *The Vietnam War: Vietnamese and American Perspectives*, eds. Jayne S. Werner and Luu Doan Huynh (Armonk, NY: M.E. Sharpe, 1993), 124.

92. Cook, *The Advisor*, 151. Michael A. Cohen, "The Myth of a Kinder, Gentler War," *World Policy Journal* 27, no. 1 (Spring 2010): 81–82. Stathis N. Kalyvas and Matthew Adam Kocher, "The Dynamics of Violence in Vietnam: An Analysis of the Hamlet Evaluation System (HES)," *Journal of Peace Research* 46, no. 3 (2009): 335.

93. Vann in Hunt, *Pacification*, 185. Abrams to Wheeler, 6 October 1969, Folder 6, Box 65, NSC Files, Vietnam Subject Files, RNL. Maj. Gen. Harris W. Hollis, 1 April 1970, Senior Officer Debriefing Reports, CMH, p. 6.

94. "Gooks" in Robert Jay Lifton, *Home from the War, Vietnam Veterans: Neither Victims nor Executioners* (New York: Simon & Schuster, 1973), 196–197. Veteran quoted in Baker, *Nam*, 171. Nick Turse argues "the stunning scale of civilian suffering" was the "inevitable outcome of deliberate policies, dictated at the highest levels of the military." *Kill Anything That Moves: The Real American War in Vietnam* (New York: Metropolitan Books, 2013), 6.

95. "Lowest people" in Heather Marie Stur, *Beyond Combat: Women and Gender in the Vietnam War Era* (New York: Cambridge University Press, 2011), 39. "Few rapes" in Bergerud, *Red Thunder, Tropic Lightning*, 229. Opportunities and temptations in Jack Crouchet, *Vietnam Stories: A Judge's Memoir* (Niwot: University Press of Colorado, 1997), 170. On this topic, see also James William Gibson, *The Perfect War: The War We Couldn't Lose and How We Did* (New York: Vintage Books, 1986), 262–265. Peter Arnett, " 'Sanitizing' a Stubborn Viet Village," *The Washington Post*, 12 August 1968.

96. Kevin M. Boylan, "Goodnight Saigon: American Provincial Advisors' Final Impressions of the Vietnam War," *Journal of Military History* 78 (January 2014): 238. USMACV, Command History, 1970, Vol. II, NARA, p. VIII-15. On enduring problems with HES, see John V. Tunney, *Measuring Hamlet Security in Vietnam: Report of a Special Study Mission* (Washington, DC: U.S. Government Printing Office, 1969), 7–8; and "The Situation in Vietnam: Overview and Outlook," 24 January 1969, Folder 1, Box 63, NSC Files, Vietnam Subject Files, RNL, pp. 6–7. For a review of the history of HES, see Erwin R. Brigham, "Pacification Measurement in Vietnam: The Hamlet Evaluation System," Folder 18, Box 3, Glenn Helm Collection, TTUVA.

97. Brig. Gen. Douglas Kinnard quoted in Kurt Jacobsen, *Pacification and Its Discontents* (Chicago: Prickly Paradigm Press, 2009), 45. Robert G. Kaiser, "New Gauge of Saigon's Control May Reduce Old Optimistic Bias," *The Washington Post*, 3 March 1970.

98. Rural Public Attitude Survey, 25 December 1969, Folder 6, Box 70, NSC Files, Vietnam Subject Files, RNL. "Analysis of Pacification Attitude Analysis System Results," 10 January 1970, Safe 71, Historians Files, CMH. "What the Vietnamese Peasant Thinks," Pacification Attitudes Analysis System, 1970, Folder 151, Thayer Papers, CMH. One report, however, argued it was an "almost hopeless task of trying to find out what the Vietnamese really think as distinct from what they say to Americans or in the presence of Americans." "Vietnam: December 1969," TTUVA, p. 2.

99. Thayer, *War without Fronts*, 174–177. Copies of the original PAAS reports are housed in MHI.

100. Vietnam Lessons Learned No. 73, "Defeat of VC Infrastructure," 20 November 1968, MACV Lessons Learned, Box 1, RG 472, NARA. Felix Belaire Jr., "U.S. Aide Defends Pacification Program in Vietnam Despite Killing of Civilians," *New York Times*, 20 July 1971. Phung Hoang Advisors Handbook, 20 November 1970, Folder 06, Box 04, United States Armed Forces Manual Collection, TTUVA. On inauguration of Phoenix, see Andradé, *Ashes to Ashes*, 72–73.

101. Abrams to Wheeler, 24 October 1968, Abrams Messages #1632, CMH. LTG Fred C. Weyand, "Intelligence Is the Key," 1 December 1968, USARV Combat Intelligence Lessons, Box 1, RG 472, NARA. Abrams saw the VCI as an "important and integral element of the effort being directed from Hanoi to overthrow and replace the government of Vietnam." Abrams to McCain, 27 December 1969, Folder 1, Box 66, NSC Files, Vietnam Subject Files, RNL. On Phoenix's link to pacification, see Editorial Note, *FRUS*, 1964–1968, VII: 762–763.

102. Colby in Sorley, *Vietnam Chronicles*, 381. Phillip Davidson, interview by Ted Gittinger, 30 March 1982, Oral History Collection, LBJL, I-I-29.

103. Colby, *Lost Victory*, 250. Figures in Andrade and Willbanks, "CORDS/Phoenix," 20. Colby's assessment in Woods, *Shadow Warrior*, 315.

104. Lucian W. Pye, *Observations on the Chieu Hoi Program* (Santa Monica, CA: RAND Corporation, 1969), ix. J. M. Carrier and C. A. H. Thomson, *Viet Cong Motivation and Morale: The Special Case of Chieu Hoi* (Santa Monica, Ca.: RAND Corporation, 1966), xiv. Figures in Thayer, *War without Fronts*, 198. On the relation between military operations and Chieu Hoi, see USMACV CORDS, Pacification Priority Area Summary, 3 September 1968, Folder 65, US Marine Corps History Division Vietnam War Documents Collection, TTUVA, p. 14; and HQ USMACV, Chieu Hoi Returnees in Support of Counterinsurgency Operations, 29 April 1967, Chieu Hoi Exploitation Folder, Box 1, Richard M. Lee Papers, MHI.

105. Herrington, *Silence Was a Weapon*, 17. Luận, *Nationalist in the Viet Nam Wars*, 345.

106. Wayne L. Cooper, "Operation Phoenix: A Vietnam Fiasco Seen from Within," 18 June 1972, Folder 05, Box 24, Douglas Pike Collection: Unit 01-Assessment and Strategy, TTUVA. Legal rights in "The Phoenix Program" January 1975, Folder 05, Box 25, Douglas Pike Collection: Unit 02-Military Operations, TTUVA. Intelligence in Prados, *The Hidden History of the Vietnam War*, 215; and Samuel A. Adams, interview by Ted Gittinger, 20 September 1984, Oral History Collection, LBJL, p. I-20. See also John R. Galvin, *Fighting the Cold War: A Soldier's Memoir* (Lexington: University Press of Kentucky, 2015), 197.

107. Andrade and Willbanks, 21. Holes in Jeffrey Race, *War Comes to Long An: Revolutionary Conflict in a Vietnamese Province* (Berkeley: University of California Press, 1972), 242. See also Ahern, *Vietnam Declassified*, 353. David Hunt, *Vietnam's Southern Revolution: From Peasant Insurrection to Total War* (Amherst: University of Massachusetts Press, 2008), 209. Mark Moyar argues, unconvincingly, that the "villagers did not assign much blame to the Allies for the attacks because they respected the power of the Allies." *Phoenix and the Birds of Prey: Counterinsurgency and Counterterrorism in Vietnam* (Lincoln: University of Nebraska Press, 1997, 2007), 302.

108. 25th Division Pacification Operations in Hau Nghia Province, 7 August 1966, US 25th Division Pacification Folder, Historians Files, CMH. Lt. Col. Boyd T. Bashore, "Revolutionary Development Support in the Republic of Vietnam: Tropic Lightning Helping Hand and 'The Other War'" (student essay, US Army War College, MHI, 19 January 1968). See also MG Fred C. Weyand, "Winning the People in Hau Nghia Province," *Army* 17, no. 1 (January 1967): 52–55.

109. Toan Thang III in J3 Inputs to Report of the MACV Effort, MHI, pp. II-80 to II-85. 25th Infantry Division Operational Report for Quarterly Period Ending 31 July 1967, 19 August 1967, Folder 08, Box 02, Ron Leonard Collection, TTUVA. MACCORDS-EVAL, Evaluation of Pacification Technique of the 2d Brigade, US 25th Infantry Division, 20 December 1968, Box 22, HQ USMACV Command Information Publications, 1967–1972, RG 472, NARA. Maj. Gen. Ellis W. Williamson, 26 September 1969, Senior Officer Debriefing Reports, Box 18, RG 472, NARA.

110. Case Study, Operation "Randolph Glen," 7 December 1969–31 March 1970, Drawer 1, Box 1, Unit History Files, 101st Airborne Division, MACV Command Historian's Collection, MHI, p. 2. For similar efforts, see Pacification Studies Group, The Infantry Company Intensive Pacification Program (ICIPP), 7 January 1970, CORDS Historical Working Group Files, 1967–1973, Box 23, Plans and Reports, RG 472, NARA.

111. HQ USMACV, US Combat Forces in Support of Pacification, Lesson Learned No. 80, 1970, Pacification Operations Folder, Historians Files, CMH, pp. 8–10.

112. Brig. Gen. H. S. Cunningham, 10 November 1970, Senior Officer Debriefing Reports, CMH. Case Study, Operation "Randolph Glen," MHI, p. 3. On problems with Washington Green, see Kevin M. Boylan, "The Red Queen's Race: Operation Washington Green and Pacification in Binh Dinh Province, 1969–70," *Journal of Military History* 73, no. 4 (October 2009): 1195–1230; and Fitzgerald, *Learning to Forget*, 30–33.

113. "Notes from a Conversation with General Abrams and Lt. General Ewell," 18 January 1970, Folder 3, Box 1009, NSC Files, Alexander M. Haig Special File, RNL, p. 4. Col. Audley C. Harris, "Youth and Revolutionary Development," *Military Review* 50, no. 5 (May 1970): 26. Combined Campaign Plan, 1968, Historians Files, CMH, pp. 7–9.

114. Collins, Senior Officer Debriefing Reports, CMH, p. 5.

115. USMACV, "One War," MACV Command Overview, CMH, p. 16

116. Figures in A Systems Analysis View of the Vietnam War: 1965–1972, Vol. 7--Report of Vietnam Armed Forces, Geog. V. Vietnam-319.1, CMH, p. 2. Halperin and Moor to Kissinger, 8 July 1969, *FRUS*, 1969-1976, VI: 289. Ngo Quang Truong, "Territorial Forces," in Sorley, *The Vietnam War*, 211. For the number of missions comprising the "eight priority pacification programs," see CORDS, Pacification Priority Area Summary, TTUVA, pp. 8–15.

117. Dong Van Khuyen, "The RVNAF," in Sorley, *The Vietnam War*, 68. CUPP in Lt. Gen. Melvin Zais, 20 August 1970, Senior Officer Debriefing Report, General Holdings, MHI, p. 16.

118. Abrams in Sorley, *Vietnam Chronicles*, 291. RF/PF casualty rates in Gibson, *The Perfect War*, 294–295. Henry A. Kissinger, Vietnam Trip Report, March 1970, Folder 2, Box 92, NSC Files, Vietnam Subject Files, RNL.

119. Pacification Studies Group, Motivation Indoctrination Program, 18 December 1969, CORDS Historical Working Group Files, 1967–1973, Box 9, RG 472, NARA. "Paper tiger" in Christian G. Appy, *Patriots: The Vietnam War Remembered from All Sides* (New York: Viking Press, 2003), 409. "Concept of nation" in Maj. Robert V. Hubbard, "The Political Army in Its Asian Context," *Military Review* 48, no. 10 (October 1968): 69. ARVN deficiencies in Memorandum for the President's File, 24 November 1970, *FRUS*, 1969–1976, VII: 190.

120. Nguyen Van Chau quoted in Andrew Wiest, *Vietnam's Forgotten Army: Heroism and Betrayal in the ARVN* (New York: New York University Press, 2008), 33. On ARVN improving, see Brian M. Jenkins, "A People's Army for South Vietnam: A Vietnamese Solution," November 1971, Folder 05, Box 04, Douglas Pike Collection: Unit 11-Monographs, TTUVA, p. 8. Lack of political training in Brigham, *ARVN*, 44–45; and Khuyen, "The RVNAF," 74.

121. Dominating land in 3rd Brigade, 82nd Airborne Division, Pacification Policy, 2 May 1969, Pacification Operations Folder, Historians Files, CMH. On controlling fragmented space, see Biggs, *Quagmire*, 185, 203; and Hunt, *Vietnam's Southern Revolution*, 174. On liberation and control, see Douglas Pike, "Liberation Is Double Speak," Folder 05, Box 20, Douglas Pike Collection, Unit 01: Assessment and Strategy, TTUVA; and Martin G. Clemis, "Competing and Incompatible Visions: Revolution, Pacification, and the Political Organization of Space during the Second Indochina War," paper presented at the Society for Military History conference, Kansas City, Missouri, 5 April 2014, p. 5.

122. USMACV, Command History, 1970, Vol. I, NARA, pp. II-4 to II-5. Plan for Pacification and Development, 1970, Historians Files, CMH, pp. 5–9. Staff optimism in Sorley, *Vietnam Chronicles*, 286; and MACV Long Range Planning Task Group, Area Security Principles and Application, Area Security Concept, 1969-1970, Historians Files, CMH, p. 34.

123. Colby, *Lost Victory*, 277–278. Eighty percent in Prados, *Lost Crusader*, 202. On little change in strategy, see Sorley, *Vietnam Chronicles*, 256; Birtle, *U.S. Army Counterinsurgency and Contingency Operations Doctrine*, 367; and Bergerud, *The Dynamics of Defeat*, 223, 242.

124. Continuing focus on security first in USMACV, Command History, 1970, Vol. II, NARA, p. VIII-3; and Plan for Pacification and Development, 1970, Historians Files, CMH, 12.

125. "Cultural production" from Robert K. Brigham, email to author, 11 July 2016. Brig. Gen. Gordon J. Duquemin, 15 September 1970, Senior Officer Debriefing Reports, CMH, p. 2. Access to the people in Gary R. Hess, *Vietnam and the United States: Origins and Legacy of War* (New York: Twayne, 1990), 99.

126. Donavan, *Once a Warrior King*, 128. See also George A. Carver, "The Faceless Viet Cong," *Foreign Affairs* 44, no. 3 (April 1966): 372; and Douglas Porch, *Counterinsurgency: Exposing the Myths of the New Way of War* (New York: Cambridge University Press, 2013), 219. One officer, though, believed the "Tet attacks of 1968 caused deep resentment against the VC in the Delta." Maj. Gen. G. S. Eckhardt, 1 July 1969, Box 4, Senior Officer Debriefing Reports, RG 472, NARA, p. 23.

127. Liberated areas in *Victory in Vietnam: The Official History of the People's Army of Vietnam, 1954–1975*, trans. Merle L. Pribbenow (Lawrence: University Press of Kansas, 2002), 238. Declining tax and recruitment base in Moyar, *Phoenix and the Birds of Prey*, 395. See also Kolko, *Anatomy of a War*, 387. Rural class in Bradley, *Vietnam at War*, 141. Changing nature of revolution in Elliott, *The Vietnamese War*, 438.

128. Trinh Duc quoted in Mark Atwood Lawrence, *The Vietnam War: An International History in Documents* (New York: Oxford University Press, 2014), 139. Coercion in Ahern, *Vietnam Declassified*, 359. John Prados, *Vietnam: The History of an Unwinnable War, 1945–1975* (Lawrence: University Press of Kansas, 2009), 328. Stanley Karnow, *Vietnam: A History* (New York: Viking Press, 1983), 603. Boylan argues that despite their troubles, the NLF was still able to "preserve their psychological hold over a large segment of the population." "Goodnight Saigon," 235.

129. CORDS evaluators in Wiesner, *Victims and Survivors*, 113. Colby quoted in Sorley, *Vietnam Chronicles*, 459. Assessment of Refugee Problem, 1968 CORDS/Refugee Division, February 1969, Folder 06, Box 31, Douglas Pike Collection: Unit 03-Refugees and Civilian Casualties, TTUVA.

130. In Allan E. Goodman and Lawrence M. Franks, "The Dynamics of Migration to Saigon, 1964-1972," *Pacific Affairs* 48, no. 2 (Summer 1975): 204. Abrams reported that the active caseload of refugees at the beginning of 1969 was roughly 1.4 million people. Abrams to Wheeler, 29 January 1970, Historians Files, CMH, p. 12.

131. HES figures in Thayer, *War Without Fronts*, 144. Socioeconomic dislocation in Robert K. Brigham, "Vietnamese Society at War," in *The Columbia History of the Vietnam War*, ed. David L. Anderson (New York: Columbia University Press, 2011), 321. See also The Military-Economic Situation in South Vietnam, 11 August 1970, Folder 1, Box 92, NSC Files, Vietnam Subject Files, RNL; and FitzGerald, *Fire in the Lake*, 411. Bergerud, *The Dynamics of Defeat*, 254.

132. Village Security Planning Guide for District and Mobile Advisory Teams, 1970, Folder 02, Box 01, Ronald Tausch Collection, TTUVA, p. 7. Political fragmentation in William J. Duiker, *Sacred War: Nationalism and Revolution in a Divided Vietnam* (Boston: McGraw-Hill, 1995), 252.

133. Duong Van Mai Elliott, *The Sacred Willow: Four Generations in the Life of a Vietnamese Family* (New York: Oxford University Press, 1999), 317. The BDM Corporation, "A Study of Strategic Lessons Learned in Vietnam," Vol. II, South Vietnam, General Holdings, MHI, p. vii. William S. Turley, *The Second Indochina War: A Concise Political and Military History*, 2nd ed. (Lanham, MD: Rowman & Littlefield, 1986, 2009), 172. Of note, Nixon recalled that "we had won the political struggle for the allegiance of the South Vietnamese people." *No More Vietnams*, 134. Moyar tends to agree. *Phoenix and the Birds of Prey*, 317.

134. Galvin, *Fighting the Cold War*, 135. Kolko, *Anatomy of a War*, 394–396.

135. Thuy Yen in Neil L. Jamieson, *Understanding Vietnam* (Berkeley: University of California Press, 1993), 249. See also Tran Van Dinh, "The Destruction of a Society," in *Why Are We Still in Vietnam?*, eds. Sam Brown and Len Ackland (New York: Random House, 1970), 65. Mass death in Heonik Kwon, *Ghosts of War in Vietnam* (New York: Cambridge University Press, 2008), 32. Collapsing structures in The Vietnamese Village, Handbook for Advisors, TTUVA, p. 1. On the role of dislocation in war, see Chris Hedges, *War Is a Force That Gives Us Meaning* (New York: Public Affairs, 2002), 106. Saturation of blood taken from roundtable comments made by Nick Turse, The Vietnam War Then and Now: Assessing the Critical Lessons, Washington, DC, 29 April 2015.

Chapter 4

1. Diffusion of power in Hal Brands, *What Good Is Grand Strategy? Power and Purpose in American Statecraft from Harry S. Truman to George W. Bush* (Ithaca, NY: Cornell University Press, 2014), 67.

2. Kissinger and Nixon quoted in Jeffrey Kimball, *The Vietnam War Files: Uncovering the Secret History of Nixon-Era Strategy* (Lawrence: University Press of Kansas, 2004), 45–46. See also Robert Dallek, *Nixon and Kissinger: Partners in Power* (New York: HarperCollins, 2007), 156; and Dorothy C. Donnelly, "A Settlement of Sorts: Henry's Kissinger's Negotiations and America's Extraction from Vietnam," *Peace & Change* 9, no. 2/3 (Summer 1983): 57. Nixon reiterated this argument in 1977 with David Frost. See John Dumbrell, *Rethinking the Vietnam War* (New York: Palgrave Macmillan, 2012), 109.

3. Don Oberdorfer, "Nixon Meets Thieu, GIs on Brief Vietnam Tour," *The Washington Post*, 31 July 1969. Melvin Small, "Containing Domestic Enemies: Richard M. Nixon and the War at Home," in *Shadow on the White House: Presidents and the Vietnam War, 1945–1975*, ed. David L. Anderson (Lawrence: University Press of Kansas, 1993), 133. On global interests and obligations outside of Asia, see William S. Turley, *The Second Indochina War: A Concise Political and Military History*, 2nd ed. (Lanham, MD: Rowman & Littlefield, 1986, 2009), 240.

4. Choosing freely in Chester L. Cooper, *The Lost Crusade: America in Vietnam* (New York: Dodd, Mead, 1970), 443. On deteriorating Sino-Soviet relations, see Qiang Zhai, *China and the Vietnam Wars, 1950–1975* (Chapel Hill: University of North Carolina Press, 2000), 181. Flexibility in Brands, 60.

5. De-ideologize in H. W. Brands, *The Devil We Knew: Americans and the Cold War* (New York: Oxford University Press, 1993), 123. Abstract crusade in Chris Tudda, *A Cold War Turning Point: Nixon and China, 1969–1972* (Baton Rouge: Louisiana State University Press, 2012), 91. Redefining US objectives in George Donelson Moss, *Vietnam: An American Ordeal*, 5th ed. (Upper Saddle River, NJ: Pearson Prentice Hill, 1990, 2006), 327–328; and Leon J. Perkowski, "Deterrence vs. Disentanglement: Military Resistance to Nixon's Troop Withdrawal from South Korea, 1969–1971," paper presented at the Society for Military History conference, Montgomery, AL, 11 April 2015, pp. 7–8. Army Chief of Staff William C. Westmoreland argued the army had to fight a limited war in Vietnam while also maintaining "its world-wide deployments in other areas of the world in support of our national interests." In "From Army of the '70s: 'A Flawless Performance,'" *Army* 20, no. 10 (October 1970): 24.

6. Max Frankel, "Vietnam Dilemma: Nixon Is Forced to 'Negotiate' on Three Fronts," *New York Times*, 23 March 1969. See also Allan E. Goodman, *The Lost Peace: America's Search for a Negotiated Settlement of the Vietnam War* (Stanford, CA: Hoover Institution Press, 1978), 49–50. On avoiding a precipitous withdrawal, see George C. Herring, *America's Longest War: The United States and Vietnam, 1950–1975*, 4th ed. (New York: McGraw-Hill, 1979, 2002), 273.

7. Richard A. Hunt, *Pacification: The American Struggle for Vietnam's Hearts and Minds* (Boulder, CO: Westview Press, 1995), 213. Pierre Asselin, *A Bitter Peace: Washington, Hanoi, and the Making of the Paris Agreement* (Chapel Hill: University of North Carolina Press, 2002), xii. Lien-Hang T. Nguyen, "Waging War on All Fronts: Nixon, Kissinger and the Vietnam War, 1969–1972," in *Nixon in the World: American Foreign Relations, 1969–1977*, eds. Fredrik Logevall and Andrew Preston (New York: Oxford University Press, 2008), 190.

8. Henry Kissinger, *White House Years* (Boston: Little, Brown, 1979), 298. Kimball, *The Vietnam War Files*, 88. On diplomatic issues from a South Vietnamese perspective, see Bùi Diễm with David Chanoff, *In the Jaws of History* (Bloomington: Indiana University Press, 1999), 231. On Cambodia's frontier breaking down, see Ben Kiernan, "The Impact on Cambodia of the U.S. Intervention in Vietnam," in *The Vietnam War: Vietnamese and American Perspectives*, eds. Jayne S. Werner and Luu Doan Huynh (Armonk, NY: M.E. Sharpe, 1993), 219.

9. Simultaneity in Guy J. Pauker, *An Essay on Vietnamization* (Santa Monica, CA: RAND Corporation, 1971), 1. Dave Richard Palmer, *Summons of the Trumpet: U.S. -Vietnam in Perspective* (San Rafael, CA: Presidio Press, 1978), 222. Kissinger recalled there were "three concurrent efforts until Saigon could stand on its own feet: American troop withdrawals; the rapid strengthening of South Vietnamese forces; and the progressive weakening of the enemy." *White House Years*, 986.

10. Considerable risk in Ewell to Abrams, 17 July 1969, Abrams Messages #3611, CMH. On multiple tasks, see J3 Inputs to Report of the MACV Effort, 1968–1970, Filing Cabinet B9, Box 3, MACV Command Historian's Collection, MHI, p. III-2; and Phillip B. Davidson, *Vietnam at War, the History: 1946-1975* (Novato, CA: Presidio Press, 1988), 538. On tensions, see Robert D. Schulzinger, *A Time for War: The United States and Vietnam, 1941–1975* (New York: Oxford University Press, 1997), 279.

11. Kissinger to Nixon, 10 September 1969, FRUS, 1969–1976, VI: 373. See also Turley, *The Second Indochina War*, 164. "Vietnam Dilemma: A First-Hand Explanation," *U.S. News & World Report*, 16 June 1969, pp. 26–29.

12. On intelligence, see Sharon A. Maneki, "The Son Tay Raid: An Intelligence Paradox," *Journal of American-East Asian Relations* 10, no. 3/4 (Fall–Winter 2001): 211–219; and

Michael B. Peterson, *The Vietnam Cauldron: Defense Intelligence in the War for Southeast Asia* (Washington, DC: Defense Intelligence Agency, 2012), 26–29. Kimball, *The Vietnam War Files*, 139. John G. Hubbell, *P.O.W.: A Definitive Account of the American Prisoner-of-War Experience in Vietnam, 1964–1973* (New York: Reader's Digest Press, 1976), 536–538. Interestingly, Hubbell called the raid a "huge success" because Hanoi now feared they may lose "their most important bargaining tool."

13. Laird to Nixon, 4 April 1970, *FRUS, 1969–1976*, VI: 766. Kissinger to Nixon, 20 January 1971, *FRUS, 1969–1976*, VII: 292.

14. On National League of Families, see Glenn Robins, "The American POW Experience," in *America and the Vietnam War: Re-examining the Culture and History of a Generation*, eds. Andrew Wiest, Mary Kathryn Barbier, and Glenn Robins (New York: Routledge, 2010), 181; Michael J. Allen, " 'Help Us Tell the Truth about Vietnam': POW/MIA Politics and the End of the American War," in *Making Sense of the Vietnam Wars: Local, National, and Transnational Perspectives*, eds. Mark Philip Bradley and Marilyn B. Young (New York: Oxford University Press, 2008), 261; and Michael J. Allen, *Until the Last Man Comes Home: POWs, MIAs, and the Unending Vietnam War* (Chapel Hill: University of North Carolina Press, 2009), 29. Political advantage in Ken Hughes, *Fatal Politics: The Nixon Tapes, the Vietnam War, and the Casualties of Reelection* (Charlottesville: University of Virginia Press, 2015), 6. On POW agreement before a ceasefire, see American Embassy, Paris, 15 January 1969, Folder 1, Box 66, NSC Files, Vietnam Subject Files, RNL. *TIME* reported, "If it was a war without heroes, many Americans were intent upon making the prisoners fill the role." Quoted in Allen, *Until the Last Man Comes Home*, 66.

15. Richard Nixon, *Public Papers of the Presidents of the United States, 1970* (Washington, DC: US Government Printing Office, 1971), 150. Allen, *Until the Last Man Comes Home*, 15–16. Allen, " 'Help Us Tell the Truth about Vietnam,' " 253.

16. Douglas Brinkley and Luke A. Nichter, eds., *The Nixon Tapes, 1971–1972* (Boston: Houghton Mifflin Harcourt, 2014), 105. See also Michael J. Allen, Review, *Passport: The Society for Historians of American Foreign Relations Review* 43, no. 3 (January 2013): 11. Hubbell argues there was "little question that Hanoi was now painfully aware that the United States was POW-conscious." *P.O.W.*, 551.

17. Allen, *Until the Last Man Comes Home*, 297. Christian Appy, *American Reckoning: The Vietnam War and Our National Identity* (New York: Viking Press, 2015), 177–264. On "new arrivals" into the POW camps being opposed to the war, see Hubbell, 581.

18. Fonda quoted in Jerry Lembke, *Hanoi Jane: War, Sex & Fantasies of Betrayal* (Amherst: University of Massachusetts Press, 2010), 23. Lembke argues persuasively that the "Hanoi Jane" persona was a postwar construction. Amy Scott, "Patriots for Peace: People-to-People Diplomacy and the Anti-war Movement," in *America and the Vietnam War*, 135.

19. Haig to Kissinger, 1 July 1969, Folder 1, Box 74, NSC Files, Vietnam Subject Files, RNL.

20. Anthony Lewis, "Hanoi Aide Says P.O.W. Agreement Can Be Separate," *New York Times*, 7 July 1971. Brinkley and Nichter, *The Nixon Tapes*, 125.

21. Notes of Meeting, 21 May 1968, *FRUS, 1964–1968*, VI: 696. Robinson Risner, *The Passing of the Night: My Seven Years as a Prisoner of the North Vietnamese* (New York: Random House, 1973), 259. On POW families favoring a rapid US withdrawal, see Allen, " 'Help Us Tell the Truth about Vietnam,' " 266–267.

22. William J. Duiker, *Sacred War: Nationalism and Revolution in a Divided Vietnam* (Boston: McGraw-Hill, 1995), 224–225. J3 Inputs to Report of the MACV Effort, MHI, p. II-6. Moor to Kissinger, 8 April 1969, Folder 6, Box 65, NSC Files, Vietnam Subject Files, RNL. Bunker to Nixon, 16 July 1969, Folder 10, Box 75, NSC Files, Vietnam Subject Files, RNL.

23. Political training in *Victory in Vietnam: The Official History of the People's Army of Vietnam, 1954–1975*, trans. Merle L. Pribbenow (Lawrence: University Press of Kansas, 2002), 242. Wheeler quoted in Lewis Sorley, ed., *Vietnam Chronicles: The Abrams Tapes, 1968–1972* (Lubbock: Texas Tech University Press, 2004), 268. Economy of force in Carver to Lemos, 21 August 1969, Folder 3, Box 91, NSC Files, Vietnam Subject Files, RNL.

24. Communist Strategy as Reflected in Lao Dong Party and COSVN Resolutions, Folder 26, Box 7, Douglas Pike Collection: Unit 06—Democratic Republic of Vietnam, TTUVA, pp. 7–12. For Abrams's assessment of these resolutions, see Abrams to Wheeler, 3 September

1969, Abrams Messages #4250, CMH; and Abrams to Moorer, 6 October 1970, Abrams Messages #8278, CMH. On how the enemy's strategy related to Vietnamization and pacification, see Abrams to Moorer, 6 October 1969, Folder 3, Box 74, NSC Files, Vietnam Subject Files, RNL.

25. COSVN Resolution No. 9, July 1969, MHI, p. 19. Ang Cheng Guan, *Ending the Vietnam War: The Vietnamese Communists' Perspective* (London and New York: Routledge Curzon, 2004), 21–22. Talk and fight strategy in James H. Willbanks, *Abandoning Vietnam: How America Left and South Vietnam Lost Its War* (Lawrence: University Press of Kansas, 2004), 67; and Lien-Hang T. Nguyen, *Hanoi's War: An International History of the War for Peace in Vietnam* (Chapel Hill: University of North Carolina Press, 2012), 130–131.

26. Kissinger to Rogers, 27 July 1969, Folder 4, Box 67, NSC Files, Vietnam Subject Files, RNL. On the PRG, see American Consul to Rogers, 16 June 1969, Folder 4, Box 67, NSC Files, Vietnam Subject Files, RNL. De facto recognition in Rostow to Johnson, 18 November 1968, *FRUS, 1964–1968*, VII: 661.

27. Nguyen, *Hanoi's War*, 142–144. Jeffrey P. Kimball, "Richard M. Nixon and the Vietnam War: The Paradox of Disengagement with Escalation," in *The Columbia History of the Vietnam War*, ed. David L. Anderson (New York: Columbia University Press, 2011), 222. Prolonged negotiations in Jeffrey Kimball, *Nixon's Vietnam War* (Lawrence: University Press of Kansas, 1998), 72. Mutual withdrawal in Jeremi Suri, *Henry Kissinger and the American Century* (Cambridge, MA: Belknap Press of Harvard University Press, 2007), 227.

28. Kissinger to Nixon, 6 September 1969, Folder 4, Box 69, NSC Files, Vietnam Subject Files, RNL.

29. Ho's last testament in *Vietnam and America: A Documented* History, eds. Marvin E. Gettleman, Jane Franklin, Marilyn Young, and H. Bruce Franklin (New York: Grove Press, 1985), 439–441. K. W. Taylor, *A History of the Vietnamese* (New York: Cambridge University Press, 2013), 611. See also *Victory in Vietnam*, 252–253.

30. Bui Tin quoted in Guan, *Ending the Vietnam War*, 29.

31. "The Situation in Vietnam: Overview and Outlook," 24 January 1969, Folder 1, Box 63, NSC Files, Vietnam Subject Files, RNL, p. 8.

32. Le Duan, "Political and Military Forces in Revolutionary Warfare," in *Guerrilla Warfare and Marxism: A Collection of Writings from Karl Marx to the Present on Armed Struggles for Liberation and for Socialism*, ed. William J. Pomeroy (New York: International Publishers, 1968), 222. William J. Duiker, "Victory by Other Means: The Foreign Policy of the Democratic Republic of Vietnam," in *Why the North Won the Vietnam War*, ed. Marc Jason Gilbert (New York: Palgrave, 2002), 69. William J. Duiker, *The Communist Road to Power*, 2nd ed. (Boulder, CO: Westview Press, 1981, 1996), 304–305.

33. Duiker, *Sacred War*, 192-193. Guan, 32-33. David W. P. Elliott, "Hanoi's Strategy in the Second Indochina War," in Werner and Huynh, *The Vietnam War*, 89.

34. Kissinger, *White House Years*, 444.

35. Kissinger to Nixon, 3 April 1969, *FRUS, 1969–1976*, VI: 181. On Abrams, see Willbanks, *Abandoning Vietnam*, 14.

36. Pace of public opinion in Kissinger to Nixon, 30 October 1969, *FRUS, 1969–1976*, VI: 476. Abrams to McCain, 2 August 1969, Abrams Messages #3735, CMH. In August 1969, the MACV order of battle summary showed a total of 234,687, including 79,641 NVA in NVA units, 17,000 to 19,000 NVA in VC units, with the remainder (136,046 to 138,046) being VC in VC units. *Records of the Military Assistance Command Vietnam*, Part 2, *Classified Studies from the Combined Intelligence Center Vietnam, 1965–1973* (Frederick, MD: University Publications of America, 1988), reel 6. Carroll Kilpatrick, "U.S. Sets GI Cut of 35,000," *The Washington Post*, 17 September 1969. Robert B. Semple Jr., "Nixon Announces New Vietnam Cut of About 35,000," *New York Times*, 17 September 1969.

37. Laird quoted in Dale Van Atta, *With Honor: Melvin Laird in War, Peace, and Politics* (Madison: University of Wisconsin Press, 2008), 201. Henry Kissinger, *Ending the Vietnam War: A History of America's Involvement in and Extrication from the Vietnam War* (New York: Simon & Schuster, 2003), 93.

38. Abrams to McCain, 23 November 1969, Abrams Messages #4748, CMH. For a similar assessment—"The military situation was tough. Throughout Vietnam, the enemy units were more

numerous than before, and our outfits were leaving one by one"—see John R. Galvin, *Fighting the Cold War: A Soldier's Memoir* (Lexington: University Press of Kentucky, 2015), 178. Kissinger felt similarly. Kissinger to Nixon, 19 January 1970, *FRUS, 1969–1976,* VI: 536.

39. Competing demands in William B. Rosson, "Four Periods of American Involvement in Vietnam: Development and Implementation of Policy, Strategy and Programs, Described and Analyzed on the Basis of Experience at Progressively Senior Levels" (Ph.D. diss., University of Oxford, 1979), 234. History of the 101st Airborne Division, Summer 1969–Summer 1970, Folder 122, Box 09, Vietnam Archive Collection, TTUVA.

40. Joseph Alsop, "Generals See Winning the War as Best Help to Negotiations," *The Washington Post,* 26 April 1968. William C. Westmoreland, *A Soldier Reports* (Garden City, NY: Doubleday, 1976), 471. On disagreeing with withdrawal timelines, see Graham A. Cosmas, *MACV: The Joint Command in the Years of Withdrawal, 1968–1973* (Washington, DC: Center of Military History, 2007), 161; William Bundy, *A Tangled Web: The Making of Foreign Policy in the Nixon Presidency* (New York: Hill and Wang, 1998), 66; and Sorley, *Vietnam Chronicles,* 186. Yitzhak Klein, however, has argued that "military planners cannot afford to agonize, Hamlet-like, over the divergent tendencies of politics and the battlefield." In "A Theory of Strategic Culture," *Comparative Strategy* vol. 10, no. 1 (January 1991): 6.

41. Mission and resources in Willard J. Webb, *The Joint Chiefs of Staff and The War in Vietnam, 1969–1970* (Washington, DC: Office of Joint History, 2002), 200. "Vietnamization: Policy Under Fire," *TIME,* 9 February 1970, 26.

42. Bunker quoted in Howard B. Schaffer, *Ellsworth Bunker: Global Troubleshooter, Vietnam Hawk* (Chapel Hill: University of North Carolina Press, 2003), 220. Alexander M. Haig Jr., with Charles McCarry, *Inner Circles: How America Changed the World, a Memoir* (New York: Warner Books, 1992), 229. Richard A. Hunt, *Melvin Laird and the Foundation of the Post-Vietnam Military, 1969–1973* (Washington, DC: Office of the Secretary of Defense Historical Office, 2015), 128–129.

43. Kissinger to Nixon, 8 March 1969, 7 July 1969, *FRUS, 1969–1976,* VI: 98, 287. Hard line in Richard M. Nixon, *RN: The Memoirs of Richard Nixon* (New York: Grosset & Dunlap, 1978), 408. See also Walter Isaacson, *Kissinger: A Biography* (New York: Simon & Schuster, 1992), 238; and David F. Schmitz, *Richard Nixon and the Vietnam War: The End of the American Century* (Lanham, MD: Rowman & Littlefield, 2014), 60.

44. Kissinger to Nixon, January 1969, Folder 3, Box 91, NSC Files, Vietnam Subject Files, RNL. Jack Anderson, "Kissinger the Hawk," *The Washington Post,* 5 October 1969. Kissinger, *White House Years,* 971. Henry Kissinger, *Diplomacy* (New York: Simon & Schuster, 1994), 682.

45. Terrence Smith, "Laird Declares Pullout Goes On Despite the Foe," *New York Times,* 14 February 1970. "G.I. Publications Asked Not to Stress Fighting," *New York Times,* 13 February 1970. Manipulating public opinion in Herring, *America's Longest War,* 283. On related budget pressures, see Hunt, *Melvin Laird,* 136.

46. Joseph Alsop, "Nixon Would Be Wise to Heed Abrams' Call for Pullout Pause," *The Washington Post,* 30 March 1970. Joseph Alsop, "A Risk Is Involved in Troop Withdrawals," *The Hartford Courant,* 30 March 1970. Joseph Alsop, "Pause in Vietnam Withdrawal Would Be Wise at This Time," *Los Angeles Times,* 31 March 1970.

47. On Nixon understanding the risks, see James Reston in Robert B. Asprey, *War in the Shadows: The Guerrilla in History* (Garden City, NY: Doubleday, 1975), 1331. Melvin Small, *Antiwarriors: The Vietnam War and the Battle for America's Hearts and Minds* (Wilmington, DE: Scholarly Resources, 2002), 109. MACV mission in Combined Campaign Plan, 1970, Historians Files, CMH, p. 2. On withdrawals based on domestic considerations rather than assessments of the enemy and friendly situations, see Douglas Kinnard, *The War Managers: American Generals Reflect on Vietnam* (New York: DaCapo Press, 1977, 1991), 141.

48. Agnew quoted in Appy, *American Reckoning,* 196. Kissinger, *White House Years,* 288, 293.

49. McGovern quoted in Robert Mann, *A Grand Delusion: America's Descent into Vietnam* (New York: Basic Books, 2001), 640. Melvin Small, *At the Water's Edge: American Politics and the Vietnam War* (Chicago: Ivan R. Dee, 2005), 141.

50. H. R. Haldeman, *The Haldeman Diaries: Inside the Nixon White House* (New York: G.P. Putnam's Sons, 1994), 100. Bockman in "Strike Against the War," *TIME,* 17 October 1969, p. 17. Israel Shenker, "Intellectuals Divided Over Effectiveness of Vietnam Moratorium in

Promoting Peace," *New York Times,* 17 October 1969. Charles DeBenedetti with Charles Chatfield, *An American Ordeal: The Antiwar Movement of the Vietnam Era* (Syracuse, NY: Syracuse University Press, 1990), 255.

51. Richard Nixon, *Public Papers of the Presidents of the United States, 1969* (Washington, DC: US Government Printing Office, 1971), 901–909. William Safire, *Before the Fall: An Inside View of the Pre-Watergate White House* (Garden City, NY: Doubleday, 1975), 172. On Nixon's own reviews, see *RN,* 404–411; and *No More Vietnams* (New York: Arbor House: 1985), 115. Jonathan Schell, *Observing the Nixon Years* (New York: Pantheon Books, 1989), 12.

52. DeBenedetti, 261–263. George Donelson Moss puts the number of protestors at "perhaps 350,000." *Vietnam,* 338. Small, *Antiwarriors,* 114–115.

53. PSU Dean Nunzio Palladino quoted in Kenneth J Heineman, *Campus Wars: The Peace Movement at American State Universities in the Vietnam Era* (New York: New York University Press, 1993), 60. Home team and Merle Haggard in Sandra Scanlon, *The Pro-War Movement: Domestic Support for the Vietnam War and the Making of Modern American Conservatism* (Amherst: University of Massachusetts Press, 2013), 188, 194.

54. Nixon quoted in George Q. Flynn, *The Draft, 1940–1973* (Lawrence: University Press of Kansas, 1993), 246. Flynn covers Nixon and the draft in chapter 9. Still, under the lottery system, college undergraduates continued to get deferments. Larry H. Addington, *America's War in Vietnam: A Short Narrative History* (Bloomington: Indiana University Press, 2000), 135. Moss, 336–337.

55. Criticisms in Selwyn P. Rogers, "An All-Volunteer Force," *Military Review* 50, no. 9 (September 1970): 89, 93. See also Morris Janowitz, "Volunteer Armed Forces and Military Purpose," *Foreign Affairs* 50, no. 3 (April 1972): 427–443. Small, *At the Water's Edge,* 136-137. Easing antiwar sentiment in Bundy, *A Tangled Web,* 67.

56. Staff officer and Abrams quoted in Sorley, *Vietnam Chronicles,* 134, 194. Troop withdrawals in Kissinger, *Ending the Vietnam War,* 141.

57. HQ, USMACV, Command History, 1969, Vol. I, Entry MACJ03, RG 472, NARA, p. 1. For other criticisms, see William M. Hammond, *Reporting Vietnam: Media and Military at War* (Lawrence: University Press of Kansas, 1998), 153. The JCS, however, directed that "officials refrain from giving the impression we are considering making any additional negotiating concessions in Paris or elsewhere." Abrams to McCain, 6 November 1969, Abrams Messages #4623, CMH.

58. Peter Arnett, "Saigon Army Improves But Big Problems Remain," *The Hartford Courant,* 16 November 1969. "Vietnam: As Shooting Dies Down. . . ," *U.S. News & World Report,* 27 October 1969, pp. 35–37. "Hanoi Troops Attack Again in Delta Area," *The Washington Post,* 9 November 1969. "Behind Optimism About Vietnam," *U.S. News & World Report,* 1 December 1969, pp. 40–42.

59. Nixon, *Public Papers of the Presidents of the United States, 1969,* 1025. Abrams quoted in Sorley, *Vietnam Chronicles,* 345.

60. Wilfred P. Deac, *Road to the Killing Fields: The Cambodian War of 1970–1975* (College Station: Texas A&M University Press, 1997), 35–40. Malcolm Caldwell and Lek Tan, *Cambodia in the Southeast Asian War* (New York: Monthly Review Press, 1973), 220. Maharaj K. Chopra, "Search for Firm Borders," *Military Review* 49, no. 11 (November 1969): 4–6. Leslie Fielding, *Before the Killing Fields: Witness to Cambodia and the Vietnam War* (London: I.B. Taurus, 2008), 41.

61. Abrams to Wheeler, 22 February 1970, Abrams Messages #5381, CMH. See also Abrams to Wheeler, 1 January 1969, Abrams Messages #2326, CMH.

62. Abrams quoted in Sorley, *Vietnam Chronicles,* 77. On restrictions to US forces operating in Cambodia and Laos, see R. B. Smith, "The International Setting of the Cambodia Crisis, 1969–1970," *International History Review* 18, no. 2 (May 1996): 311–312. On earlier "secret" operations into Cambodia, see Deac, 46–47. *U.S. News & World Report* called the Ho Chi Minh Trail the communists' "lifeline." "If You Wonder What U.S. Is Doing in Laos," 5 January 1970, p. 28.

63. Rosson, "Four Periods of American Involvement in Vietnam," 261. Willbanks, *Abandoning Vietnam,* 29.

64. Turley, *The Second Indochina War*, 166–167. Bundy, *A Tangled Web*, 72. Sihanouk's role in Safire, *Before the Fall*, 182. Greg Grandin has called the bombing of Cambodia "illegal in its conception, deceitful in its implementation, and genocidal in its effect." *Kissinger's Shadow: The Long Reach of America's Most Controversial Statesman* (New York: Metropolitan Books, 2015), 68. On similar deception over Laos, see Robert Shaplen, "Our Involvement in Laos," *Foreign Affairs* 48, no. 3 (April 1970): 482.

65. Kissinger to Nixon, 16 March 1969, Folder 5, Box 89, NSC Files, Vietnam Subject Files, RNL. Kissinger to Nixon, 27 May 1969, Folder 7, Box 67, NSC Files, Vietnam Subject Files, RNL. Kissinger's private admission in Ken Hughes, *Chasing Shadows: The Nixon Tapes, the Chennault Affair, and the Origins of Watergate* (Charlottesville: University of Virginia Press, 2014), 90–91. Defoliation in Caldwell and Tan, *Cambodia in the Southeast Asian War*, 212. "Between April 18 and May 14, 1969, U.S. spray planes destroyed nearly 40,000 acres of rubber." On the relationship between bombing and diplomacy, see Peter G. Drivas, "The Cambodian Incursion Revisited," *International Social Science Review* 86, no. 3/4 (June 2011): 138.

66. Haig, *Inner Circles*, 236. John Prados, *The Blood Road: The Ho Chi Minh Trail and the Vietnam War* (New York: John Wiley & Sons, 1999), 19.

67. Rosson to McCain, 2 January 1970, Folder 1, Box 12, Official Correspondence–Army Chief of Staff Back Channel Messages, Incoming, William C. Westmoreland Collection, MHI. "The Situation in Vietnam," RNL, p. 3. Sorley, *Vietnam Chronicles*, 397.

68. "Sharp increase" in Abrams to Wheeler, 28 January 1970, Folder 4, Box 12, Official Correspondence–Army Chief of Staff Back Channel Messages, Incoming, William C. Westmoreland Collection, MHI. Tons in James P. Harrison, "History's Heaviest Bombing," in Werner and Huynh, *The Vietnam War*, 131. See also Prados, *The Blood Road*, 303. Chinese and Soviet support from Mark Clodfelter, *The Limits of Airpower: The American Bombing of North Vietnam* (New York: The Free Press, 1989), 135. Not bringing Hanoi to terms in *The Pentagon Papers: The Defense Department History of United States Decisionmaking on Vietnam* [The Sen. Gravel Edition, 5 vols.], Vol. IV (Boston: Beacon Press, 1971–1972), 53. On why Rolling Thunder continued, despite its shortcomings, see William Conrad Gibbons, *The U.S. Government and the Vietnam War: Executive and Legislative Roles and Relationships, Part IV: July 1965–January 1968* (Washington, DC: US Government Printing Office, 1994), 188.

69. JCS in McCain to Wheeler, 16 December 1969, Folder 1, Box 66, NSC Files, Vietnam Subject Files, RNL. Conversation between Nixon and Kissinger, 20 January 1972, *FRUS*, 1969-1976, VIII: 9–10. Hanoi committed "some 60 percent of North Vietnam's air defense capability . . . to protecting its lines of communications." John M. Shaw, *The Cambodian Campaign: The 1970 Offensive and America's Vietnam War* (Lawrence: University Press of Kansas, 2005), 11.

70. Haldeman, *The Haldeman Diaries*, 153. On morale at home, see David L. Anderson, *The Vietnam War* (New York: Palgrave Macmillan, 2005), 92.

71. Untenable in Morris, Lord, and Lake to Kissinger, 22 April 1970, *FRUS*, 1969–1976, VI: 857. Bold move in Kissinger to Nixon, 22 April 1970, ibid., 845. Inducing uncertainty in Bunker to Kissinger, 8 April 1970, ibid., 799. Public exposure in Abrams to Wheeler, 13 March 1970, Abrams Messages #5559, CMH.

72. "Reveal Note to Nixon Led to Cambodia," *Chicago Tribune*, 25 May 1970. Joseph R. Cerami lays out the major objectives in "Presidential Decisionmaking and Vietnam: Lessons for Strategists," *Parameters* 26, no. 4 (Winter 1996–97): 70.

73. Abrams to McCain and Wheeler, 13 March 1970, Folder 4, Box 91, NSC Files, Vietnam Subject Files, RNL. Kissinger, *White House Years*, 493–494. On reasons the president was "compelled to act forcefully," see "If Cambodia Falls to the Reds--Why Nixon Acted," *U.S. News & World Report*, 11 May 70. On link to Vietnamization, see Kimball, *Nixon's Vietnam War*, 202. See also Robert G. Kaiser, "Vietnam Allies Anxiously Await Effects of Cambodian Coup," *The Washington Post*, 3 April 1970.

74. Kissinger to Nixon, 19 March 1970, *FRUS*, 1969–1976, VI: 703–706. Keith William Nolan, *Into Cambodia: Spring Campaign, Summer Offensive, 1970* (Novato, CA: Presidio Press, 1990), 73–75. On economic crisis, see Smith, "The International Setting of the Cambodia Crisis," 314. Political crisis in Caldwell and Tan, 219, 256; and Deac, 51.

75. Nixon, *RN*, 447. Hanoi diplomats in Isaacson, *Kissinger*, 258; and Drivas, "The Cambodian Incursion Revisited," 141. Withdraw of diplomats in Zhai, *China and the Vietnam Wars*, 189.

76. Wheeler to Abrams, 26 March 1970, Abrams Messages #5714, CMH. Abrams quoted in Bundy, *A Tangled Web*, 151. Max Lerner, "Reds Have Lost Cambodian Sanctuaries; Now What?" *Los Angeles Times*, 2 April 1970.

77. Rogers in Haldeman, 155. On bypassing Laird as well, see Hunt, *Melvin Laird*, 157–158; and Isaacson, *Kissinger*, 266–267. Nixon, *RN*, 450. Nixon, *No More Vietnams*, 119.

78. Thieu quoted in Caldwell and Tan, 266. MACV intelligence in Shaw, *The Cambodian Campaign*, 38. Of note, Hanoi also used the coup as an excuse to expand its operations inside Cambodia. See Dale Andrade, "Crossing the Line: Assault into Cambodia," *MHQ: Quarterly Journal of Military History* (Winter 2001): 23.

79. Kissinger quoted in A. J. Langguth, *Our Vietnam: The War, 1954-1975* (New York: Simon & Schuster, 2000), 565. On blaming Hanoi, see Kimball, *Nixon's Vietnam War*, 198. Political calculations also drove Hanoi's "fight-while-talking" approach. See Combined Campaign Plan, 1970, Historians Files, CMH, pp. A-1, A-9.

80. Tran Von Don, *Our Endless War: Inside Vietnam* (San Rafael, CA: Presidio Press, 1978), 187. Communicating will and strength in James William Gibson, *The Perfect War: The War We Couldn't Lose and How We Did* (New York: Vintage Books, 1986), 407.

81. Laird in Van Atta, *With Honor*, 260–261; and John Prados, *Vietnam: The History of an Unwinnable War, 1945-1975* (Lawrence: University Press of Kansas, 2009), 363. On excluding the Vietnamese from planning, see Shaw, 29. Lack of intelligence in LTG Michael S. Davison, Senior Officer Debriefing Reports, CMH, p. 6.

82. "Dink-bastards" in Sewall Menzel, *At the Cutting Edge: Cold War Campaigning with the U.S. Army in Vietnam, Cambodia, and Laos, 1967-1971* (CreateSpace, 2005), 135. One NSC staff, reviewing Abrams's plan, "was horrified by its brevity and sloppiness." William Shawcross, *Sideshow: Kissinger, Nixon, and the Destruction of Cambodia*, rev. ed. (New York: Cooper Square Press, 1979, 2002), 143. Of note, even MACV planners had "no idea" of the secret bombing of Cambodia. See Douglas Kinnard in Christian G. Appy, *Patriots: The Vietnam War Remembered from All Sides* (New York: Viking Press, 2003), 324. For Abrams's assessment, see Abrams to McCain, 30 March 1970, Box 11, Creighton W. Abrams Papers, 1969–1970, MHI.

83. Haig to Kissinger, 3 April 1970, *FRUS, 1969–1976*, VI: 754. Nixon, *RN*, 448. Troop levels in Drivas, 144-145. On the internal debate over the 20 April announcement, see Kissinger, *White House Years*, 475–477; and Hunt, *Melvin Laird*, 133–134.

84. "The World," *New York Times*, 26 April 1970. Abrams's displeasure in Willbanks, *Abandoning Vietnam*, 69. Lloyd Gardner, "The Last Casualty? Richard Nixon and the End of the Vietnam War, 1969–1975," in *A Companion to the Vietnam War*, eds. Marilyn B. Young and Robert Buzzanco (Malden, MA: Blackwell, 2002), 246.

85. Nixon, *Public Papers of the Presidents of the United States, 1970*, 405–410. On *Patton*, see Safire, 183; and Evan Thomas, *Being Nixon: A Man Divided* (New York: Random House, 2015), 262–263. Authorization in National Security Council Decision Memorandum 57, 26 April 1970, *FRUS, 1969–1976*, VI: 889.

86. For a contemporary assessment of the decision, see Tad Szulc, "Threat to U.S. Troops in Vietnam Termed Basis for Nixon Decision," *New York Times*, 30 April 1970. Christian Appy argues that the "fear of impotence and loss was as primal with Nixon as it was with LBJ." *American Reckoning*, 89. Others saw the speech as Nixon judging Cambodia not as a real crisis but as a "test." See Gibson, *The Perfect War*, 407.

87. Minimum of publicity in Notes of Washington Special Actions Group Meeting, 28 April 1970, *FRUS, 1969–1976*, VI: 908. On the Cambodian planning, see Willbanks, 77–79; Shaw, *The Cambodian Campaign*, 59–77; Nolan, *Into Cambodia*, 75–81; and J. D. Coleman, *Incursion: From America's Chokehold on the NVA Lifelines to the Sacking of the Cambodian Sanctuaries* (New York: St. Martin's Press, 1991), 222–229.

88. NVA casualties in Cosmas, *MACV*, 302. Haig to Young for Kissinger, 18 May 1970, Folder 3, Box 1000, NSC Files, Vietnam Subject Files, RNL.

89. Abrams in Sorley, *Vietnam Chronicles*, 415. 25th Infantry assistant commander quoted in Nolan, 294. Harassment and COSVN in Shaw, 102, 120.

90. Wayne Thompson, *To Hanoi and Back: The United States Air Force and North Vietnam, 1966–1973* (Washington, DC: Air Force History and Museums Program, 2000), 172–174. "Hardest blow" in Abrams to Wheeler, 11 May 1970, Folder 4, Box 88, NSC Files, Vietnam Subject Files, RNL. On Nixon at the Lincoln Memorial, see Bundy, *A Tangled Web*, 155; and Thomas, *Being Nixon*, 271–274.

91. Haig and MACV staff in Sorley, *Vietnam Chronicles*, 420. Kissinger to Nixon, 25 May 1970, *FRUS, 1969–1976*, VI: 1005–1007. Gallup poll in Hunt, *Melvin Laird*, 162. On press criticism of the incursion, see William M. Hammond, *Public Affairs: The Military and the Media, 1968–1973* (Washington, DC: Center of Military History, 1996), 336–341.

92. Memorandum of Conversation, 31 May 1970, *FRUS, 1969–1976*, VI: 1016–1028. One week later, Abrams reported that he was "maintaining pressure on all fronts in Laos, Cambodia and South Vietnam." Abrams to Moorer, 8 June 1970, Abrams Messages #7391, CMH.

93. Wheeler to Abrams, 5 May 1970, Messages About Cambodian Operations Folder, Box W, Cables, The Creighton Abrams Papers, MHI. Vast amounts in II FFORCEV Commander's Evaluation Report-Cambodian Operations, 31 July 1970, Folder 01, Box 00, Bud Harton Collection, TTUVA, 10.

94. Casey quoted in Nolan, *Into Cambodia*, 438. Toughest setback in Kissinger to Nixon, 27 July 1970, *FRUS, 1969–1976*, VII: 9. ARVN morale in Headquarters, USMACV, "One War," MACV Command Overview, 1968–1972, Historians Files, CMH, p. 91. Nixon recalled that the "Cambodian incursion was the most successful military operation of the entire Vietnam War." *No More Vietnams*, 122.

95. CIA in Coleman, *Incursion*, 265 Looting in Davison to Abrams, 24 May 1970, Abrams Messages #7145, CMH. B-52s in Collins to Abrams, Observations on Dak Seang—Dak Pek Operations, 7 May 1970, Box 5, A. S. Collins Papers, MHI, p. 2.

96. Schell, *Observing the Nixon Years*, 35. ARVN Brig. Gen. Tran Dinh Tho believed the incursion posed "little more than a temporary disruption of North Vietnam's march toward domination of all of Laos, Cambodia, and South Vietnam." "The Cambodian Incursion," in *The Vietnam War: An Assessment by South Vietnam's Generals*, ed. Lewis Sorley (Lubbock: Texas Tech University Press, 2010), 548. Not eliminating the threat in "Smashing Red Sanctuaries: The Gains So Far," *U.S. News & World Report*, 25 May 1970, 32. Sweep in "The Cambodian Venture: A 'Decisive' Move?," *The Washington Post*, 10 May 1970.

97. Laird to Kissinger, 3 September 1970, *FRUS, 1969–1976*, VII: 66. "Cambodia: Now It's 'Operation Buy Time,'" *Time*, 25 May 1970. One report noted that HES figures "showed a national regression" in April 1970, the final month before the Cambodian operation. USMACV, "One War," MACV Command Overview, CMH, 44.

98. Abrams to Zumwalt, Davison, Collins, and McCown, 30 April 1970, Abrams Messages #6368, CMH. Bunker to Nixon, 24 April 1970, Folder 21, Box 01, Douglas Pike Collection: Other Manuscripts—Ellsworth Bunker Papers, TTUVA. Laird quoted in Jeffrey J. Clarke, *Advice and Support: The Final Years, 1965–1973* (Washington, DC: Center of Military History, 1988), 421.

99. Refugees in Abrams to Wheeler, McCain, 7 May 1970, Abrams Messages #6674, CMH. Pressure in Abrams to Wheeler, McCain, 26 May 1970, Abrams Messages #7189, CMH. Air strikes in Abrams to Wheeler, McCain, 16 May 1970, Abrams Messages #6953, CMH. Hardest blow in Abrams to Laird, Wheeler, McCain, 11 May 1970, Abrams Messages #6792, CMH. Offensive mood in Abrams to Moorer, 14 May 1970, Abrams Messages, CMH. On problems with the incursion, see Shawcross, *Sideshow*, 151.

100. Abrams quoted in Clarke, *Advice and Support*, 421. RF/PF in Abrams to Wheeler, 23 May 1970, Abrams Messages #7162, CMH. Zais to Abrams, 21 May 1970, Abrams Messages #7071, CMH. Julian Ewell noted their continuing problem was to get the ARVN to "grind away . . . to dig and fight the enemy out of the woodwork." "Notes from a Conversation with General Abrams and Lt. General Ewell," 18 January 1970, Folder 3, Box 1009, NSC Files, Vietnam Subject Files, RNL.

101. Kissinger to Laird, 15 June 1970, Folder 4, Box 91, NSC Files, Vietnam Subject Files, RNL. Economic problems in "Fighting Slows Down, But Saigon's Woes Increase," *U.S. News & World Report*, 17 August 1970; and Kissinger to Nixon, 10 August 1970, *FRUS, 1969–1976*, VII: 32–33. Threat to stability in USMACV, Command History, 1970, Vol. I, NARA,

p. I-4. Laird to Nixon, 4 April 1970, *FRUS, 1969–1976*, VI: 761. MACV also reported on the sounding of an "ominous note" with labor unions joining student protests. Davison to Abrams, 30 May 1970, Abrams Messages #7266, CMH.

102. GVN tension in Kissinger to Nixon, 24 August 1970, *FRUS, 1969–1976*, VII: 54. 50-50 chance in Arthur J. Dommen, "U.S. Pullout to Put Thieu in Political Peril," *Los Angeles Times*, 19 February 1970. Andrew Wiest argues the "ARVN, more than any other organ of the South Vietnamese state, had demonstrated the most progress in the period since the Tet Offensive." *Vietnam's Forgotten Army: Heroism and Betrayal in the ARVN* (New York: New York University Press, 2008), 180.

103. Kissinger, *White House Years*, 515. On the link between negotiations and political liberalization, see Pauker, *An Essay on Vietnamization*, 5. On problems inside Cambodia, see "Cambodia: December 1970: A Staff Report Prepared for the Use of The Committee on Foreign Relations, United States Senate" (Washington, DC: US Government Printing Office, 1970), 2.

104. Davison, Senior Officer Debriefing Reports, CMH, p. 27. Under siege in "Operation Successful; Outcome Uncertain," *Newsweek*, 18 May 1970, p. 52. Chinese rebuff in Tudda, *A Cold War Turning Point*, xii. Henry Kamm, "In Cambodia, Gloom Returns After the U.S. Pullout," *New York Times*, 4 July 1970. Dale Andrade argues that "in the long run, the incursion was only a temporary setback for Hanoi." "Crossing the Line," 29.

105. "Bums" in footnote 2, *FRUS, 1969–1976*, VI: 917. For a timeline of events at Kent State, see Philip Caputo, *13 Seconds: A Look Back at the Kent State Shootings* (New York: Chamberlain Bros., 2005), 123–131.

106. "U.S. Students Assail War, Deaths of 4," *Chicago Tribune*, 6 May 1970. Joseph Lelyveld, "Protests on Cambodia and Kent State Are Joined by Many Local Schools," *New York Times*, 6 May 1970. Nixon echoed Mayor Lindsay, stating that "when dissent turns to violence it invites tragedy." In Safire, *Before the Fall*, 191.

107. Crocker Snow Jr., "Cambodia and Kent—A Generation Alienated," *Boston Globe*, 6 May 1970. For a similar assessment from a historian, see Shawcross, *Sideshow*, 134.

108. Haldeman, 162. Matthew Storin, "Nixon Vows Quick Cambodia Pullout," *Boston Globe*, 6 May 1970. Small, *At the Water's Edge*, 151–152. Nixon, *RN*, 457.

109. Caputo, *13 Seconds*, 12. On Cooper and Church, see P. Edward Haley, *Congress and the Fall of South Vietnam and Cambodia* (East Brunswick, NJ: Fairleigh Dickinson University Press, 1982), 31; and Schmitz, *Richard Nixon and the Vietnam War*, 92–93.

110. Laird quoted in George C. Wilson, "GI Casualty Rate Held 'Top Concern,'" *The Washington Post*, 9 May 1970. USMACV, Command History, 1970, Vols. I and II, NARA, pp. III-100, XII-1. Abrams quoted in Sorley, *Vietnam Chronicles*, 627.

111. Casey to Davison, 17 May 1970, Abrams Messages #6984, CMH. Staff officer in Sorley, *Vietnam Chronicles*, 466. Even during the incursion, advisors to the White House, like Sir Robert Thompson, thought the communists were only "*temporarily* very stretched." "Balance Sheet on Cambodia," *U.S. News & World Report*, 1 June 1970, p. 32.

112. John T. Wheeler, "Reds Cut or Threaten 3 Cambodian Highways," *The Washington Post*, 2 October 1970. USMACV, Command History, 1970, Vol. II, NARA, p. VII-98. Abrams to McCain, 13 December 1970, Abrams Messages #9085, CMH. Eric M. Bergerud has called the American participation in the Cambodian incursion a "monumental blunder." *The Dynamics of Defeat: The Vietnam War in Hau Nghia Province* (Boulder, CO: Westview Press, 1991), 287.

113. Terence Smith, "U.S. Vietnam Policy: An Assessment," *New York Times*, 3 June 1970.

114. Rowland Evans and Robert Novak, "Viet Troops' Splendid Performance in Cambodia Surprises U.S. Generals," *The Washington Post*, 29 May 1970.

115. Lewis Sorley, *A Better War: The Unexamined Victories and Final Tragedy of America's Last Years in Vietnam* (New York: Harcourt Brace, 1999), 217. Sorley, *Vietnam Chronicles*, 387, 404. For an alternative view, see William J. Shkurti, *Soldiering On in a Dying War: The True Story of the Firebase Pace Incidents and the Vietnam Drawdown* (Lawrence: University Press of Kansas, 2011), 224–225; and Tad Szulc, "Expert Now Gloomy in Report to Nixon on Vietcong Power," *New York Times*, 3 December 1970.

116. Samuel L. Popkin, "Pacification: Politics and the Village," *Asian Survey* 10, no. 8 (August 1970): 664. Another report found that the communists and their supporters had "not faded away" but "merely changed tactics." "The U.S. Maps Its Progress," *Newsweek*, 26 October 1970, p. 33. Komer to Kissinger, 29 July 1970, R. Hunt VSSG Folder, OSDHO. The 1970 USMACV Command History noted that at year's end, "problems in security persisted." Vol. I, NARA, p. I-3.

117. Kevin M. Boylan, "Goodnight Saigon: American Provincial Advisors' Final Impressions of the Vietnam War," *Journal of Military History* 78 (January 2014): 249. Memorandum of Conversation, 23 July 1970, *FRUS, 1969–1976*, VII: 7.

118. Rosson to McCain, 1 June 1970, Folder 1, Box 13, Official Correspondence–Army Chief of Staff Back Channel Messages, Incoming, William C. Westmoreland Collection, MHI. Diplomatic issues in Prados, *Vietnam*, 404.

119. French officer quoted in David L. Schalk, *War and the Ivory Tower: Algeria and Vietnam* (New York: Oxford University Press, 1991), 29. Senior Officer Debriefing Report, LTG W. J. McCaffrey, 5 September 1972, Box 10, HQ USARV Command History Senior Officer Debriefing Reports, RG 472, NARA, p. 4.

120. Nixon, *Public Papers of the Presidents of the United States, 1970*, 476–477. "Nixon Says Goal Achieved in Cambodia," *The Hartford Courant*, 4 June 1970.

121. Kissinger to Nixon, 27 August 1970, *FRUS, 1969–1976*, VII: 58–59. Kissinger to Nixon, 13 October 1970, *FRUS, 1969–1976*, VII: 128. British counterinsurgency "expert" Sir Robert Thompson, however, declared to Nixon that the "main force war is virtually over." On enduring problems, see Bundy, *A Tangled Web*, 158.

122. Maynard Parker, "Vietnamization Is Not Peace," *Newsweek*, 23 November 1970. George McArthur, "Nixon-Thieu Accord May Hide Differences," *Los Angeles Times*, 22 October 1970.

123. "Cambodia: A Cocky New ARVN," *TIME*, 8 June 1970. Joseph Kraft, "Further War Troubles," *The Washington Post*, 7 October 71. Critics worried that "present RVNAF force levels are already too large to be supportable by the RVN for any extended period." See S. Canby, B. Jenkins, and R. B. Rainey, *A Ground Force Structure and Strategy for Vietnam in the 1970s* (Santa Monica, CA: RAND Corporation, 1970), 1.

124. J3 Inputs to Report of the MACV Effort, MHI, p. III-19. Trooper quoted in Keith W. Nolan, *Ripcord: Screaming Eagles under Siege, Vietnam 1970* (Novato, CA: Presidio Press, 2000), 403. On Operation Texas Star and the lead-up to the Ripcord siege, see Robert D. Sander, *Invasion of Laos, 1971: Lam Son 719* (Norman: University of Oklahoma Press, 2014), 75–78.

125. Nixon, *Public Papers of the Presidents of the United States, 1970*, 540. Nguyen, *Hanoi's War*, 135.

126. "Absolutely exhausted" in Thomas Noel, interview by Steve Glick, Senior Officers Debriefing Program, Creighton Abrams Story, MHI, p. 29. On Abrams's health and those who believed "he never got all the way back," see Cosmas, *MACV*, 182–183.

127. USMACV, Command History, 1970, Vol. I, NARA, p. I-6. Insane life in Schell, *Observing the Nixon Years*, 28. On morale problems, see Robert Dallek, *Nixon and Kissinger: Partners in Power* (New York: HarperCollins, 2007), 252. For one view on the relationship between morale and policy, see David Cortright, *Soldiers in Revolt: The American Military Today* (Garden City, NY: Anchor Press, 1975), 153. Questioning assumptions of South Vietnam's survival in Mark M. Boatner III, "Withdrawal, Redeployment or Cop Out," *Army* 21, no. 4 (April 1971): 16.

Chapter 5

1. Simpson quoted in *The Vietnam War: A Documentary Reader*, ed. Edward Miller (Malden, MA: Wiley Blackwell, 2016), 134.

2. Fred Widmer quoted in Michael Bilton and Kevin Sim, *Four Hours in My Lai* (New York: Viking Press, 1992), 39–40. "Part of the problem" on p. 85. On US patrols receiving harassing fire and losing men before the assault, see Tom Tiede, *Calley: Soldier or Killer?* (New York: Pinnacle Books, 1971), 23. Pilot Larry Colburn believed "these guys were really out for revenge." In Christian G. Appy, *Patriots: The Vietnam War Remembered from All Sides* (New York: Viking Press, 2003), 348.

3. Dean Fields quoted in William Thomas Allison, *My Lai: An American Atrocity in the Vietnam War* (Baltimore: Johns Hopkins University Press, 2012), 39. A summary of rapes can be found in James S. Olson and Randy Roberts, eds., *My Lai: A Brief History with Documents* (Boston: Bedford/St. Martin's, 1998), 99–102.

4. On the aftermath and the decision to investigate, see Allison, 53–78. "Disbelief" on p. 78. See also Seymour M. Hersh, *Cover-Up* (New York: Random House, 1972).

5. Packard to Nixon, 4 September 169, *FRUS, 1969–1976*, VI: 356–357.

6. Seymour Hersh, "New Viet Murder Charge," *Boston Globe*, 13 November 1969. Peter Braestrup, "Trial in Pinkville Massacre Case to Be Heard at Ft. Benning, Ga.," *The Washington Post*, 30 November 1969.

7. Richard L. Stout, "Grim Story May Be Year's Biggest," *The Christian Science Monitor*, 29 November 1969. Murrey Marder, "Pinkville Sets Back U.S. Strategists, Gives Reds a Propaganda Windfall," *The Washington Post*, 1 December 1969. On Abrams's response in enforcing and elaborating on MACV's rules of engagement in the aftermath of My Lai, see Graham A. Cosmas, *MACV: The Joint Command in the Years of Withdrawal, 1968–1973* (Washington, DC: Center of Military History, 2007), 228.

8. Body counts in Colin L. Powell with Joseph E. Persico, *My American Journey* (New York: Random House, 1995), 146. See also Daniel Southerland, "'Body Count' Doubted," *The Christian Science Monitor*, 14 February 1970. Futility in Robert M. Smith, "26 Are Investigated in Vietnam Deaths," *New York Times*, 22 November 1969. See also Peter Braestrup, "Frustration Could Have Caused Alleged Viet Killings," *The Washington Post*, 23 November 1969. Dehumanization in Patrick Hagopian, *The Vietnam War in American Memory: Veterans, Memorials, and the Politics of Healing* (Amherst: University of Massachusetts Press, 2009), 53. For an argument that civilian suffering was "the inevitable outcome of deliberate policies," see Nick Turse, *Kill Anything That Moves: The Real American War in Vietnam* (New York: Metropolitan Books, 2013), 6.

9. James T. Wooten, "My Lai Defendant Accuses Abrams," *New York Times*, 29 October 1970. Secretary of the Army Stanley R. Resor dismissed the charges, saying that there was "no evidence" that Abrams "concealed any mistreatment of prisoners and detainees." "Abrams Is Cleared of Soldier's Charge," *New York Times*, 5 December 1970. "3 Ex-Officers Attack Viet Body Count," *The Washington Post*, 16 April 1971. William F. Buckley Jr., "The Guilt for My Lai May Hit Very Close to Home," *Lost Angeles Times*, 12 December 1969.

10. Moral vacuum in Bilton and Sim, *Four Hours in My Lai*, 79. Mother in Seymour M. Hersh, *The Price of Power: Kissinger in the Nixon White House* (New York: Summit Books, 1983), 135. Decline of officer quality in Richard A. Gabriel and Paul L. Savage, *Crisis in Command: Mismanagement in the Army* (New York: Hill and Wang, 1978), 10. VFW support in Tiede, *Calley*, 130.

11. On Nixon, see Melvin Small, *At the Water's Edge: American Politics and the Vietnam War* (Chicago: Ivan R. Dee, 2005), 168; and Hagopian, *The Vietnam War in American Memory*, 62. On relating Calley to Christ, see Tiede, 16.

12. Animals in Malcolm W. Browne, *The New Face of War*, rev. ed. (Indianapolis: Bobbs-Merrill, 1965, 1968), 337. Richard Harwood and Laurence Stern, "Pinkville Symbolizes Brutalization That Inevitably Afflicts Men at War," *The Washington Post*, 26 November 1969. Saving South Vietnam in Jonathan Schell, *Observing the Nixon Years* (New York: Pantheon Books, 1989), 18. Soul in Seymour Melman, ed., *In the Name of America: The Conduct of the War in Vietnam by the Armed Forces of the United States as Shown by Published Reports* (New York: Clergy and Laymen Concerned About Vietnam, 1968), 11.

13. Stuart Auerbach, "Excess of Viet Killing Blamed on Marijuana," *Los Angeles Times*, 11 May 1970. Richard L. Strout, "Tragic Human Costs of War," *The Christian Science Monitor*, 24 November 1969.

14. Haines to Westmoreland, 11 September 1970, Abrams Messages #8072, CMH. Permissiveness in "Memoirs," 2d rev., Part II, Box 9, Donald A. Seibert Papers, MHI, p. 1049; and "Armed Forces: Disorder in the Ranks," *TIME*, 9 August 1971, p. 21. Others worried the "spillover" would work the other way, as young veterans brought their problems back into society. See William L. Hauser, *America's Army in Crisis: A Study in Civil-Military Relations* (Baltimore: Johns Hopkins University Press, 1973), 124. For a dissenting voice on blaming society, see Gabriel and Savage, *Crisis in Command*, 26.

15. Perverse pride in George McArthur, "GIs Gripe, But Do the Job," *The Washington Post*, 21 December 1970. On the state of discipline being "generally appalling," see BG DeWitt C. Armstrong, 9 May 1972, Senior Officer Debriefing Reports, CMH, p. 3.

16. On this point, see C. L. Sulzberger, "Rotten Eggs or Sick Chickens?," *New York Times*, 25 February 1972.

17. Michael Herr, *Dispatches* (New York: Alfred A. Knopf, 1968, 1978), 6. George McT. Kahin, "The Nixon Strategy," in *Why Are We Still in Vietnam?*, eds. Sam Brown and Len Ackland (New York: Random House, 1970), 38–39. See also Schell, *Observing the Nixon Years*, 36–37. Embedded in US culture in William Braden, "Today's Angry GI—Does He Enjoy Killing?," *Los Angeles Times*, 4 December 1969.

18. Scott H. Bennett, *Radical Pacifism: The War Resisters League and Gandhian Nonviolence in America, 1915–1963* (Syracuse, NY: Syracuse University Press, 2003), 239–240. Charles DeBenedetti with Charles Chatfield, *An American Ordeal: The Antiwar Movement of the Vietnam Era* (Syracuse, NY: Syracuse University Press, 1990), 96–101. Melvin Small, *Antiwarriors: The Vietnam War and the Battle for America's Hearts and Minds* (Wilmington, DE: Scholarly Resources, 2002), 17. Nancy Zaroulis and Gerald Sullivan, *Who Spoke Up? American Protest Against the War in Vietnam, 1963–1975* (Garden City, NY: Doubleday, 1984), 12–13.

19. Teach-ins in DeBenedetti, 107–115. Bombing protests in Small, *Antiwarriors*, 20. War supporters in Washington, DC, held rallies against the teach-ins, with supporters holding "Burn The Teach-In Professors" signs. Terry H. Anderson, "Vietnam Is Here: The Antiwar Movement," in *The War That Never Ends: New Perspectives on the Vietnam War*, eds. David L. Anderson and John Ernst (Lexington: University Press of Kentucky, 2007), 248.

20. SDS statement in *Major Problems in the History of the Vietnam War*, 2nd ed., ed. Robert J. McMahon (Lexington, MA: D.C. Heath, 1995), 467–468. For a broader history of SDS, see James Miller, *"Democracy Is in the Streets" From Port Huron to the Siege of Chicago* (New York: Simon & Schuster, 1987). Committee for Nonviolent Action rally in Zaroulis and Sullivan, 61.

21. John Prados, "The Veterans Antiwar Movement in Fact and Memory," in *A Companion to the Vietnam War*, eds. Marilyn B. Young and Robert Buzzanco (Malden, MA: Blackwell, 2002), 403. Mitchell K. Hall, "The Vietnam Era Antiwar Movement," *OAH Magazine of History* 18, no. 5 (October 2004): 14.

22. King in *A Vietnam War Reader: A Documentary History from American and Vietnamese Perspectives*, ed. Michael H. Hunt (Chapel Hill: University of North Carolina Press, 2010), 169–170. See also Zaroulis and Sullivan, 108–109. On links to Great Society, see Anderson, "Vietnam Is Here," 250. According to the *Los Angeles Times*, King accused the president of bringing Westmoreland home "to silence dissent against the Vietnam war and encourage support for escalation of the conflict." "Westmoreland Home to Silence Dissent—King," 1 May 1967.

23. Signs in Zaroulis and Sullivan, 138. Anderson, 245. Norman Mailer covered the Pentagon protests in *The Armies of the Night: History as a Novel, the Novel as History* (New York: New American Library, 1968).

24. Stone quoted in DeBenedetti, *An American Ordeal*, 228. "Nightstick city" in George C. Herring, *America's Longest War: The United States and Vietnam, 1950–1975*, 4th ed. (New York: McGraw-Hill, 1979, 2002), 261.

25. Student Leverett Millen quoted in Kenneth J. Heineman, *Campus Wars: The Peace Movement at American State Universities in the Vietnam Era* (New York: New York University Press, 1993), 158. On the problems of revitalizing patriotic culture and the war's moral ambiguity, see Michael S. Sherry, *In the Shadow of War: The United States since the 1930s* (New Haven, CT: Yale University Press, 1995), 298.

26. Blair Clark, "Westmoreland Appraised: Questions and Answers," *Harper's* (November 1970): 98. On Westmoreland's concerns, see Charles F. Brower IV, "Strategic Reassessment in Vietnam: The Westmoreland 'Alternate Strategy' of 1967–1968," *Naval War College Review* Vol. 44, no. 2 (Spring 1991): 45. The general argued that violent protestors "went beyond the bounds of reasonable debate and fair dissension," while their "actions helped prolong the war." William C. Westmoreland, *A Soldier Reports* (Garden City, NY: Doubleday, 1976), 503.

27. Kissinger quoted in Larry Berman, *No Peace, No Honor: Nixon, Kissinger, and Betrayal in Vietnam* (New York: The Free Press, 2001), 63. Mainstream in Melvin Small, *Covering Dissent: The Media and the Anti-Vietnam War Movement* (New Brunswick, NJ: Rutgers University Press, 1994), 86.

28. "Commentary by Religious Leaders on the Erosion of Moral Constraint in Vietnam" in Melman, *In the Name of America*, 1–8.
29. Robert F. Kennedy, "Conflict in Vietnam and at Home," Landon Lecture, 18 March 1968, Kansas State University, transcript available at https://www.k-state.edu/landon/speakers/robert-kennedy/transcript.html.
30. Wheeler in Lewis Sorley, *A Better War: The Unexamined Victories and Final Tragedy of America's Last Years in Vietnam* (New York: Harcourt Brace, 1999), 157. On "no mounting sense of excitement" with the inauguration of Nixon in relation to ending the war, see Robert R. Tomes, *Apocalypse Then: American Intellectuals and the Vietnam War, 1954–1975* (New York: New York University Press, 1998), 206.
31. Department of State to Embassy in France, 14 October 1968, *FRUS, 1964–1968*, VII: 173. See also William Colby with James McCargar, *Lost Victory: A Firsthand Account of America's Sixteen-Year Involvement in Vietnam* (Chicago: Contemporary Books, 1989), 364.
32. Abrams quoted in Lewis Sorley, ed., *Vietnam Chronicles: The Abrams Tapes, 1968–1972* (Lubbock: Texas Tech University Press, 2004), 347. Moorer quoted in Anderson, "Vietnam Is Here," 262. Col. Robert B. Rigg, apparently suggesting the need for some form of national censorship, argued the United States had failed by giving "too much information to the enemy on the home-front of public opinion. This has handicapped us in Hanoi for many years, and it is now plaguing us in the Paris peace talks." "How Not to Report a War," *Military Review* 49, no. 6 (June 1969): 15.
33. Dave Richard Palmer, *Summons of the Trumpet: U.S.-Vietnam in Perspective* (San Rafael, CA: Presidio Press, 1978), xix. On not separating stateside and front line resistance groups, see Penny Lewis, *Hardhats, Hippies, and Hawks: The Vietnam Antiwar Movement as Myth and Memory* (Ithaca, NY: Cornell University Press, 2013), 127.
34. Brig. Gen. Theodore C. Mataxis, "This Far, No Farther," *Military Review* 50, no. 3 (March 1970): 74. James Reston, "Washington: The Stupidity of Intelligence," *New York Times*, 17 October 1965. On the Weathermen, see Small, *At the Water's Edge*, 126; Heineman, *Campus Wars*, 192; and Zaroulis and Sullivan, *Who Spoke Up?*, 311–312. On stopping the war more popular than continuing it, see David L. Anderson, review, *Passport: The Society for Historians of American Foreign Relations Review* 43, no. 3 (January 2013): 16. DeBenedetti found "no evidence that protest prolonged the war." *An American Ordeal*, 397–398.
35. Jeremi Suri considers the "global disruption of 1968" in chapter 5 of *Power and Protest: Global Revolution and the Rise of Détente* (Cambridge, MA: Harvard University Press, 2003). Henry Kissinger, *Diplomacy* (New York: Simon & Schuster, 1994), 677. DeBenedetti, 217.
36. *The Guardian* quoted in John Dumbrell, *Rethinking the Vietnam War* (New York: Palgrave Macmillan, 2012), 156. Conspiracy in Small, *Antiwarriors*, 49.
37. Critic Herman Kahn quoted in Gerard J. DeGroot, *A Noble Cause? America and the Vietnam War* (Harlow, Essex, UK: Longman, 2000), 261. John Tirman, *The Deaths of Others: The Fate of Civilians in America's Wars* (New York: Oxford University Press, 2011), 170–171. Of South Vietnam, Michael Herr noted, "A lot of people knew the country could never be won, only destroyed." *Dispatches*, 59.
38. McGovern quoted in Steven Casey, *When Soldiers Fall: How Americans Have Confronted Combat Losses from World War I to Afghanistan* (New York: Oxford University Press, 2014), 196.
39. Westmoreland, *A Soldier Reports*, 443. Small, *Antiwarriors*, 80. DeBenedetti, *An American Ordeal*, 135. On the "hippie" culture in South Vietnam, see Olga Dror, "Raising Vietnamese: War and Youth in the South in the Early 1970s," *Journal of Southeast Asian Studies* 44, no. 1 (February 2013): 85–86.
40. On working class, see Lewis, *Hardhats, Hippies, and Hawks*, 15. On media coverage, see Small, *Covering Dissent*, 165. National unity in Sandra Scanlon, *The Pro-War Movement: Domestic Support for the Vietnam War and the Making of Modern American Conservatism* (Amherst: University of Massachusetts Press, 2013), 197.
41. Henry Kissinger, *White House Years* (Boston: Little, Brown, 1979), 301. On the paradox of opposing the war "while simultaneously opposing those who opposed the war," see Jerry Lembke, *Hanoi Jane: War, Sex & Fantasies of Betrayal* (Amherst: University of Massachusetts Press, 2010), 120.

42. Richard Nixon, *No More Vietnams* (New York: Arbor House: 1985), 127. H. R. Haldeman, *The Haldeman Diaries: Inside the Nixon White House* (New York: G.P. Putnam's Sons, 1994), 77. Veterans in Andrew E. Hunt, *The Turning: A History of Vietnam Veterans Against the War* (New York: New York University Press, 1999), 2. On the media focusing on the movement, not what it had to say, see Daniel C. Hallin, *The "Uncensored War": The Media and Vietnam* (New York: Oxford University Press, 1986), 199.

43. On elements within the antiwar coalition, see Zaroulis and Sullivan, 345. There is debate within the Vietnam War historiography as to when the antiwar movement peaked. For those arguing that moment occurred in 1969, see Small, *Antiwarriors*, 119; and Hall, "The Vietnam Era Antiwar Movement," 15. Penny Lewis places it later, in 1971. See *Hardhats, Hippies, and Hawks*, 136–137.

44. Anthony Lewis, "Death in the Abstract," *New York Times*, 4 January 1971. Polling in William L. Lunch and Peter W. Sperlich, "American Public Opinion and the War in Vietnam," *Western Political Quarterly* 32, no. 1 (March 1979): 31.

45. Nixon's "mindless rioters" and silencing domestic critics in Anderson, "Vietnam Is Here," 257. Nixon's paranoia in Philip Caputo, *13 Seconds: A Look Back at the Kent State Shootings* (New York: Chamberlain Bros., 2005), 113. On not changing the overall goals, Paul Joseph, "Direct and Indirect Effects of the Movement against the Vietnam War," in *The Vietnam War: Vietnamese and American Perspectives*, eds. Jayne S. Werner and Luu Doan Huynh (Armonk, NY: M.E. Sharpe, 1993), 168. Hanoi's views of the antiwar movement in Small, *Antiwarriors*, 162.

46. On evaluating the effectiveness of the antiwar movement, see Dumbrell, *Rethinking the Vietnam War*, 149; DeBenedetti, 398–405; and Jeffrey Kimball, "How Wars End: The Vietnam War," *Peace & Change* 20, no. 2 (April 1995): 194. Gil Merom argues "American ground forces were pulled out of Vietnam largely because of domestic, and in particular, campus pressure." *How Democracies Lose Small Wars: State, Society, and the Failures of France in Algeria, Israel in Lebanon, and the United States in Vietnam* (New York: Cambridge University Press, 2003), 237.

47. George Q. Flynn, *The Draft, 1940–1973* (Lawrence: University Press of Kansas, 1993), 170–171, 192–194. David L. Anderson, *The Columbia Guide to the Vietnam War* (New York: Columbia University Press, 2002), 113–114. D. Michael Shafer, "The Vietnam-Era Draft: Who Went, Who Didn't, and Why It Matters," in *The Legacy: The Vietnam War in the American Imagination*, ed. D. Michael Shafer (Boston: Beacon Press, 1990), 67–70. John Helmer, *Bringing the War Home: The American Soldier in Vietnam and After* (New York: The Free Press, 1974), 3–8. For an overview of draft policies, see Alfred B. Fitt, interview by Dorothy Pierce, 25 October 1968, Oral History Collection, LBJL. Fitt served as the assistant secretary of defense for manpower and reserve affairs.

48. LTG W. R. Peers, Senior Officer Debriefing Report, 23 June 1969, General Holdings, MHI, p. 12. Bradley D. Helton, "Revolving Door War: Former Commanders Reflect on the Impact of the Twelve-Month Tour Upon Their Companies in Vietnam" (master's thesis, North Carolina State University, 2004), 8–11. Marines endured a thirteen-month tour.

49. Ngo Quang Truong, "RVNAF and US Operational Cooperation and Coordination," in *The Vietnam War: An Assessment by South Vietnam's Generals*, ed. Lewis Sorley (Lubbock: Texas Tech University Press, 2010), 173. Robert D. Ramsey III, *Advising Indigenous Forces: American Advisors in Korea, Vietnam, and El Salvador* (Fort Leavenworth, KS: Combat Studies Institute Press, 2006), 55. Turbulence in Julian J. Ewell, "Impressions of a Division Commander in Vietnam," 17 September 1969, Box 1, Elvy B. Roberts Papers, MHI, p. 1. Inexperienced leaders in the BDM Corporation, "A Study of Strategic Lessons Learned in Vietnam," Vol. VII, The Soldier, General Holdings, MHI, pp. 2–23. Lack of institutional memory in R.W. Komer, *Bureaucracy Does Its Thing: Institutional Constraints on U.S. -GVN Performance in Vietnam* (Santa Monica, CA: RAND Corporation, 1972), 67. On the need for "extended practical experience and rapport with indigenous counterparts" during counterinsurgency operations, see David R. Holmes, "Some Tentative Thoughts After Indochina," *Military Review*, 57, no. 8 (August 1977): 85.

50. Christian G. Appy, *Working-Class War: American Combat Soldiers and Vietnam* (Chapel Hill: University of North Carolina Press, 1993), 37. Lawrence M. Baskir and William

A. Strauss, *Chance and Circumstance: The Draft, the War, and the Vietnam Generation* (New York: Alfred A. Knopf, 1978), 48–49.

51. James E. Westheider, *Fighting on Two Fronts: African Americans and the Vietnam War* (New York: New York University Press, 1997), 29. Christian G. Appy, *Patriots: The Vietnam War Remembered from All Sides* (New York: Viking Press, 2003), 325. Small, *At the Water's Edge*, 107.

52. Whether Vietnam was a "class war" or not remains somewhat of a debate. Two of the more important works are James Fallows, "What Did You Do in the Class War, Daddy?," *The Washington Monthly* (October 1975): 5–19; and Appy, *Working-Class War*. One statistical analysis questioned these claims, finding little correlation between neighborhood incomes and per capita Vietnam deaths. See Arnold Barnett, Timothy Stanley, and Michael Shore, "America's Vietnam Casualties: Victims of a Class War?," *Operations Research* 40, no. 5 (September–October 1992): 856–866. See also Shafer, "The Vietnam-Era Draft," 68. Both Fallows and Appy responded, as did Barnett and Stanley, in *The Atlantic Monthly* (August 1993): 12–14.

53. Rhodes scholar quoted in Baskir and Strauss, 7. "Proles" in Fallows, "What Did You Do in the Class War, Daddy?," 16.

54. On "little association between income and per capita death rates," see Barnett, Stanley, and Shore, 865. Alienation in Hearings before the Committee on Foreign Relations, United States Senate, Ninety-First Congress, *Second Session on Moral and Military Aspects of the War in Southeast Asia* (Washington, DC: US Government Printing Office, 1970), 4; and Helmer, *Bringing the War Home*, 48–49. Lewis, *Hardhats, Hippies, and Hawks*, 118–121, 194.

55. Poster in *The Vietnam War: A History in Documents*, eds. Marilyn B. Young, John J. Fitzgerald, and A. Tom Grunfeld (New York: Oxford University Press, 2002), 118. On how Hanoi used allusions to the antiwar movement in negotiations with Kissinger, see John Prados, *Vietnam: The History of an Unwinnable War, 1945–1975* (Lawrence: University Press of Kansas, 2009), 448.

56. "The Week in Review," *New York Times*, 21 September 1969. "As U.S. Seeks a New Strategy for Vietnam. . . ," *U.S. News & World Report*, 22 September 1969, 37–38.

57. Kevin Klose, "Ft. Belvoir GIs Start Antiwar Paper," *The Washington Post*, 25 March 1969. Randy Hoelzen quoted in James R. Ebert, *A Life in a Year: The American Infantryman in Vietnam, 1965-1972* (Novato, CA: Presidio Press, 1993), 318.

58. James Reston, "A Whiff of Mutiny in Vietnam," *New York Times*, 27 August 1969. "The Alpha Incident," *Newsweek*, 8 September 1969. See also James Landers, *The Weekly War: Newsmagazines and Vietnam* (Columbia: University of Missouri Press, 2004), 113. For an alternate view, see James P. Sterbas, "G.I.'s in Battle Area Shrug Off the Story of Balky Company A," *New York Times*, 29 August 1969.

59. Carrot-and-stick in "Cambodia: 'We're Cache Counters,'" *Newsweek*, 25 May 1970, 45. *Vietnam Courier* in Richard R. Moser, *The New Winter Soldiers: GI and Veteran Dissent during the Vietnam War* (New Brunswick, NJ: Rutgers University Press, 1996), 45. Combat refusals and dissent in "A New GI: For Pot and Peace," *Newsweek*, 2 February 1970, 24, 28; and "Incident on Route 9," *TIME*, 5 April 1971, 25. One senior officer, describing a combat refusal incident to Abrams, noted that the soldiers "felt that they were justified in refusing the mission on the basis of their unpreparedness to engage at night an enemy force of the size they believed" was present in the area. Sutherland to Abrams, 29 March 1971, Abrams Messages #9813, CMH.

60. Company commander quoted in George McArthur, "Average 'Grunt' in War Wants Only to Get Out," *Los Angeles Times*, 12 December 1970. George McArthur, "GIs Gripe, But Do the Job," *The Washington Post*, 21 December 1970.

61. John Sarr, "You Can't Just Hand Out Orders," *LIFE*, 23 October 1970, 31–36, 57. Utermahlen's defense in John R. Galvin, *Fighting the Cold War: A Soldier's Memoir* (Lexington: University Press of Kentucky, 2015), 205–207, 215–216. On popular officers avoiding unnecessary risks, see Ron Milam, *Not a Gentleman's War: An Inside View of Junior Officers in the Vietnam War* (Chapel Hill: University of North Carolina Press, 2009), 144. One lieutenant even disclosed that "I don't feel that my job here is to kill Gooks but to keep my men happy." "Boredom and Drugs Biggest Viet Enemies," *The Harford Courant*, 28 October 1971.

62. Hill quoted in "No Punishment Planned for GIs Who Balked," *The Washington Post*, 23 March 1971. See also Moser, 46. Investigation in HQ, USMACV, Command History, 1971, Vol. II, Entry MACJ03, RG 472, NARA, p. X-33. On Mary Ann, see Keith William Nolan, *Into Laos: The Story of Dewey Canyon II/Lam Son 719; Vietnam 1971* (Novato, CA: Presidio Press, 1986), 24.

63. "Kennedy Asks Probe of GI Plea," *The Washington Post*, 16 October 1971. Craig R. Whitney, "Army Says Some G.I.'s Balked Briefly at Patrol," *New York Times*, 12 October 1971. See also Guenter Lewy, "The American Experience in Vietnam," in *Combat Effectiveness: Cohesion, Stress, and the Volunteer Military*, ed. Sam C. Sarkesian (Beverly Hills, CA: SAGE, 1980), 97–98. The best treatment of this episode, and its context to the larger war, is William J. Shkurti, *Soldiering On in a Dying War: The True Story of the Firebase Pace Incidents and the Vietnam Drawdown* (Lawrence: University Press of Kansas, 2011), 58–62.

64. Col. James M. Lee, 14 February 1970, VNIT Folder 253, CMH. Col. Volney F. Warner, End of Tour Report, 14 January 1970, Box 1, Volney F. Warner Papers, MHI.

65. Colby, *Lost Victory*, 326. As early as July 1969, Nixon, then visiting South Vietnam, admitted to soldiers in the 1st Infantry Division that "this is the first time in our history when we have had a lack of understanding of why we are here, what the war is all about, where we have had real division at home." Richard Nixon, *Public Papers of the Presidents of the United States, 1969* (Washington, DC: US Government Printing Office, 1971), 587.

66. Galvin, *Fighting the Cold War*, 203. Keith Nolan called "the American fighting man who was facing the North Vietnamese along the Laotian front in 1971 . . . perhaps the least motivated in U.S. history." *Into Laos*, 20.

67. LTC J. R. Meese, interview, 30 July 1968, VNIT Folder 239, CMH. As an example of the focus on self-preservation, see Appy, *Working-Class War*, 198.

68. Donald Kirk, "Who Wants to Be the Last American Killed in Vietnam?," *New York Times*, 19 September 1971. See also D. Michael Shafer, "The Vietnam Combat Experience," in Shafer, *The Legacy*, 84. Ronald H. Spector argues the army after Tet had become "an organization that lacked any true sense of identity, continuity of leadership, or purpose." *After Tet: The Bloodiest Year in Vietnam* (New York: The Free Press, 1993), 45.

69. Anonymous death in Nicholas C. Proffitt, "Soldiers Who Refuse to Die," *Newsweek*, 25 October 1971, 67–68. Roger Steffens quoted in Doug Bradley and Craig Werner, *We Gotta Get Out of This Place: The Soundtrack of the Vietnam War* (Amherst: University of Massachusetts Press, 2015), 86.

70. Hostile press in LTG A. S. Collins Jr., Senior Officer Debriefing Report, 18 January 1971, Box 2, RG472, NARA, p. 13. Merron quoted in Hugh A. Mulligan, "Armed Forces Mirror Society's Ills," *The Hartford Courant*, 23 May 1971. On love of service and contempt for the war, see Herr, *Dispatches*, 185. Herr noted that younger captains and majors ultimately could not reconcile the two.

71. Drug use in McCaffrey to Kerwin, 16 November 1970, Folder 4, Box 1007, NSC Files, Alexander M. Haig Special File, RNL. "Abrams Cautions on Laxity by G.I.'s," *New York Times*, 27 May 1971. For an example of the armed forces attempting to limit the influence of domestic dissent, see Richard Halloran, "Army Orders the Seizure of Antiwar Mail Sent to G.I.'s in Vietnam," *New York Times*, 31 March 1971.

72. Allison, *My Lai*, 110–111. Richard M. Nixon, *RN: The Memoirs of Richard Nixon* (New York: Grosset & Dunlap, 1978), 363. William Greider, "Calley Becomes a Symbol," *The Washington Post*, 24 January 1971. Herbert Brucker, "Fort Benning Trial Recalls Nuremberg," *The Hartford Courant*, 15 January 1971.

73. Medina quoted in Tiede, *Calley*, 127. Rifkin in Richard W. McManus, "'Unofficial Atrocities' Attributed to Pentagon," *The Christian Science Monitor*, 18 May 1970. Capt. Jordan J. Paust argued the war had "lessened the spirit and conscience of America." "My Lai and Vietnam: Norms, Myths, and Leader Responsibility," *Military Law Review* 57 (Summer 1972): 187.

74. Davidson to Abrams, 1 May 1970, Abrams Messages #6434, CMH. Abrams to McCain, 4 May 1970, Backchannel Messages, Creighton W. Abrams Papers, MHI. On subordinates' views of My Lai, see Mildren to Abrams, 3 April 1970, Abrams Messages #6360, CMH; and McCown to Abrams, 30 April 1970, Abrams Messages #6386, CMH. On My Lai and the GVN, see

Nguyễn Công Luận, *Nationalist in the Viet Nam Wars: Memoirs of a Victim Turned Soldier* (Bloomington: Indiana University Press, 2012), 362. For an argument suggesting that the massacre was partly a result of US policy, see David Cortright, *Soldiers in Revolt: The American Military Today* (Garden City, NY: Anchor Press, 1975), 27. Robert Jay Lifton argued My Lai was "exceptional only in its dimensions." *Home from the War, Vietnam Veterans: Neither Victims nor Executioners* (New York: Simon & Schuster, 1973), 42.

75. McArthur, "GIs Gripe, But Do the Job." On the psychological scars, see Norman M. Camp, *US Army Psychiatry in the Vietnam War: New Challenges in Extended Counterinsurgency Warfare* (Fort Sam Houston, TX: Borden Institute, 2015), 160–161.

76. Opportunity versus burden in Westheider, *Fighting on Two Fronts*, 2; and C. L. Sulzenberger, "Foreign Affairs: The Spin-Out," *New York Times*, 21 May 1969. Carmichael quoted in John Darrell Sherwood, *Black Sailor, White Navy: Racial Unrest in the Fleet during the Vietnam War Era* (New York: New York University Press, 2007), 19.

77. Anderson quoted in James E. Westheider, *The African American Experience in Vietnam: Brothers in Arms* (Lanham, MD: Rowman & Littlefield, 2008), 139. Jones quoted in Westheider, *Fighting on Two Fronts*, 67.

78. Ken Moorefield in Al Santoli, *To Bear Any Burden: The Vietnam War and Its Aftermath in the Words of Americans and Southeast Asians* (Bloomington: Indiana University Press, 1999), 189. Larry H. Addington, *America's War in Vietnam: A Short Narrative History* (Bloomington: Indiana University Press, 2000), 124. Zaroulis and Sullivan, *Who Spoke Up?*, 163–164.

79. Eldridge Cleaver quoted in Curtis Austin, "The Black Panthers and the Vietnam War," in *America and the Vietnam War: Re-examining the Culture and History of a Generation*, eds. Andrew Wiest, Mary Kathryn Barbier, and Glenn Robins (New York: Routledge, 2010), 105. See also "'I'll Bleed for Myself,' Says Black U.S. Soldier in Europe," *New York Times*, 11 October 1970.

80. James S. White, "Race Relations in the Army," *Military Review* 50, no. 7 (July 1970): 6. Ralph Blumenthal, "'Pervasive' Racial Unrest Is Found in Armed Forces," *New York Times*, 29 November 1969.

81. Abrams to Palmer, Cushman et al., 6 April 1968, Abrams Messages #424, CMH. Stanley Williford and William Endicott, "Military Racial Harmony Fades: Reasons Why," *Los Angeles Times*, 5 September 1969.

82. Ali quoted in Anderson, "Vietnam Is Here," 251. See also Westheider, *The African American Experience in Vietnam*, 31; and Small, *Antiwarriors*, 64.

83. Sanders quoted in Appy, *Working-Class War*, 224.

84. Zalin B. Grant, "The Other War: Whites against Blacks in Vietnam," *The New Republic* 160, no. 3 (18 January 1969): 15–16. David Cortright, "Black GI Resistance during the Vietnam War," *Vietnam Generation* 2, no. 1 (Spring 1990): 57. Herman Graham III, *The Brothers' Vietnam War: Black Power, Manhood, and the Military Experience* (Gainesville: University Press of Florida, 2003), 91–92. John T. Wheeler, "Black Power Comes to Vietnam as Racial Tensions Increase," *The Washington Post*, 20 April 1969. "Tensions of Black Power Reach Troops in Vietnam," *New York Times*, 13 April 1969.

85. "Back Power in Viet Nam," *TIME*, 19 September 1969, 22–23. Westheider, *The African American Experience in Vietnam*, 64–65.

86. 9th Infantry soldier quoted in Westheider, *Fighting on Two Fronts*, 115.

87. Officer quoted in Grant, "The Other War," 16. Course in Westheider, ibid., 134. Abrams in Sorley, *Vietnam Chronicles*, 605.

88. Moratorium in Bradley and Werner, *We Gotta Get Out of This Place*, 128. On Latinos, see also Kyle Longley, *Grunts: The American Combat Soldier in Vietnam* (Armonk, NY: M.E. Sharpe, 2008), 130–131. For the best treatment of unrest in the US Navy, see Sherwood, *Black Sailor, White Navy*.

89. "GIs' Drug Use Said Hurting War Effort," *The Hartford Courant*, 10 August 1970. "Marijuana—The Other Enemy in Vietnam," *U.S. News & World Report*, 26 January 1970, 68–69. See also "Drug Use on the Battlefield," *Los Angeles Times*, 23 August 1970.

90. Michael Getler, "Pentagon Moves to Stem 'Alarming' Drug Abuse," *The Washington Post*, 21 August 1970. USMACV Directive 190–4, Military Police Drug Abuse Suppression Program, 10 December 1970, Folder 4, Box 1011, NSC Files, Alexander M. Haig Special File, RNL. Haig believed the drug problem had "received serious attention only since July" 1970. Major Conclusions and Recommendations, *FRUS*, 1969–1976, VII: 231.

91. Soldier quoted in Jeremy Kuzmarov, "The Myth of the 'Addicted Army': Drug Use in Vietnam in Historical Perspective," *War & Society* 26, no. 2 (October 2007): 132. On self-medication, see Camp, *US Army Psychiatry in the Vietnam War*, 362.

92. DoD survey in Jeremy Kuzmarov, *The Myth of the Addicted Army: Vietnam and the Modern War on Drugs* (Amherst: University of Massachusetts Press, 2009), 26. On the problems of reporting the extent of drug use in the command, see William M. Hammond, *Public Affairs: The Military and the Media, 1968–1973* (Washington, DC: Center of Military History, 1996), 389.

93. McCaffrey to Kerwin, 16 November 1970, RNL. On rear area drug use and urinalysis testing, see Kuzmarov, *The Myth of the Addicted Army*, 35, 131.

94. No fingerprints in Stanley Karnow, *Vietnam: A History* (New York: Viking Press, 1983), 632. Statistics in William Thomas Allison, *Military Justice in Vietnam: The Rule of Law in an American War* (Lawrence: University Press of Kansas, 2007), 79.

95. Ritual in Eugene Linden, "Army's Deadly Internal War," *Los Angeles Times*, 9 January 1972. See also Jack Foise, " 'Fragging' Increase Proves Only Mild Surprise to Servicemen," *Los Angeles Times*, 25 April 1971. Insensitive to soldier frustrations in Milam, *Not a Gentleman's War*, 159. Ticket punching and John Wayne tactics in George Lepre, *Fragging: Why U.S. Soldiers Assaulted Their Officers in Vietnam* (Lubbock: Texas Tech University Press, 2011), 84–85.

96. Congressional panel in Lepre, 32. On rear areas, see Meredith H. Lair, *Armed with Abundance: Consumerism & Soldiering in the Vietnam War* (Chapel Hill: University of North Carolina Press, 2011), 32, 90. See also Terry H. Anderson, "The GI Movement and the Response from the Brass," in *Give Peace a Chance: Exploring the Vietnam Antiwar Movement*, eds. Melvin Small and William D. Hoover (Syracuse, NY: Syracuse University Press, 1992), 105.

97. Eugene Linden, "Fragging and Other Withdrawal Symptoms," *Saturday Review*, 8 January 1972, 12. Fraggings in Lepre, 99–100.

98. Veteran quoted in Michael Putzel, "GI Attacks on Leaders Increase in Rear Area," *The Washington Post*, 14 January 1971. See also Westheider, *Fighting on Two Fronts*, 44. Abrams quoted in C. L. Sulzberger, "Rotten Eggs or Sick Chickens?," *New York Times*, 25 February 1972.

99. "The Troubled U.S. Army in Vietnam," *Newsweek*, 11 January 1971, 29–31, 34, 37. See also "As Fighting Slows in Vietnam: Breakdown in GI Discipline," *U.S. News & World Report*, 7 June 1971, 16–17. West Pointer in Drew Middleton, "Morale Sag Afflicts Career Servicemen," *New York Times*, 26 October 1970.

100. Strong quoted in Wallace Terry, *Bloods: An Oral History of the Vietnam War by Black Veterans* (New York: Random House, 1984), 56. This lack of faith in the war effort had an impact on unit cohesion as well. One soldier, disillusioned with the war, noted, "I quit learning people's names after a short period of time." Tom Weiner, *Called to Serve: Stories of Men and Women Confronted by the Vietnam War Draft* (Amherst, MA: Levellers Press, 2011), 69.

101. Pennsylvanian veteran and Pentagon official quoted in Douglas E. Kneeland, "War Stirs More Dissent among G.I.'s," *New York Times*, 21 June 1970. Tobias Wolff, *In Pharoah's Army: Memories of the Lost War* (New York: Alfred A. Knopf, 1994), 68. On officers reacting to the changes within the army's ranks, see Lt. Gen. Arthur S. Collins Jr., Senior Officers Oral History Program, interview by Chandler P. Robbins III, 1982, MHI, p. 347. Avoiding defeat in F. Charles Parker IV, *Vietnam: Strategy for a Stalemate* (New York: Paragon House, 1989), 3.

102. Sacrificed in Shelby L. Stanton, *The Rise and Fall of an American Army: U.S. Ground Forces in Vietnam, 1965–1973* (Novato, CA: Presidio Press, 1985), 368. Rumors in William F. Buckley Jr., "Expert on Vietnam Refutes Reports of Conduct of GIs," *Los Angeles Times*, 30 December 1970.

103. Col. Robert D. Heinl Jr., "The Collapse of the Armed Forces," *Armed Forces Journal* 108, no. 19 (7 June 1971): 30–37. Col. David H. Hackworth, "Army Leadership Is Ineffective," *The Wall Street Journal*, 29 June 1971. For a similar argument, see "The State of the Army," *The Christian Science Monitor*, 25 May 1971.

104. The first report in the series was Haynes Johnson and George C. Wilson, "The U.S. Army: A Battle for Survival," *The Washington Post*, 12 September 1971. Maj. Gen. R. F. K. Goldsmith, "An Army in Trouble," *Military Review* 51, no. 11 (November 1971): 51–55.

105. Plague in Cortright, *Soldiers in Revolt*, 47. Courts martial figures in Allison, *Military Justice in Vietnam*, 70–71. For a snapshot of how MACV was dealing with these problems, see Abrams to McCain, "Military Discipline," 15 June 1971, Folder 01, Box 14, George J. Veith Collection, TTUVA.

106. US Army War College, "Study on Military Professionalism," 30 June 1970, Carlisle Barracks, PA, MHI Library, p. v. See also Ronald H. Spector, "The Vietnam War and the Army's Self-Image," in *The Second Indochina War: Proceedings of a Symposium Held at Airlie, Virginia, 7–9 November 1984*, ed. John Schlight (Washington, DC: Center of Military History, 1986), 172; and Edward L. King, *The Death of the Army: A Pre-mortem* (New York: Saturday Review Press, 1972), 75. On how the study remained a text "without institutional practice," see James William Gibson, *The Perfect War: The War We Couldn't Lose and How We Did* (New York: Vintage Books, 1986), 442.

107. Abrams quoted in Sorley, *A Better War*, 289.

108. Cushman quoted in Hauser, *America's Army in Crisis*, 104.

109. Helmer, *Bringing the War Home*, 89–90. Small, *Anitwarriors*, 141. Lewis, *Hardhats, Hippies, and Hawks*, 128–129.

110. Sociologist Charles C. Moskos Jr., "Military Made Scapegoat for Vietnam," in *A Short History of the Vietnam War*, ed. Allan R. Millett (Bloomington: Indiana University Press, 1978), 69. Veterans also joined to connect with fellow soldiers as a way to deal with the psychological wounds of war. See Lifton, *Home From the War*, 103–107.

111. Soldier quoted in Anderson, "The GI Movement and the Response from the Brass," 106. Operation RAW in Hunt, *The Turning*, 43–54. Ronald Sullivan, "Veterans for Peace Simulate the War," *New York Times*, 5 September 1970.

112. Al Hubbard's term "criminal policy" quoted in Helmer, 91. See also Addington, *America's War in Vietnam*, 132. For similar condemnations, see John Lengel, "Five Officers Seek War Crimes Inquiry," *The Washington Post*, 13 January 1971; and Barbara Carlson, "Veterans Against War Describe Torture, Destruction in Vietnam," *The Hartford Courant*, 24 March 1971.

113. Veteran Scott Camil quoted in Hunt, *The Turning*, 70. For a counter to the argument that atrocities were part of formal US policy, see Milam, *Not a Gentleman's War*, 133–134.

114. Limited incursion in Zaroulis and Sullivan, *Who Spoke Up?*, 355. Spoiled children in Hunt, 77. Hatfield in Lloyd Gardner, "The Last Casualty? Richard Nixon and the End of the Vietnam War, 1969–75," in *A Companion to the Vietnam War*, 408.

115. Emerson quoted in Marilyn B. Young, *The Vietnam Wars, 1945–1990* (New York: HarperCollins, 1991), 257. Gold Star mothers on p. 258.

116. Constitutionality in Hunt, 108. DAR encounter on p. 97. DeBenedetti argues the "VVAW protest carried the weight of tested patriotism" and "conveyed no ideology except love of country." *An American Ordeal*, 310.

117. Kerry testimony in *Landmark Speeches on the Vietnam War*, ed. Gregory Allen Olson (College Station: Texas A&M University Press, 2010), 170–179. See also Michael J. Allen, *Until the Last Man Comes Home: POWs, MIAs, and the Unending Vietnam War* (Chapel Hill: University of North Carolina Press, 2009), 298.

118. VVAW member quoted in *The American Experience in Vietnam: A Reader*, ed. Grace Sevy (Norman: University of Oklahoma Press, 1989), 65.

119. Vet quoted in Andrew J. Huebner, *The Warrior Image: Soldiers in American Culture from the Second World War to the Vietnam Era* (Chapel Hill: University of North Carolina Press, 2008), 230. Hunt, *The Turning*, 113–114.

120. Daniel Ellsberg, *Secrets: A Memoir of Vietnam and the Pentagon Papers* (New York: Viking Press, 2002), 249, 276. See also Ken Hughes, *Chasing Shadows: The Nixon Tapes, the Chennault Affair, and the Origins of Watergate* (Charlottesville: University of Virginia Press, 2014), 81, 99.

121. Neil Sheehan, "Vietnam Archive: Pentagon Study Traces 3 Decades of Growing U.S. Involvement," *New York Times*, 13 June 1971. Alexander Haig on the "security breach" in

Douglas Brinkley and Luke A. Nichter, eds., *The Nixon Tapes, 1971–1972* (Boston: Houghton Mifflin Harcourt, 2014), 171. Kissinger quoted in Greg Grandin, *Kissinger's Shadow: The Long Reach of America's Most Controversial Statesman* (New York: Metropolitan Books, 2015), 104.

122. Supreme Court in Robert D. Schulzinger, *A Time for War: The United States and Vietnam, 1941–1975* (New York: Oxford University Press, 1997), 291. Nixon, *RN*, 511. Secret diplomacy in Chris Tudda, *A Cold War Turning Point: Nixon and China, 1969–1972* (Baton Rouge: Louisiana State University Press, 2012), 81.

123. Hunt, *The Turning*, 144.

124. Morale problems in USMACV, Command History, 1970, Vol. I, NARA, p. VII-21. Leadership issues on p. VII-24 and desertion rates on p. VII-31. National Police numbers in USMACV, Command History, 1971, Vol. I, NARA, p. I-5.

125. Luận, *Nationalist in the Viet Nam Wars*, 389. On links between the army's expansion and its impact on South Vietnamese society, see Nguyen Duy Hinh and Tran Dinh Tho, "The South Vietnamese Society," in Sorley, *The Vietnam War*, 721.

126. Pay and inflation in Andrew Wiest, *Vietnam's Forgotten Army: Heroism and Betrayal in the ARVN* (New York: New York University Press, 2008), 39. Divided society in Guenter Lewy, "Some Political-Military Lessons of the Vietnam War," in *Assessing the Vietnam War: A Collection from the Journal of the U.S. Army War College*, eds. Lloyd J. Matthews and Dale E. Brown (Washington, DC: Pergamon-Brassey's International Defense Publishers, 1987), 143. Robert K. Brigham quoted one US advisor, "We had to make sure that the ARVN weren't alienating the local population by stealing their food." "Dreaming Different Dreams: The United States and the Army of the Republic of Vietnam," in Young and Buzzanco, *A Companion to the Vietnam War*, 153. Jeffrey Race argues the NLF's social policies led to "superior motivation." "How They Won," *Asian Survey* 10, no. 8 (August 1970): 639.

127. Lack of decisive battles and its impact in Sarkesian, *Combat Effectiveness*, 101. Strategic purpose in Colin S. Gray, *Modern Strategy* (New York: Oxford University Press, 1999), 45. One US Army captain suggested, "We might have to reorient ourselves to the limited kinds of victory which alone are feasible in this age." James R. Holbrook, "Volunteer Army: Military Caste?," *Military Review* 51, no. 8 (August 1971): 95.

128. Soldier Dan Vandenberg quoted in Eric M. Bergerud, *The Dynamics of Defeat: The Vietnam War in Hau Nghia Province* (Boulder, CO: Westview Press, 1991), 291. Family survival in Robert K. Brigham, *ARVN: Life and Death in the South Vietnamese Army* (Lawrence: University Press of Kansas, 2006), 121. On lack of South Vietnamese political community, see Guenter Lewy, *America in Vietnam* (New York: Oxford University Press, 1978), 218.

Chapter 6

1. Plenum decree in Pierre Asselin, *A Bitter Peace: Washington, Hanoi, and the Making of the Paris Agreement* (Chapel Hill: University of North Carolina Press, 2002), 25. Sino-Soviet split and antiwar crackdown in Lien-Hang T. Nguyen, *Hanoi's War: An International History of the War for Peace in Vietnam* (Chapel Hill: University of North Carolina Press, 2012), 116, 157.

2. On terminating American presence, see Gil Merom, *How Democracies Lose Small Wars: State, Society, and the Failures of France in Algeria, Israel in Lebanon, and the United States in Vietnam* (New York: Cambridge University Press, 2003), 233; and John Prados, *Vietnam: The History of an Unwinnable War, 1945–1975* (Lawrence: University Press of Kansas, 2009), 443.

3. On the linkages between the battlefield and the negotiating table, see David W. P. Elliott, "Hanoi's Strategy in the Second Indochina War," in *The Vietnam War: Vietnamese and American Perspectives*, eds. Jayne S. Werner and Luu Doan Huynh (Armonk, NY: M.E. Sharpe, 1993), 89.

4. Captured documents in John Prados, *The Hidden History of the Vietnam War* (Chicago: Ivan R. Dee, 1995), 246; and William J. Duiker, *Sacred War: Nationalism and Revolution in a Divided Vietnam* (Boston: McGraw-Hill, 1995), 232. Setting back revolution in Nguyen, *Hanoi's War*, 112.

5. Kissinger to Nixon, 21 January 1971, *FRUS*, 1969–1976, VII: 294–295.

6. William Beecher, "Vietnamization: A Few Loose Ends," *Military Review* 20, no. 11 (November 1970): 15. Laotian buildup in James H. Willbanks, *A Raid Too Far: Operation Lam Son 719 and Vietnamization in Laos* (College Station: Texas A&M University Press, 2014), 27.

7. NLF cadre quoted in Konrad Kellen, *Conversations with Enemy Soldiers in Late 1968/Early 1969: A Study of Motivation and Morale* (Santa Monica, CA: RAND Corporation, 1970), 55. Analysis questions in Kissinger to Nixon, 16 November 1970, *FRUS*, 1969-1976, VII: 167, 192. Nguyen, 196.

8. Abrams to McCain, 9 September 1970, Abrams Messages #8065, CMH. Abrams to McCain, 18 September 1970, Abrams Messages #8126, CMH. The MACV evaluation of the RVNAF at the end of 1970 highlighted the lingering problems with, and thus limited influence of, the US advisory effort. See MACV SEER Report, Part I, 4th Qrtr. CY 70, File HRC, Geog V Vietnam 319.1, CMH, p. 3.

9. On leverage, see Lawrence E. Grinter, "Bargaining Between Saigon and Washington: Dilemmas of Linkage Politics During War," *Orbis*, Vol. 18, no. 3 (Fall 1974): 847–848.

10. Strategic Guidance, HQ, USMACV, Command History, 1970, T.S. Supplement, Secretary of Joint Staff (MACJ03), Military History Branch, Box 8, RG 472, NARA. Combined Campaign Plan, 1971, Historians Files, CMH, pp. 4–5. On change in US role to support and assist, see LTG James W. Sutherland, 31 August 1971, Senior Officer Debriefing Reports, CMH, p. 4; and HQ, USMACV, Command History, 1971, Vol. I, Entry MACJ03, RG 472, NARA, pp. II-7 to II-8.

11. Critical of Abrams in Moorer, 3 April 1972, *FRUS*, 1969–1976, VIII: 185. Not thinking creatively in Nixon and Kissinger conversation, 5 February 1972, ibid., 83. A year earlier, Kissinger told Chairman of the Joint Chiefs Thomas H. Moorer that the president "was having absolute fits" with Abrams. Conversation, 18 April 1971, *FRUS*, 1969–1976, VII: 563.

12. Study quoted in Robert B. Asprey, *War in the Shadows: The Guerrilla in History* (Garden City, NY: Doubleday, 1975), 1328.

13. Max Boot, *The Savage Wars of Peace: Small Wars and the Rise of American Power* (New York: Basic Books, 2002), 336–337. On the United States having a "long experience in 'restoring order' on behalf of the civil authority in troubled lands," see G. C. Reinhardt, *Guerrilla-Combat, Strategy and Deterrence in Southeast Asia* (Santa Monica, CA: RAND Corporation, 1964), 11. On Nixon not having a mandate from the public, the press, or the government bureaucracy, see Carolyn Eisenberg, "Remembering Nixon's War," in *A Companion to the Vietnam War*, eds. Marilyn B. Young and Robert Buzzanco (Malden, MA: Blackwell, 2002), 260.

14. Mansfield to Johnson, 24 March 1965, *FRUS*, 1964–1968, II: 477. Fulbright quoted in Joseph A. Fry, *Debating Vietnam: Fulbright, Stennis, and Their Senate Hearings* (Lanham, MD: Rowman & Littlefield, 2006), 31. See also Randall B. Woods, "Dixie's Dove: J. William Fulbright, the Vietnam War, and the American South," in *Vietnam and the American Political Tradition: The Politics of Dissent*, ed. Randall B. Woods (New York: Cambridge University Press, 2003), 161–162.

15. Rostow to Johnson, 1 August 1967, *FRUS*, 1964–1968, V: 653. Sen. Richard Russell told LBJ, "What everybody wants is an end to the war. It's been a miserable war—worse than Korea." Notes of meeting, 14 October 1968, *FRUS*, 1964–1968, VII: 194. Wheeler to Westmoreland and H. K. Johnson, 2 August 1967, Folder 1, Box 6, Series I, Official Correspondence, WC Westmoreland Collection, MHI.

16. "U.S.: Rising Voice of the War Critics," *U.S. News & World Report*, 18 March 1968, p. 10. Robert F. Kennedy, *Thirteen Days: A Memoir of the Cuban Missile Crisis* (New York: W.W. Norton, 1968, 1999), 139.

17. Richard M. Nixon, *RN: The Memoirs of Richard Nixon* (New York: Grosset & Dunlap, 1978), 350. Robert D. Schulzinger, "Richard Nixon, Congress, and the War in Vietnam, 1969–1972," in Woods, 284. Fry, 154.

18. Richard Nixon, *Public Papers of the Presidents of the United States, 1970* (Washington, DC: US Government Printing Office, 1971), 145. On the pro-war lobby, see Sandra Scanlon, *The Pro-War Movement: Domestic Support for the Vietnam War and the Making of Modern American Conservatism* (Amherst: University of Massachusetts Press, 2013), 118.

19. Nixon, *RN*, 350. Kyle Longley, "Congress and the Vietnam War: Senate Doves and Their Impact on the War," in *The War That Never Ends: New Perspectives on the Vietnam War*, eds.

David L. Anderson and John Ernst (Lexington: University Press of Kentucky, 2007), 302. Schulzinger, 289. See also "Showdown on War—Congress vs. Nixon," *U.S. News & World Report*, 25 May 1970, p. 35.

20. McGovern quoted in in *The Vietnam War: A Documentary Reader*, ed. Edward Miller (Malden, MA: Wiley Blackwell, 2016), 183. Church quoted in "GI's Into Cambodia—Americans React," *U.S. News & World Report*, 11 May 1970, p. 19. Schulzinger argues this congressional assertiveness "represented a sea change in the deference lawmakers had accorded presidents during the Cold War years" (p. 283).

21. Kissinger to Nixon, 7 September 1970, *FRUS, 1969–1976*, VII: 92–93. Henry Kissinger, *White House Years* (Boston: Little, Brown, 1979), 513. "Sharp downturn" from Sen. Robert Dole (R-Kansas), quoted in "GI's Into Cambodia—Americans React," 19.

22. Bruce Palmer, interview by Ted Gittinger, 9 November 1982, Oral History Collection, LBJL, p. II-36. On Congress preparing for re-election, see Longley, 300.

23. On the bipartisan antiwar movement led by Sens. Church and Cooper, see David F. Schmitz, "Congress Must Draw the Line: Senator Frank Church and the Opposition to the Vietnam War and the Imperial Presidency," in Woods, 133–137; and Fry, *Debating Vietnam*, 156.

24. Church quoted in Schmitz, 139.

25. "The Congress Moves to Reassert Its War Power," *The Washington Post*, 1 January 1971. Schmitz, 138–141. For a negative view, see Joseph Alsop, "Cooper-Church Amendment Leads Senate in Ballet Dance," *The Washington Post*, 19 June 1970.

26. Sparkman quoted in "Goodby to Tonkin Gulf!," *The Washington Post*, 8 January 1971. Peter A. Jay, "Laird Calls War Trend Heartening," *The Washington Post*, 12 January 1971. Repeal in William Bundy, *A Tangled Web: The Making of Foreign Policy in the Nixon Presidency* (New York: Hill and Wang, 1998), 224.

27. Nixon quoted in Fry, 156.

28. Abrams quoted in Lewis Sorley, ed., *Vietnam Chronicles: The Abrams Tapes, 1968–1972* (Lubbock: Texas Tech University Press, 2004), 26. Military action in Laos in Abrams to McCain, 26 October 1970, Abrams Messages #8473, CMH.

29. "Gen. Weyand to 4-Star; Abrams' Deputy," *The Hartford Courant*, 2 November 1970. Dale Van Atta, *With Honor: Melvin Laird in War, Peace, and Politics* (Madison: University of Wisconsin Press, 2008), 339.

30. MACV staff assessment in Sorley, 509; and Keith William Nolan, *Into Laos: The Story of Dewey Canyon II/Lam Son 719; Vietnam 1971* (Novato, CA: Presidio Press, 1986), 12. Abrams's request in George C. Wilson and Michael Getler, "Military See Cambodia as Key Front," *The Washington Post*, 13 December 1970. Alvin Shuster, "Laird Expects Wider Pullout of Troops," *New York Times*, 12 January 1971.

31. Duiker, *Sacred War*, 232–233. David W. P. Elliott, *NLF-DRV Strategy and the 1972 Spring Offensive* (Ithaca, NY: Cornell University International Relations of East Asia Project, 1974), 17.

32. "Hanoi Steps Up Laos Infiltration," *The Hartford Courant*, 2 February 1971. George McArthur, "Hanoi Gets Soviet War Gear at Record Rate," *Los Angeles Times*, 6 January 1971.

33. Quoted in Robert Buzzanco, *Masters of War: Military Dissent and Politics in the Vietnam Era* (New York: Cambridge University Press, 1996), 241–242.

34. Unger to State Department, 13 September 1964, Box 268, National Security Files, LBJL. JCS to CINCPAC, 3 November 3 1966, Box 271, National Security Files, LBJL. JCS to Secretary of Defense, 21 March 1968, DoD Electronic Reading Room, http://www.dod.mil/pubs/foi/Reading_Room/International_Security_Affairs/701.pdf. For an overview of this earlier period, see Seth Jacobs, *The Universe Unraveling: American Foreign Policy in Cold War Laos* (Ithaca, NY: Cornell University Press, 2012).

35. Preemptive defensive raid in Nolan, *Into Laos*, 11. Haig to Kissinger, 15 December 1970, *FRUS, 1969–1976*, VII: 219–220.

36. Memorandum of conversation, 22 December 1970, *FRUS, 1969–1976*, VII: 233–235. Westmoreland, however, shared his concerns with Kissinger that "whether you can expand Vietnamese forces generally is debatable" (p. 263).

37. Memorandum of meeting conversation, 26 January 1971, *FRUS, 1969–1976*, VII: 306–307.

38. Memorandum for the record, 23 December 1970, *FRUS, 1969–1976*, VII: 243. Memorandum of meeting conversation, 27 January 1971, ibid., 328. See also Michael J. Allen, review,

Passport: The Society for Historians of American Foreign Relations Review 43, no. 3 (January 2013): 11. Dramatic fashion in Nguyen, *Hanoi's War*, 202. On the president attempting to maintain strategic flexibility, see Robert B. Semple Jr., "Nixon Refuses to Rule Out Wider Air Role in the War or a Saigon Push to North," *New York Times*, 18 February 1971.

39. Indefinitely in "The Last Big Push—Or a Wider War?," *Newsweek*, 15 February 1971, p. 24. Of course, the United States was already in a wide-ranging air war in Laos, on a very large scale. US bomb tonnage on Laos had been 515,000 tons in 1969 and 453,000 tons in 1970. Data from House Judiciary Committee, *Statement of Information*, Book XI, *Bombing of Cambodia* (Washington, DC: US Government Printing Office, 1974), pp. 90–103. Laird quoted in "Widening the War to Wind It Down?," *Newsweek*, 8 February 1971, p. 19. On Nixon being comfortable with the political risks at home, see Alvin Shuster, "Plan to Cut Enemy's Lines in Laos, Long Rejected, Was Revived 3 Months Ago," *New York Times*, 9 February 1971. As one source noted, "He knew there would be troubles at home, but he also knew that they could be offset by mid-April when he announces another substantial reduction in American forces."

40. Judd quoted in Scanlon, *The Pro-war Movement*, 155. On the long-held assumptions over northern aggression, see Andrew Preston, *The War Council: McGeorge Bundy, The NSC, and Vietnam* (Cambridge, MA: Harvard University Press, 2006), 93. MACV long proposing an invasion of Laos in Richard A. Hunt, *Melvin Laird and the Foundation of the Post-Vietnam Military, 1969–1973* (Washington, DC: Office of the Secretary of Defense Historical Office, 2015), 175. US embassy support in Howard B. Schaffer, *Ellsworth Bunker: Global Troubleshooter, Vietnam Hawk* (Chapel Hill: University of North Carolina Press, 2003), 224.

41. Laos incursion being "transitory" from Stephen Randolph, "The President's Daily Brief: Delivering Intelligence to Nixon and Ford," Richard Nixon Presidential Library and Museum, Yorba Linda, CA, 24 August 2015. Senior official quoted in "Why U.S. Stepped Up War in Indo-China," *U.S. News & World Report*, 15 February 1971, p. 22.

42. Moorer quoted in Hunt, 177. Kissinger and Westmoreland conversation, 12 April 1971, *FRUS, 1969–1976*, VII: 537–538.

43. Peter A. Jay, "Campaign in Laos 'Critical' to Pullout, Abrams Says," *The Washington Post*, 25 February 1971. Richard Nixon, *Public Papers of the Presidents of the United States, 1971* (Washington, DC: US Government Printing Office, 1972), 392. Kissinger quoted in Greg Grandin, *Kissinger's Shadow: The Long Reach of America's Most Controversial Statesman* (New York: Metropolitan Books, 2015), 87. ARVN in Willbanks, *A Raid Too Far*, 30.

44. Bruce Palmer Jr., *The 25-Year War: America's Military Role in Vietnam* (Lexington: University Press of Kentucky, 1984), 108. See also Willbanks, 30–32. On narrow aims, see Kissinger, *White House Years*, 989; and Robert D. Sander, *Invasion of Laos, 1971: Lam Son 719* (Norman: University of Oklahoma Press, 2014), 88.

45. Abrams to McCain, 12 December 1970, Abrams Messages #9068, CMH. Abrams to McCain, 18 October 1970, Abrams Messages #8385, CMH.

46. On no existing plan, see Willbanks, 31.

47. Cut and disrupt in "General Abrams' Report on Laos Operation," 14 February 1971, Folder 1, Box 81, NSC Files, Vietnam Subject Files, RNL. Four phases in Memorandum for the Record, 19 January 1971, *FRUS, 1969–1976*, VII: 288. See also Graham A. Cosmas, *MACV: The Joint Command in the Years of Withdrawal, 1968–1973* (Washington, DC: Center of Military History, 2007), 324; and Hunt, 178.

48. Cooper-Church in Willbanks, 35.

49. CIA analysis in Kissinger to Nixon, 26 January 1971, *FRUS, 1969–1976*, VII: 319. On Hanoi knowing about the invasion, see John Prados, *The Blood Road: The Ho Chi Minh Trail and the Vietnam War* (New York: John Wiley & Sons, 1999), 323. According to Keith Nolan, the ARVN "were not overly enthused" by Abrams's plan, instead supporting a "short hit-and-run raid" as Westmoreland had advocated. *Into Laos*, 34.

50. Palmer, 110. Kissinger, *White House Years*, 992. Lt. Gen. James W. Sutherland Jr. reported to Abrams on 10 March 1971 that the "enemy has had foreknowledge of every move planned by I Corps in Lamson 719." Abrams Messages #9659, CMH.

51. Abrams quoted in Sorley, *Vietnam Chronicles*, 531. Abrams was referring to both his American and South Vietnamese subordinates. Opening rounds in Jim E. Fulbrook, "Lam Son 719,

Part II: The Battle," *U.S. Army Aviation Digest* (July 1986): 38–39. On alerting the NVA, see Sander, 104,117.

52. Headquarters, USMACV, "One War," MACV Command Overview, 1968–1972, Historians Files, CMH, p. 98. NVA preparations in Willard J. Webb and Walter S. Poole, *The Joint Chiefs of Staff and the War in Vietnam, 1971–1973* (Washington, DC: Office of Joint History, 2007), 6–7.

53. On General Lãm, see Nolan, *Into Laos*, 104. Lãm shared that meetings with President Thieu had "at times involved bitter oral exchanges." Sutherland to Abrams, 10 March 1971, Abrams Messages #9660, CMH. Assault waves in USMACV, "One War," MACV Command Overview, 1968–1972, Historians Files, CMH, p. 98.

54. Abrams quoted in Kissinger to Nixon, 14 February 1971, *FRUS*, 1969–1976, VII: 399. Kissinger quoted in William M. Hammond, *Public Affairs: The Military and the Media, 1968–1973* (Washington, DC: Center of Military History, 1996), 451.

55. Abrams quoted in Sorley, *Vietnam Chronicles*, 558. Nixon, conversation with Kissinger, 18 February 1971, *FRUS*, 1969-1976, VII: 404. Thieu's decision in Webb and Poole, 12–14. For an example of the negative press Nixon hoped to avoid, see "Laos: What Is the Objective?," *Newsweek*, 8 March 1971, pp. 14–15.

56. Kissinger to Bunker, 9 March 1971, *FRUS*, 1969–1976, VII: 450. 11 March briefing in Hunt, *Melvin Laird and the Foundation of the Post-Vietnam Military*, 190.

57. Kissinger to Bunker, 1 March 1971, *FRUS*, 1969–1976, VII: 438–440. Alexander M. Haig Jr., with Charles McCarry, *Inner Circles: How America Changed the World, a Memoir* (New York: Warner Books, 1992), 275. H. R. Haldeman, *The Haldeman Diaries: Inside the Nixon White House* (New York: G.P. Putnam's Sons, 1994), 250.

58. Haldeman, 259. In April, Nixon maintained his ire, telling Kissinger he was "getting sick of the military, anyway. They drag their feet about everything." Douglas Brinkley and Luke A. Nichter, eds., *The Nixon Tapes, 1971–1972* (Boston: Houghton Mifflin Harcourt, 2014), 89. On Haig's trip and Laird's defense, see Hunt, 191–192. During the visit, Haig believed "a serious debacle could evolve in the absence of firm ARVN command and control." Davison to Abrams, 19 March 1971, Abrams Messages #9726, CMH.

59. Conversation, Nixon and Kissinger, 7 June 1971, *FRUS*, 1969–1976, VII: 674. Abrams also lost the respect of his peers as well. Gen. John D. Ryan, the Air Force chief of staff, believed Abrams "did not have a feel for the intensity with which Washington viewed the Lam Son 719 operation." Webb and Poole, 16. The campaign even "jarred" the faith of Abrams's deputy commander, Fred Weyand. In Lewis Sorley, *Thunderbolt: General Creighton Abrams and the Army of His Times* (New York: Simon & Schuster, 1992), 314.

60. Editorial Note, conversations, 14 September 1971, *FRUS*, 1969–1976, VII: 905–907. Abrams, for his part, shared with the MACV staff his irritation with "Washington as an ethnic group" not understanding the war. In Sorley, *Vietnam Chronicles*, 565.

61. Murrey Marder, "Nixon Says Foe Is Seriously Hurt by Laos Assault," *The Washington Post*, 5 March 1971. "Nixon Calls Laos Operation a Success," 5 March 1971.

62. Kissinger to Nixon, 21 March 1971, Folder 1, Box 82, NSC Files, Vietnam Subject Files, RNL. "The Most Decisive Turn Since Tet," *Newsweek*, 22 February 1971, p. 31. On numbers of enemy losses reported, see Kissinger to Nixon, 27 March 1971, Folder 1, Box 80, NSC Files, Vietnam Subject Files, RNL. Kissinger shared Abrams's upbeat assessment with the president on 15 March 1971. *FRUS*, 1969–1976, VII: 454–457.

63. Haig, 278. ARVN losses in Andrew Wiest, *Vietnam's Forgotten Army: Heroism and Betrayal in the ARVN* (New York: New York University Press, 2008), 224. Enemy losses in Kissinger to Nixon, 16 April 1971, *FRUS*, 1969–1976, VII: 552–553; and "Balance Sheet on Laos—Victory or Defeat?," *U.S. News & World Report*, 5 April 1971, p. 15. On comparisons to Cambodia, see Weyand in Sorley, *Vietnam Chronicles*, 578.

64. Davison to Abrams, 14 April 1971, Abrams Messages #9901, CMH. Kissinger to Nixon, 20 March 1971, Folder 4, Box 82, NSC Files, Vietnam Subject Files, RNL. "Severely hurt" in Sutherland to Abrams, 21 March 1971, Abrams Messages #9741, CMH. Dale Van Atta agrees, arguing "Lam Son seriously disrupted the Ho Chi Minh Trail." *With Honor*, 351. Seymour M. Hersh, however, called the invasion a "classic military failure." *The Price of Power: Kissinger in the Nixon White House* (New York: Summit Books, 1983), 307.

65. "Lam Son Talking Points," 19 April 1971, Folder 4, Box 82, NSC Files, Vietnam Subject Files, RNL. Alvin Shuster, "The Campaign in Laos," *New York Times*, 24 March 1971. ". . . Increases the Credibility Gap," *New York Times*, 24 March 1971. John Saar, "An Ignominious and Disorderly Retreat," *LIFE*, 2 April 1971, 24–28.

66. Conversation, Nixon and Kissinger, 21 April 1971, *FRUS*, 1969–1976, VII: 567. Conversation, Nixon and Kissinger, 23 April 1971, ibid., 575. Abandoning in Bernard Brodie, *War and Politics* (New York: Macmillan, 1973), 207. On "Nixon's impulse to blame the press for the defeat," see Robert Dallek, *Nixon and Kissinger: Partners in Power* (New York: HarperCollins, 2007), 261.

67. Shelby L. Stanton, *Anatomy of a Division: The 1st Cav in Vietnam* (Novato, CA: Presidio Press, 1987), 241. Peter A. Jay, "After 5½ Years, First 'Cav' to Leave Vietnam," *The Washington Post*, 27 March 1971.

68. Abrams to Clay, McCaffrey, et al., 5 July 1971, Abrams Messages #10163, CMH. LTG James W. Sutherland Jr., Debriefing Report, 1 June 1971, Folder 06, Box 17, Douglas Pike Collection: Unit 02-Military Operations, TTUVA, p. 37. At the White House, Kissinger guessed in April that "the South Vietnamese aren't going anywhere where they're going to suffer casualties right now." Brinkley and Nichter, 77.

69. National Intelligence Estimate, 29 April 1971, *FRUS*, 1969–1976, VII: 596–597. Willbanks argues the "problems that were prevalent during Operation Lam Son 719 in Laos in 1971 were still there in 1972." *A Raid Too Far*, 197.

70. William J. Lederer, *Our Own Worst Enemy* (New York: W.W. Norton, 1968), 27. Stuart A. Herrington, *Silence Was a Weapon: The Vietnam War in the Villages* (Novato, CA: Presidio Press, 1982), 192. Michael Herr argued that "trying to read the faces of the Vietnamese . . . was like trying to read the wind." *Dispatches* (New York: Alfred A. Knopf, 1968, 1978), 3.

71. Ngo Cong Duc quoted in Miller, *The Vietnam War*, 186–188. ARVN letter in Neil L. Jamieson, *Understanding Vietnam* (Berkeley: University of California Press, 1993), 350. Growing resentment in Sutherland, Debriefing Report, TTUVA, 21. See also Tran Quanh Minh, "A Decade of Public Service: Nation-Building During the Interregnum and Second Republic (1964–75)," in *Voices from the Second Republic of South Vietnam (1967–1975)*, ed. K. W. Taylor (Ithaca, NY: Cornell Southeast Asia Program Publications, 2014), 75.

72. *Victory in Vietnam: The Official History of the People's Army of Vietnam, 1954-1975*, trans. Merle L. Pribbenow (Lawrence: University Press of Kansas, 2002), 277. Hanoi's overestimation in Nguyen, *Hanoi's War*, 228. Abrams quoted in Cosmas, *MACV*, 339.

73. Thompson to Kissinger, 1 April 1971, Folder 5, Box 92, NSC Files, Vietnam Subject Files, RNL. Minutes of Meeting, 24 May 1971, *FRUS*, 1969-1976, VII: 637, 640. Major quoted in Peter Osnos, "New Mood of Gloom Developing in Saigon," *The Washington Post*, 17 April 1971.

74. Bruce Palmer Jr. claimed that if a strong US advisory element remained, there was "at least a 50–50 chance for South Vietnam to 'hack it.'" *The 25-Year War*, 94. On labor and military accessions, see Douglas C. Dacy, *Foreign Aid, War, and Economic Development: South Vietnam, 1955–1975* (New York: Cambridge University Press, 1986), 17.

75. "But Who Hath Measured the Ground?," *TIME*, 15 March 1971. On Abrams not allocating personnel to Phoenix, see John Prados, *Lost Crusader: The Secret Wars of CIA Director William Colby* (New York: Oxford University Press, 2003), 232.

76. Alvin Shuster, "Colby, U.S. Chief of Pacification for Vietnam, Gives Up Duties and Returns Home," *New York Times*, 1 July 1971. George McArthur, "'Soft Spots' Show Up in S. Viet Pacification," *Los Angeles Times*, 23 July 1971. On the enemy attacking the pacification program, see Ang Cheng Guan, *Ending the Vietnam War: The Vietnamese Communists' Perspective* (London and New York: Routledge Curzon, 2004), 74.

77. Richard Nixon, *Public Papers of the Presidents of the United States, 1972* (Washington, DC: US Government Printing Office, 1974), 284. During that same time period, Kissinger reported the GVN controlled 70 percent of the population. Kissinger to Nixon, n.d., *FRUS*, 1969–1976, VIII: 43.

78. Alvin Shuster, "Kissinger and Thieu Confer on Pullout," *New York Times*, 5 July 1971. Hurting Thieu politically in Jeffrey Kimball, *Nixon's Vietnam War* (Lawrence: University Press of Kansas, 1998), 246. On the resiliency of these problems, see Clarence R. Wyatt, *Paper Soldiers: The American Press and the Vietnam War* (New York: W.W. Norton, 1993), 198.

79. "The Mudslingers," *Newsweek*, 2 August 1971, 38. Sorley, *Vietnam Chronicles*, 619. USMACV, Command History, 1971, Vol. I, NARA, p. II-8.

80. Jack Anderson, "Polls Show Viet Resentment of Chaos," *The Washington Post*, 26 January 1972. On land reform tied to political development, see MG R. Wetherill, 14 May 1971, Senior Officer Debriefing Reports, CMH, p. C-23; and Tran Dinh Tho, "Pacification," in *The Vietnam War: An Assessment by South Vietnam's Generals*, ed. Lewis Sorley (Lubbock: Texas Tech University Press, 2010), 251–252. Resentment in Peter King, "The Political Balance in Saigon," *Pacific Affairs* 44, no. 3 (Autumn 1971): 408; and Duong Van Mai Elliott, *The Sacred Willow: Four Generations in the Life of a Vietnamese Family* (New York: Oxford University Press, 1999), 314. On "omnipresence of 'cliques,'" see Joseph W. Dodd, "Faction and Failure in South Vietnam," *Asian Affairs* 2, no. 3 (January-February 1975): 175.

81. Officials quoted in George McArthur, "Vietnam: One Man-One Vote," *Los Angeles Times*, 29 August 1971. Social revolution and agricultural output in Simon Toner, "'The Life and Death of our Republic': Modernization, Agricultural Development and the Peasantry in the Mekong Delta in the Long 1970s," in *Decolonization and the Cold War: Negotiating Independence*, eds. Leslie James and Elisabeth Leake (London: Bloomsbury, 2015), 48, 51. Strongman in Bùi Diễm with David Chanoff, *In the Jaws of History* (Bloomington: Indiana University Press, 1999), 289. Corruption in Cushman to Abrams, 7 June 1971, Abrams Messages #10065, CMH. Lack of social mobility in Jeffrey Race, *War Comes to Long An: Revolutionary Conflict in a Vietnamese Province* (Berkeley: University of California Press, 1972), 274. Herbert Mitgang called the October 1971 political campaign an "uncontested nonelection." "The Nonwar War," *New York Times*, 27 September 1971.

82. Motto in *Vietnam and America: A Documented History*, eds. Marvin E. Gettleman, Jane Franklin, Marilyn Young, and H. Bruce Franklin (New York: Grove Press, 1985), 464. Acres in the Committee of Concerned Asian Scholars, *The Indochina Story: A Fully Documented Account* (New York: Pantheon Books, 1970), 113. For an overview on chemical warfare, see Edwin A. Martini, *Agent Orange: History, Science, and the Politics of Uncertainty* (Amherst: University of Massachusetts Press, 2012); and Peter Sills, *Toxic War: The Story of Agent Orange* (Nashville, TN: Vanderbilt University Press, 2014).

83. J3 Inputs to Report of the MACV Effort, 1968-1970, Filing Cabinet B9, Box 3, MACV Command Historian's Collection, MHI, p. II-149. Frank Mankiewicz and Tom Braden, "The Defoliation Deception," *The Washington Post*, 29 December 1970. Victor Cohn, "Vietnam Defoliation Called a Failure," *The Washington Post*, 30 December 1970. On Laird and MACV phase-out, see Wilbur H. Morrison, *The Elephant and the Tiger: The Full Story of the Vietnam War* (New York: Hippocrene Books, 1990), 469–471.

84. On the long-term problems of redefining social and political spaces, see Shaun Kingsley Malarney, *Culture, Ritual and Revolution in Vietnam* (Honolulu: University of Hawaii Press, 2002), chapter 1. Supporting government bureaucracy in Charles A. Joiner, *The Politics of Massacre: Political Processes in South Vietnam* (Philadelphia: Temple University Press, 1974), 54–55.

85. Pham Quoc Thuan, "A Vietnam Solution," *Military Review* Vol. 51, no. 6 (June 1971): 91. Abrams to Milloy, Vann, Wagstaff, and Cushman, 5 June 1971, Box V, Creighton W. Abrams Papers, May 1971–June 1972, MHI. See also Abrams to Clay, McCaffrey, et al., 5 July 1971, ibid. In July, Abrams was still focused on the "removal and replacement of ineffective leaders." COMUSMACV to CINCPAC, RVNAF Leadership, 11 July 1971, RVNAF Assessments 1971, Historians Files, CMH. Jack Foisie, "Vietnamese Blame Departing Americans for War Woes," *The Washington Post*, 14 October 1971.

86. Abrams quoted in Sorley, *Vietnam Chronicles*, 633. Air support in Haig, The Situation in the Countryside, September 1971, Folder 1, Box 1014, NSC Files, Alexander M. Haig Special File, RNL, p. 5. See also Iver Peterson, "Resor, in Vietnam, Expects Difficulties as Troops Pull Out," *New York Times*, 4 May 1971.

87. Abrams in Sorley, 647. Peter Osnos, "The War: Uneasy Lull," *The Washington Post*, 1 August 1971. On decline in "combat results," see Cushman to Abrams, 17 September 1971, Abrams Messages #10390, CMH. Minutes of a Meeting of the Senior Review Group, 24 May 1971, *FRUS, 1969–1976*, VII: 629. Moorer in Webb and Poole, *The Joint Chiefs of Staff and The War in Vietnam*, 101.

88. Haig to Kissinger, 27 September 1971, Folder 1, Box 1014, NSC Files, Alexander M. Haig Special File, RNL. ARVN commanders in MR3 still saw an attack by "enemy divisions as their primary threat," thus complicating MACV efforts to focus on pacification. Wagstaff to Abrams, 12 July 1971, Abrams Messages #10190, CMH.

89. May diplomatic "package" in David F. Schmitz, *Richard Nixon and the Vietnam War: The End of the American Century* (Lanham, MD: Rowman & Littlefield, 2014), 129. "Decent interval" in Jeffrey Kimball, *The Vietnam War Files: Uncovering the Secret History of Nixon-Era Strategy* (Lawrence: University Press of Kansas, 2004), 186–187. Kimball sees this document as "incontrovertible 'incriminating' proof" of Nixon and Kissinger's support. See also Ken Hughes, *Fatal Politics: The Nixon Tapes, the Vietnam War, and the Casualties of Reelection* (Charlottesville: University of Virginia Press, 2015), 44.

90. Kissinger to Nixon, 26 July 1971, *FRUS, 1969–1976*, VII: 836–839. See also Allan E. Goodman, *The Search for a Negotiated Settlement of the Vietnam War* (Berkeley: Institute of East Asian Studies, 1986), 62–63. Kissinger on Abrams in Brinkley and Nichter, *The Nixon Tapes*, 167.

91. On "illusory peace," see Edward Miller, review of Schmitz, *The Journal of Military History* 80, no. 3 (July 2016): 964. Winston Lord, interview by Charles Stuart Kennedy and Nancy Bernkopf Tucker, 28 April 1998, Association for Diplomatic Studies and Training Foreign Affairs Oral History Project, p. 260.

92. More recently, Kissinger argued, "We who made the agreement thought it would be the beginning, not of peace in the American sense, but the beginning of a period of coexistence which might evolve, as it did in Korea, into two states." In Ralph Blumenthal, "The Ones Who Were Left Behind: Ghosts of Vietnam in Rory Kennedy's Documentary," *The New York Times*, 28 August 2014.

93. "Big play" in Brinkley and Nichter, 298. Kissinger acknowledged that a "swift collapse in South Vietnam . . . would seriously endanger [Nixon's] effort to shape a new foreign policy role for this country." To Nixon, 18 September 1971, *FRUS, 1969–1976*, VII: 918. Robert K. Brigham offered sound advice on this paragraph. Email to author, 25 October 2016.

94. Sino-US negotiations in Guan, *Ending the Vietnam War*, 75. Kissinger, To Nixon, 18 September 1971, *FRUS, 1969–1976*, VII: 919. Bitter pill from John M. Carland, email to author, 25 September 2016.

95. Kissinger to Bunker, 23 August 1972, *FRUS, 1969–1976*, VII: 886. State Department in Kissinger, *White House Years*, 1032. Thieu's authority on p. 1034.

96. Embassy judgment in Editorial Note, *FRUS, 1969–1976*, VII: 975. Mikva quoted in Gettleman, *Vietnam and America*, 460. Coup warnings in Larry Berman, *No Peace, No Honor: Nixon, Kissinger, and Betrayal in Vietnam* (New York: The Free Press, 2001), 99. Berger quoted in Sorley, *Vietnam Chronicles*, 717.

97. "Combat Unit Deactivated in Vietnam," *The Washington Post*, 1 November 1971. Nixon, *Public Papers of the Presidents of the United States, 1971*, 1101. "As Vietnam Gets Set for Faster Pullout—," *U.S. News & World Report*, 15 November 1971, p. 45.

98. Nixon, *RN*, 584. Michael Getler and George McArthur, "Abrams' Bombing Rationale," *The Washington Post*, 30 December 1971. William McGaffin, "Abrams Request Cited as Reason for N. Viet Raids," *Los Angeles Times*, 1 January 1972. Evelyn Keene, "Nixon 'New Barbarian' Drinan Says at Protest," *Boston Globe*, 2 January 1972.

99. Abrams to Lavelle, McCaffrey, et al., 20 February 1972, Abrams Messages #11328, CMH. "Advisory Unit Only to Be Left When Abrams Leaves Vietnam," *Los Angeles Times*, 14 January 1972. "U.S. Troop Commander to Leave South Vietnam," *The Hartford Courant*, 15 January 1972.

100. Combined Campaign Plan, 1972, Historians Files, CMH, p. 2. USMACV, Command History, 1968, Vol. I, NARA, p. 13.

101. Realities in Elliott, *NLF-DRV Strategy and the 1972 Spring Offensive*, 40. 1971 planning in Guan, 85–85; and Webb and Poole, 83–85.

102. Offensive objectives in *Victory in Vietnam*, 283; and Stephen P. Randolph, *Powerful and Brutal Weapons: Nixon, Kissinger, and the Easter Offensive* (Cambridge, MA: Harvard University Press, 2007), 26. Consensus in Nguyen, *Hanoi's War*, 234. See also Hunt, *Melvin Laird*, 213–214.

103. Martin F. Nolan, "Nixon Calls Viet Talks '3½-Year Filibuster,'" *Boston Globe*, 25 March 1972. Terse response in Qiang Zhai, *China and the Vietnam Wars, 1950–1975* (Chapel Hill: University of North Carolina Press, 2000), 200. Chinese pressures in Mark Atwood Lawrence, *The Vietnam War: An International History in Documents* (New York: Oxford University Press, 2014), 156. Links to airpower in Brinkley and Nichter, 394.

104. Territory in relation to negotiations in Allan E. Goodman, *The Lost Peace: America's Search for a Negotiated Settlement of the Vietnam War* (Stanford, CA: Hoover Institution Press, 1978), 117–118. Nguyen Hue in Dale Andrade, *America's Last Vietnam Battle: Halting Hanoi's 1972 Easter Offensive* (Lawrence: University Press of Kansas, 1995, 2001), 29.

105. Final plans in *Victory in Vietnam*, 289–290. Spearheads in Col. G. H. Turley, *The Easter Offensive: Vietnam, 1972* (Novato, CA: Presidio Press, 1985), 29.

106. Tank sightings in Vann to Abrams, 26 January 1972, Abrams Messages #11106, CMH. Abrams to Dolvin, Van, et al., 7 February 1972, Abrams Messages #11199, CMH. Abrams's views in Abrams to Moorer, McCain, 1 February 1972; and Kissinger to Nixon, 29 January 1972, *FRUS, 1969-1976*, VIII: 37.

107. General Lâm quoted in Dolvin to Abrams, 5 March 1972, Abrams Messages #11449, CMH. Inconclusive intelligence in HQ PACAF Directorate of Operations Analysis, "The 1972 Invasion of Military Region I: Fall of Quang Tri and Defense of Hue," 15 March 1973, Folder 1055, Box 16, Vietnam Archive Collection, TTUVA, p. 7. See also Thomas H. Lee, "Military Intelligence Operations and the Easter Offensive," Folder 18, Box 03, Glenn Helm Collection, TTUVA. On Ho Chi Minh Trail, see Andrade, 6.

108. Any day in Sorley, *Vietnam Chronicles*, 777. Abrams to Lavelle, Dolvin, and Vann, 31 January 1972, Box V, Creighton W. Abrams Papers, MHI. On advocating border strikes, see Vann to Abrams, 2 February 1972, Abrams Messages #11154, CMH. Conversation, Nixon and Kissinger, 20 January 1972, *FRUS, 1969–1976*, VIII: 10.

109. Laird to Kissinger, Situation in Southeast Asia, 10 March 1972, Folder 3, Box 1014, NSC Files, Alexander M. Haig Special File, RNL, p. 5. Peter Osnos, "US Air Strikes at 1½-Year High," *Boston Globe*, 13 February 1972.

110. Ian Ward, "Why Giap Did It: Report from Saigon," *Conflict Studies*, no. 27 (October 1972): 3. HQ PACAF Directorate of Operations Analysis, TTUVA, p. 13. According to Nguyễn Công Luận, in Hué "the small number of police and military police were unable to control the mass of refugees and soldiers." *Nationalist in the Viet Nam Wars: Memoirs of a Victim Turned Soldier* (Bloomington: Indiana University Press, 2012), 401.

111. "North Viet Attack Across DMZ Sends Saigon Troops Running," *The Hartford Courant*, 3 April 1972. Nixon, *RN*, 587. JCS to CINCPAC, 4 April 1972, Folder 1, Box 1016, NSC Files, Alexander M. Haig Special File, RNL. Andrade, *America's Last Vietnam Battle*, 59.

112. Editorial Note, *FRUS, 1969–1976*, VIII: 155. Moorer quoted in Webb and Poole, 156.

113. Jack Anderson, "Nixon War Move May Have Backfired," *The Washington Post*, 13 April 1972. Nixon was furious over ARVN being "taken by surprise," since MACV was "in charge of the goddamned intelligence out there." Conversation, Nixon and Kissinger, 3 April 1972, *FRUS, 1969–1976*, VIII: 163.

114. Conversation, Nixon, Kissinger, Laird, and Moorer, 17 April 1972, *FRUS, 1969–1976*, VIII: 272–273. Paul Houston, "More B-52s Sent to Counter Hanoi Drive," *Los Angeles Times*, 5 April 1972.

115. Effectiveness in Abrams to Laird, 2 May 1972, Abrams Messages #11966, CMH. See also Lewis Sorley, "Courage and Blood: South Vietnam's Repulse of the 1972 Easter Offensive," *Parameters* 29, no. 2 (Summer 1999): 48. Countering NVA tanks in Laird to Nixon, Tanks in the ARVN, 30 April 1972, Folder 6, Box 117, NSC Files, Vietnam Subject Files, RNL. Psychological setback in HQ PACAF Directorate of Operations Analysis, TTUVA, 50. Haig, *Inner Circles*, 287.

116. NVA losses in Andrade, 171. Off balance in Latimer to Kissinger, 7 May 1972, Folder 6, Box 117, NSC Files, Vietnam Subject Files, RNL. "Vietnamization: A Policy Under the Gun," *TIME*, 17 April 1972, p. 30. See also David Halberstam, "Nixon Was Fated to Try Vietnamization—and Fail," *Boston Globe*, 14 May 1972.

117. Nixon, *Public Papers of the Presidents of the United States, 1972*, 550–554. Darius Jhabvala, "Nixon to Continue Pullout, Bombing," *Boston Globe*, 27 April 1972. Two weeks earlier,

Moorer made it clear there was no intention of committing additional US ground troops. Rudy Abramson, "Moorer Has Optimistic Viet of Viet Situation," 12 April 1972.

118. Moscow Summit in Walter Isaacson, *Kissinger: A Biography* (New York: Simon & Schuster, 1992), 425–426; and Bundy, *A Tangled Web*, 314–315. Abrams to Laird, 26 April 1972, Abrams Messages #11906, CMH.

119. American Embassy, Saigon to Secretary of State, 11 May 1972, Folder 6, Box 117, NSC Files, Vietnam Subject Files, RNL. Craig R. Whitney, "Pessimism in Saigon," *New York Times*, 3 May 1972.

120. David E. Hoffman, "Secret Archive Offers Fresh Insight into Nixon Presidency," *The Washington Post*, 11 October 2015. Linebacker objectives in Moorer to Laird, 15 May 1972, *FRUS*, 1969–1976, VIII: 559–561; and John Schlight, *A War Too Long: The USAF in Southeast Asia, 1961–1975* (Washington, DC: Air Force History and Museums Program, 1996), 92–96. Destructor campaign in Moorer to Laird, 12 October 1972, *FRUS*, 1969–1976, IX: 117. Campaign overview in Mark Clodfelter, *The Limits of Airpower: The American Bombing of North Vietnam* (New York: The Free Press, 1989), 158–163.

121. Sorties in Peter Osnos, "Bombing of North Spreads to Nonmilitary Targets," *The Washington Post*, 24 May 1972; and A. J. C. Lavalle, ed., *Airpower and the 1972 Spring Invasion* (Washington, DC: US Government Printing Office, 1976), 106. "US Widens Bombing of North Vietnam," *Boston Globe*, 24 May 1972. John Paul Vann on ARVN leadership in Andrade, 217. Staying power in Abrams to Laird, 1 May 1972, Abrams Messages #11960, CMH. Nixon to Kissinger, 9 May 1972, *FRUS*, 1969–1976, VIII: 520.

122. Moorer to Abrams, 8 April 1972, *FRUS*, 1969–1976, VIII: 231. Moorer, diary entry, 12 April 1972, ibid., 237–238. Haldeman, *The Haldeman Diaries*, 440. Soviet response in Col. Walter L. Harris, "The Linebacker Campaigns: An Analysis" (Air War College Research Report, Maxwell Air Force Base, 1987), 9.

123. Haldeman, diary entry, 4 May 1972, *FRUS*, 1969–1976, VIII: 252. Kissinger to Bunker, ibid., 433. On losing confidence, see Hughes, *Fatal Politics*, 67. Haig report, 18 April 1972, Folder 1, Box 1016, NSC Files, Alexander M. Haig Special File, RNL.

124. Disgusted in Nixon to Kissinger and Haig, 19 May 1972, Folder 2, Box 1006, NSC Files, Alexander M. Haig Special File, RNL. No imagination and drinking in Conversation, Nixon, Kissinger, and Moorer, 3 April 1972, *FRUS*, 1969–1976, VIII: 17; and conversation, Nixon and Kissinger, 4 April 1972, ibid., 212.

125. Laird support in Laird to Abrams, 16 April 1972, Abrams Messages #11831, CMH. Editorial note, *FRUS*, 1969–1976, VIII: 392. Negroponte to Kissinger, 2 May 1972, ibid., 427–428. Conversation, Nixon and Kissinger, 5 May 1972, ibid., 449.

126. Nixon in Brinkley and Nichter, 494. Tran Van Dinh, "The Destruction of a Society," in *Why Are We Still in Vietnam?*, eds. Sam Brown and Len Ackland (New York: Random House, 1970), 58. For an American perspective, see John Prados, ed., *In Country: Remembering the Vietnam War* (London: Ivan R. Dee, 2011), 271.

127. Laotian quoted in Fred Branfman, ed., *Voices from the Plain of Jars: Life under an Air War* (Madison: University of Wisconsin Press, 1972, 2013), 111. Refugees in George, McCarthur, "With Saigon's Army Busy, Red Guerillas Gain in Countryside," *Los Angeles Times*, 31 May 1972. Craig Whitney, "Pacification Hopes Battered in Vietnam," *New York Times*, 21 June 1972. Thousands of tons of bombs in Jonathan Schell, *Observing the Nixon Years* (New York: Pantheon Books, 1989), 134.

128. Abrams quoted in Sorley, *Vietnam Chronicles*, 832. Kissinger to Bunker, n.d., Folder 2, Box 80, NSC Files, Vietnam Subject Files, RNL.

129. Conversation, Nixon and Kissinger, 6 May 1972, Chronological File, May 6–8, 1972, Box 14, Kissinger Telephone Conversations, Presidential Materials, NARA.

130. Editorial Note, *FRUS*, 1969–1976, VIII: 512–513. On the port closings, see Randolph, *Powerful and Brutal Weapons*, 172–182.

131. Antiwar activity in Hammond, *Public Affairs*, 570. Henry Kissinger, *Ending the Vietnam War: A History of America's Involvement in and Extrication from the Vietnam War* (New York: Simon & Schuster, 2003), 268. Slowdown of negotiations in Negroponte to Kissinger, 14 April 1972, *FRUS*, 1969–1976, VIII: 255. Thomas Oliphant, "Nixon Orders Blockade of N. Vietnam," *Boston Globe*, 9 May 1972.

132. Joseph Alsop, "An Loc Defense Heroic Saga," *The Hartford Courant*, 23 May 1972. Bomb numbers in George McArthur, "An Loc—the Battle That Couldn't Be Lost," *Los Angeles Times*, 19 June 1972. Thieu in Andrade, 451. Abrams use of B-52s in Abrams to Agnew, 17 May 1972, Abrams Messages #12113, CMH; and "B52s Retaliate After Foe Renews Attack on An Loc," *Boston Globe*, 21 April 1972.

133. Advisor quoted in McArthur, "An Loc." Bulldozers in General Tran Van Nhut, *An Loc: The Unfinished War* (Lubbock: Texas Tech University Press, 2009), 125. Casualties in James H. Willbanks, *The Battle of An Loc* (Bloomington: Indiana University Press, 2005), 147–148. "Control" in Lam Quang Thi, *Hell in An Loc: The 1972 Easter Invasion and the Battle That Saved South Vietnam* (Denton: University of North Texas Press, 2009), 218.

134. Abrams quoted in Kissinger to Nixon, 19 May 1972, *FRUS, 1969–1976*, VIII: 611; and Sorley, *Vietnam Chronicles*, 842. Air Force Gen, John W. Vogt Jr. views of the "screwed up" ground war in Webb and Poole, 188. NVA casualties in Andrade, 329, 487. "Test" in William Colby with James McCargar, *Lost Victory: A Firsthand Account of America's Sixteen-Year Involvement in Vietnam* (Chicago: Contemporary Books, 1989), 321.

135. Haig, *Inner Circles*, 292. Michael Parks, "Vietnam Assessment: The South Is Unable to Stand Alone," *Boston Globe*, 25 June 1972. See also "Assessment of Easter Offensive: June 24 1972," Folder 04, Box 24, Douglas Pike Collection: Unit 01-Assessment and Strategy, TTUVA.

136. New lease in Trip Report, 1–3 July 1972, Folder 3, Box 1016, NSC Files, Alexander M. Haig Special File, RNL. Nixon to Kissinger and Haig, 15 May 1972, Folder 2, Box 1006, ibid. Laird support in Seymour M. Hersh, "Abrams Is Choice as Chief of Staff," *New York Times*, 1 June 1972. No public ceremonies in Andrade, 173. See also Richard Levine, "Nixon to Nominate Abrams as Army Chief; Move Unlikely to Help Service's Image," *Wall Street Journal*, 21 June 1972.

137. On Lavelle, see Mark Clodfelter, *Violating Reality: The Lavelle Affair, Nixon, and the Parsing of the Truth* (Washington, DC: National Defense University Press, 2016); and Schlight, *A War Too Long*, 85–86. Lavelle quoted in "Gen. Abrams on the Griddle," *Boston Globe*, 3 July 1972. Abrams responded on 15 June 1972 to a Laird information request that air strikes in North Vietnam were "directed within authorities prescribed by higher authority." Abrams Messages #12338, CMH.

138. Joseph Kraft, "Gen. Lavelle a Scapegoat?," *Boston Globe*, 19 June 72. Edward L. King, "Civilian Control Is Still the Issue," *The Washington Post*, 1 October 1972. "Civilian Control. . . ," *New York Times*, 17 September 1972.

139. Stennis in "Gen. Abrams on the Griddle." Joseph B. Treaster, "In Command in Vietnam," *New York Times*, 4 July 1972.

140. Smith quoted in "Senator Hits Abrams for 'Failing Duty,'" *The Hartford Courant*, 12 October 1972. Rudy Abramson, "Senate Oks Abrams as Army Chief, 84 to 2," *Los Angeles Times*, 13 October 1972. Conversation, Nixon, Kissinger, and Haig, 14 December 1972, *FRUS*, 1969–1976, IX: 666. On Nixon's continuing distrust of Abrams, see Randolph, 89.

141. Doubts on South Vietnam's survival in Brinkley and Nichter, *The Nixon Tapes*, 605.

142. Memorandum of conversation, 6 December 1972, Box 865, NSC Files, Nixon Presidential Materials, NARA.

143. Settle in Jack Anderson, "Nixon Is Deferring Viet Showdown," *The Washington Post*, 18 May 1972. Nixon and Kissinger quoted in Miller, *The Vietnam War*, 214. See also Craig R. Whitney, "U.S. Aides in Vietnam See an Unending War," *New York Times*, 1 September 1972. Links to election in Grandin, *Kissinger's Shadow*, 87–88.

144. Battlefield assessments in Guan, 104; and Asselin, *A Bitter Peace*, 73. Bundy argues the "United States had to make a deal with Hanoi that would sit badly with Thieu, almost regardless of its specific terms." *A Tangled Web*, 356.

145. Robert K. Brigham, *Guerrilla Diplomacy: The NLF's Foreign Relations and the Viet Nam War* (Ithaca, NY: Cornell University Press, 1999), 104–108. Michael H. Hunt and Steven I. Levine, *Arc of Empire: America's Wars in Asia from the Philippines to Vietnam* (Chapel Hill: University of North Carolina Press, 2012), 233. Schaffer, *Ellsworth Bunker*, 240–241.

146. Negroponte to Kissinger, Some Thoughts on Where We Stand on Negotiations, 4 October 1972, Folder 1, Box 1017, NSC Files, Alexander M. Haig Special File, RNL.

147. Resupply provisions in Arnold R. Isaacs, *Without Honor: Defeat in Vietnam and Cambodia* (Baltimore: Johns Hopkins University Press, 1983), 37. Haig memorandum, 20 October 1972, *FRUS*, 1969–1976, IX: 218. Thieu dissatisfaction with the October draft in Goodman, *The Lost Peace*, 144–145. Nixon quoted in Brinkley and Nichter, 622. Nixon told Thieu the "most important provision" is that the GVN would "remain intact after the ceasefire has been observed." 16 October 1972, *FRUS*, 1969-1976, IX: 169.

148. Abrams selling the war in Hughes, *Fatal Politics*, 114; and Murrey Marder, "He, Abrams to Bargain With Thieu," *The Washington Post*, 18 October 1972. Thieu quoted in Asselin, 90. Not wanting *any* peace in Nhut, *An Loc*, 175. Isaacson treats this episode in *Kissinger*, 446–456.

149. Willing partner in Pierre Asselin, H-Diplo FRUS Reviews, No. 21, 17 April 2013, 2. Hard line and honor in Nixon to Kissinger, 24 November 1972, *FRUS*, 1969–1976, IX: 443. Fox Butterfield, "Thieu Is Reported Adamant in Talks with Nixon Envoy," *New York Times*, 11 November 1972.

150. Thieu's objections in Goodman, *The Search for a Negotiated Settlement of the Vietnam War*, 98–99. NSC staffer quoted on p. 97. Asselin, *A Bitter Peace*, 111. Isaacs, 50–53.

151. Settlement in Haldeman, 555. Bomb the hell out of Hanoi in Conversation, Nixon and Haig, 12 December 1972, *FRUS*, 1969–1976, IX: 586. Diplomatic cable in Goodman, 107.

152. Nixon, *RN*, 733. Blow in *FRUS*, 1969–1976, IX: 586. JCS in conversation, Moorer and Vogt, ibid., 680.

153. Conversation, Nixon and Kissinger, 17 December 1972, *FRUS*, 1969–1976, IX: 717. Hanoi Radio in "Massive Bombing of North Resumed," *The Hartford Courant*, 19 December 1972, 42,000 bombs in Harris, "The Linebacker Campaigns," 24. Targeting Hanoi's will in Clodfelter, *The Limits of Airpower*, 182. For a campaign overview, see Wayne Thompson, *To Hanoi and Back: The United States Air Force and North Vietnam, 1966-1973* (Washington, DC: Air Force History and Museums Program, 2000), chapter 10.

154. "McGovern Criticizes Renewal of Bombing," *The Hartford Courant*, 19 December 1972. Robert R. Bowie, "The Agony of Vietnam," *The Christian Science Monitor*, 27 December 1972. "Paper Hits Nixon on Bombing," *Boston Globe*, 22 December 1972.

155. Thieu in Haig, *Inner Circles*, 310. See also Donald Kirk, "Haig Assures Thieu U.S. Won't Force Surrender on South Viet," *Chicago Tribune*, 20 December 1972; and Isaacs, 60. General Cao Van Vien, *The Final Collapse* (Washington, DC: US Army Center of Military History, 1985), 154–155.

156. "15th B-52 Downed as U.S. Jets Pound North for 11th Day," *Los Angeles Times*, 29 December 1972. Haig, 310. U. S. Grant Sharp, *Strategy for Defeat: Vietnam in Retrospect* (San Rafael, CA: Presidio Press, 1978), 255. Sir Robert Thompson stated the war was won. See also Moorer in Guenter Lewy, "Some Political-Military Lessons of the Vietnam War," in *Assessing the Vietnam War: A Collection from the Journal of the U.S. Army War College*, eds. Lloyd J. Matthews and Dale E. Brown (Washington, DC: Pergamon-Brassey's International Defense Publishers, 1987), and Vogt in "Air Power & The 1972 Easter Offensive: 9/72," Folder 02, Box 19, Douglas Pike Collection: Unit 02-Military Operations, TTUVA.

157. Agreement comparisons in Prados, *Vietnam*, 513. Infiltration in Kissinger to Nixon, 14 March 1973, *FRUS*, 1969–1976, X: 144. The efficacy of this final air campaign remains hotly debated. Kissinger's aide John Negroponte, for instance, argued, "We bombed the North Vietnamese into accepting our concessions." Quoted in Susan A. Brewer, *Why America Fights: Patriotism and War Propaganda from the Philippines to Iraq* (New York: Oxford University Press, 2009), 224.

158. On effective governance, see Volney F. Warner, interview by Dean M. Owen, 1983, Senior Officers Oral History Program, Box 1, Volney F. Warner Papers, MHI. Peace Nixon could live with in Kissinger, *Ending the Vietnam War*, 111.

159. LTG Ninh Loc, "National Defense: The Key to Vietnam Survival," *Military Review* 51, no. 7 (July 1971): 94. On cohering force to political purpose, see Rupert Smith, *The Utility of Force: The Art of War in the Modern World* (New York: Alfred A. Knopf, 2007), 21. On leaving behind an ARVN that could fight a war by themselves, see Stephen T. Hosmer, Konrad Kellen, and Brian M. Jenkins, *The Fall of South Vietnam: Statements by Vietnamese Military and Civilian Leaders* (New York: Crane, Russak, 1980), 88. Political corollary to military power from Robert K. Brigham, conversation with author, 12 October 2016.

Epilogue and Conclusions

1. H. R. Haldeman, *The Haldeman Diaries: Inside the Nixon White House* (New York: G.P. Putnam's Sons, 1994), 572. Richard Nixon, *No More Vietnams* (New York: Arbor House: 1985), 18. On how the agreement's articles were carried out, see Arnold R. Isaacs, *Without Honor: Defeat in Vietnam and Cambodia* (Baltimore: Johns Hopkins University Press, 1983), 64–68.
2. Frances FitzGerald, "Vietnam: A Long Way From Peace," *The Washington Post*, 28 January 1973. See also Bernard Gwertzman, "The Cease-Fire Accords and Beyond: Some Questions and Answers," *New York Times*, 26 January 1973. Kissinger quoted in Laurence Stern, "Serious Pitfalls Facing 'Evolution' of Peace Agreement," *The Washington Post*, 27 January 1973.
3. Conversation, Kissinger and Haig, 15 March 1973, *FRUS, 1969–1976*, X: 149. Sylvan Fox, "Saigon and the Vietcong Charge Fighting Goes On; U.S. Aides Term It 'Light,'" *New York Times*, 30 January 1973. Kissinger recalled that he believed the "agreement could have worked." *Ending the Vietnam War: A History of America's Involvement in and Extrication from the Vietnam War* (New York: Simon & Schuster, 2003), 428.
4. Intense political activity in Kissinger to Nixon, 9 March 1973, *FRUS, 1969–1976*, X: 143. POW return in Walter Scott Dillard, *Sixty Days to Peace: Implementing the Paris Peace Accords, Vietnam 1973* (Honolulu: University Press of the Pacific, 2003), 73–74. NVA recruits in James H. Willbanks, *Abandoning Vietnam: How America Left and South Vietnam Lost Its War* (Lawrence: University Press of Kansas, 2004), 192. North's goal of control in USMACV, Command History, 1972, Entry MACJ03, RG 472, NARA, p. 1. Time bomb in Stuart A. Herrington, *Peace with Honor? An American Reports on Vietnam, 1973–1975* (Novato, CA: Presidio Press, 1983), 34.
5. "Text of Talks by U.S. General on Leaving Vietnam," *New York Times*, 30 March 1973. George McArthur, "America's Last Farewell to Vietnam—Some Even Cried," *Los Angeles Times*, 29 March 1973. Joseph B. Treaster, "U.S. Forces Out of Vietnam; Hanoi Frees the Last P.O.W.," *New York Times*, 30 March 1973.
6. Crocker Snow Jr., "The Vietnam Withdrawal," *Boston Globe*, 1 April 1973. Laird to Shillitoe, 25 October 1972, *FRUS, 1969–1976*, IX: 301–303. As these efforts related to the ceasefire agreement, see Dillard, 19.
7. On Enhance Plus, see William E. Le Gro, *Vietnam from Cease-Fire to Capitulation* (Washington, DC: US Army Center of Military History, 1981), 17–18; and Willard J. Webb and Walter S. Poole, *The Joint Chiefs of Staff and the War in Vietnam, 1971–1973* (Washington, DC: Office of Joint History, 2007), 213–215. On criticisms of the program, see Bui Diem in Stephen T. Hosmer, Konrad Kellen, and Brian M. Jenkins, *The Fall of South Vietnam: Statements by Vietnamese Military and Civilian Leaders* (New York: Crane, Russak, 1980), 32–33. $750 million in William S. Turley, *The Second Indochina War: A Concise Political and Military History*, 2nd ed. (Lanham, MD: Rowman & Littlefield, 1986, 2009), 211. NLF in John M. Gates, "People's War in Vietnam," *Journal of Military History* 54, no. 3 (July 1990): 338. Thomas W. Lippman, "Saigon Fights to Regain Land, People," *The Washington Post*, 30 September 1973.
8. War Powers Resolution in P. Edward Haley, *Congress and the Fall of South Vietnam and Cambodia* (East Brunswick, NJ: Fairleigh Dickinson University Press, 1982), 41–42; and Robert D. Schulzinger, *A Time for War: The United States and Vietnam, 1941–1975* (New York: Oxford University Press, 1997), 314. Economic woes and declining aid in George J. Veith, *Black April: The Fall of South Vietnam, 1973–75* (New York: Encounter Books, 2012), 55. On Watergate in relation to Vietnam, see Michael S. Sherry, *In the Shadow of War: The United States since the 1930s* (New Haven, CT: Yale University Press, 1995), 333; and George C. Herring, *America's Longest War: The United States and Vietnam, 1950–1975*, 4th ed. (New York: McGraw-Hill, 1979, 2002), 328.
9. Strategic opportunity in *Victory in Vietnam: The Official History of the People's Army of Vietnam, 1954-1975*, trans. Merle L. Pribbenow (Lawrence: University Press of Kansas, 2002), 341. Consolidation in Le Gro, 33. 1973 tasks in Ang Cheng Guan, *Ending the Vietnam War: The Vietnamese Communists' Perspective* (London and New York: RoutledgeCurzon, 2004), 151; and General Cao Van Vien, *The Final Collapse* (Washington, DC: US Army Center of Military History, 1985), 39.

10. Le Duan quoted in *A Vietnam War Reader: A Documentary History from American and Vietnamese Perspectives*, ed. Michael H. Hunt (Chapel Hill: University of North Carolina Press, 2010), 189. On preparation for final offensive, see Veith, 75–87.

11. For explanations on the causes of South Vietnam's collapse, see Lam Quang Thi, "A View from the Other Side of the Story: Reflections of a South Vietnamese Soldier," in *Rolling Thunder in a Gentle Land: The Vietnam War Revisited*, ed. Andrew Wiest (New York: Osprey, 2006), 133; Hosmer, Kellen, and Jenkins, 159; and Veith, 6, 498–499. On Hanoi's planning, see Merle L. Pribbenow, "North Vietnam's Final Offensive: Strategic Endgame Nonpareil," *Parameters* 29, no. 4 (Winter 1999-2000): 58-71.

12. On the agreement being seen as a "temporary truce," see Isaacs, 83. See also Larry Berman, *No Peace, No Honor: Nixon, Kissinger, and Betrayal in Vietnam* (New York: The Free Press, 2001), 76; and Pierre Asselin, *A Bitter Peace: Washington, Hanoi, and the Making of the Paris Agreement* (Chapel Hill: University of North Carolina Press, 2002), xi.

13. Van Vien, 37. Children in Nguyễn Công Luận, *Nationalist in the Viet Nam Wars: Memoirs of a Victim Turned Soldier* (Bloomington: Indiana University Press, 2012), 424.

14. Thieu quoted in Hunt, *A Vietnam War Reader*, 190.

15. Kissinger in Irwin Abrams, ed., *Nobel Lectures: Peace, 1971–1980* (River Edge, NJ: World Scientific, 1997), 54. On American reactions, see Jeremi Suri, *Henry Kissinger and the American Century* (Cambridge, MA: Belknap Press of Harvard University Press, 2007), 232; and Schulzinger, 313.

16. Richard Nixon, *Public Papers of the Presidents of the United States, 1971* (Washington, DC: US Government Printing Office, 1972), 252. Four No's in Mark Atwood Lawrence, *The Vietnam War: A Concise International History* (New York: Oxford University Press, 2008), 162.

17. Nixon, conversation with Monica Crowley, quoted in Berman, *No Peace, No Honor*, 7. Nixon also told Crowley that "looking back I think the biggest flaw with the Paris Peace Accords of 1973 was that the cease-fire provisions allowed the North Vietnamese forces to stay in some territory captured in the '72 invasion" (p. 234). William J. Duiker argues Nixon's greatest success was "in redefining the terms of the conflict." *Sacred War: Nationalism and Revolution in a Divided Vietnam* (Boston: McGraw-Hill, 1995), 238–239.

18. Kissinger, *Ending the Vietnam War*, 556-560. Johnson's Secretary of State Dean Rusk recalled "two things we could not turn over to the Nixon administration: a unified congress and a unified people." *As I Saw It* (New York: W.W. Norton, 1990), 491.

19. On Abrams "being spared the agony" of South Vietnam's collapse, see Bruce Palmer Jr., *The 25-Year War: America's Military Role in Vietnam* (Lexington: University Press of Kentucky, 1984), 133. Arrogance in U.S. Grant Sharp, *Strategy for Defeat: Vietnam in Retrospect* (San Rafael, CA: Presidio Press, 1978), 268.

20. Westmoreland quoted in Cincinnatus, *Self-Destruction: The Disintegration and Decay of the United States Army during the Vietnam Era* (New York: W.W. Norton, 1981), 21. Funding in John C. "Doc" Bahnsen Jr., *American Warrior: A Combat Memoir of Vietnam* (New York: Citadel Press, 2007), xv. Democracy in Phillip B. Davidson, *Vietnam at War, the History: 1946–1975* (Novato, CA: Presidio Press, 1988), 717. On this point, see also Ira A. Hunt, *Losing Vietnam: How American Abandoned Southeast Asia* (Lexington: University Press of Kentucky, 2013), 322. Gutless in Eric M. Bergerud, *Red Thunder, Tropic Lightning: The World of a Combat Division in Vietnam* (Boulder, CO: Westview Press, 1993), 302, quoting Kenneth Stumpf.

21. Fight and win in Maj. Marc B. Powe, "The US Army after the Fall of Vietnam: A Contemporary Dilemma," *Military Review* Vol. 56, no. 2 (February 1976): 3. No "peace dividend" in Harry G. Summers Jr., "The United States Army Institutional Response to Vietnam," in *Proceedings of the 1982 International Military History Symposium*, ed. Charles R. Shrader (Washington, DC: US Army Center of Military History, 1984), MHI Holdings, p. 300. George C. Herring argues the debates in the memoirs of the participants had "not captured the attention of the media or the public." "American Strategy in Vietnam: The Postwar Debate," *Military Affairs* 46, no. 2 (April 1982): 57.

22. Veteran quoted in Kathy Burke, "War Is Over—but Vietnam Vets Find No Peace," *Los Angeles Times*, 5 May 1975. Rusk, 491.

23. Powe, 12. Human rights in Patrick Hagopian, *The Vietnam War in American Memory: Veterans, Memorials, and the Politics of Healing* (Amherst: University of Massachusetts Press, 2009), 34.

24. Carter quoted in Andrew J. Bacevich, *The Limits of Power: The End of American Exceptionalism* (New York: Metropolitan Books, 2008), 32–33.

25. Reagan 1980 "noble cause" speech in Mark Atwood Lawrence, *The Vietnam War: An International History in Documents* (New York: Oxford University Press, 2014), 177–179. For assessments, see Marilyn B. Young, *The Vietnam Wars, 1945-1990* (New York: HarperCollins, 1991), 315; and Thomas G. Paterson, "Historical Memory and Illusive Victories: Vietnam and Central America," *Diplomatic History* 12, no. 1 (Winter 1988): 5. Moral confusion in Arnold R. Isaacs, *Vietnam Shadows: The War, Its Ghosts, and Its Legacy* (Baltimore: Johns Hopkins University Press, 1997), 8. For an example of military officers blaming politicians, see William C. Westmoreland, "Vietnam in Perspective," *Military Review* 59, no. 1 (January 1979): 38.

26. Unwillingness in George C. Herring, "The Vietnam Syndrome," in *The Columbia History of the Vietnam War*, ed. David L. Anderson (New York: Columbia University Press, 2011), 409. Reagan quoted in Hagopian, 32.

27. Nixon, *No More Vietnams*, 19. For a similar argument, see Sen. Robert Kasten (R-Wisconsin) in David Fromkin and James Chace, "What Are the Lessons of Vietnam?," *Foreign Affairs* 63, no. 4 (Spring 1985): 741.

28. Shame in Robert K. Brigham, "Monument or Memorial? The Wall and the Politics of Memory," *Historical Reflections* 25, no. 1 (Spring 1999): 171. Lin quoted in Sabine Behrenbeck, "Versailles and Vietnam: Coming to Terms with War," in *America, the Vietnam War, and the World: Comparative and International Perspectives*, eds. Andreas W. Daum, Lloyd C. Gardner, and Wilfried Mausbach (New York: Cambridge University Press, 2003), 138. On commemorations being therapeutic, see Hagopian, 19.

29. Reagan quoted in Hunt, *A Vietnam War Reader*, 202. On changing images of the Vietnam veteran after 1980, see James S. Olson and Randy Roberts, *Where the Domino Fell: America and Vietnam, 1945–2010*, 6th ed. (West Sussex, UK: Wiley Blackwell, 2014), 241. Meredith H. Lair suggests that within this process, few distinctions were made between combat veterans and those who served in the relatively safer rear areas. *Armed with Abundance: Consumerism & Soldiering in the Vietnam War* (Chapel Hill: University of North Carolina Press, 2011), 59.

30. William Colby with James McCargar, *Lost Victory: A Firsthand Account of America's Sixteen-Year Involvement in Vietnam* (Chicago: Contemporary Books, 1989), 367, 371. "Stand tall" in Young, *The Vietnam Wars*, 314. On links between Vietnam and Reagan's interventionist policies, George Donelson Moss, *Vietnam: An American Ordeal*, 5th ed. (Upper Saddle River, NJ: Pearson Prentice Hill, 1990, 2006), 432. Herring argues this revisionist history "simply did not take" in the early 1980s. "The Vietnam Syndrome," 414.

31. Veterans quoted in Cecil B. Currey, "How Different Is the Military Today Because of the Vietnam War?," *The American Experience in Vietnam: A Reader*, ed. Grace Sevy (Norman: University of Oklahoma Press, 1989), 147. Norman B. Hannah, *The Key to Failure: Laos and the Vietnam War* (Lanham, MD: Madison Books, 1987), xxi.

32. Robert E. Osgood, *Limited War Revisited* (Boulder, CO: Westview Press, 1979), 46–47. See also Herring, "American Strategy in Vietnam," 60; and Robert E. Osgood, "The Reappraisal of Limited War," in *Problems of Modern Strategy*, ed. Alastair Buchan (New York: Praeger, 1970), 107–108.

33. On prestige, see F. B. Schoomaker, "The Apparent Similarities and Significant Differences Between the Vietnamese and the Malayan Insurgencies," 19 January 1966, US Army War College Student Paper, Folder 6, Box 132, Series II Official Papers, Harold K. Johnson Collection, MHI, p. 10. On the tendency of American strategists to separate military strategy from political reality, see Richard Shultz, "Coercive Force and Military Strategy: Deterrence Logic and the Cost-Benefit Model of Counterinsurgency Warfare," *Western Political Quarterly* 32, no. 4 (December 1979): 465.

34. Robert C. Dennison Jr., "The Importance of South Vietnam," 5 February 1962, Student Thesis, US Army War College, MHI, p. iii.

35. Nixon quoted in Douglas Brinkley and Luke A. Nichter, eds., *The Nixon Tapes* (Boston: Houghton Mifflin Harcourt, 2014), 360. Officer quoted in Guenter Lewy, "Some Political-Military Lessons of the Vietnam War," in *Assessing the Vietnam War: A Collection from the Journal of the U.S. Army War College*, eds. Lloyd J. Matthews and Dale E. Brown

(Washington, DC: Pergamon-Brassey's International Defense Publishers, 1987), 145. Making armed force purposeful in Bacevich, 152.

36. Nixon quoted in Brinkley and Nichter, 182. On fears about global effects of a defeat in Vietnam, see Johannes Kadura, *The War After the War: The Struggle for Credibility during America's Exit from Vietnam* (Ithaca, NY: Cornell University Press, 2016), 118.

37. Cult in David Halberstam, *The Best and the Brightest* (New York: Random House, 1969), 548. On speculation of a new strategy embarrassing Abrams, see Andrew J. Birtle, "In Pursuit of the Great White Whale: Lewis Sorley's *Westmoreland: The General Who Lost Vietnam*," *Army History* (Summer 2012): 29. *Newsweek*, 29 September 1969, 32. On only minor changes in strategy, see Graham A. Cosmas, *MACV: The Joint Command in the Years of Withdrawal, 1968–1973* (Washington, DC: Center of Military History, 2007), 410; and Andrew J. Birtle, *U.S. Army Counterinsurgency and Contingency Operations Doctrine, 1942-1976* (Washington, DC: Center of Military History, 2006), 366. One study, in fact, argued, "None of the four legs of the US strategy was new." The BDM Corporation, "A Study of Strategic Lessons Learned in Vietnam," Vol. VI, Conduct of the War, General Holdings, MHI, pp. 4–14.

38. Col. Volney F. Warner, End of Tour Report, 14 January 1970, Box 1, Volney F. Warner Papers, MHI, p. 2. Mutual exhaustion in Michael H. Hunt and Steven I. Levine, *Arc of Empire: America's Wars in Asia from the Philippines to Vietnam* (Chapel Hill: University of North Carolina Press, 2012), 236.

39. Deeply conventional in Thomas E. Ricks, *The Generals: American Military Command from World War II to Today* (New York: Penguin Press, 2012), 426. Improving dramatically in Mark Moyar, *A Question of Command: Counterinsurgency from the Civil War to Iraq* (New Haven, CT: Yale University Press, 2009), 161. Everything different in Thomas Powers, "Warrior Petraeus," *The New York Review of Books*, 7 March 2013.

40. On using Vietnam as a case study for a "clear and hold" strategy in Iraq, see Fred Kaplan, *The Insurgents: David Petraeus and the Plot to Change the American Way of War* (New York: Simon & Schuster, 2013), 194; and Robert M. Cassidy, *Counterinsurgency and the Global War on Terror: Military Culture and Irregular War* (Westport, CT: Praeger Security International, 2006), 136-137. On criticisms of this use of history, see Gian Gentile, *Wrong Turn: America's Deadly Embrace of Counterinsurgency* (New York: The New Press, 2013), 61; and Ken Hughes, *Fatal Politics: The Nixon Tapes, the Vietnam War, and the Casualties of Reelection* (Charlottesville: University of Virginia Press, 2015), 200.

41. Abrams quoted in Lewis Sorley, ed., *Vietnam Chronicles: The Abrams Tapes, 1968–1972* (Lubbock: Texas Tech University Press, 2004), 672. Peter Arnett, "Pride Worn Thin," *The Washington Post*, 12 August 1972.

42. Mark Moyar, "Abandoning Vietnam," *The Wall Street Journal*, 4 May 2012.

43. USMACV, Command History, 1972, NARA, p. 1. On this point, see also Martin G. Clemis, "The Control War: Communist Revolutionary Warfare, Pacification, and the Struggle for South Vietnam, 1968–1975" (Ph.D. diss., Temple University, 2015), 489. Assumptions on transforming society in Gary R. Hess, *Vietnam: Explaining America's Lost War* (Malden, MA: Blackwell, 2009), 123.

44. Luu Van Loi and Ngueyn Anh Vu's "great difficulties" quoted in Lewis Sorley, "Reassessing ARVN," Lecture, Vietnam Center, Texas Tech University, Lubbock, TX, 17 March 2006, p. 24. "One war" in USMACV Quarterly Evaluation Report, 1 April–30 June 1969, MHI, p. 5. Political vision in Hunt and Levine, 227.

45. Restructuring society in Lewis Sorley, "The Quiet War: Revolutionary Development," *Military Review* 47, no. 11 (November 1967): 14. Credibility in Arnold Isaacs, "The Limits of Credibility," in *Major Problems in the History of the Vietnam War*, 2nd ed., ed. Robert J. McMahon (Lexington, MA: D.C. Heath, 1995), 450. On the paradox of waging war to achieve power, see Jeffrey S. Milstein, *Dynamics of the Vietnam War: A Quantitative Analysis and Predictive Computer Simulation* (Columbus: Ohio State University Press, 1974), 145–150.

46. Colby in Richard A. Hunt, *Pacification: The American Struggle for Vietnam's Hearts and Minds* (Boulder, CO: Westview Press, 1995), 215. On the war not being entirely in US hands, see Nixon, *Public Papers of the Presidents of the United States, 1971*, 255. Robert Kaiser, "Thieu Defies U.S. and Makes It Pay," *The Washington Post*, 12 September 1969.

47. Lack of leverage in James H. Lebovic, *The Limits of U.S. Military Capability: Lessons from Vietnam and Iraq* (Baltimore: Johns Hopkins University Press, 2010), 205; Stanley Karnow, *Vietnam: A History* (New York: Viking Press, 1983), 635; and Neil Sheehan, "Military Frustration," *New York Times*, 4 July 1967.

48. Gerald C. Hickey, *U.S. Strategy in South Vietnam: Extrication and Equilibrium* (Santa Monica, CA: RAND Corporation, 1969), 10. Schell quoted in Kurt Jacobsen, *Pacification and Its Discontents* (Chicago: Prickly Paradigm Press, 2009), 2. Phillip B. Davidson argued the prolonged war also "eroded the domestic support for the conflict within the United States." *Secrets of the Vietnam War* (Novato, CA: Presidio Press, 1990), 152.

49. US casualty figures from Stephen J. Lofgren, Chief, Historical Support Branch, Histories Directorate, US Army Center of Military History. Email to author, 19 November 2016. Vietnamese casualties drawn from Thomas C. Thayer, *War Without Fronts: The American Experience in Vietnam* (Annapolis, MD: Naval Institute Press, 1985, 2016), 104–107. See also Charles Hirschman, Samuel Preston, and Vu Manh Loi, "Vietnamese Casualties during the American War: A New Estimate," *Population and Development Review* 21, no. 4 (December 1995): 783–812.

50. Irrelevant in Larry Cable, *Unholy Grail: The US and the Wars in Vietnam, 1965–8* (London: Routledge, 1991), 234. For an example on placing blame, see American officer quoted in Frances FitzGerald, *Fire in the Lake: The Vietnamese and the Americans in Vietnam* (Boston: Little, Brown, 1972), 407; and George Ball in Paterson, 8. Leverage in John Prados, *Vietnam: The History of an Unwinnable War, 1945–1975* (Lawrence: University Press of Kansas, 2009), 331. Legitimacy between social orders in Timothy J. Lomperis, *The War Everyone Lost—and Won: America's Intervention in Viet Nam's Twin Struggles* (Washington, DC: CQ Press, 1993), 100.

51. Haig quoted in Christian G. Appy, *Patriots: The Vietnam War Remembered from All Sides* (New York: Viking Press, 2003), 397. For an alternate view, see Davidson, *Secrets of the Vietnam War*, 127. On the emergence of a Vietnamese nationalism, see Pierre Brocheux and Daniel Hémery, *Indochina: An Ambiguous Colonization, 1858–1954* (Berkeley: University of California Press, 2009), 292–300.

52. Legitimacy defined in Eqbal Ahmad, "Revolutionary War and Counter-Insurgency," in *Revolutionary War: Western Response*, eds. David S. Sullivan and Martin J. Sattler (New York: Columbia University Press, 1971), 5. Evolution in Nguyen Thai, *Is South Vietnam Viable?* (Manila: Carmelo & Bauermann, 1962), 11. Italics in the original.

53. Westmoreland to Wheeler, 11 November 1965, Pacification Folder, Box 4, Paul L. Miles Papers, MHI. Imagined political community in Michael E. Latham, *Modernization as Ideology: American Social Science and "Nation Building" in the Kennedy Era* (Chapel Hill: University of North Carolina Press, 2000), 146. Political competitiveness in Jeffrey Record, *The Wrong War: Why We Lost in Vietnam* (Annapolis, MD: Naval Institute Press, 1998), 94. On anticommunism, see Andrew E. Hunt, *The Turning: A History of Vietnam Veterans against the War* (New York: New York University Press, 1999), 9.

54. Allan E. Goodman, *Politics in War: The Bases of Political Community in South Vietnam* (Cambridge, MA: Harvard University Press, 1973), 250. Urban population in Simon Toner, "The Counter-Revolutionary Path: South Vietnam, the United States, and the Global Allure of Development, 1968–1973" (Ph.D. diss., London School of Economics, 2015), 190–191.

55. My thanks to Heather Stur, who greatly assisted me with the complex deliberations over Vietnamese identity. Email to author, 18 April 2016. Rootless movement in Olga Dror, "Raising Vietnamese: War and Youth in the South in the Early 1970s," *Journal of Southeast Asian Studies* 44, no. 1 (February 2013): 94. On this point, see also Nu-Anh Tran, "South Vietnamese Identity, American Intervention, and the Newspaper *Chính Luận* [Political Discussion], 1965–1969," *Journal of Vietnamese Studies* 1, no. 1–2 (February/August 2006): 179. Mobilizing and pacifying the countryside in Laurence E. Grinter, "How They Lost: Doctrines, Strategies and Outcomes of the Vietnam War," *Asian Survey* 15, no. 12 (December 1975): 1115.

56. Broad political alliance in Peter King, "The Political Balance in Saigon," *Pacific Affairs* 44, no. 3 (Autumn 1971): 403. Governmental processes in Goodman, 188. Reforms in Davidson, *Vietnam at War*, 720. Viable in the BDM Corporation, "A Study of Strategic Lessons Learned in Vietnam," Vol. II, South Vietnam, General Holdings, MHI, p. vii.

57. General Cao Van Vien, "Vietnam: What's Next?," *Military Review* 52, no. 4 (April 1972): 30.

58. On the importance of an integrative vision for Vietnam's future, see Mark Philip Bradley, *Vietnam at War* (New York: Oxford University Press, 2009), 23. Voluntary participation in Operational Guidelines for Advisory Support of Revolutionary Development Cadre, 13 June 1966, Revolutionary Development Folder #2, Box 1, Richard M. Lee Papers, MHI, p. 5.

INDEX